Historical and Cultural Dictionaries of Asia
edited by Basil C. Hedrick

Historical and Cultural Dictionary of VIETNAM

by

DANNY J. WHITFIELD

Historical and Cultural Dictionaries of Asia, No. 7

The Scarecrow Press, Inc.

Metuchen, N.J.   1976

Library of Congress Cataloging in Publication Data

Whitfield, Danny J
  Historical and cultural dictionary of Vietnam.

  (Historical and cultural dictionaries of Asia ; no. 7)
  Bibliography: p.
  1. Vietnam--Dictionaries and encyclopedias.
I. Title. II. Series: Historical and cultural
dictionaries of Asia series ; no. 7.
DS556.25.W48   959.704'003   75-38729
ISBN 0-8108-0887-0

EDITOR'S FOREWORD

All of the authors or compilers of the Historical
and Cultural Dictionaries of Asia Series have been
given the charge to select, in a more or less arbi-
trary manner--based on the experience and knowledge
for which they were chosen--the materials for in-
clusion in the various volumes. The intent of the
series is to provide a source where both the scholar
and the casual and interested reader may find factual,
somewhat balanced, and certainly helpful information
pertinent to the various nations of Asia.

The Series is not intended necessarily to be an
exhaustive listing, nor should it be viewed as an
encyclopedia. It is intended as a "ready reference"
work which, in some instances, may turn out to be a
most definitive work, owing to the relative dearth of
factual knowledge in the Western World about many of
the nations included in the Series.

Mr. Danny J. Whitfield, the author of this
present work, is uniquely qualified, for an Occidental,
to write knowledgeably about Vietnam. He received
his Baccalaureate Degree from the Delaware Valley
College of Science and Agriculture in Doylestown,
Pennsylvania, in 1961 and thereafter did graduate work
at Southern Illinois University at Carbondale. Sub-
sequent to approximately eight years of work in Viet-
nam as a Volunteer with the International Voluntary
Services; as Area Development Officer, USAID; as
Recruiting Officer, USAID/Washington; as Backstop
Officer for AID's Vietnam Field Programs; as Area
Development Officer, Vietnam Senior Civilian Pro-
vincial Advisor and as Director of IVS/VN, Mr.
Whitfield served as Assistant to the Director in the
Center for Vietnamese Studies at Southern Illinois
University at Carbondale from January, 1970 until
July 1, 1974. Decorated three times for services in
Vietnam, Mr. Whitfield has a good command of the
Vietnamese language and a humanitarian spirit and
love toward and for all Vietnamese. It is with
distinct pleasure that we welcome him to the group
of authors represented in this Series.

The Editor wishes to acknowledge particularly
Ms. Judy Grimes and Ms. Vicky Wuehler for their

iii

extraordinary performance in the editing of this
manuscript.

Basil C. Hedrick
Director
University Museum
Southern Illinois University
   at Carbondale

CONTENTS

PREFACE

The term "dictionary" may be misleading, for the reader may be expecting to find short, Webster-like definitions of a selected list of words. This volume, however, represents an attempt to provide both the serious scholar and the casual reader with a handy and practical reference tool. One of the more difficult aspects of this compilation has been the necessity to maintain brevity in each entry while limiting the number of entries. Literally speaking, a book-length treatise could be written on virtually every entry. For a more detailed description of the subject matter, the reader is referred to the bibliography at the end of the book.

The format is designed to be the most workable for the English speaking, non-Vietnamese reader. Therefore, the system of alphabetization is adapted from the Vietnamese. For instance, no distinction is made for purposes of word order between the D and Đ. Nor are the words beginning with TR or TH handled as individual letter categories. The use of hyphens in the Vietnamese language, even among Vietnamese scholars, varies. The system used herein claims no universal acceptance, but is intended to be both usable for the reader and palatable for the grammarians. As a general rule, hyphens are used for place names, personal names (only in given names) and in Sino-Vietnamese words.

A major caveat should be noted: that "north Vietnam", "central Vietnam" and "south Vietnam" refer in all instances herein to the three geographical regions in Vietnam. The nation states are referred to as the Democratic Republic of Vietnam and the Republic of Vietnam in the north and south respectively. Thus, when referring to the north or north Vietnam, the reader should not confuse it with the nation (Democratic Republic of Vietnam). Also, when referring to the Vietnamese monarchs, the title Emperor is used throughout. While the Vietnamese rulers sought recognition from China as vassal kings in a tributary relationship to China, they established imperial dynasties and were considered as emperors within their own borders. For clarity, the dates of reign appear after the initial mention of every monarch in each entry. The date of reign of each dynasty is likewise noted. Finally, the term "traditional Vietnam" is used to denote Vietnam prior to or void of Western influence. Naturally, there was and is an overlap so that even today there exists a "traditional Vietnam" and a "modern Vietnam."

Special and sincere thanks go to Professor
Chingho A. Chen who reviewed the manuscript and
gave invaluable advice and help, and to Miss
Nguyễn Hồng-Cúc who proofread the entire volume--
and in some parts, several times.

1974
Carbondale, Illinois   D.W.

-A-

ADMINISTRATIVE DIVISIONS. The system of administrative divisions varied with each period or dynasty in Vietnamese history. The first real administrative centralization of the country began as early as the Lý Dynasty (1010-1225). Emperor Lý Thái-Tổ, (1010-1028) divided the country into twenty-four provinces (Lộ) which were governed by members of the royal family or by military officers. These provinces, which were later governed by civilian mandarins, were subdivided into prefectures (Phủ), districts (Huyện) and villages (Xã). The civil service or mandarinate developed and grew through successive dynasties, coming under heavy influence from the Chinese Confucian philosophy, especially under the Lê Dynasty (1428-1788). The Nguyễn Dynasty (1802-1945) divided the country into three regions: North, Central and South. The Central Region was under the direct authority of the Court while the North and South were governed by Imperial Delegates called Tổng Trấn. Each region was divided into provinces (Trấn), prefectures (Phủ), and districts or subdistricts (Huyện). Within the Huyện the village (Xã) maintained its local autonomy. The French continued to distinguish between the three regions. They established French Protectorates in North and Central Vietnam and asserted direct control over South Vietnam which became the French colony of Cochinchina. The essentials of the Vietnamese system of administrative divisions were maintained throughout the French era. The Democratic Republic of Vietnam established two highland autonomous regions in 1955. At present there are twenty-three provinces, one special zone and two municipalities in the Democratic Republic of Vietnam. The Republic of Vietnam is divided into four military tactical areas and the capitol district of Saigon. Additionally there are forty-five provinces and eleven autonomous municipalities. The following represents the territorial administrative units used at various times in Vietnamese history in descending order of size:

1. Region...........Bộ, Châu, Đạo
2. Province.........Tỉnh, Lộ, Trấn
3. Prefecture.......Phủ

1

4. Subprefecture or
    District..............Quận, Huyện, Châu
5. Canton................Tổng
6. Village...............Xã, Làng
7. Hamlet................Ấp, Thôn

See ẤP, HUYỆN, PHỦ, QUẬN, TỈNH, XÃ.

ADRAN, BISHOP OF. See PIGNEAU DE BEHAINE, BISHOP.

AGRICULTURE. Rice is by far the most important agricultural commodity in the Vietnamese diet and
   economy. Under normal conditions it occupies
   about eighty percent of the total cultivated land,
   and most of the labor force is engaged in its
   cultivation. Wet (paddy) rice is cultivated on
   dry soil in the highland areas. Under favorable
   conditions three crops of rice a year can be
   grown on the same land. Other significant crops
   include sugarcane, sweet potatoes, manioc, coffee,
   tea, rubber, bamboo, cinnamon, timber, coconut,
   pork, and various kinds of fruits and vegetables.
      Democratic Republic of Vietnam: Agriculture
   in the Democratic Republic of Vietnam (North Vietnam) is characterized by almost complete collect-
   ivization. North Vietnam has traditionally been
   a food-deficit area, importing rice from the South.
   According to reports, rice acreage increased by
   seventeen percent between 1939 and 1956 and the
   average yields per acre increased from twenty-
   eight to thirty-eight bushels. The following
   production figures were given for 1963 (in metric
   tons):

Rice...........	4,296,000	Cotton Seed.....	5,900
Sugarcane......	732,000	Jute...........	16,200
Peanuts........	34,500	Hemp...........	1,000
Soybeans.......	7,900	Reed...........	22,000
Sesame.........	2,400	Tobacco........	4,200
Castor Beans...	1,700	Tea............	3,600

   Republic of Vietnam: The Republic of Vietnam (South Vietnam) has experienced a steady drop
in agricultural production as the security and
economy has been disrupted by the war since 1961.
The introduction of the new high-yield rice varieties has helped reduce this trend. The following production figures were given for 1970 (in
metric tons):

Rice..........	5,651,000	Banana........	218,460
Corn..........	31,730	Rubber........	29,780
Soybeans......	7,570	Tea...........	5,650

Fruits....... 257,075   Coffee........ 4,500
Sugarcane..... 442,125

See RICE CULTURE.

ẢI-NAM-QUAN (Also called TRẤN-NAM-QUAN or NAM-QUAN).
A strategic pass on the Chinese border in Lạng-
Sơn Province. It is located eighteen kilomaters
(eleven miles) north of the city of Lạng-Sơn. The
pass has been a traditional route into Vietnam from
China. It was, therefore, named Ải-Nam-Quan, (Gate-
way-to-the-South Pass). It is also the site on
·which the famous Vietnamese hero, Nguyễn-Trãi,
lamented his father's forced exile from Vietnam.
See LẠNG-SƠN PROVINCE, NGUYỄN-TRÃI

ẢI-VÂN PASS. See HẢI-VÂN PASS.

ALEXANDER OF RHODES. See RHODES, MONSIGNOR ALEXANDER DE.

ALOES WOOD. See TRAM-HUONG WOOD.

ÂM-LỊCH. (Lunar calendar). The dating system used by
the Chinese and Chinese-related cultures. It
starts from the year 2,647 B.C. The year 1973
thus corresponds to the year 4,610 of the lunar
calendar. The lunar calendar is divided into
sixty-year cycles (vạn-niên lục-giáp). The year
1973 (Quý-Sửu) falls into the seventy-eighth cycle,
1924-1984. Each year is designated by two words.
The first refers to one of the ten "celestial
trunks" (Thập-Can). The second word refers to one
of the twelve "terrestrial branches" (Thập-Nhị-Chi)
or the twelve animals of the zodiac.

Thập-Can	Thập-Nhị-Chi
1. Giáp Mọc (Wood)	1. Tí (Rat)
2. Ất	2. Sửu (Water Buffalo)
3. Bính Hỏa (Fire)	3. Dần (Tiger)
4. Đinh	4. Mão (Cat)
5. Mậu Thổ (Soil)	5. Thìn (Dragon)
6. Kỷ	6. Tỵ (Snake)
7. Canh Kim (Metal) ·	7. Ngọ (Horse)
8. Tân	8. Mùi (Goat)
9. Nhâm Thủy (Water)	9. Thân (Monkey)
10. Quý	10. Dậu (Rooster)
	11. Tuất (Dog)
	12. Hợi (Pig)

The ten celestial trunks or stems (Thập-Can) cor-
respond to the five basic elements on which,

according to the Chinese tradition, the order of
the universe is based. The first year of the
cycle, 1924, is designated by the combination of
the first celestial trunk (Giáp) with the first
terrestrial branch (Tí), i.e., Giáp-Tí. The
second year, 1925, is designated by combining the
second term in each category, i.e., Ắt-Sửu. The
eleventh year is referred to by combining the first
celestial trunk with the eleventh terrestrial
branch, Giáp-Tuất. Thus, each sixty-year cycle is
composed of six ten-year cycles and five twelve-
year cycles.

AN-DƯƠNG-VƯƠNG. The founder and first king of the
legendary Thuc Dynasty. He ruled over the Kingdom of Âu-Lạc from 257-208 B.C. According to
legend, An-Dưỡng-Vưỡng received a magic bow from
the fairy Kim-Qui. He was told that when he used
the bow in battle tens of thousands of the enemy
would be destroyed by a single arrow. For this
reason, the Chinese General Triệu-Đà could not
defeat him. Triệu-Đà sent his son to marry An-
Dưỡng-Vưỡng's daughter, Mị-Châu. Mị-Châu showed
the magic bow to her husband, Trọng-Thỉ, who stole
it away and gave it to his father. Triệu-Đà then
used it to defeat An-Dưỡng-Vưỡng and established
the Triệu Dynasty (207-111 B.C.). See ÂU-LẠC,
CỔ-LOA, THỤC DYNASTY, TRIỆU-ĐÀ.

ĂN-GIẠM. (Lễ Ăn-Giạm, also called Lễ Vấn-Danh). A
pre-betrothal ceremony. The Lễ Ăn-Giạm is held
after the formal expression of interest in the
marriage is made and the boy's family has visited
the girl's family. The matchmaker guides the boy's
family to the girl's home. They carry with them
the betel nut, tea and wine for the occasion. The
purpose of the ceremony is to afford an opportunity
for the parents of the boy to request the birth
certificate of the girl indicating the date and
time of birth. This is then taken to an astrol-
oger to see if the couple is compatible. See
CHẠM-NGÕ, ĂN-HỎI, HÔN-NHÂN.

AN-GIANG PROVINCE. A Mekong Delta province in south
Vietnam. It is located north of Kiến-Giang Province, east of Châu-Đốc Province, west of Phong-
Dinh and Sa-Đéc provinces and south of Kiến-
Phong Province. The population of the province
is 605,497 (1971) and the area is 1,903 square
kilometers, (734 square miles). The provincial
capital is Long-Xuyên, which is located on the
lower Mekong River (Sông Hậu-Giang) and is linked

by road to Châu-Đốc and Cần-Thơ. An-Giang was one
of six provinces comprising South Vietnam under
Emperor Minh-Mạng (1820-1840). The French divided
An-Giang into six smaller provinces; Châu-Đốc,
Long-Xuyên, Sa-Đec, Cần-Thơ, Sốc-Trăng and Bạc-Liêu.
In 1956, Long-Xuyên and Châu-Đốc were combined to
form An-Giang Province. In 1964, Châu-Đốc Province
was reestablished leaving An-Giang identical to the
former Long-Xuyên Province under the French. An-
Giang is perhaps best known as the center of the
Hòa-Hảo religious sect, although the heart of the
religion, Hòa-Hảo village, is now located in Châu-
Đốc Province. An-Giang is a major producer of
soybean, mung bean, corn, sweet potatoes, tobacco,
rice, and fish. Floating rice is planted extensively in An-Giang Province. See HÒA-HẢO, LONG-
XUYÊN.

ĂN HỎI.   (Lễ Ăn Hỏi, also called Lễ Nạp-Tệ). A pre-
betrothal engagement ceremony. The Lễ Ăn-Hỏi is
held after the two families have agreed to the
marriage. The family of the groom takes the
ceremonial dishes to the house of the bride. These
include rice cakes (bánh trái), other varieties of
cakes, sausage (nem), tea, wine, and betel nut.
These are received by the girl's parents and distributed to the members of the girl's family and
close friends as an indication of the acceptance
of the boy's family and their proposal of marriage.
In modern times, the boy's family also brings the
engagement announcements which are then distributed by both families. From this time on, the
couple is considered engaged. In traditional
Vietnam, the engaged boy was then obligated to
bring offerings to the girl's family on the
occasion of the major holidays and family celebrations and rituals. In some cases, the boy was
expected to live and work at the bride-to-be's
house for a period of time prior to the marriage
ceremony. At one time it was common for the engagement period to last for one to three years.
It is now usually a matter of months. See HÔN-
NHÂN, SÊU, LÀM RỂ.

AN-KHÊ. A small chain of mountains (average height of
500 meters or 1,600 feet) in Bình-Định Province
in central Vietnam. A steep and scenic pass of
the same name runs through the mountains along
highway nineteen which connects Qui-Nhơn with
Kontum. This area was the home of Nguyễn-Huệ and
Nguyễn-Nhạc, the leaders of the Tây-Sơn rebellion
(1771-1788). See BÌNH-ĐỊNH PROVINCE, TÂY-SƠN
REBELLION.

AN-LỘC. The capital city of Bình-Long Province. Population of the city is given as 21,972 (1971). The
city is in a mountainous area and is inhabited by
both ethnic Vietnamese and highland ethnic minority
people. An-Lộc was decimated in a well-publicized
battle in 1972. See BÌNH-LONG PROVINCE.

An-NAM. (Literally means peaceful or pacified south).
1. The name of the Chinese colony (later to become Vietnam) under the T'ang Dynasty (603-939).
The actual name used during this period was An-
Nam Đô-Hộ-Phủ.
2. The name applied to the country under the
occupation of the Chinese Ming Dynasty (1407-1427).
3. The name given to Vietnam by China since 1497
as the various Vietnamese emperors sought recognition from and paid tribute to China. The full
name used was An-Nam Quốc (Kingdom of An-Nam).
4. The name applied by the French to designate
central Vietnam. An-Nam (or Annam) was established as a French protectorate in 1902 and was
administered by a Resident Superieur until the
Japanese took control of the country in 1941.

AN-NAM CHÍ-LƯỢC. (Literally, Description of An-Nam).
A history of Vietnam written by the scholar Lê-
Tắc in the thirteenth century. It was written in
classical Chinese in twenty volumes, but the last
volume was lost. The work was published in 1340.
See LÊ-TẮC.

AN-NAM-QUAN. See NGANG PASS.

AN-XUYÊN PROVINCE. The southernmost province in south
Vietnam. The province borders on Kiến-Giang,
Bặc-Liêu and Chửơng-Thiện provinces and the South
China Sea and the Gulf of Thailand. The population is 279,113 (1971) and the area is 5,029
square kilometers (1,941 square miles). The provincial capital is Quản-Long, also known as Cà-
Mau. An-Xuyên has one of the lowest population
densities in south Vietnam--55 persons per square
kilometer. The province occupies the Cà-Mau
Peninsula. The lower U-Minh Forest is located in
the northwestern part of the province. A large
number of the Khmer minority group live in An-
Xuyên. The main products of the province are
fish, pineapples, and rice. See CÀ-MAU PENINSULA,
QUẢN-LONG, U-MINH FOREST.

ANCESTOR WORSHIP. See CULT OF THE ANCESTORS.

ANH CẢ. The eldest brother in a nuclear family. In
traditional Vietnam upon the death of the father,
the anh ca assumed the responsibilities for rearing his siblings, managing the family property,
maintaining the family altar, and performing all
of the family rituals.

ANNAM CORDILLERA. See TRƯỜNG-SỔN MOUNTAIN RANGE.

AÓ DÀI. (Literally, long dress). The women's national
dress of Vietnam. It is a contoured, full-length
dress worn over black or white loose fitting
trousers. The dress splits into a front and back
panel from the waist down. There is great stylish
variation in color and collar design. Originally,
the aó dài was loosely tailored with four panels,
two of which tied in front while the other two
were tied in back. In 1932, a nationalistic
literary group called the Tự-Lực Văn–Đoàn designed what is essentially now the ao dai. A
similar costume is worn by the men and is also
called an aó dài. However, the man's dress is
shorter (knee length) and fits looser. The color
of the brocade and the embroidery indicated the
rank and status of the wearer in traditional
Vietnamese society. Gold brocade with embroidered
dragons was worn only by the Emperor. Purple was
the color reserved for high-ranking mandarins while
blue was worn by those mandarins of lower rank.
The dresses for mourning have frayed fringes or a
line up the back and may be either white or black,
although white is the standard color for mourning.

ẤP. Hamlet. The ấp is a subdivision of a Xã (village)
and is usually determined by the geographical
grouping of a number of houses. The size and
shape of a hamlet varies from region to region.
Although the Xã has traditionally been the lowest
official administrative unit recognized by the
central government, the ấp has been a functional
and practical subdivision for the day-to-day
affairs of the community. The hamlet was given
particular importance in the Republic of Vietnam
with the establishment of the strategic hamlet
(ấp chiến lược) program in 1963. See XÃ.

ẤP THÁI-HÀ BATTLE (Trận Ấp Thái-Hà). See ĐỐNG–ĐA
BATTLE.

ARCHITECTURE. Vietnamese architecture shows definite
Chinese influence and yet is distinct and unique.
Religious architecture has been most strongly

influenced by the Chinese tradition, especially
the temples and pagodas. The Vietnamese pagoda,
however, has its own layout plan and includes the
three main halls, the front hall, the center hall
and the main altar hall. The đình (communal temple), while built in the traditional style, is
unique to Vietnam and not found anywhere in China.
Military architecture dates back to before the
Christian era. A number of fortified cities
(citadels) were built throughout Vietnam's history
culminating with the Huế citadel in 1805-1831,
which was built with French material and personnel
assistance and shows noticeable French influence.
The Vietnamese house varies in style and substance
according to region and social class. Since most
Vietnamese practice ancestor worship, the home is
a place of worship as well as a dwelling. It
tends, therefore, to be a harmonious structure,
emphasizing the aesthetic and balance rather than
comfort and convenience. The Vietnamese home
usually consists of three bays (nhà ba căn). Located at the very axis of the central bay the
family altar (bàn thờ gia-tiên), dedicated to the
ancestors, is placed against the wall and opposite
the main entrance and over or behind a one-piece
large wooden bed. This central room serves as a
living room, bedroom and the holy center of the
house where all the important family rituals take
place. The more well-to-do houses might have a
verandah added all along the length of the house
in the front. Unlike the Chinese houses, the
Vietnamese kitchen is always separate from the
main building. The kitchen is a small outbuilding
and is located in back of the main structure.
Another outbuilding serves as a utility shed,
granary and storage room. Contemporary urban
architecture shows strong Western influence,
especially the governmental buildings which were
designed in the French tradition. See BÀN THỜ
GIA-TIÊN, CITADELS, CÔNG-NGÕ, ĐÌNH, HOUSING.

ART.   Vietnamese art can be dated back to prehistoric
times. The most famous specimens are the bronze
drums unearthed at Đồng-Sơn in north Vietnam.
However, works in metals and stone were rare and
did not survive the ravages of war and political
upheaval. Similarly, most architectural structures
were made of bamboo, wood and baked earth which
do not withstand the tropical climate. Traditional Vietnamese architecture has been called landscape painting, referring to the Vietnamese concept of art as an hommage to nature and an attempt

to achieve harmony and unity with the natural order. The best examples of Vietnamese architecture
are found in the pagodas, temples, and royal tombs
as well as the common thatch roofed houses and
village structures. Traditional Vietnamese painting was limited to religious and mythological
representations until the period of French domination when it came under the influence of Western
tradition. The ancient Asian art of silk painting
has recently gained popularity. Sculpture was
never strong in Vietnam, especially when compared
to Champa or neighboring Cambodia. On the other
hand, the minor arts, such as ceramics, wood
carving, lacquerware, and embroidery have been
highly developed and have flourished. The scholarly
art of calligraphy was very popular in traditional
Vietnam but is no longer widely practiced. The
more modern medium of photography has become quite
popular and is one at which Vietnamese excel. See
ARCHITECTURE, CERAMICS, ĐINH, ĐỒNG-SỒN, LACQUER-
WARE, MIẾU, PAGODA, PRINTING.

ARVN. An acronym used by Americans to refer to the army
of the Republic of Vietnam.

ASSOCIATION FOR THE MODERNIZATION OF VIETNAM. See
VIỆT-NAM DUY-TÂN HỘI.

ASSOCIATION FOR THE RESTORATION OF VIETNAM. See
VIỆT-NAM QUANG-PHỤC HỘI.

ÂU-CƠ. One of the legendary ancestors of the ethnic
Vietnamese race. Âu-Cơ was the fairy who married
Lạc-Long Quân and gave birth to one hundred eggs.
These eggs hatched out one hundred boys, fifty of
whom went with their mother to the mountains. The
other fifty went with their father to live by the
sea, and thus were the procreators of the ethnic
(lowland) Vietnamese. The group that went to the
mountains became the founders of the highland
(montagnard) people's race. See HỒNG-BẰNG, LẠC-
LONG-QUÂN.

ÂU HỌC NGŨ NGÔN THI. A book of five-word verses for
children. It is a textbook of 278 five-word
verses describing the delights of learning as well
as the dream of a student wishing to receive the
degree of "First Doctor of the First Class" (Trạng
Nguyên).

ÂU-LẠC. The kingdom founded in 257 B.C. by An-Dương-
Vương, the first king of the Thục Dynasty. The

capital of Âu-Lạc was established at Phong-Khê in
what is now Vĩnh-Phú province of north Vietnam.
An-Dương-Vương had a tall spiral citadel built,
the remains of which can still be seen. The unusual citadel contributed to the use of several
names for the capital, including Loa-Thanh, Co-
Loa-Thành and Cổ-Loa. Âu-Lạc was under constant
pressure from the Chinese Ch'in Dynasty. Finally,
in 208 B.C. under the leadership of the Chinese
General Triệu-Đà, the kingdom of Âu-Lạc was conquered and the kingdom of Nam-Việt (Nan-Yueh) was
founded. See AN-DƯƠNG-VƯƠNG, CỔ-LOA, TRIỆU-ĐÀ.

AUGUST REVOLUTION. The takeover of Vietnam in August,
1945, by the Việt-Minh upon the defeat of the
Japanese by the Allies. The Japanese had assumed
control of the country in March, 1945, by ousting
the French. A provisional government under Trần
Trọng-Kim was established. On August 7, 1945,
after the Hiroshima blast, Hồ Chí-Minh announced
the formation of the "Committee for the Liberation
of the Vietnamese People", and mobilized the
guerilla army which had been organized and trained
under Võ Nguyên-Giáp. On August 15, 1945, the
Việt-Minh held a party conference which adopted
the national flag and national anthem of what is
now the Democratic Republic of Vietnam and laid
out a political and military strategy for the
takeover. With the fall of the Japanese and the
absence of any other organized group, the Việt-
Minh attracted broad nationalist support. Emperor Bảo-Đại abdicated in favor of the establishment of the Democratic Republic. On September 2, 1945, at Ba-Đình Square in Hà-Nội, Hồ Chí-
Minh delivered the Declaration of Independence.
The day is still celebrated as Independence Day
in the Democratic Republic of Vietnam. The newly
unified Vietnam was short-lived and immediately
challenged by the returning French, culminating
in the French Indochina War (1945-1954). The
August Revolution is celebrated today as the
occasion that gave birth to the Democratic Republic of Vietnam. See BẢO-ĐẠI, HỒ CHÍ-MINH,
DEMOCRATIC REPUBLIC OF VIETNAM, VIỆT-MINH

-B-

BÁ. Count, a rank of nobility. See NOBILITY.

BA-BỂ LAKE. A famous and unusual lake located in

Bắc-Thái Province in the highlands of north Vietnam. It is situated at an elevation of 145 meters
(400 feet) and is surrounded by formidable mountain
ranges. The lake is seven kilometers (4.3 miles)
long and reaches a width of three kilometers (1.9
miles), and a depth of thirty meters (ninety-eight
feet). There are small islands scattered throughout the lake. It is one of the most scenic spots
in the north Vietnamese highlands, complete with
waterfalls, fresh springs, caves and grottoes in
the vicinity of the lake. It is not, however,
accessible enough to be a tourist center.

BA-ĐEN MOUNTAIN. (Núi Bà-Đen or Black Lady Mountain).
A mountain located in Tây-Ninh Province in south
Vietnam. It stands over 900 meters (3,000 feet).
Legend has it that a magical Buddhist statue was
located on the summit of the mountain. A woman
named Hương used to visit the statue while wait-
ing for her husband to complete his military service. One day she was returning home from the
mountain when she was attacked by kidnappers.
Rather than give in, she jumped off a high cliff
in order to keep her promise to her husband that
she would wait for him. She reappeared in a
vision to a monk who lived on the mountain and
relayed her story. The mountain has also been the
site of fierce fighting during the French Indochina war and the more recent conflict involving
the Americans.

BA-ĐINH SQUARE. A public square in downtown Hà-Nội.
It was from this square on September 2, 1945, that
Hồ Chí-Minh delivered the Declaration of Indepen-
dence. See AUGUST REVOLUTION, DEMOCRATIC REPUBLIC
OF VIETNAM.

BÀ MAI. (Also called Bà Mối). Matchmaker. In traditional Vietnam the marriage partner was chosen
and the wedding arranged for by the parents. The
Bà Mai would serve as a go-between to determine
the interest and availability of the families concerned. She was usually employed by the boy's
family and took an active role in negotiating the
particulars of the wedding. In some cases the
matchmaker would be a man (Ông Mai). See LỄ HÔN-
NHÂN.

BA-NGÒI. A small town near the bay of Cam-Ranh on the
national highway number one. It has become the
residence for people employed at the Cam-Ranh port
facilities as well as for fishermen and entrepre-
neurs. See CAM-RANH.

BÀ-RỊA PROVINCE. See PHƯỚC-TUY PROVINCE.

BA RIVER (Sông Ba). See ĐÀ-RĂNG RIVER.

BA-THÊ MOUNTAIN. A small mountain in An-Giang Province
   in south Vietnam. It is only 210 meters (700 feet)
   high, but it has many interesting grottoes.
   Archaeologists have unearthed several stone objects that date back to the kingdom of Funan,
   including a Buddha head which is possibly from
   India. See SÂM MOUNTAIN, FUNAN.

BA-VÌ MOUNTAIN. See TẢN-VIÊN MOUNTAIN.

BA-XUYÊN PROVINCE. A coastal province in the Mekong
   Delta area of south Vietnam. It is located
   north of Bạc-Liêu Province and south of Vĩnh-
   Bình Province. The population is 436,668 (1971)
   and the area is 2,583 square kilometers (997
   square miles). The provincial capital is Khanh-
   Hưng, formerly known as Sóc-Trăng. The lower
   Mekong River flows through the province and
   empties into the sea at Cửa Tranh-Đề. The provincial capital is located on highway number four
   which runs from Sài-Gòn to Cà-Mau. Ba-Xuyên
   Province was originally called Sóc-Trăng Province.
   It was made a part of Bạc-Liêu Province under
   the French, but was reestablished as a separate
   province in 1955. The chief products include
   rice, pork, and fish. There is a sizable Khmer
   population in the province. See KHÁNH-HƯNG.

BẮC-BỘ. See BẮC-PHẦN.

BẮC-CẠN PROVINCE. See BẮC-THÁI PROVINCE.

BẮC-GIANG CITY. The capital city of Hà-Bắc Province
   in north Vietnam. It is situated on the road
   and rail routes between Lạng-Sởn and Hà-Nội,
   forty-nine kilometers (thirty miles) from Hà-Nội.

BẮC-GIANG PROVINCE. See HÀ-BẮC PROVINCE.

BẮC-GIANG RIVER (Sông Bắc-Giang). A river in north
   Vietnam. It originates in the Nguyên-Bình
   Plateau, flows through Cao-Bằng Province and
   empties into the Kỳ-Cung River near Thất-Khê.

BẮC-KỲ. See BẮC-PHẦN.

BẠC-LIÊU CITY. The capital city of Bạc-Liêu Province.
   Population is 65,678 (1971). The city was
   formerly known as Vĩnh-Lợi. It is located several
   miles from the coast on highway number four, which
   runs from Sài-Gòn to Ca-Mau. See BẠC-LIÊU PROVINCE.

miles from the coast on highway number four, which
runs from Sai-Gòn to Cà-Mau. See BẠC-LIÊU PROVINCE.

BẠC-LIÊU PROVINCE. A coastal province in south Vietnam.
It is located north of An-Xuyên Province and south
of Ba-Xuyên Province. Bạc-Liêu Province was
established in 1964 from parts of Ba-Xuyên and
Chường-Thiện provinces. The population of the
province is 352,230 (1971) and the land area is
2,559 square kilometers (988 square miles). The
provincial capital is Bạc-Liêu City, formerly
known as Vĩnh-Lội. The city is located on highway
number four. The main crops of the province are
rice, pork, and fish. There is a large Khmer
population in the province.

BẮC-NINH PROVINCE. See HÀ-BẮC PROVINCE.

BẮC-PHẦN. (Also known as Bắc-Bộ, Bắc-Kỳ and Miền Bắc).
North Vietnam, the area of Vietnam north of Thanh-
Hóa Province. North Vietnam is one of three
regions of Vietnam (the other two being central
and south Vietnam), and should not be confused
with the Democratic Republic of Vietnam. This
region includes the mountainous Thượng-Du region
in the north and northwest, the heavily populated
Trung-Châu around the Red River Delta and the
plateau area of Trung-Du in-between. It is
bordered by China to the north, Laos to the west,
central Vietnam to the south and the South China
Sea to the east. North Vietnam, particularly
the Red River Delta, is known as the cradle
of Vietnamese civilization. It was from there
that the ethnic Vietnamese spread southward.
The people of north Vietnam have maintained their
cultural individuality. The language of the
north is a distinct dialect from central and
south Vietnam but has been considered as the
standard language of Vietnam. See NORTHERN
COASTAL PLAIN, RED RIVER DELTA, THƯỢNG-DU,
TRUNG-DU.

BẮC-SƠN CIVILIZATION. (Also called Bắc-Sơnian culture).
A prehistoric culture of the neolithic (late stone
age) era which existed in what is now north Vietnam. It takes its name from the Bắc-Sơn mountain
range in which the vestiges of the civilization
were first found. The characteristic tool used
by these cave dwellers was the short axe which
was made by splitting a bifacial tool and polish-
ing it at the cutting edge on one side only.
Primitive pottery has been found along with
indications that these people practiced a rudi-

mentary form of agriculture. They also had
domesticated the dog. There also appears to have
been an elaborate burial ritual practiced by these
people. A study of the numerous skulls and skull
fragments found in Bắc-Sơn indicates that people
with strong melanesoid-australoid characteristics
existed during the late stone age in north Vietnam, including types similar to the present inhabitants of Melanesia, Indonesia and Australia.
Like the Hoà-Bình civilization, these people
settled in the caves and grottoes of the limestone
formations but did not venture near the coast.
The Bắc-Sơn civilization can be said to be a
transition period between the mesolithic and neolithic eras. See HOÀ-BÌNH CIVILIZATION, PRE-
HISTORY.

BẮC-SƠN MOUNTAIN RANGE. (Dãy Bắc-Sơn or Dãy Cai-Kinh).
A chain of mountains extending from the Thất-Khê
highlands in Lạng-Sơn Province down along the
Thương River to Bắc-Giang in Hà-Bắc Province.

BẮC-SƠN UPRISING (1940). The uprising of the Thổ
minority peoples against the French. The uprising
was coordinated with an attack on the border town
of Lạng-Sơn by the Japanese who had just concluded
an agreement with the Vichy Government for the
entry of the Japanese troops into Indochina.

BẮC-THÁI PROVINCE. (Formerly Bắc-Cạn and Thái-Nguyên
Provinces). An inland province located in the
mountains and foothills of north Vietnam. Bắc-
Thái Province was formed by merging Bắc-Cạn and
Thái-Nguyên provinces and is presently part of
the Việt-Bắc Autonomous Region (Khu Việt-Bắc Tự-
Trị). The provincial capital, Thái-Nguyên city,
is located on the Cầu River, seventy-six kilometers (forty-seven miles) from Hà-Nội. The land
mass of the province is approximately 8,600 square
kilometers (3,330 square miles) and the population
is estimated at 376,219 (1960). Bắc-Thái is inhabited predominantly by the Thổ and Nung ethnic
groups. There are also Dao, Chinese and a small
number of ethnic Vietnamese living in the province.
Thái-Nguyên is an industrial center due largely
to the steel mills and coal mines. The main
agricultural crops of the province are rice,
coffee, tea and lumber. Under the French, much
of the land was divided into plantations. The
former province of Bắc-Cạn was established in
1900. Prior to that it was a prefecture (Phủ)
under several names. Like the former Province of
Thái-Nguyên, it was under the direct control of

the Thô. There are several military outposts of
historical as well as current importance. See
INDUSTRY, THÁI-NGUYÊN, THÁI-NGUYÊN REVOLT, BA-BÊ
LAKE.

BẮC-THUỘC. (Thời Bắc-Thuộc). The period of Chinese
domination, 111 B.C.--938 A.D. This period is
divided into three phases, each phase being inter-
rupted by a short period of independence:

1. First Period 111 B.C.--39 A.D.

   Trung Dynasty 40-43 A.D.

2. Second Period 44-544 A.D.

   Early Lý Dynasty 544-602 A.D.

3. Third Period 603-939 A.D.

   Ngô Dynasty 939-965 A.D.

These thousand years of Chinese domination were
marked by the strong infusion of Chinese culture
resulting in the Sinization of Vietnam. New
agricultural technology was introduced by the
Chinese colonizers as well as Confucianism, Taoism,
Buddhism and Chinese education. It was also during
this period that the people of Giao-Chỉ and later
Giao-Châu changed from a matrilineal descent system
to a patrilineal descent system. The Chinese also
ruled Vietnam from 1414 to 1427 under the Ming
Dynasty. They were driven out by the national hero,
Lê-Lợi, the founder of the Lê Dynasty.

BẠCH-ĐẰNG BATTLE. There were actually two battles on
the Bạch-Đằng River--one in 939 A.D. and the other
in 1288. In both battles the Chinese were defeated
by the Vietnamese who used the same decisive techniques. In 938, Ngô-Quyền had iron spikes driven
into the river bottom so that at high tide they
were hidden. The Chinese boats were allowed to
come up the river. When the tide went down, the
boats were pierced by the spikes leaving the
enemy trapped. Again in 1288, Trần Hưng-Đạo laid
the same trap for the invading Mongols. He sent
troops to maneuver the Chinese fleet into position,
then ambushed the Mongols as the tide went out.
Again, as in 938, the Bạch-Đằng Battle was the
deciding victory and resulted in the total defeat
of the Chinese invaders. See BẠCH-ĐẰNG RIVER,
NGÔ-QUYỀN, TRẦN HƯNG-ĐẠO.

BẠCH-ĐẰNG RIVER. A river in north Vietnam. It flows
through the provinces of Hà-Bắc, Hải-Hưng and
empties into the South China Sea near Quảng-Yên.
See BẠCH-ĐẰNG BATTLE.

BACH-VIỆT. (Literally, one hundred Viets). The name
of the region in southern China, north of Âu-Lạc
around the time of the Hồng-Bàng Dynasty and the
Thục Dynasty. It is also the generic term indicating the various ethnic groups scattered throughout the southeastern parts of mainland China during
the Chin and Han Dynasties (around 200 B.C. through
400 A.D.). See HỒNG-BÀNG DYNASTY, THỤC DYNASTY.

BAHNAR. An ethno-linguistic minority group of highland
people located in Pleiku, and Phú-Bồn provinces
and parts of Darlac, Phú-Yên and Bình-Định Provinces. The Bahnar is the largest Mon-khmer
speaking group in Vietnam, numbering around 59,000
(1965). The Bahnar were once a very powerful
people. From the fifteenth to the eighteenth
centuries, they fought against the ethnic Vietnamese and the Chàm. They also were recognized
by the Khmer King. During the nineteenth century,
the Bahnar were almost eliminated by the war-like
Harai and Dedang. With the coming of the Europeans,
the Bahnar developed a strong loyalty to the French,
particularly to the missionaries. The first French
Catholic mission to the Bahnar tribe was founded
in 1849 in Kontum. There are several subgroups of
the Bahnar including the Bonam, Hrui, Konko, Roh,
Tolo, Monam, Rongao and the Alakong. Each subgroup is distinguished by individual dialects as
well as differences in customs. The Bahnar are
one of the few groups to have had a written
language for many years. Their script, resembling
the Vietnamese Quốc-Ngữ, was developed by missionaries in 1861. Several books have been published
in the Bahnar language. The Bahnar society is
based on the nuclear family as the basic unit.
The kinship system is bilateral. Lineage is
determined through both the male and female sides
of the family. Marriage may be proposed by either
the boy's or girl's family. The young married
couples normally divide their place of residence
between their parents' homes until they establish
their own household. Personal property is inherited by blood relatives and common property is
distributed among the surviving spouse and blood
relatives. The Bahnar religion is animism, including the worship of spirits of animate and in-
animate objects. They have a subsistence economy
based primarily on the slash-and-burn (swidden)

cultivation of upland rice. Secondary crops include corn, squash, yams, cucumbers, eggplant and
tobacco. Livestock are also kept but are primarily for sacrificial purposes. It has been
estimated (1972) that there are over 100,000
Bahnar.

BẪI-BÙN POINT. (Mũi Bẫi-Bùn). The southernmost point
in south Vietnam. It is located at the southern
tip of the Cà-Mau peninsula in An-Xuyên Province.

BAMBOO. (Tre). Bamboo is by far the most versatile
product in Vietnam and one of the most important.
There are two types of bamboo grown in Vietnam.
Tre is the thick bamboo with cylindrical stalks,
tough knots and a thick durable lining. Núi is a
thin and slender variety with well spaced knots
and a fine lining. These two varieties are the
basis of the paper industry at Ðáp-Cầu and the
manufacture of cellulose paste at Việt-Trì in
north Vietnam. The young shoots are eaten as a
vegetable. The mature plant is used in housing
construction, fencing, and for innumerable other
minor uses.

BAN-MÊ-THUỘT. The capital city of Darlac Province and
the largest city in the central highlands. Population 64,585 (1971). Ban-Mê-Thuột is the unofficial capital of the central highlands. Under
the French, it was known as a center for big game
hunting. There is a normal school in the city
which is designed primarily to serve the highland
minority people. A large and important agricultural experiment station (Ea-Kmat) is located
nearby. The city is located on highway number
fourteen, 642 kilometers (140 miles) north of
Sài-Gòn.

BÀN THỜ GIA-TIÊN. (Also called Bàn Thờ Tổ-Tiên).
Family altar. The family altar is located in the
middle of the house and used to worship the spirits
of the ancestors of a nuclear family. This is not
to be confused with a nhà thờ họ or bàn thờ họ
which is used to worship the ancestors of an extended family. Each family altar is arranged
differently, but all usually have a pair of candles,
incense burner, ancestral tablets (thần-chủ), joss
stocks, a box containing the dishes and utensils
for worship and pictures of the deceased ancestors.
   The family altar varies greatly in size
according to the wealth of the family. It is
quite modest in poorer families, sometimes con-

sisting of a table and the basic necessities for
the rituals. In the homes of the aristocracy it
is very often elaborate, occupying the area equivalent to a small room, resplendent with banners,
models of ancient weapons, wooden plaques with
parallel sentences (câu đối), pictures and carved
wooden plaques indicating the rank of mandarin or
nobility of the ancestor(s). Ornate curtains
separate the various parts of the altar as well as
the altar itself from the rest of the house. The
entire area occupied by the altar is referred to
as the gia-từ. The bàn thờ gia-tiên is by far the
most important part of the Vietnamese home. See
CULT OF THE ANCESTORS.

BÀN THỜ HỌ. (Also called Bàn Thờ Thủy-Tổ or Nhà Thờ Họ).
The household altar used to worship the ancestors
of an extended family or clan (họ). This is not
to be confused with the bàn thờ gia-tiên, which is
used for the worship of the ancestors of the
nuclear family. The bàn thờ họ is usually maintained by the head of the họ (trưởng-tộc). On the
altar is kept the ancestral tablets (bài-vị) which
proclaims the name of the clan, plus other ornaments and instruments for the ritual such as
candles, offering (sacrifice) trays and incense
burners. Sometimes in place of an altar, a stele
is placed in the open air with the name of the
various ancestors in the family. This is used
for worship on the anniversary of the death of
the founder of the extended family. See CULT OF
THE ANCESTORS, NGÀY GIỖ HỌ.

BÁNH CHƯNG. A special cake made for the Tết (lunar
new year) celebration. It is made from sticky
rice, pork and soybeans wrapped in green banana
and rush leaves. It is steamed all night over an
open fire. Legend has it that King Hùng-Vương VIII
had many sons and could not choose a successor. He
told them all to seek out the finest, most delicious dish in the land. The one to return and
present him with the best dish would become the
heir apparent. All of his sons left to scour the
countryside except one who did not want to leave
his aging father alone. Although he would not
leave his father's side, he also had to obey his
command to present him with a new dish. Word of
his predicament reached a sage who instructed the
son to make two cakes from sticky rice; a round
cake representing the heavens to be called Bánh
Giầy, and a square cake representing the earth to
be called Bánh Chưng. The son not only presented
his father with the most delicious dish, but

honored him by relating the significance attached
to each cake. See BANH GIẤY.

BÁNH ĐA. A rice wafer made from rice paste and often
covered with sesame seeds. It is dried on racks
in the sun until crisp, then sometimes toasted
over an open fire. Banh Đa is a common food
throughout Vietnam.

BÁNH ĐÚC. A rice cake made from white rice. The rice
is ground into flour and combined with a little
powdered limestone and water to make a paste. Then
as it cools it jells into the shape of the mold
or container in which it was placed. It is eaten
by itself or together with other condiments such
as pork sausage. Banh đúc is a very popular dish
among the rich and poor alike.

BÁNH GIẤY. A rice cake made from glutinous rice. It
is often served together with banh chung on special
occasions such as engagement ceremonies, weddings
or funerals. For the legendary origins of banh
giầy see BANH CHỨNG.

BẢO-ĐẠI (1926-1945). The thirteenth and last emperor
of the Nguyễn Dynasty (1802-1945). He was the only
son of Emperor Khải-Định, who took him to France to
be educated. Bảo-Đại proved to be a powerless
emperor, a puppet in the hands of France. He was
not even allowed to give honorary titles without
French approval. He came to the throne in 1926 at
the age of twelve, but he stayed in France to complete his education. He finally returned to Vietnam in 1932. The Japanese occupied Vietnam during
World War II at which time Bảo-Đại proclaimed independence and asked Trần Trọng-Kim to form a new
government. Several months later, he was forced
to abdicate by the revolutionary Việt-Minh. After
his abdication on August 25, 1945, he was made
high counselor to the new government of the Democratic Republic of Vietnam. In June of 1949 after
two years of negotiations with France, the French
government approved of limited independence for
the State of Vietnam. Bảo-Đại became the Chief
of State, a position which he held until October,
1955, when his Prime Minister, Ngô Đình-Diệm,
called for and won a national referendum calling
for the country to become a republic under his
leadership as chief of state. Bảo-Đại then retired and returned to France where he has remained
since. See AUGUST REVOLUTION, NGÔ ĐÌNH-DIỆM,
NGUYỄN DYNASTY, TRẦN TRỌNG-KIM.

BẢO-LỘC. (Also known as Blao). The capital city of
Lâm-Đồng Province. Population 29,752. It is
located on highway number twenty, the main route
between Sài-Gòn and Đà-Lạt. A large segment of
the inhabitants are from north Vietnam and settled
there in 1954. Bảo-Lộc is best known as a center
of tea production. A large modern tea processing
plant built recently under the Colombo plan is
located in the town. There is a small silk industry maintained chiefly by the north Vietnamese.
A college of agriculture was established there
but because of the war, it has been converted to
an agricultural high school. See LÂM-ĐỒNG
PROVINCE.

BẢO-NGHIÊM STONE TOWER. (Tháp Bảo-Nghiêm). A well-
known tower part of the Ninh-Phúc pagoda in Hà-
Bắc Province, eighteen kilometers (eleven miles)
north of Hà-Nội. It was built with large square
blocks in 1647. It stands five stories high,
measures ten meters (thirty-three feet) high and
is octagonal in shape. The top of the tower is
in the shape of a pen brush. Consequently, the
tower is sometimes called the pen-brush tower.

BASSAC RIVER. See HẬU-GIANG RIVER.

BÁT-CÚ. A form of classical poetry (Dường-Luật) in
which each verse has eight lines, five of which
rhyme.

BEAU, JEAN-BAPTISTE-PAUL (1857-1926). Governor General
of Indochina from October, 1902 to February, 1908.
He opened the first Indochinese University. He
also provided for the direct Vietnamese participation in the lower ranks of the colonial administration, organized medical assistance and abolished certain corporal punishments.

BẾN-HẢI RIVER. (Sông Bến-Hải also known as Sông Hiền-
Lường). A river in central Vietnam. It originates
in the mountains of Laos and empties into the South
China Sea at Cửa Tùng in Quảng-Trị Province. The
Bến-Hải River is located at approximately the
seventeenth parallel, and has served as the de-
marcation line separating the Democratic Republic
of Vietnam from the Republic of Vietnam since
July 22,,1954. See DEMARCATION LINE, DEMILITARIZED
ZONE, CỬA TÙNG, QUẢNG-TRỊ PROVINCE.

BẾN-NGHÉ RIVER. See SÀI-GÒN RIVER.

BẾN-TRÉ. See TRÚC-GIANG.

BERT, PAUL (1838-1886). Resident General for Annam
    and Tongking from February to November, 1886. A
    physician and professor, he instituted a number
    of reforms in the interest of the Vietnamese. He
    restored some of the prestige to the scholars and
    emperor, founded the Tongkinese Academy and the
    Council of Tongkinese Notables. His last official
    request before his death was for funds to build
    an electric plant on the Red River.

BETEL NUT. See TRẦU.

BÍCH-CẦU KỲ NGỘ. A classic epic poem written in nôm
    by an unknown author. The poem contains 648 lines
    and is written in the lục-bát (6-8) style. The
    story is one which was recorded by several authors
    and took place during the Lê Dynasty (1428-1788).
    See LỤC-BÁT, NÔM.

BIÊN-HOA CITY. The capital city of Biên-Hòa Province.
    The population is given as 177,513 (1971). The
    city was established by the Chinese refugees and
    immigrants in the 1680's, and was originally
    called Đồng-Nai Đại-Phố. The present city is
    located on the east bank of the Đồng-Nai River.
    It is situated thirty-two kilometers (twenty
    miles) north of Sài-Gòn. It is connected to Sài-
    Gòn by the Biên-Hòa highway, a four lane highway
    along which the Biên-Hòa industrial park is lo-
    cated. See BIÊN-HOA PROVINCE, ĐỒNG-NAI RIVER.

BIÊN-HOA PROVINCE. An inland province in south Vietnam.
    Biên-Hòa was one of six original provinces of
    south Vietnam, created in 1832 by Emperor Minh-
    Mạng (ruled 1820-1840). Prior to that time the
    region was known as Trấn-Biên. In accordance with
    the treaty of 1862, Biên-Hòa was relinquished to
    the French. With the treaty of 1874, the French
    acquired the three remaining provinces. These six
    provinces were then divided into twenty of which
    Biên-Hòa was one. The province is located north
    of Sài-Gòn and south of Long-Khánh Province. The
    provincial capital, Biên-Hòa City, is located on
    the Đồng-Nai River. The population of the pro-
    vince is 496,638 (1971) and the area is 2,407
    square kilometers (929 square miles). The pro-
    vince has always been agriculturally productive,
    the chief products being rubber, sugar cane, rice,
    coffee, tobacco and a grapefruit-like fruit called
    trai bưởi, (pamelo). Biên-Hòa Province also has
    a few small quarries which supply rock and gravel
    for road construction and sand for other construc-
    tion needs. More recently, the province has been

the site of several new industries, including a
cement plant, textile mills, and a glass factory.
The area along the highway running between Sài-
Gòn and Biên-Hòa City is designed to be an in-
dustrial park. A large airfield and headquarters
base was built by the United States Army at Long-
Bien, near the provincial capital. See BIÊN-HÒA
CITY, INDUSTRY.

BINDWEED. See RAU-MUỐNG.

BÌNH-ĐỊNH PROVINCE. A large coastal province in central Vietnam. The province is located south of
Quảng-Ngãi and north of Phú-Yên Province. It has
a land mass of 9,429 square kilometers (3,640
square miles) and an estimated population of
754,150 (1971). The area now covered by Bình-
Định Province was once a part of the kingdom of
Champa (Chiêm-Thành). The capital, (Vijaya) was
once located here. Vijaya was conquered by the
Vietnamese in 1470, during the Lê Dynasty (1428-
1788). In 1600, Nguyễn-Hoàng named the city Qui-
Nhơn. In 1771, Nguyễn-Nhạc captured it and it
became the capital for the Tây-Sơn Dynasty (1788-
1802). The provincial capital, Qui-Nhơn, is located
on the coast, 680 kilometers (422 miles) north of
Sài-Gòn and 400 kilometers (248 miles) south of
Huế. Qui-Nhơn has developed into an important
deep water port and commercial center. Much of
the rice land is comparatively rich, especially
in the districts of Phú-Mỹ and Hoài-Nhơn. The
principal occupations of the inhabitants of Bình-
Định Province are farming and fishing. The main
products are rice, fish, salt, coconut, and mung
bean. National highway number one and the railroad run from north to south through the province.
Highway nineteen connects Qui-Nhơn with Pleiku and
Kontum via the An-Khê Pass. Besides the ethnic
Vietnamese, there are Chàm, Hroy, and Bahnar
people living in the province. See AN-KHÊ, QUI-
NHƠN, TÂY-SƠN REBELLION.

BÌNH-ĐỊNH-VƯƠNG. (Literally, King of Pacification).
The title assumed by Lê-Lợi during the Lam-Sơn
resistance movement (1418-1427) and before he became Emperor Lê Thái-Tổ (1428-1433). See LAM-SƠN
UPRISING, LÊ-LỢI, LÊ THÁI-TỔ.

BÌNH-DƯƠNG PROVINCE. (Formerly Thủ-Dầu-Một Province).
An inland province in south Vietnam. It is situ-
ated north of Sài-Gòn bordering on Tây-Ninh
Province to the west and Biên-Hòa Province to the

east. The provincial capital of Bình-Dương Province is Phú-Cường. The population is 257,900
and the land mass is 2,033 square kilometers (784
square miles). The main products of the province
include rice, sugarcane, peanuts, fruits, and
handicrafts. The province is especially well-
known for the lacquerware which is produced in
and around the provincial capital. See LACQUER-
WARE, PHÚ-CƯỜNG.

BINH-GIA CIVILIZATION. The oldest known-stone age
civilization in Vietnam. It is named for the
village of Bình-Gia in Lạng-Sơn Province in north
Vietnam. A piece of an anthropoid (ape) tooth
was unearthed in this location which is believed
to represent the oldest traces of mankind in what
is now Vietnam. This archaeological find has been
dated at about 300,000 years B.C. See PREHISTORY.

BINH-NGÔ ĐẠI-CAO. (The Great Proclamation). A proclamation written by Nguyễn-Trãi as authorized by
Lê-Lợi after he defeated the Chinese in 1427 and
thus ended the Chinese occupation of Vietnam. In
this classic work, the author recounts all the
hardships, difficulties and sufferings of the Vietnamese during the period of Chinese domination and
during the war for independence. See LAM-SƠN UP-
RISING, LÊ-LỢI, NGUYỄN-TRÃI.

BINH-NGUYÊN. See ĐỒNG-BẰNG.

BINH-PHÚ-KHÁNH-NINH PLAINS. (Đồng-Bằng Bình-Phú-Khánh-
Ninh). The part of the central coastal plain
which extends from the Ẻn Peninsula in Bình-Định
Province to the Dinh Peninsula in Ninh-Thuận Province. The area measures 5,560 square kilometers
(2,146 square miles) and includes the lowland portions of Bình-Định, Phú-Yên, Khánh-Hòa, and Ninh-
Thuận provinces. The main rivers of the region
are the Đà-Rằng River (Phú-Yên Province) and the
Giang River (Khánh-Hòa Province). The two chief
ports of the plains area are located in Cam-Ranh
and Nha-Trang. The seaward side of the plains is
known for its resort beaches, sea food and salt
fields. The bulk of the land between the coast
and the mountains is used for rice production. A
large amount of coconut is produced along the
coast. See CENTRAL COASTAL PLAIN.

BINH-SƠN TOWER. (Tháp Bình-Sơn), A tower (temple) in
Lập-Thạch District, Vĩnh-Phú Province in north
Vietnam. It was built under the Lý Dynasty (1010-
1225) and is considered to be an excellent example

of Vietnamese architecture. It stands 15.5 meters
(51 feet) high and has fourteen stories of which
only eleven still remain. The tower is made of
large bricks of various sizes. It displays a
harmonious style and is ornately decorated with
designs and archways.

BÌNH-THUẬN PROVINCE. A coastal province in central
Vietnam located south of Ninh-Thuận Province and
north of Bình-Thuy Province. It has a population
of 284,929 (1971) and a land mass of 5,000 square
kilometers (1,930 square miles). The provincial
capital, Phan-Thiết, is situated on national highway number one 200 kilometers (124 miles) north of
Sài-Gòn and 880 kilometers (546 miles) south of
Huế. Phan-Thiết is a coastal town famous for its
fishing industry and nước mắm production. Bình-
Thuận was once a part of Champa. In 1693, the
Nguyễn lords captured the Chàm king and negotiated
the release of Thuận-Phủ, which under Emperor Gia-
Long (1802-1819) became Bình-Thuận. Two important
towns in the province are Sông-Mao, a railroad
town with a large Nùng population, and Phan-Lý-Chàm,
a center of the Chàm culture. Phan-Ri (also called
Phan-Ri-Cửa) is a fishing center at the mouth of
the Lũy River. In addition to the Nùng and Chàm
people, the province has a large number of the
Raglai and Rai ethno-linguistic minority groups.
Many vestiges of the Chàm empire and culture are
located in Bình-Thuận. The southernmost Cham
tower (tháp-Chàm) is located in An-Hải Village of
Hải-Long District. A walled fortification pro-
tecting the banks of the Lũy River was constructed
around 1692 and is still preserved in Hải-Ninh
District. About seventeen kilometers (ten miles)
west of Sông-Mao is the Yan-Yin Mountain, where
legend says that the spirit Yan-Yin made a spring
and a pond to go fishing and spend his leisure
time. Bình-Thuận is the southernmost province of
central Vietnam. In addition to the north-south
highway number one which runs through the province,
the capital, Phan-Thiết is linked by road to Đà-
Lạt to the northwest. See NƯỚC-MẮM, CHÀM, SÔNG-
MAO, PHAN-THIẾT.

BÌNH-TRỊ-THIÊN PLAINS. (Đồng-Bằng Bình-Trị-Thiên).
That portion of the central coastal plains which
extends from the Hoành-Sởn mountains in Quảng-
Bình Province to the Ải-Vân Pass just north of
Đà-Nẵng in Thừa-Thiên Province. It includes the
lowland areas of Quảng-Bình, Quảng-Trị and Thừa-
Thiên provinces. The area measures some 2,000
square kilometers (772 square miles) and includes

the delta areas of the Perfume River, Bến-Hải
River and the Đại-Giang River. It is extremely
narrow, measuring only a few miles in certain
places. The soil is poor and subject to salt
water intrusion, flooding and drought. The coastal area is sandy and barren for the most part and
is dotted with fishing villages. See CENTRAL
COASTAL PLAIN.

BINH-TUY PROVINCE. A coastal province in south Vietnam.
It is situated south of Binh-Thuận Province and
north of Phước-Tuy. The population of Binh-Tuy
Province is 74,315 (1971). It covers an area of
3,696 square kilometers (1,427 square miles). The
provincial capital, Hàm-Tân, is located near the
coast. The province is mostly mountainous. The
chief products include timber, fish and wild game
such as deer, tiger, and wild boar. See HÀM-TÂN.

BINH-XUYÊN. A bandit-type political sect which was
active in and around Sài-Gòn between 1945 and 1955.
The sect was led by Lê Văn-Viên, alias Bảy-Viên
who started with a band of river pirates that operated along the marshy stretches of Chợ-Lớn,
working first with the Viet-Minh against the
French. Some hold the Binh-Xuyên responsible for
the 1945 massacre of 150 French women and children.
in a Sài-Gòn city block where they had been in-
terned by the Japanese. The Binh-Xuyên changed
loyalties and was recognized by the French and the
Sài-Gòn regime in 1948. While continuing their
illegal activities, such as extortion and gambling,
they also participated in local and national politics. In 1953 they received nine seats in the
national congress. However, in March of 1955 the
Binh-Xuyên broke with the government of Premier
Ngô Đình-Diệm. Then, a brief but bloody civil
war in and around Sài-Gòn ensued which resulted
in the complete elimination of the Binh-Xuyên as
an effective political force.

BLACK FLAGS. (cờ đen). A private army comprised
mainly of Chinese, who, after the failure of the
Tai-Ping Revolt of 1865, had fled into north Vietnam. There, many of them actually became pirates.
They pillaged the villages, engaged in illegal
opium traffic and even traded in slaves. Some,
however, were hired by the court at Huế to keep
order in Tongking before the French took Hà-Nội.
Later, particularly in 1873 and 1882, they fought
for the Vietnamese government against the French.
After the French established themselves in Hà-Nội,
the Black Flags made common cause with the

resistance movement against the French. The central figure and leader of the Black Flags was Lưu
Vĩnh-Phúc. See LƯU VĨNH-PHÚC.

BLACK RIVER. See ĐÀ-GIANG RIVER.

BLACK THÁI. (Thái Đen). An ethno-linguistic group of
highland people located in north Vietnam. They
are so named because of the characteristic black
color of the women's costume. The Black Thái together with the White Thái, Red Thái, and the Tày
(Thổ) are the principal Thai speaking groups of
north Vietnam. The Black Thai are concentrated
in the area between the Red and Black rivers and
can also be found in northern Laos. The population estimates for the Black and White Thai are
given at 350,000 (1969). A small number of Black
and White Thai have resettled in Tùng-Nghĩa
(Tuyên-Đức Province) in central Vietnam. See THÁI.

BLAO. See BÁO-LỘC.

BỜ-RIVER. (Sông Bờ). See ĐÀ-GIANG RIVER.

BOLLAERT, EMILE. High Commissioner to Indochina from
March, 1947 to October, 1948.

BONARD, LOUIS-ALDOPHE (1805-1867). The first Governor
of Cochinchina. He took command of the French
forces in November, 1861, and proceeded to conquer Biên-Hòa and pushed deep into Vĩnh-Long Province. On June 6, 1862, he signed a preliminary
treaty with Phan Thanh-Giản which left France in
possession of the three northern provinces (Gia-
Định, Định-Tường, and Biên-Hòa) as well as the
island of Puolo Condore (Côn-Sơn). Bonard had
had previous experience in Algiers and tried to
set up a similar type of French protectorate in
which the administrative responsibilities are
assumed by the indigenous inhabitants. However,
the mandarins would not cooperate. They left and
took the official records, thus forcing him into
direct administration. He carried the treaty to
Huế for the Emperor's signature in April, 1863,
and then took the signed copy to France, turning
the governorship over to de la Grandiere. See
TREATY OF SÀI-GÒN.

BREVIE, JULES. Governor General of Indochina from
January, 1937, to August, 1939. He brought about
many liberal reforms including the authorization
of Vietnamese political parties and their newspapers to operate openly.

BROU. See BRŨ.

BRŨ. (Also known as Brou). An ethno-linguistic
minority group of highland people native to Quảng-
Trị Province and adjacent parts of Laos. The Brũ
are closely related to the Pacoh of Thừa-Thiên
Province. Both tribes are often categorized as
part of a larger grouping called the Van-Kiêu.
The Brũ language is in the Mon-Khmer language
family and is classified as a member of the Katuic
branch. Brũ society is patriarchal and the lineage
and inheritance follow the male line. In 1965 it
was estimated that there were over 22,000 Bru in
the Republic of Vietnam. However, war, especially
the battle of Khê-Sanh (1968) and the general
offensive against the Republic of Vietnam (1972),
have caused major dislocation and dispersal of
the Brũ people, making it impossible to give an
accurate population figure, except for those
living in refugee camps. See VAN-KIÊU.

BÚA-LIÊM NEWSPAPER. (Literally, hammer and sickle
newspaper). The first Vietnamese communist newspaper. It was published from late 1929 by the
Communist Party and later by the Indochinese
Communist Party. It was designed to disseminate
the policy and propaganda of the party and to promote the revolutionary struggle throughout Vietnam.

BUDDHISM. (Phật-Giáo). The predominant religion in
Vietnam. Buddhism was introduced into Vietnam
simultaneously via sea from India (Theravada Buddhism) and overland from China (Mahayana Buddhism).
Mâu-Tử is credited with introducing Buddhism to
Vietnam from China around 194-195 A.D. Although
it was first carried to Vietnam by pilgrims and
refugees, it was promoted and supported by diplo-
mats, merchants and immigrants. The religion did
not gain popularity with the masses until much
later.
     Emperor Đinh-Tiên-Hoàng (968-979) instituted
a policy of royal support to Buddhism which was
continued by the Early Lê Dynasty (980-1009) and
reached a high point under the Lý Dynasty (1010-
1225). This support included recognition and elevation of the Buddhist hierarchy, construction
of pagodas, financial support and an active role
for the clergy in the rule of the country. Emperor Lý Anh-Tông (1138-1175) proclaimed Buddhism
as the official state religion. By the eleventh
century Buddhism had filtered down to the village

level. By this time it was mixed with Taoism and
Confucianism and as such became an indigenous part
of the popular beliefs of the common people.
Under the Trần Dynasty (1225-1400) Buddhism began
to experience competition from Confucianism as
the main religion of the court. Confucian scholars
gradually replaced Buddhist clergy in the mandarin
corps. In 1414 the invading Chinese brought re-
newed vigor to the encouragement of Confucianism
as well as the destruction of many pagodas and
Buddhist writings. The Nguyễn lords reversed this
trend for political reasons. In 1601, Nguyễn-
Hoàng ordered the construction of the famous Thiên-
Mụ Pagoda in Huế. But the discipline of the religion continued to decline and became thoroughly
mixed with mysticism, animism, polytheism and
tantrism (rituals derived from Hinduism). In 1920,
Buddhism began a revival throughout Vietnam.
Starting in 1931 formal Buddhist organizations
were established in Hà-Nội, Huế and Sài-Gòn. This
organizational emphasis has continued to the
present. Most recently (1963), the Buddhist church
played a major role in the overthrow of President
Ngô Đình-Diệm which reflects the strength of Buddhism in the Republic of Vietnam.
     The Mahayana or Greater Wheel (Bắc-Tông or
Đại-Thừa) school of Buddhism is predominant in
Vietnam, especially in north and central Vietnam.
The largest sect of Mahayana Buddhism in Vietnam
is the Thiền (Dhyana or Zen) sect, otherwise
known as the school of meditation. The second
most important sect is the pure land school (Đạo
Trang) and is practiced mainly in the south.
     Theravada Buddhism or Lesser Wheel (Nam-Tông
or Tiểu-Thừa) is practiced mainly in the ten delta
provinces of south Vietnam. Its adherents are
chiefly ethnic Cambodian (Khmer). The principal
sect of Vietnamese Theravada Buddhism is the dis-
ciplinary school (Luật-Tông).
     Recent organizational attempts have been made
to unite the various factions of Buddhism in Vietnam. Most notably was the Fourth Buddhist Congress
in 1958 which was held in Hà-Nội and the Unified
Buddhist Church of Vietnam (Giáo Hội Phật-Giáo
Việt-Nam Thống-Nhất) which was organized in Sài-Gòn
in 1964. There is one Buddhist university (Văn-
Hạnh University) which is located in Sài-Gòn. See
PAGODAS, RELIGION.

-C-

CA-DAO. Folk songs. Ca-dao are a vital part of the
    oral literature of Vietnam. These short songs are
    usually written in the lục-bát (six-eight) form,
    although other forms include song-thất (double-
    seven) and nối-lối. Ca-dao, by its very nature,
    reflects the soul of the common people, of a given
    period. See LỤC-BÁT, NỐI-LỐI, SONG-THẤT.

CA HUẾ. (Also known as hát lý). Huế songs. A form
    of traditional entertainment music performed in
    the Huế court. It was probably introduced under
    a different name in the thirteenth century, with
    a heavy influence from the music of Champa. How-
    ever, it has become known by the present name and
    style only since the founding of Huế as the cap-
    ital in 1802. Ca Huế can be played in solo, duet,
    trio or quartet. The poetic lyrics must follow
    rigid rules of composition.

CÀ-MAU PENINSULA. An area at the southern tip of south
    Vietnam. It is bordered on the west by the Gulf
    of Thailand and on the east by the South China Sea.
    It includes all of An-Xuyên Province and parts of
    Kiên-Giang, Chương-Thiện, and Bạc-Liêu provinces.
    The area was originally part of Cambodia and was
    called Tuk Khmau (Black Country) in Cambodian.
    Under the French it was a district of Bạc-Liêu
    Province. After the Geneva agreements, the penin-
    sula was designated as a regrouping place for the
    Việt-Minh before they went north. The term Cà-Mau
    is often applied to that area that is presently
    occupied by An-Xuyên Province. See AN-XUYÊN
    PROVINCE.

CẢ PASS. (Đèo Cả). A coastal mountain pass in the
    Trường-Sơn mountains in central Vietnam. The pass
    separates the two provinces in Khánh-Hòa and Phú-
    Yên.

CẢ RIVER. (Sông Cả). A river in central Vietnam. It
    originates in the mountains of Laos and flows
    through Nghệ-An Province where it empties into the
    South China Sea at Bến-Thủy, near Vinh. The river
    is 400 kilometers (248 miles) long. An important
    tributary of the Cả River is the Con River.

CAI-ĐÁM. A person elected by the village to be in charge
    of the village religious ceremonies and rituals in
    traditional Vietnam. Strict requirements were

prescribed in order to be eligible for this position. One had to be a third generation native
of the village, healthy and not widowed, handi-
capped or in mourning. A person in this position
was required to reside in the temple, not visit
his wife or an expectant mother or attend a funeral. Since he was preoccupied with the worship of
the village spirits he had to relinquish similar
responsibility for ancestral worship within his
own family. Tenure in this position was usually
for one year or more. The villager who served as
cai-dảm was expected to always be on hand at the
temple, especially on holy days. He was responsible for all religious aspects of the temple and
for performing certain rituals at predetermined
times and dates.

CẢI-LƯỜNG. The modern musical theater of the south.
This theater form was introduced in 1917 by a
group of Vietnamese musicians who combined several
existing forms of music. Cải-lường employs a
variety of combinations of instruments, including
at times, western instruments. Singing is the
most important feature of this type of theater,
and the most important style of song is the vọng-
cổ, a form representing nostalgia and sadness.
Often performed by traveling groups, cải-lường
has steadily grown in popularity, especially in
the south and especially with the advent of modern
communications.

CẢI RIVER. (Sông Cái, also known as Sông Thu-Bồn, Sông
Bùng or Sông Bổng). A river in central Vietnam.
It originates in the mountains in the western part
of Quảng-Nam Province and flows past Hội-An where
it empties into the South China Sea. The Cái
River is often called the Thu-Bồn River. However,
the Thu-Bồn River is actually a tributary of the
Cái River. See CỬA-ĐẠI, HỘI-AN, QUẢNG-NAM.

CẢI-TÁNG. (Also called cát-táng or bốc-mộ). The process
of exhuming and washing the bones of a deceased
person in order to bury them in a final grave chosen by a geomancer. This is done in cases where
the original burial site was chosen hurriedly or
for some other reason a good location was not
available. It is also done if there is reason to
believe that the spirit of the deceased is restless or not compatible with the original site.
Sometimes when a family cannot afford a proper
burial site the first time it will exhume and wash
the remains and rebury them when it can finance a

better burial and do justice to their ancestors.
The process of cải-táng is usually carried out
three or four years after the death. The remains
are unearthed, the bones washed carefully with
perfumed water and placed in a clay pot. Care
is taken not to let the sunlight shine on the
remains. The pot is then taken to the new site
and buried. This practice was popular in traditional Vietnam, especially in the north. See
ĐƯA-ĐÁM, MỘC-DỤC.

CAM-LỘ RIVER. (Sông Cam-Lộ). See HIẾU-GIANG RIVER.

CAM-RANH. (Also known as Cam-Lâm). A port and autonomous municipality located in central Vietnam
between Khánh-Hòa and Ninh-Thuận provinces. The
port is situated on Cam-Ranh Bay, near Ba-Ngòi
and is considered to be an excellent natural harbor. It was used by the Russian fleet in 1904
during the Russian-Japanese war. The Japanese
also used it during World War II. More recently
the Americans established a major military base
there, constructed a large airstrip and extensive
port facilities. The municipality of Cam-Ranh
was established in 1965 and has a population of
104,666 (1971).

CẦN-LAO NHÂN-VỊ CÁCH-MẠNG ĐẢNG. Revolutionary Personalist Labor Party, also known as the Cần-Lao
Party. A secret, elite, political organization
in the Republic of Vietnam founded by Ngô Đình-
Nhu (brother of President Ngô Đình-Diệm) in 1954.
The Cần-Lao Party was composed of selectively
recruited intellectuals, labor leaders, civil
service members and military officers. The exact
membership of the party has never been clearly
established; however, estimates seem to place the
membership at 20,000-25,000 during its most active
period, i.e., from 1954-1963. The Cần-Lao Party
never sought a mass following nor did it compete
openly in elections. Rather, it was designed to
effect a certain amount of political and economic
control through intelligence gathering and report-
ing, and through the support by the local membership to elections campaigns, public demonstrations,
and governmental programs. The theoretical base
for the party's philosophy came from the Personalist Doctrine (Thuyết Nhân-Vị) - a synthesis of
eastern and western ideologies developed by Ngô
Đình-Nhu. The party employed several distinct
methods and techniques which were identical to
the traditional communist approach, including

cells, front organizations, political study classes, clandestine operations, etc. While Ngô Đinh-Nhu maintained control of most of the Cần-Lao Party, his brother, Ngô Đinh-Cẩn, retained control of the party in central Vietnam. After the overthrow of Ngô Đinh-Diệm in 1963, the Cần-Lao Party became practically inactive and, in fact, was the target of widespread hostility from the population. However, it has recently resumed its activity albeit very low key. See NGÔ ĐINH-CẨN, NGÔ ĐINH-DIỆM, NGÔ ĐINH-NHU.

CẦN-THỞ. The capital city of Phong-Dinh Province and the principal city in the Mekong Delta. Population 153,769. It is located on the west bank of the lower Mekong River. It is also located on highway number four which runs from Sài-Gòn to Cà-Mau. The city is directly connected by road to An-Giang and Châu-Đốc provinces and to most other population centers in the delta by an intricate system of canals and rivers. Consequently, it is the transportation and communication center of the Mekong Delta. The city is the site of the University of Cần-Thở which opened in 1966 and is one of the five major universities in the Republic of Vietnam. The city of Cần-Thở was established as an autonomous municipality on September 30, 1970. See PHONG-DINH PROVINCE.

CẦN-VUỐNG MOVEMENT. (Literally, Loyalty to the King Movement). The resistance movement formed around the deposed Emperor Hàm-Nghi. The name of the movement was taken from the edict which was issued on July 13, 1885 and was widely distributed. It called on the citizenry, especially the scholars, to rally around Hàm-Nghi against the French. This short-lived royalist movement was characterized by numerous local revolts which were led by such groups as the Bãi-Sậy Front in the north and the Nghĩa-Hội in the center. The movement was subdued when Hàm-Nghi was captured in November, 1888. Only the famous patriot, Phan Đinh-Phùng continued the struggle by leading his resistance army of 3,000 men against the French. He kept up his campaign until 1895 when he died of dysentery. Other famous patriots affiliated with the movement included Cao-Thắng, Trần Văn-Du and Hoàng Hoa-Thám (Đề-Thám). See CAO-THẮNG, ĐỀ-THÁM, HÀM-NGHI, PHAN ĐINH-PHÙNG.

CANTON. See TỔNG.

CAO BÁ-QUÁT (?-1854). A scholar and poet in the Nguyễn
Dynasty (1802-1945). He was from Bắc-Ninh Province.
He studied with his father and in 1831 successfully
passed the regional examinations in Hà-Nội. He
was a brilliant, easygoing and precocious student
who repeatedly took the examinations and failed
them, mainly because of his insolent wit and un-
conformity. In 1841, Cao Bá-Quát was chosen to
go to Singapore with an official delegation.
Upon his return he was ordered to a post in Sơn-
Tây. There after becoming disenchanted with the
court and bureaucracy, he quit his post in order
to support a revolt against the court. Together
with an alleged descendant of the Lê Dynasty
(1428-1788), Lê Duy-Cự, he led a revolt in 1854
in the area of Sơn-Tây that is known as the
"Locust Revolt". The revolt failed. Cao Bá-Quát
was captured and executed in the same year. His
poems, in both classical Chinese (Hán) and Nôm
are still famous. Even Emperor Tự-Đức (1848-1883)
against whom he revolted, praised his work. See
LOCUST REVOLT.

CAO-BẰNG CITY. The capital city of Cao-Bằng Province
in north Vietnam. It is located 292 kilometers
(181 miles) from Hà-Nội. See CAO-BẰNG PROVINCE.

CAO-BẰNG PROVINCE. A mountainous province in north
Vietnam. Cao-Bằng Province borders on China to
the north and is situated between Lạng-Sơn and
Hà-Giang provinces. It is presently part of the
Việt-Bắc Autonomous Region. The estimated population of the province is 274,069 (1968) and it
covers an area of 9,897 square kilometers (3,821
square miles). The provincial capital, Cao-Bằng
City is located 292 kilometers (181 miles) north
of Hà-Nội. The province is inhabited mainly
by highland tribal groups, specifically the Thổ,
Nùng, Dao and Mèo ethno-linguistic groups. There
is also a significant number of ethnic Vietnamese
living in the province. Cao-Bằng Province was
part of the original Chinese province of Giao-
Châu. After the first period of independence in
the tenth century, the area was placed under the
rule of the local Thái (Thổ) tribal chieftains
where it remained almost continually up until
modern times. It was also the last stronghold of
the Mạc Dynasty (1527-1592). The principal products of the province include livestock (beef, pork
and goats), zinc and lumber. The area is also
known for its wild game. There are many scenic
locations in the province including waterfalls

and grottoes, some of which are quite famous and extensive.

CAO-ĐAI. (Đại-Đạo Tam-Kỳ Phổ-Độ). A religion native to south Vietnam. Cao-Daiism was founded by a visionary and spiritualist, Ngô Văn-Chiêu. In 1919, he is said to have received a divine revelation setting forth the tenets of the Cao-Đai doctrine. The Cao-Đai religion is actually a composite of several religions and includes elements of Buddhism, Christianity, Islamism, Taoism, and Confucianism. Among its many Saints are Victor Hugo, Sir Winston Churchill, Dr. Sun Yat Sen and the Vietnamese prophet, Trạng-Trình. The center of the Cao-Đai faith is the city of Tây-Ninh. The church is strongest in the Mekong Delta area although, Cao-Đai temples can be found throughout south and central Vietnam. It is estimated that between one and a half and two million people are followers of the Cao-Đai religion. The essence of the doctrine is the belief that there were three major revelations to mankind. The first was to several saints of various religions including Moses. The second came later to Jesus, Confucius, Lao-Tse, Buddha and Muhammad. The third came to Ngô Văn-Chiêu who founded the "Cao-Đai", or the "Doctrine of the Third Revelation." The main articles of the faith include the belief in one God, respect for the dead, maintenance of the cult of the ancestors, the existence of the soul and the use of mediums to communicate with the spiritual world. The Cao-Đai Church has been a formidable political force. At one time it maintained an independent army which received support from the Japanese and later from the French. The church is still a determining force in the political affairs of Tây-Ninh Province and surrounding areas. See NGÔ VĂN-CHIÊU, TÂY-NINH CITY, TÂY-NINH PROVINCE.

CAO-LÃNH. The capital city of Kiên-Phong Province in south Vietnam. Population 31,836. The city is located on the south edge of the Plain of Reeds. It is situated near the east bank of the upper Mekong River.

CAO-NGUYÊN TRUNG-PHẦN. See CENTRAL HIGHLANDS.

CAO THẮNG. A patriot and comrade of Phan Đình-Phùng. Cao Thắng was born in Hà-Tĩnh Province and adopted by Phan Đình-Phùng's brother. When Phan Đình-Phùng set out to organize a resistance army Cao

Thắng followed him and became one of his lieutenants. In 1887, Phan Đình-Phùng went north to
solicit support. Cao Thắng reorganized the army,
recruited more troops and equipped them. Of
special note was Cao Thắng's accomplishment at
reproducing the newest French rifles. In 1895 the
French went all out to defeat the resistance forces.
As they applied an increasing amount of pressure,
the army was forced to move its base. In October,
1893, he volunteered to lead a desperate attack on
Nghệ-An. He took three French posts on the way,
but was killed while engaging the fourth. Cao
Thắng was a man of small stature but great intellect and resourcefulness. See PHAN ĐÌNH-PHÙNG.

CAOLAN. An ethno-linguistic minority group of highland people located in the provinces of Tuyên-
Quang, Hà-Bắc and Bắc-Thái in north Vietnam. They
speak a Sino-Thai language of the Sino-Tibetan
language family. According to the 1960 census,
the Caolan numbered 22,543.

CAP ST. JACQUES. See VŨNG-TÀU.

CAPE PADARAN. See DINH POINT.

CÁT-BÀ ISLAND. (Đảo Cát-Bà). A large island in the
Gulf of Tongking. It was formerly in Quảng-Yên
Province but is now included in the municipality
of Hải-Phong. The northern side of the island is
the southern boundary of Hạ-Long Bay. See HẠ-
LONG BAY.

CATHOLICISM. (Công-giáo). See CHRISTIANITY.

CATROUX, GEORGES. Governor General of Indochina from
August, 1939, to July, 1940. He was a career
military officer and diplomat.

CÂU ĐỐI. (Parallel sentences). A literary art form of
Chinese origin. A cau đối, which literally means
"sentence pair", consists of two sentences or
lines. Each line corresponds with the other in
meaning as well as tone pattern and individual
word meaning. The cau đối is usually used to
convey good wishes on the Tết (Lunar New Year)
holidays. It is a highly specialized form of
poetry.

CÂU-HAI LAGOON. (Đầm Câu-Hai). A saltwater lagoon in
Thừa-Thiên Province in central Vietnam. It is
located in the southeast section of the province

and is connected to the Hà-Trung Lagoon.

CAU MA. See MAA.

CẦU RIVER. (Sông Cầu). A river in north Vietnam. It
     originates in the highlands near Bà-Bể Lake in
     Bắc-Thái Province. It flows southward past Thái-
     Nguyên and Bắc-Giang where it meets the Thái-Bình
     River at Phả-Lại. It is the largest tributary of
     the Thái-Bình River.

CAU SRÊ. See SRÊ.

CÂY NÊU. (Nêu Tree). A bamboo pole stripped of its
     leaves except for a tuft on top. Red paper
     decorates the tree which is planted outside the
     house during the Tết (Lunar New Year) holidays.
     It is supposed to ward off the evil spirits during
     the absence of the spirit of the hearth (Táo-Quân)
     who leaves the family at this time to visit the
     palace of the Jade Emperor. See GIAO-THỪA, TÁO-
     QUÂN, TẾT.

CÂY RIVER. (Sông Cây, also known as Sông Dinh or Sông
     Phan-Rang). A river in Ninh-Thuận Province in
     central Vietnam. It originates in the Lâm-Viên
     Highlands and flows past An-Phước and Phan-Rang.
     It has several smaller tributaries and empties
     into the South China Sea. It also carries water
     from the Đa-Nhim Dam.

CENTRAL COASTAL PLAIN. (Đồng-Bằng Trung-Phần, also
     called central lowlands). An area of coastal
     flatlands wedged between the Trường-Sơn mountain
     range and the South China Sea. It extends from
     Thanh-Hóa Province southward to Bình-Thuận Pro-
     vince. The central coastal plain is naturally
     divided into several smaller plains areas. The
     divisions are caused by mountains extending to the
     sea coast in numerous locations. The central
     coastal plain covers an area of about 6,750 square
     kilometers (2,606 square miles). The area forms
     a strip that is generally narrow, although it
     reaches a maximum of sixty-four kilometers (forty
     miles) in width at certain points. The land is
     poor and unproductive compared to the rich rice-
     lands of the Red River and Mekong Deltas. Those
     areas near the mountains are rocky which makes
     cultivation difficult. The parts near the sea are
     sandy and subject to saltwater intrusion and wind
     erosion. Irrigation is a problem partly because
     of extremes in rainfall and partly because much of
     the land sets too low. The private individual

landholdings in this region have always been small
while large communal or village owned lands are
traditional and common. The natural (mountainous)
communication barriers between the various smaller
plains have caused distinct differences in the
spoken language, even though one dialect (central
Vietnamese) is spoken throughout the entire area.
See THANH-NGHỆ-TỈNH PLAINS, BÌNH-TRỊ-THIÊN PLAINS,
NAM-NGÃI PLAINS, BÌNH-PHÚ-KHÁNH-NINH PLAINS,
TRUNG-NAM PLAINS.

CENTRAL HIGHLANDS. (Cao-Nguyên Trung-Phần). A plateau
area in the southern part of the Trường-Son Mountain Range. It covers an area about 160 kilometers (100 miles) wide and 320 kilometers (200
miles) long which totals over 51,500 square kilometers (20,000 square miles). It has an estimated populated of 976,747 and is divided into
several distinct minor plateaus. The Lâm-Viên
Plateau is centered in Tuyên-Đúc Province. The
Gia-Lai Plateau covers most of Pleiku and Kontum
provinces. The southernmost plateau is called
the Di-Linh Plateau and is located in Quảng-Đúc
and Lâm-Đồng Provinces. The central highlands are
inhabited by highland ethno-linguistic minority
groups, chief among them are the Rhade, Jarai,
and Koho. There are some plantations in the area,
mainly for the production of coffee and tea.
Vegetables are also shipped to Sài-Gòn and Nha-
Trang from the Đà-Lạt region. The Central Highlands, although sparsely populated, have always
been considered to be of great strategic military
importance. See ĐA-LẠT, DI-LINH PLATEAU, GIA-LAI
PLATEAU, LÂM-VIÊN PLATEAU, TRƯỜNG-SỞN MOUNTAIN
RANGE.

CENTRAL LOWLANDS. See CENTRAL COASTAL PLAIN.

CENTRAL VIETNAM. See TRUNG-PHAN.

CERAMICS. (Gốm). An indigenous Vietnamese art.
Ceramics were made in ancient Vietnam by coating
a wicker mold with clay or sand and then baking
it. Each period in Vietnamese history is marked
by distinctive and characteristically predominant
motifs. The period of Chinese domination (111
B.C.-938 A.D.) featured elephants; the Lý Dynasty
(1010-1225) - worm-shaped dragons and lotus
flowers; the Trần Dynasty (1225-1400) - egrets and
fish. Vietnamese ceramics reached a high level of
perfection in the Lý and Trần Dynasties with marked
national and folk features. The silicious clay of
"Bát-Tràng" from Hải-Ninh produces excellent

ceramic pieces. Ceramics are presently produced
in both the Democratic Republic of Vietnam and
the Republic of Vietnam. See HANDICRAFTS.

CHẢ GIÒ. A very popular dish in Vietnam. A mixture
of crabmeat, pork, noodles and chopped vegetables
is rolled in a thin rice paper wrapping into
small two to four inch rolls. These are deep
fried and served with fresh lettuce and nuoc mam.

CHẢ TÔM. A Vietnamese dish comprised of individual
sticks of sugar cane around which is rolled a
spiced shrimp paste. This is then grilled over
an open fire and eaten by hand off of the cane.

CHAINE ANNAMITIQUE. See TRƯỜNG-SƠN MOUNTAIN RANGE.

CHẢM. An ethno-linguistic group of people located in
central Vietnam centering around Phan-Rang and in
Châu-Đốc Province in the Mekong Delta. The Chàm
people speak an Austronesian (Malayo-Polynesian)
language which is related to certain language
groups in Indonesia and Melanesia. This points
to an early migration northward. They were already in place on the Indochinese Peninsula when
the first beginnings of Indianization of the area
took place around the start of the Christian era.
The Chàm were greatly influenced by the Indian
tradition, first by Hinduism and later by Islam.
They founded the kingdom of Champa, first known
as Lâm-Ấp, which flourished until the eleventh
century when the Vietnamese began a protracted
period of southward expansion. The last Chàm
king or chieftain, relinquished the throne in
1822. The Chàm are today an important minority
group in the Republic of Vietnam. They have a
traditional script of Indian origin and a Romanized script devised by the French. They have also
adopted many Vietnamese customs - house style,
clothes, lunar calendar and, in many cases, language. Chamic society is matriarchal, descent is
reckoned through matrilineal lines. During the
imperial phase of Chàm history, the society was
divided into four castes, but this is no longer
adhered to. The men usually wear a "sarong", a
kind of long skirt while the women dress in a
white or blue tunic with narrow sleeves and, generally, a scarf. The Chàm of central Vietnam are
ordinarily Brahmanist while the groups living in
the Mekong Delta are Muslim. A number of Chàm
also live in the Tôn-Lê-Sap area of Cambodia and
are usually more orthodox in the practice of Islam. There are an estimated 56,820 (1971) Chàm

people living in Vietnam, over 36,000 of which are
in the provinces of Ninh-Thuận, and Binh-Thuận.
See CHAMPA.

CHÂM-CỨU. Acupuncture. This form of traditional medicine has been practiced in Vietnam since early
times. Acupuncture is of Chinese origin but is
quite popular in all regions of Vietnam. A
specialist in acupuncture is often also trained
in western medicine.

CHẠM-NGỎ. (Lễ Chạm-Ngỏ, also called Lễ Chạm-Mặt). A
pre-betrothal ceremony. The Lễ Chạm-Ngỏ is held
after the informal agreement of marriage is made
between the two families. The boy's family visits
the girl's family and brings betel nut, tea and
wine for the occasion. The purpose of the exercise is to afford the future bride and groom an
opportunity to meet each other (it was sometimes
called Lễ Xem Mặt or "ceremony to see each other's
face"), and to allow the groom's family to learn
more about the homelife of the bride. Since the
parents arranged for the marriage and chose the
marriage partner this would sometimes be the
first time that the engaged couple would meet each
other. See HÔN-NHÂN.

CHAMPA. 1. A kingdom founded between 190-193 A.D. by
the Chàm people. Champa was an Indianized state
extending south to what is now Binh-Tuy Province,
west into the Mekong Valley of present-day Cambodia and southern Laos and as far north as
Quảng-Binh Province. The state of Giao-Chỉ and
later the kingdom of Champa was known by the
Chinese as Lin-Yi (Lâm-Ấp) and centered around
Quảng-Nam Province. Champa was at constant war
with the Vietnamese to the north and the Cambodians to the west. The Chams even took Ankor in
the twelfth century and invaded the Tongking Delta,
sacking Hà-Nội in the fourteenth century. Champa
flourished with her capital located at Đông-Dưởng
(Indrapura) in Quảng-Nam Province until the eleventh century when the Vietnamese began a protracted period of expansion and aggression that
culminated in the cession of Indrapura to the
Vietnamese in 1402 and the conquest of the new
Chàm capital at Vijaya in Binh-Định Province in
1471. The kingdom continued to exist but was
divided into several smaller states and grew
steadily weaker until 1822 when the last Chàm king
or chieftain, Pô Chởn relinquished the throne.
2. Champa is the Sino-Vietnamese equivalent of

"Champapura", which was adopted by the Cham people
to indicate their country during the period 860-
1471.

CHARAI. See JARAI.

CHARNER, LEONARD-VICTOR-JOSEPH (1797-1869). Commander
of French forces in Cochinchina from February,
1861, to December, 1861. He fought a major battle
against the Vietnamese at Chi-Hòa and later captured Mỹ-Tho. It was under Charner that the
French occupied and controlled much of Biên-Hòa,
Gia-Định and Định-Tường Provinces, an area which
extends from the ocean to the Cambodian border.
He returned to France in 1862 and became a senator.

CHÂU. District. An administrative unit first used
under Emperor Lê Thái-Tổ (1428-1433). Several
Châu comprised a Trấn (Province). One Châu was
divided into smaller Huyện (Sub-districts). The
word châu is still used to designate an administrative unit of district size in some highland
areas of north Vietnam. The chief of a Châu is
called a Tri-Châu. See ADMINISTRATIVE UNITS.

CHÂU-ĐỐC CITY. The capital city of Châu-Đốc Province
in the Mekong Delta area of south Vietnam. Population 40,383. It is located on the west bank
of the lower Mekong River, also known as the
Bassac River. It is connected by road to Long-
Xuyên and Cần-Thơ. There is a sizeable Chinese
and Khmer population in the city. See CHÂU-ĐỐC
PROVINCE.

CHÂU-ĐỐC PROVINCE. A province in the Mekong Delta area
of south Vietnam. It borders on Cambodia to the
west and is situated north of Kiên-Giang Province,
south of Kiên-Phong Province and west of An-Giang
Province. The population is 576,818 (1971) and
the area is 2,075 square kilometers (801 square
miles). The provincial capital city is Châu-Đốc
city, formerly called Châu-Phú, and is located
on the lower Mekong River. It is connected by
road to Long-Xuyên and Cần-Thơ. Châu-Đốc was
originally part of Cambodia. It was given to the
Nguyễn lord, Nguyễn Phúc-Khoát (1738-1765) after
he put down a local rebellion and saved the Khmer
throne. At this time it was called Châu-Đốc-Đạo.
In 1831, Emperor Minh-Mạng established the province of An-Giang which included present-day Châu-
Đốc. The French divided An-Giang Province into
six provinces; Bạc-Liêu, Sốc-Trăng, Cần-Thơ,

Long-Xuyên, Sa-Đéc and Châu-Đốc. In 1956, Châu-
Đốc and Long-Xuyên were combined to form An-Giang.
Then, in 1964, Châu-Đốc was reestablished as a
separate province. The province has a large Khmer
population as well as the largest Chàm settlement
in the delta (estimated at over 8,500). There are
also a large number of the Hòa-Hảo religious sect.
Hòa-Hảo Village, which is the center of the Hòa-
Hảo Buddhist religion, is located in Châu-Đốc
Province. The principal products of the province
are rice, corn, fruits and beef. There is a large,
active and well-known cattle market located near
the capital. There is also a small silk production industry. See CHÂU-ĐỐC CITY, HÒA-HẢO,
THẤT-SƠN MOUNTAINS, SAM MOUNTAIN.

CHẢY RIVER. (Sông Chảy). A river in north Vietnam
and a tributary of the Lô River. It originates
near the Kiêu-Lùu-Ti Mountain Hà-Giang Province,
near the Chinese border. It parallels the Red
River and passes through the provinces of Lào-
Cai, Yên-Bảy and Tuyên-Quang where it meets the
Lô River just south of Tuyên-Quang City.

CHÈ. A light dessert-type of dish. This sweet pudding
or custard is made in many different ways and can
include corn, noodles, coconut, mung bean, lotus
seeds or other beans. It is served by street
vendors and also made in the home.

CHEO. (Nạp cheo). The custom of paying a betrothal
fee to the village. This custom was common in
traditional Vietnam. Nạp cheo included bringing
offerings to the patron saint of the bride's
village and paying a fee into the village treasury.
This was then recorded in the official records of
the village. See LỄ HÔN-NHÂN.

CHEO-REO. See HẬU-BỔN.

CHESS. See CỜ-TƯỚNG.

CHI-LĂNG. A village in Lạng-Sơn Province in the highlands of north Vietnam. It was the site of a
famous battle in which Lê-Lợi defeated the invading Chinese in 1427. See LÊ-LỢI.

CHIÊM-HOA MOUNTAIN RANGE. A chain of mountains in
north Vietnam. It is located between the Gâm
River and the Lô River in Hà-Giang and Tuyên-
Quang provinces. The mountain range runs north-
south from the Chinese border to where the two
rivers meet in Tuyên-Quang Province.

CHIÊM-THÀNH. The Vietnamese word for Champa or Champapura, the Indianized nation of the Chàm people.
See CHÀM, CHAMPA, LÂM-ẤP.

CHIL. See CIL.

CHINESE. The Chinese constitute the largest ethno-
linguistic minority group in the Republic of Vietnam numbering about 1.2 million or 6.6 percent of
the total population. However, less than 200,000
are located in the Democratic Republic of Vietnam
mainly in the Hà-Nội and Hải-Phong areas. Most
of the Chinese in the Republic of Vietnam are
centered in the Chợ-Lớn area of metropolitan Sài-
Gòn. They are active in commerce, particularly in
rice trading, real estate and banking. About
45,000 Chinese moved to the south after the signing of the 1954 Geneva accords. A small number
of Chinese also live near the Vietnam/Chinese
border in north Vietnam.

CHINH-PHỦ CÁCH-MẠNG LÂM-THỜI CỘNG-HÒA MIỀN NAM VIỆT-
NAM. (Provisional Revolutionary Government of
the Republic of South Vietnam, also known as the
PRG). The official communist governing body of
the Republic of (South) Vietnam. It was established by the Congress of People's Representatives
of the Republic of South Vietnam which met from
June 6-8, 1969. Huỳnh Tấn-Phát, a southern
architect was elected President. The PRG assumed
responsibility for foreign representation and
administration of the communist controlled areas
of the Republic of Vietnam. Although the National
Front for the Liberation of South Vietnam continues
to function, the PRG succeeded it in many aspects.
The headquarters were originally located in or
near Tây-Ninh Province. See MẶT-TRẬN DÂN-TỘC
GIẢI-PHÓNG MIỀN NAM VIỆT-NAM, HUỲNH TẤN-PHÁT.

CHINH-PHỤ-NGÂM. (Lament of a Warrior's Wife). A
classic poem written in Chinese by Đặng Trần-Côn
in the early eighteenth century. The poem was
popularized by Đoàn Thị-Điểm who translated it
into nôm. The translation is actually the most
well-known version. See ĐOÀN THỊ-ĐIỂM.

CHỢ-BỜ. A town in Hòa-Bình Province in north Vietnam.
It is located on the Hắc-Giang River. Chợ-Bờ was
the capital of Hòa-Bình Province until 1891 when
the Mường people captured and burned the town. It
is a transportation center for goods shipped to
and from the highlands and the lowlands.

CHỢ-LỚN. (Literally, Great Market). The Chinese
quarter of the Sài-Gòn metropolitan area. Originally a settlement of overseas Chinese, Chợ-Lớn
was distinct and separate from Sài-Gòn. Recently,
however, the two communities have fused together
due to the rapid urbanization and population growth.
Chợ-Lớn once had a gangland reputation. It is now
the home of most of south Vietnam's one million
Chinese. Chợ-Lớn was also the name of one of the
sixteen southern provinces during the French
administration. It included parts of what are
now Gia-Định, Gò-Công and Định-Tường provinces.

CHRAU. See CHROO.

CHRISTIANITY. The vast majority of Vietnamese Christians are Catholic. Protestantism is relatively
new and accounts for only a fraction of the total
population. Catholicism was introduced into
Vietnam in the sixteenth century by missionaries
from Spain, France and Portugal. The Portuguese
Dominicans and the French Jesuits were particularly active in the sixteenth and seventeenth
centuries. The first bishops were assigned to
Vietnam by Pope Alexander VII in 1659. The first
Vietnamese Catholic priests were ordained in 1668.
By 1685 it was estimated that there were 800,000
Catholics in Vietnam. One of the most prominent
of the missionaries was the Jesuit Father Alexandre de Rhodes who established himself at Hà-Nội,
studied the history and culture of Vietnam,
travelled widely and was instrumental in the development of the Romanized script (quốc-ngữ).
Even though the Catholic Church continued to grow
in Vietnam, it met with constant resistance and,
at times, was harshly and severely repressed. As
early as 1533 a decree was issued by Emperor Lê
Trang-Tông (1533-1548), which forbade the teaching
of Christianity by a missionary in Nam-Định Province. During the seventeenth and eighteenth
centuries persecution of the foreign missionaries
and their converts took place throughout the
country. Under Emperor Gia-Long (1802-1819), the
Church enjoyed a short respite because of his
gratitude to a French bishop who helped him secure
the throne. However, the persecutions resumed
with his successor. The Vietnamese monarchs
feared that the Catholic faith would undermine the
traditional Confucianist order. Under the French,
the Catholic Church flourished in Vietnam and, in
fact, received preferential status by the colonial
administration. Today, an estimated eight to ten

percent of all Vietnamese are Catholic. See LA-
VANG BASICALLA; PIGNEAU DE BEHAINE BISHOP; RE-
LIGION; RHODES, MONSIGNOR ALEXANDRE DE.

CHROO. (Also called Chrau). An ethno-linguistic
minority group of highland people located in the
southern part of the central highlands, particularly in Long-Khánh, Bình-Tuy, Phước-Tuy and Biên-
Hòa provinces. They are actually a subgroup of the
Koho linguistic group and as such, speak a dialect
of Koho, a Mon-khmer language. Population estimates were given in 1972 as around 15,000. There
are several subgroups of the Chroo all of which
share the same culture, social system and general
lifestyle with other groups of the Koho. See
KOHO.

CHRU. (Also known as Churu). An ethno-linguistic
group of highland people located in the Dran valley between Đà-Lạt and Phan-Rang. They speak a
language of the Malayo-Polynesian (Austronesian)
stock and number around 5,000.

CHỮ NHO. See NHO.

CHỮ NÔM. See NÔM.

CHU RIVER. (Sông Chu). A river in central Vietnam.
It originates in Laos and flows through Thanh-Hoa
Province where it empties into the South China Sea
at Sầm-Sởn. There is an important irrigation dam
located at Bái-Thượng on the Chu River. The river
is connected to the Mã River in the delta of the
Mã River.

CHU VĂN-AN (?-1370). A scholar, mandarin and teacher
during the Trần Dynasty (1225-1400). Born in
Hà-Đông Province he became the tutor of the crown
prince under Emperor Trần Minh-Tông (1314-1329).
During the reign of Emperor Trần Dụ-Tông (1341-
1369) he demanded that the Emperor execute seven
corrupt officials. The Emperor ignored him so
he retired to the countryside to become a teacher.
He authored several books in the classical (Chinese) form. See TRẦN DỤ-TÔNG.

CHÚA. Lord or prince. An hereditary title used during
the later part of the Lê Dynasty (1428-1788). The
Chúa ruled in place of the Lê emperor and were
members of the Trịnh family north of the eighteenth
parallel and of the Nguyễn family to the south.
Thus, they are referred to as the Chúa Trịnh (Trịnh

Lords) and the Chúa Nguyễn (Nguyễn Lords) respectively. Both families were at constant war
with each other and each ruled simultaneously in
their respective territories. The reign of the
Trịnh and Nguyễn lords was terminated by the Tây-
Sơn Rebellion (1771-1788) which briefly unified
the country. See LÊ DYNASTY, NGUYỄN LORDS, TÂY-
SƠN REBELLION, TRỊNH LORDS, TRỊNH-NGUYỄN INTERNE-
CINE WAR.

CHÙA. See PAGODA

CHƯƠNG-THIỆN PROVINCE. An inland province in south
    Vietnam. Chương-Thiện Province was created in
    1961 from parts of Ba-Xuyên, Kiên-Giang and Phong-
    Dinh provinces. It is located south of Phong-Dinh
    Province and north of An-Xuyên and Bạc-Liêu pro-
    vinces. The population is 285,517 and the area is
    2,292 square kilometers (884 square miles). The
    provincial capital is Vị-Thanh. Chương-Thiện is
    part of the rich Mekong Delta area. The chief
    means of transportation is via canals. The main
    products are rice and fruits. See VỊ-THANH.

CIL. (Also known as Kil or Chil). An ethno-linguistic
    minority group of highland people located in the
    central highlands, primarily in western Khánh-Hòa
    Province. The Cil are actually a subgroup of the
    Koho linguistic group and speak a dialect of Koho,
    a language of Mon-khmer stock. The Cil are est-
    imated to number around 18,000 (1972). They are
    probably the least sophisticated (technologically)
    subgroup of the Koho. See KOHO.

CITADELS. The Vietnamese have traditionally used cita-
    dels as a defensive fortification. The Chinese
    citadel, with its characteristic square-like ar-
    rangement was used as a model until the nineteenth
    century. The earliest recorded citadel, Loa-Thành,
    was built in 255 B.C. by An Dương-Vương at Cô-Loa
    in present-day Vĩnh-Phú Province. In the nine-
    teenth century, a system of citadels was built
    throughout Vietnam. These structures showed
    European influence but still maintained the basic
    Chinese symmetrical design. Citadels were built
    during this period at: Sài-Gòn (1790), Nha-Trang
    (1793), Huế and Ha-Nội (1805), Quảng-Ngãi (1807),
    Khánh-Hòa (1810), Bình-Định (1817), Sơn-Tây (1882),
    Cao-Bằng, Nghệ-An, Quảng-Nam, Lạng-Sơn, Phú-Yên, and
    Biên Hòa (1824-1838). See CÔ-LOA, HUẾ, TÂY-ĐÔ
    CITADEL.

CLIMATE. The climate of Vietnam ranges from tropical in the south to subtropical in the north. At no time is plant life suspended because of cold climate. Being subject to the monsoon, Vietnam has a wet and dry season. The timing, length and intensity of these two seasons varies throughout the country. The winter monsoon reaches the Red River Delta area in north Vietnam about mid-September and continues until April. This is characterized by constant fog and drizzle with typhoons common from August through October. In Huê, in central Vietnam, the heaviest rains occur from September through January. The rainy season in Sài-Gòn lasts from April through December with two peak periods, one in June and one in September. The average rainfall for these three cities is Hà-Nội - 72 inches; Huê - 117 inches; Sài-Gòn - 81 inches. The range of temperature in the north is much greater than in the south because of the difference in latitude. In Hà-Nội the temperature ranges from 41°F. to 107°F. with an average temperature of 63°F. The temperature in Sài-Gòn ranges only 6.2°F from 78.8°F to 85°F. Coastal typhoons are common in north and north-central Vietnam from July to November. The plateaus in the central highlands are marked by hot, dry and sometimes violent summer winds known as Gió-Lao (Winds of Laos). Floods and droughts are common especially in central Vietnam. Snow is practically unknown in the south, but frost and snow appear infrequently in the mountains of north Vietnam. Hail occurs but rarely in the mountain areas of central Vietnam, usually accompanied by heavy thunderstorms.

CỜ ĐEN. See BLACK FLAGS.

CỔ-LOA. (Also known as Cổ Loa-Thành or Loa-Thành). The capital city of the kingdom of Âu-Lạc under the Thục Dynasty (257-208 B.C.) and again established as the national capital under the Ngô Dynasty (939-965). Cổ-Loa is located in present-day Vĩnh-Phú Province. The first fortified citadel recorded in Vietnamese history was built at Cổ-Loa by King An Dương-Vương in 255 B.C. Vestiges of the structure can still be seen today. A well-known temple (Đền Cổ-Loa) was built there in honor of King An-Dương-Vương. Traditionally there is a festival held there from the sixth to the sixteenth of the first lunar month, also in honor of King An Dương-Vương. See AN DƯƠNG-VƯƠNG, ÂU-LẠC, CITADELS, THỤC DYNASTY.

CỔ-PHÁP TEMPLE. (Đền Cổ-Pháp). A famous temple in
    Đình-Bảng Village of Hà-Bắc Province. It is ded-
    icated to the Lý Dynasty (1010-1225). Inside the
    temple is a large courtyard housing, on one side,
    an altar to the Emperor Lý Chiêu-Hoàng (1125),
    and numerous statues of people wearing the costumes
    of the Lý period. Nearby are located the tombs of
    the various Lý emperors. See ĐỀN, LÝ DYNASTY.

CỔ-PHONG. An early form of poetry written either in the
    ngũ-ngôn style (each line containing five words)
    or the thất-ngôn style (each line containing seven
    words).

CỔ-TƯỚNG. (Chess). Cổ-tướng is a form of chess of
    Chinese origin and is played extensively through-
    out Vietnam. It is similar in principle to west-
    ern chess, but is played with small round buttons
    marked with a Chinese character and a paper or
    wooden chess board. There are also variations in
    the moves and pieces which distinguish it from
    western chess. An early encounter with the game
    was recorded during the reign of Trần Dụ-Tông
    (1341-1369). A Chinese ambassador to Vietnam
    challenged the Emperor to a game of chess. Since
    he did not know the game he ordered a search for
    someone who did. A man named Vũ-Huyền came for-
    ward to help. He posed as one of the Emperor's
    guards during the game and held a parasol for the
    Emperor to shade him from the sun. By means of a
    small hole in the parasol, Vũ-Huyền was able to
    direct the Emperor's moves with a small point of
    light on the chess board. The Emperor won three
    consecutive games. It is said that when word
    reached China, the Chinese were so impressed by
    the talent and intellect of the Vietnamese that
    they dismissed previous plans to conquer Vietnam.

COCHINCHINA. (Cochinchine). A term which was used to
    refer to south Vietnam as contrasted to north
    Vietnam (Tongking) and central Vietnam (Annam)
    during the French period. It is generally agreed
    that the term is of Portuguese origin meaning
    "Cochin in China" to distinguish it from the Port-
    uguese colony of Cochin in India. Cochinchina was
    first used to refer to the lower Mekong Delta but
    after the seventeenth century it referred to all
    the territory ruled by the Nguyễn Lords. The
    later French colonists applied it to central Viet-
    nam while referring to south Vietnam as lower Co-
    chinchina. Then, between 1870-1880, Annam was
    used for central Vietnam and Cochinchina was re-

served for the south. Through a series of military conquests and diplomatic negotiations, the
French brought Cochinchina under direct French
rule as a colony of France. Annam and Tongking,
on the other hand, were established as protectorates. See NAM-PHẦN.

COCONUT MONK. See ÔNG ĐẠO DỪA.

COL DES NUAGES. See HẢI-VÂN PASS.

CON CẢ. The eldest child in a nuclear family. The
oldest child is naturally given a disproportionate
amount of responsibility, especially in rearing
and tutoring the younger siblings. The con cả has
added duties in such family rituals as the death
anniversaries (ngày giỗ) and funerals.

CON RIVER. (Sông Con). A river in central Vietnam and
a tributary of the Cả River. It originates in
Thanh-Hóa Province and flows southward through
Nghệ-An Province where it joins the Cả River at
Làng Bình-Lang.

CÔN-SƠN ISLAND. (Also known as Côn-Lôn, Côn-Nôn, Con-
dur or Poulo Condore Island). A group of fourteen islands off the southeastern coast of Vietnam. It is located in the South China Sea 280
kilometers (218 miles) from Sài-Gòn and 180 kilometers (156 miles) from the point of Vũng-Tàu.
Côn-Sơn is administered as a province. It has a
population of 3,300 (1971) and a land mass of
sixty-seven square kilometers (twenty-five square
miles). The capital city is Côn-Sơn City. Nguyễn
Phúc-Anh (who later became Emperor Gia-Long (1802-
1819)) and his party fled to Côn-Sơn Island during
the Tây-Sơn Rebellion (1771-1788). The island is
known for its harsh prisons, used especially for
political prisoners since the time of French
colonization.

CÔN-SƠN MOUNTAIN. (Núi Côn-Sơn). A mountain located
in Hải-Hưng Province, sixty kilometers (thirty-
seven miles) from Hà-Nội. It was the site where
Nguyễn-Trãi, a famous Vietnamese hero, held
classes and resided in retirement. The location
is now preserved as a national shrine.

CON-VOI MOUNTAIN RANGE. (Dãy Con-Voi). A chain of
mountains in Yên-Bay Province in north Vietnam.
It lies to the northeast of and runs parallel to
the Red River. There are no tall mountains or

peaks in the chain.

CONFUCIANISM. (Nho-Giáo, or Khổng-giáo). While not a
formal organized religion, Confucianism has been
an important force in shaping Vietnamese history,
life and thought. Confucianism was introduced
into Vietnam by the Chinese who dominated the
country during the thousand year "Bắc-Thuộc"
period (111 B.C. - 938 A.D.). It was continued
by the Vietnamese during independence and it com-
peted with Buddhism as the major moral and phil-
osophic force in the Vietnamese dynastic system.
By the end of the fourteenth century, it had replaced Buddhism as the most important "religion"
or philosophy in Vietnam. It is one of the three
components of the Tam-giáo (three religions) which
were promoted under the Lý Dynasty (1010-1225).
The triennial or mandarinal examinations in the
Confucianist tradition, used for the selection
of mandarins, were one of the most significant
contributions to the development of Vietnam.
These were first held in 1070. They encouraged
a respect for intellectual and literary accomplishments which persists today.
        Confucianism strongly influenced the social
system and structure of Vietnam by prescribing
rules for social interaction, holding up the
patriarchal family as the ideal human institution,
stressing self-perfection (in both accomplishment
and behavior), and by providing for clear-cut
social classes and the potential for social mobility for all citizens. The concepts of imperial
rule by the mandate of heaven and the autonomy of
the village are also products of the Confucianist
tradition. And, of no lesser importance are the
concepts of filial piety and the practice of
maintaining the cult of the ancestors, both of
which are results of the teachings of the great
sage. Although Confucianism is not an organized
religion as such, there are temples and shrines
dedicated to Confucius which are located throughout Vietnam. See RELIGION.

CÔNG. Duke, a rank of nobility. See NOBILITY.

CÔNG ĐIỀN. (Also called Công-Thổ). Public or communal lands. These were lands which were granted to
the village at the time of the formation of the
village in traditional Vietnam. The amount of
public land was then increased by the land given
to the village by wealthy villagers or by land
that was abandoned. Public land could also be

derived from land that was offered to the village pagoda. These lands were then rented or farmed for village income.

CÔNG-NGÕ. The entrance or gateway to a house or village. In traditional Vietnam, great importance was attached to the entrance of a house. It was considered a reflection on the family living inside. A well-kept, neat entrance way was indicative of a neat orderly family.

CONICAL HAT. See NÓN.

CONSTANS, JEAN-ANTOINE-ERNEST. Governor General of Indochina from November, 1887 to March, 1888.

COOKING. See FOOD.

CORNULIER-LUCINIERE, COUNT ALPHONSE (1811-1886). Interim Governor of Cochinchina 1870-1871. He was in office during the outbreak of the Franco-German war at which time he declared a state of emergency and prepared defenses against a possible attack by Prussian ships. He requested to be relieved of his command because of ill health.

COUNCIL OF NOTABLES. See HỘI-ĐỒNG KỲ-MỤC.

COURBET, AMEDEE-ANATOLE-PROSPER. Rear Admiral in the French navy and commander-in-chief of land and sea forces in Annam and Tongking from 1883-1884. He commanded the force that bombarded Hue on August 20, 1883.

CÙ-LAO. Island. See ĐẢO.

CÙ-LAO CHÀM. An island southeast of Đà-Nẵng and northwest of Hội-An in the South China Sea. It is formed by the extension of the same mountain formation that forms the Hải-Vân Pass. See HẢI-VÂN PASS.

CUA. (Also called Khua, Kor, or Kol). An ethno-linguistic minority group of highland people located in Quảng-Ngãi Province of central Vietnam. The Cua is one of the least known ethnic groups in Vietnam. In 1965 there were approximately 11,500 in the official population estimates. The Cua language belongs to the Mon-khmer language family and is closely related to the Hre language found in the neighboring tribe to the south. The Cua

society is patriarchal, the lineage and inheritance
follow the male line. The eldest male is the head
of the extended family and the key figure in the
society.

CỦA CUNG-HẬU. The mouth of one of the branches of the
upper Mekong River (Sông Tiền-Giang) in Vĩnh-Bình
Province.

CỦA-ĐẠI. The mouth of the Cái River (also known as the
Thu-Bồn River) in Quảng-Nam Province. It was for-
merly known as Đại-Chiếm Hải-Khẩu. See CÁI RIVER,
HỘI-AN, QUẢNG-NAM PROVINCE.

CỦA SÔNG. Estuary, river mouth. Individual river
mouths are listed under separate entires. See
CỦA CUNG-HẬU, CỦA-ĐẠI, CỦA SÔNG SAI-GÒN, CỦA
TRANH-ĐỀ, CỦA-TÙNG, CỦA-VIỆT.

CỦA SÔNG SAI-GÒN. The mouth of the Sai-Gòn River. It
actually forms the border between Gò-Công Province
and Gia-Định Province. See SAI-GÒN RIVER.

CỦA TRANH-ĐỀ. The mouth of one of the branches of the
upper Mekong River (Sông Tiền-Giang) in Vĩnh-Bình
Province.

CỦA-TÙNG. The mouth of the Bến-Hải River in Quảng-
Trị Province in central Vietnam. See BẾN-HẢI
RIVER, DEMILITARIZED ZONE, QUẢNG-TRỊ PROVINCE.

CỦA-VIET. The mouth of the Hiếu-Giang River (also
called Cam-Lộ River) in Quảng-Trị Province. See
HIẾU-GIANG RIVER, QUẢNG-TRỊ PROVINCE.

CULT OF THE ANCESTORS. (Thờ-Phụng Tổ-Tiên). Ancestral
worship. While Buddhism is the predominant organized religion, ancestral worship exerts a pro-
found influence on the daily life and outlook of
the Vietnamese people and is compatible, even en-
hanced, by the other major religions and philosophies. The cult of the ancestors is based on
the belief that the human soul survives after
death and becomes the natural protector of the
family line. If there are no descendants, the
soul of the dead is doomed to eternal wandering
for the lack of hommage and honor on the occasions
of traditional feasts and holidays. Since the
spirits of one's ancestors exert an influence in
the world of the living, to have them restless or
angry would not only be shameful, but dangerous.
Thus it is that the ancestors (and elders) are

venerated and honored regularly. Sacrifices and
prayers are offered to ancestral spirits implor-
ing, for example, the curing of a sick child or
success in business. Important elements in the
cult of the ancestors are the family altar (bàn
thờ gia-tiên), a piece of land, legally designated for the support of the ancestors (hương-hỏa)
and a senior male in the direct line of descent to
assume the obligation for celebrations and family
rituals (Đích-tôn). The most important celebration is the anniversary of the death of an ancestor (ngày-giỗ) during which religious rites
are performed before the family altar and sacrificial offerings are made to both the god of the
household and the spirit of the ancestor. Besides
the annual death anniversary, whenever there is
an occasion of family joy or sorrow such as a
wedding, success in examinations or death, the
ancestors are informed. See BÀN THỜ GIA-TIÊN,
BÀN THỜ HỌ, ĐÍCH-TÔN, HƯƠNG-HỎA.

CULT OF THE GUARDIAN SPIRIT. See THÀNH-HOÀNG.

CUNG HOÀNG-ĐẾ. See LỄ CUNG-HOÀNG.

CUNG-OÁN NGÂM-KHÚC. (Lament of a Courtmaid). An epic
poem written by Nguyễn Gia-Thiều (1741-1798).
This poem was composed in the style of sông-thất
lục-bát (7-7-6-8 syllabic lines) and in nôm characters. The story concerns the life of a royal
concubine who enjoyed the favor of the Emperor
only to be later abandoned by him. The poem shows
strong Buddhist philosophical influence. See
NGUYỄN GIA-THIỀU.

CƯỜNG-ĐỀ (1882-1951). A direct descendant of Emperor
Gia-Long (1802-1819) and pretender to the throne.
He was chosen by Phan Bội-Châu in 1903 as a pref-
erable alternative to Emperor Thành-Thái (1889-
1907) and titular head of the anti-French movement. In 1903 he went to Japan to study and
while there he took out Chinese citizenship. In
1909, because of Japanese pressure, he fled to
China. When the Việt-Nam Quang-Phục Hội was organized in 1912, Cường-Đề was chosen chairman. He
travelled extensively through Asia and Europe
actively soliciting support for the anti-colonial
cause. When the Japanese seized control of Vietnam in March, 1945, a faction in Japan supported
the installation of Cường-Đề as Emperor under the
Japanese overlordship. He travelled to Bangkok
but those in opposition to him prevented his re-

turn. He spent most of his life in exile heading
the restoration movement together with Phan Bội-
Châu. Cường-Để died in Tokyo on April 6, 1951 at
the age of 69. See NGUYỄN DYNASTY, PHAN BỘI-CHÂU,
VIỆT-NAM QUANG PHỤC-HỘI.

CYCLO. (Also spelled xích-lô). A three-wheeled pedi-
cab used primarily in the urban areas of Vietnam.
A motorized version of the cyclo called the cyclo-
máy is used in some of the larger cities. The
cyclo offers a practical and economic means of
transportation for all classes of people.

-D-

ĐA-BẠCH RIVER. (Sông Đà-Bạch). A river in north Vietnam. It receives its flow from smaller tributaries
in the Đồng-Triều mountain range as well as the
Thái-Bình River. It is exceptionally wide is some
places, reaching a width of two kilometers (1.2
miles). It empties into the Gulf of Tongking and
is one of several outlets of the Thái-Bình River.
See THÁI-BÌNH RIVER.

ĐA-GIANG RIVER. (Sông Đà-Giang, also known as Sông Bờ,
Sông Hắc-Giang, Sông Đà or Black River). A major
river in north Vietnam. It is a tributary of the
Red River. The Đà-Giang River originates in China
and flows southeasterly past Lai-Châu, Vạn-Yên,
Chờ Bờ and Hòa-Bình. It meets the Red River at
Việt-Trì. The Đà-Giang River passes through the
provinces of Lai-Châu, Sơn-La, and Hòa-Bình. It
is 850 kilometers (528 miles) long although only
550 kilometers (341 miles) of the river are in
Vietnam. There are three tributaries of the Đa-
Giang River: the Nam River, the Ma River and the
Mắc River.

ĐA-LẠT. A mountain resort city in the central highlands.
It was founded in 1912 upon the recommendation of
Dr. Alexander Yersin, a famous French scientist.
Đa-Lạt now occupies an area of 155 square kilometers (60 square miles) and has a population of
86,636 (1971). It is located 305 kilometers
(190 miles) northeast of Sài-Gòn. The climate
is exceptionally good with a temperature that
averages between 60° and 70° the year round. Đà-
Lạt is also an important agricultural center. It
is especially well-known for its flowers, lettuce,
cabbage and strawberries. Fruits and vegetables

are shipped to Sài-Gòn and Nha-Trang, and are
sometimes exported. The most popular tourist
attractions are the Hồ Xuân-Hương Lake, the Pongour Waterfalls, the Liên-Khương waterfalls, the
Suối-Vàng (Golden Brook), the Hồ Than-Thở Lake,
and the Lâm-Viên Mountain. Also located in Đà-
Lạt are the Atomic Energy Agency, Đà-Lạt University, the Pasteur Institute, and the Đà-Lạt Military Academy. Đà-Lạt served as the capital city
of Tuyên-Đức Province until 1970 when the capital
was moved to Tùng-Nghĩa. See YERSIN, ALEXANDRE.

ĐÀ-NẴNG. (Also called Tourane). A major port and the
second largest city in the Republic of Vietnam.
Đà-Nẵng is located in central Vietnam, 970 kilometers (600 miles) north of Sài-Gòn and 89 kilometers (50 miles) south of Huế. It has a total
population of 437,668 (1971) and is an important
center of commerce because of its transportation
and shipping facilities. The city is located on
the north/south rail line and highway number one.
A large airport has been constructed at Da-Nang
for both military and civilian operations. The
port facilities enable Đà-Nẵng to serve as a
focal point for coastal shipping and oceangoing
craft. The city of Đà-Nẵng was originally known
as Cửa-Hàn. The French named it Tourane, which
was later changed to Đà-Nẵng during the Japanese
occupation. It became a major port at the end
of the nineteenth century as the larger oceangoing vessels could no longer be accommodated by
the port city of Hội-An. In 1847 the French Navy,
under Captain LaPierre, entered the Đà-Nẵng Bay
to demand the release of a French Bishop who was
imprisoned at Huế. Unable to elicit a response,
he shelled the city, sank five Vietnamese ships
and left. In September, 1857, the French forces
returned and captured the city, thus beginning the
French conquest of Indochina. The city remained
primarily a French city until the French left in
1954. The Americans built a large military base
(air, naval and ground) there in the late 1960's.
Đà-Nẵng served as the capital of Quảng-Nam Province until 1964 at which time it was declared an
autonomous city and the provincial capital moved
to Hội-An. Among the more well-known points of
interest in and around Đà-Nẵng are the Hải-Vân
Pass, Non-Nước Mountain (Marble Mountain), and
the Chàm Museum. Although Protestant and Catholic missionaries have long been active and established in Đà-Nẵng, the Buddhist Church is predominant and most influential. Đà-Nẵng is also

the name of the adjacent bay and point on the
South China Sea coast northwest of the city. See
HẢI-VÂN PASS, NON-NƯỚC MOUNTAIN.

ĐA-NHIM RIVER DAM. A hydroelectric power plant at Đôn-
Dương on the Đa-Nhim River southeast of Đà-Lạt in
the central highlands. The project was financed
under a war reparations agreement by the Japanese
Government. It cost $50 million. The dam is
1,585 yards long across the Đa-Nhim River. The
waters of the river have been backed up to create
a lake which covers 3.7 square miles. The water
falls 2,500 feet producing enough power to turn
four generator turbines.

ĐÁ POINT. (Mũi Đá). A cape or point extending into
the South China Sea southwest of Hàm-Tân in Bình-
Tuy Province of south Vietnam.

ĐA-RĂNG RIVER. (Sông Đa-Rằng, also known as the Sông
Ba). A river in central Vietnam. It flows from
Kontum Province through Cheo-Reo in Phú-Bổn Province to Tuy-Hoà in Phú-Yên Province where it
empties into the South China Sea. It served as
the border between Vietnam and Champa around
1578.

ĐÀ RIVER. (Sông Đà). See ĐÀ-GIANG RIVER.

ĐẮC-LẮC PLATEAU. (Also known as the Darlac Plateau).
A plateau area centering around Ban-Mê-Thuột in
the central highlands. The plateau extends from
the Ayun River Valley (around Phú-Bổn Province)
to the Srepok River near the Cambodian border.
The area is about 1,000 meters (3,280 feet) above
sea level. The region is inhabited mainly by
Rhade. See BAN-MÊ-THUỘT, RHADE.

ĐẮC-LẮC PROVINCE. See DARLAC PROVINCE.

ĐẠI-CỔ-VIỆT. The name given to the country of Vietnam
in 969 A.D. by Emperor Đinh Tiên-Hoàng (968-979)
and used until 1054.

ĐẠI-ĐẠO TAM-KỲ PHỔ-ĐỘ. See CAO-ĐÀI.

ĐẠI-GIANG RIVER. (Sông Đại-Giang). A river in central
Vietnam. It originates in the mountains near Laos
at Đông-Hiểm and empties into the South China Sea
at Đồng-Hới in Quảng-Bình Province.

ĐẠI-HỌC. (Literally, Great Learning). One of four

famous Chinese books (Tứ-Thư) dealing with the
philosophy and doctrine of Confucius. Đại-Học is
a treatise concerning Confucius' conception of
the superior man. This book was used by scholars
and students in traditional Vietnam. It was
particularly important because the mandarinal
examinations were partially based on it. See
EDUCATION, THI-ĐÌNH, THI-HỘI, THI-HƯƠNG, TỨ-THƯ.

ĐẠI-LA. (Also called Đại-La-Thành). The name of the
ninth century town on the site of present-day Hà-
Nội. It was renamed Thăng-Long in 1010 A.D. when
Emperor Lý Thái-Tổ (1010-1028) established it as
the capital.

ĐẠI-NAM. (Literally, Great South). The name applied
to the country of Vietnam under the Nguyễn Dynasty (1802-1945). Đại-Nam was actually first
used by Emperor Minh-Mạng (1820-1840). Prior to
that time the country was known as Việt-Nam.

ĐẠI-NAM NHẤT-THỐNG-CHÍ. (Literally, Geography of
United Đại-Nam). A twenty-eight volume geography
of Vietnam written by the court historians under
Emperor Tự-Đức (1848-1883). The compilation was
started in 1865 and finished in 1882. Each volume covers one province and contains topographic
and demographic information, historical sites and
resources, etc. This is the most complete geography written by the court at Huế. The total
work is divided into three sections: Bắc-Ky
(Northern Area); Trung-Kỳ (Central Area) and,
Nam-Kỳ (Southern Area).

ĐẠI-NAM QUỐC-SỬ DIỄN-CA. (Literally, National History
of Đại-Nam in Poetic Style). A history of Vietnam covering the period from the Hồng-Bàng Dynasty
through the Lý Dynasty (1010-1225). It was the
first history written in the Vietnamese language
(nom) and was titled Sử-Ký Quốc-Ngữ-Ca. The first
volume covered only the relations with the Minh
Dynasty in China. A continuation was written in
1858 by Lê Ngô-Cát and Trương Phục-Hào resulting
in a volume called Việt-Sử Quốc-Ngữ. It was revised by Phạm Xuân-Quế and again by Phạm Đình-
Thoái which finally yielded the 1021-line epic
poem known today as Đại-Nam Quốc-Sử Diễn-Ca.

ĐẠI-NAM THỰC-LỤC. (Literally, Veritable Records of
Đại-Nam). A 538-volume collection of history
books written by the court historians during the
Nguyễn Dynasty (1802-1945). The works record

the events under the Nguyễn Lords (1600-1778) and under the Nguyễn Dynasty. Đai-Nam Thực-Luc is comprised of the following individual works:

Đai-Nam Thực-Lục Tiền-Biên. Twelve volumes covering the history of central and southern Vietnam under the Nguyễn Lords (1558-1777).

Đai-Nam Liệt-Truyên Tiền-Biên. Six volumes of biographies of the nobility and eminent people under the Nguyễn Lords (1558-1777).

Đai-Nam Thực-Luc Chính-Biên, Đê-Nhất-Kỳ. Sixty volumes of history under the rule of Emperor Gia-Long (1802-1819).

Đai-Nam Chính-Biên, Liệt-Truyên Sơ-Tập. Thirty-three volumes, a collection of biographies of eminent people. Also includes descriptions of Cambodia, Siam, Burma, Luang-Pra-Bang and Vieng-Chang under the reign of Emperor Gia-Long (1802-1819).

Đai-Nam Thực-Luc Chính-Biên, Đê-Nhi-Kỳ. Two hundred twenty volumes, a history of the reign of Emperor Minh-Mạng (1820-1840).

Đai-Nam Thực-Luc Chính-Biên, Đê-Tam-Kỳ. Seventy-two volumes, a history of the reign of Emperor Thiệu-Tri (1841-1847).

Đai-Nam Thực-Luc Chính-Biên, Đê-Tứ-Kỳ. Seventy volumes, a history of the reign of Emperor Tự-Đức (1847-1883).

Đai-Nam Thực-Luc Chính-Biên, Đe-Ngũ-Kỳ. Eight volumes, a history of the reign of Emperor Kiến-Phúc (1883-1884).

Đai-Nam Thực-Luc Chính Biên, Đe-Luc-Kỳ. Eleven volumes a history of the reign of Emperor Đồng-Khanh (1885-1889).

Đai-Nam Chính-Biên Liet-Truyen, Nhi-Tap. Forty-six volumes of biographies of eminent people during the reign of Minh-Mạng (1820-1840), Thiệu-Tri (1841-1847) and Tự-Đức (1848-1883). See NGUYỄN DYNASTY.

ĐAI-NGU. The name of Vietnam under the Hồ Dynasty (1400-1407 A.D.).

Đại-Tướng
                                58

ĐẠI-TƯỚNG. (Ngày Đại-Tường or Ngày Giỗ-Hết). The
  second anniversary of the death of a member of
  the family. The second anniversary is a larger
  celebration and is considered more important
  than the first anniversary (Ngày Tiểu-Tường). The
  observance of the occasion includes rituals of
  ancestral worship and a banquet. Friends and
  relatives are invited to the festivities. See
  CULT OF THE ANCESTORS, NGÀY GIỖ.

ĐẠI-VIỆT. The name applied to the country of Vietnam
  under the Lý and Trần Dynasties (1010-1400 A.D.).
  The name Đại-Việt was also used to designate the
  country of Vietnam during the Lê Dynasty (1428-
  1788), and under the Nguyễn Lords (1600-1778).

ĐẠI-VIỆT PARTY. See ĐẢNG ĐẠI-VIỆT.

ĐẠI-VIỆT SỬ-KÝ. (Literally, History of Đại-Việt). A
  history of Vietnam covering the period from the
  Triệu Dynasty (207-111 B.C.) through the Lý Dynasty (1010-1225). This work was written by Lê
  Văn-Hưu at the command of Emperor Trần Thái-Tông
  (1225-1258). This history was written in thirty
  volumes and is considered to be the first official
  history of Vietnam. The work was completed in
  1272. See LÊ VĂN-HƯU.

ĐẠI-VIỆT SỬ-KÝ TOÀN-THƯ. (Literally, Complete History
  of Vietnam). A history of Vietnam covering the
  period from the Hồng-Bàng Dynasty to the reign of
  Emperor Lê-Thái-Tổ (1428-1433). This work was
  completed in 1479. It was written in fifteen
  volumes and was divided into two parts. The
  compilation was authored by Ngô Sĩ-Liên at the
  command of Emperor Lê Thanh-Tông (1460-1497).
  See NGÔ SĨ-LIÊN.

ĐẠI-VIỆT SỬ-KÝ TỤC-BIÊN. (Literally, Supplement History of Đại-Việt). A history of Vietnam covering the period from the Trần Dynasty (1225-1400)
  to the founding of the Lê Dynasty (1428-1788). It
  was written by Phan Phu-Tiên at the command of
  Emperor Lê Nhân-Tông (1443-1459). Đai-Việt Sử-Ký
  Tục-Biên is actually a continuation of Đại-Việt
  Sử-Ký by Lê Văn-Hưu which covered the period up
  to 1224. See ĐẠI-VIỆT SỬ-KÝ.

ĐẠI-VIỆT THỐNG-GIÁM THỐNG-KHẢO. (Literally, Comments
  on the General History of Đại-Việt). A history
  of Vietnam covering the period from the Hồng-Bàng
  Dynasty to the reign of Emperor Lê Thái-Tổ (1428-

1433). This work was written by Vũ-Quỳnh at the
command of Emperor Lê Tưởng-Dục (1510-1516). This
history was written in twenty-six volumes and is
divided into two parts. It was incorporated into
the Chinh hoa edition (1697) of the larger history
Ðai-Việt Sử-Ký Toàn-Thư.

ÐẮM-BÓP. (Also called tẩm-quất). Massage. A form of
traditional Vietnamese therapy. Actually, massage
was not used as a treatment for a particular illness as much as it was as a conditioner or for
relief of general aches and pains. In the urban
areas of north Vietnam, the masseur would hawk
his services through the streets much like a food
vendor. See Y-DƯỢC.

ÐÁM CƯỚI. Wedding procession. See LỄ HÔN-NHÂN.

ÐÀN BẦU. (Also called Ðàn Ðộc-Huyền). A uniquely
Vietnamese musical instrument. It is a one-
stringed instrument using a wooden sounding board
and a gourd-shaped wooden resonator, sometimes an
empty coconut shell.

ÐÀN ÐÁY. (Singer's lute). A three-stringed musical
instrument unique to Vietnam and found mainly in
the north. The dan day was used in traditional
Vietnam to accompany the professional singers,
the ả-đào, similar to the Japanese geishas. See
HÁT-Ả-ÐÀO.

ÐÀN NGUYỆT. (Also called Ðàn Kim). Moon-shaped lute.
A two-stringed musical instrument used in traditional Vietnamese music.

ÐÀN TRANH. A popular zither-type of musical instrument
used in traditional Vietnamese music. The đàn
tranh has sixteen strings with movable bridges. It
is held horizontally from a sitting position and
plucked with finger picks.

ÐẢNG ÐẠI-VIỆT. (Literally, Great Việt Party). A
nationalist anti-communist political party formed
in 1939 by Trưởng Tử-Anh with support from university students, civil servants and the military.
It was immediately suppressed by the French and
consequently went underground. The party has
undergone many changes. In 1941, a merger of
major nationalist parties took place to form the
Ðại-Việt Quốc-Gia Liên-Minh. The party has
always been known as a bourgeois party with membership drawn from upper or upper-middle class

society. In 1945, the interim government of
Trần Trọng-Kim which was formed in April of that
year, was strongly backed by the Đại-Việt Party.
The Đại-Việt maintained their ultra-nationalist
stand and continued to be active in the Vietnamese
political arena. It has become one of the most
prominent political parties in the Republic of
Vietnam. Among the names of well-known people
associated with the Đại-Việt are Dr. Phan Quang-
Đán, Phan Huy-Quát, Đặng Văn-Sung and Trần Trọng-
Kim.

ĐẢNG DÂN-CHỦ VIỆT-NAM. See VIỆT-NAM DÂN-CHỦ ĐẢNG.

ĐẢNG LAO-ĐỘNG VIỆT-NAM. (Vietnam Worker's Party). The
Vietnamese Communist Party. It was founded in May,
1951, at the same time that the Việt-Nam Độc-Lập
Đồng-Minh Hội (Việt-Minh) was dissolved. The
Workers Party actually replaced the Việt-Minh. The
Lao-Động Party is the ruling political party in the
Democratic Republic of Vietnam. Although it exists
outside the formal governmental structure, the
party is decisively influential on policy in every
aspect of life at every level of government. The
party also serves as the principal channel for
social mobility and political advancement. The
party is headed by a Politburo which is comprised
of eleven members and two alternates. As of 1970
there were an estimated 1,100,000 party members
(five percent of the population). See DEMOCRATIC
REPUBLIC OF VIETNAM, VIỆT-NAM ĐỘC-LẬP ĐỒNG-MINH
HỘI.

ĐẢNG XÃ-HỘI VIỆT-NAM. (Vietnamese Socialist Party).
A minor political party in the Democratic Republic
of Vietnam. It represents the intelligentsia.
The party organ is the magazine Tổ-Quốc.

ĐẢNG XUÂN-KHU. See TRƯỜNG-CHINH.

DAO. (Also known as Man, Zao or Yao). An ethno-linguistic minority group in north Vietnam. See
MAN.

ĐẢO. Island. Same as Cù-Lao. Individual islands are
listed under separate entries. See CÁT-BÀ ISLAND,
CÔN-SƠN ISLAND, CÙ-LAO CHÀM, PARACELS ISLANDS,
PHÚ-QUỐC ISLAND, SPRATLEY ISLANDS.

ĐẠO. An administrative and military unit used first
by Emperor Lê Thái-Tổ (1428-1433). The country
was divided into five regions (Đạo). The regions
were then broken down into provinces (Trấn). See

ADMINISTRATIVE DIVISIONS.

ĐÀO DUY-TỪ (1572-1634). A scholar and military strategist under the Nguyễn Lords. Although he was born
in the north, (Thanh-Hóa Province), his family was
poor so he cound not take the mandarinal examinations. He went to the south to seek his fortune.
He studied on his own and eventually came to the
attention of the court. He was appointed to the
court at Huế and advanced to the position of
Commander and Chief of the Armed Forces. Đao Duy-
Từ built the defensive wall in Quảng-Bình Province
(approximately twelve kilometers or seven miles
long) which was instrumental in preventing in-
vasions of the Trịnh from the north. He also
created an armada to protect the coastline and
later, built the famous strategic wall in Quảng-
Bình Province known as the Lũy-Thầy (Master's
Wall). He also wrote extensively on military
tactics and strategy. See ĐÒNG-HỒI WALL, NHẬT-LỆ
WALL, TRỊNH-NGUYỄN INTERNECINE WAR.

ĐẠO GIÁO. See TAOISM.

D'ARGENLIEU, ADMIRAL GEORGES THIERRY. First High
Commissioner to Indochina (1945-1947).

D'ARIES, JOSEPH-HYACINTHE (1813-1878). Commander in
Chief of French Forces in Indochina from April,
1860, to February, 1861. He graduated from the
French Naval Academy in 1829. He was given command of the French forces in Sài-Gòn when Admiral
Theogene-Francois Page was called to China. His
forces were constantly attacked by the Vietnamese.
He managed to always keep his communications open
to the sea. It was d'Aries who handed the citadel of Vĩnh-Long over to Phan Thanh-Giản in accordance with the treaty of 1862. See TREATY OF
SÀI-GÒN.

DARLAC PROVINCE. (Also known as Đắc-Lắc Province).
A mountainous province in the central highlands.
It borders on Cambodia to the west and is located
south of Pleiku Province and north of Quảng-Đúc
Province. The population is 244,772 and it
covers an area of 10,552 square kilometers (6,552
square miles). The provincial capital, Ban-Mê-
Thuột, is well-known as the focal point of highland affairs in the Republic of Vietnam. The
province was noted for its big game hunting prior
to the recent war. The province is inhabited primarily by the Rhade ethno-linguistic group. See

BAN-MÊ-THUỘT, RHADE.

DÃY. Mountain range. Individual mountain ranges are
listed under separate entries. See AN-KHÊ, BẮC-
SƠN MOUNTAIN RANGE, CHIÊM-HÓA MOUNTAIN RANGE,
ĐÔNG-TRIỀU MOUNTAIN RANGE, HOÀNG-LIÊN-SƠN MOUN-
TAIN RANGE, HOÀNH-SƠN MOUNTAIN RANGE, LÀO-CAI
MOUNTAIN RANGE, NAM-KIM MOUNTAIN RANGE, NGÂN-SƠN
MOUNTAIN RANGE, SA-PHIN MOUNTAIN RANGE, SÔNG GÂM
MQUNTAIN RANGE, TRƯỜNG-SƠN MOUNTAIN RANGE, YÊN-
BINH MOUNTAIN RANGE, YÊN-LẠC MOUNTAIN RANGE.

ĐÀY-THƯỢNG RIVER. (Sông Đày-Thượng). A river in
north Vietnam and a tributary of the Red River.
It originates in Tuyên-Quang Province and joins
the Red River near Việt-Tri.

DE CHAMPEAUX, LOUIS-EUGENE. French Charge d'Affairs
in Huê from 1880-1881 and Consul at Hải-Phòng
in 1883.

DE COURCY, COUNT PHILIPPE-MARIE-HENRI ROUSSEL. General in the French army and Resident General for
Annam and Tongking from 1885-1886.

DE LA GRANDIERE, PIERRE-PAUL-MARIE (1807-1876). Second Governor of Cochinchina from 1863-1868. De
la Grandiere was a career navy officer. He relieved Admiral Bonard as Governor in May, 1863.
By June, 1867, he had annexed the southern provinces of Vĩnh-Long, Sóc-Trăng and Châu-Đốc,
thereby completing the French conquest of Cochinchina. While in office he founded the monthly
magazine, COURRIER DE SAIGON. He was instrumental
in launching the scientific exploration of the
upper Mekong River by Doudart de Lagree. He was
also a prime force in extending French control
over Cambodia.

DE LANESSAN, JEAN-MARIE-ANTOINE (1843-1919). Governor
General of Indochina from June, 1891, to December
1894. A physician, explorer, and professor, he
came to Indochina in 1886 on a study mission of
the colonies. While in office he tried to restore
the direct administration of Vietnam to the mandarins.

DE TASSIGNY, JEAN DE LATTRE. High Commissioner of Indochina from December, 1950, to December, 1951,
and Commander-in-Chief of French Forces in Indochina at the same time.

ĐỀ-THÁM. (Hoàng Hoa-Thám). A revolutionary and re-
    sistance leader during the anti-colonial move-
    ment in the early 1900's. He was born in Bắc-
    Giang Province into a family of revolutionaries,
    who took refuge in the mountains of Yên-Thế. Đề-
    Tham established his headquarters in Yên-Thế and
    launched a thirty year campaign against the
    French. He is sometimes identified with the Cần-
    Vương Movement. Unable to eliminate his forces,
    the French conceded the area around Yên-Thế to
    Đề-Thám. The agreement was short-lived as Đề-
    Thám renewed his fight against the French in
    1896. In 1898, he launched an attack against
    Hà-Nội and again in 1905. He was also involved
    in the unsuccessful attempt to poison the French
    troops in the Hà-Nội garrison in 1908. This
    spurred the French on to an all-out effort to
    capture him. Although they succeeded in dis-
    persing his troops, Đề-Thám eluded capture.
    Finally, on March 18, 1913, he was assassinated
    by a former ally and his head was presented to
    the French for a large reward. See CẦN-VƯƠNG
    MOVEMENT.

DECOUX, ADMIRAL JEAN. Commander-in-Chief of the French
    Far-Eastern Fleet in 1939 and Governor General of
    Indochina from 1940-1945.

DEJEAN, MAURICE. Resident Commissioner General of
    Indochina from July, 1953, to June, 1954.

DEMARCATION LINE. The line separating the Democratic
    Republic of Vietnam (sometimes referred to as
    North Vietnam) from the Republic of Vietnam (some-
    times referred to as South Vietnam). It was es-
    tablished as a cease-fire line on July 22, 1954.
    Although it does not coincide exactly with the
    seventeenth parallel, it approximates it enough
    that the two terms are often used interchangeably.
    The line follows the Bến-Hải River in the eastern
    half and follows a path parallel to the seven-
    teenth parallel in the western part. The demar-
    cation line was established by the Geneva accords
    as a provisional boundary pending general elections
    which never took place. See DEMILITARIZED ZONE,
    GENEVA CONFERENCE.

DEMILITARIZED ZONE (DMZ). A zone of five kilometers
    on each side of the demarcation line established
    along the Bến-Hải River in central Vietnam in
    July, 1954. The purpose of the zone, in the terms
    of the Geneva accords, is to act as a buffer zone
    in or

in order to avoid the resumption of hostilities.
The part of the zone south of the Bến-Hải River
is administered as the district of Trung-Lương by
the Republic of Vietnam. That part of the zone to
the north of the river became the Vĩnh-Linh Special
Zone under the Democratic Republic of Vietnam.
See DEMARCATION LINE, GENEVA CONFERENCE, VĨNH-LINH
SPECIAL ZONE.

DEMOCRATIC REPUBLIC OF VIETNAM. See VIỆT-NAM DÂN-CHỦ
   CỘNG-HÒA.

ĐỀN. A village temple used to honor and worship the
   spirit of a hero, popular ruler or one of the
   lesser spirits of the supernatural world at the
   village level. It is usually smaller than the
   đình but larger than the miểu - and is used only
   for worship. It is believed that spirits live
   in the đền and only inhabit the đình on holy days
   in order to be honored. If the village worships
   more than one major spirit in addition to the
   patron saint, then each spirit must have a separate đền. Urban residents have for the most
   part, abandoned the use of a đình, but many urban
   communities still maintain a đền. The ceremonies
   for most village festivals and holy days include
   a procession from the đền to the đình. Like the
   đình, the đền is located away from the residen-
   tial area of the village. The structure of the
   den is similar to that of the đình. There are
   two main buildings, front and back, and a small
   courtyard. The đền is also distinct from the
   Buddhist pagoda, although certainly not in competition or conflict. The village usually se-
   lects one person to reside in the den to oversee
   the grounds and maintain the altar, incense and
   other religious paraphernalia. He is called the
   Thủ-Tự. See ĐINH, MIỂU, THỦ-TỰ.

ĐEO. Mountain pass. Individual mountain passes are
   listed under separate entries. See ẢI-NAM-QUAN,
   CẢ PASS, HẢI-VÂN PASS, MỤ-GIA PASS, NGANG PASS,
   TAM-ĐIỆP PASS.

DI-LINH. (Djiring). A highland town in Lâm-Đồng Province. It is located on highway number twenty
   between Bảo-Lộc and Đà-Lạt. The surrounding area
   is chiefly used for tea plantations and fruit
   groves. The altitude (1200 meters or 3,937 feet),
   and mild climate make it suitable for agricultural
   production. The town is inhabited by both ethnic

Vietnamese and highland people of the Koho ethno-
linguistic group. See KOHO, LÂM-ĐỒNG.

DI-LINH PLATEAU. The plateau area south of the Lâm-
     Viên Plateau in the central highlands. It covers
     the area centering around Lâm-Đồng Province and
     includes portions of Quảng-Đức and Bình-Tuy pro-
     vinces. The plateau is inhabited mainly by the
     Koho ethno-linguistic highland group and is known
     for its fruit, tea and coffee production. This
     area represents the southernmost reaches of the
     Trường-Sơn Mountain Range. The climate is cool
     and comfortable.

ĐICH-TÔN. (Cháu đich-tôn). A grandfather's eldest
     son's son. The đich-tôn has special responsibil-
     ities to carry on the rites and rituals of an-
     cestral worship. See CULT OF THE ANCESTORS.

DIE. (Also called Jeh). An ethno-linguistic minority
     group of highland people located in southwestern
     Quảng-Nam, western Quảng-Tín and northwestern
     Kontum provinces. Population estimates were placed
     at 15,000 in 1972. The Die are of Mon-Khmer ethnic
     and language stock. The basic unit of social or-
     ganization is the patrilineal extended family
     headed by the eldest male. Men select their wives
     from neighboring villages. Their religion is
     animistic and includes animal sacrifices and wor-
     ship of the forces of nature as well as the spirits
     of inanimate objects. The Die practice slash-and-
     burn rice cultivation and also grow papayas, ba-
     nanas, guavas, pineapples and corn. Farming is
     supplemented by gathering, hunting and fishing.
     Although they are ethnically closely related to
     the Sedeng, the two groups have traditionally
     been enemies.

ĐIỆN-BIÊN-PHỦ. The site of a decisive battle in early
     1954 in which the Việt-Minh defeated the French.
     Điện-Biên-Phủ is located in Lai-Châu Province,
     sixteen kilometers (ten miles) from the Lao border.
     The French garrison was located in a flat, heart-
     shaped paddy field basin about nineteen kilometers
     (twelve miles) long and thirteen kilometers (eight
     miles) wide. It was fringed by low but steep and
     heavily wooded hills. The decision to reinforce
     Điện-Biên-Phủ was made by General Henri Navarre
     in order to engage the Việt-Minh if they attemp-
     ted to cross into Laos. The French concentrated
     a force of twelve battalions at Điện-Biên-Phủ,
     one third of whom were Vietnamese. They were

equipped with artillery and mortars together with
six fighter bombers and ten light tanks. In the
course of the battle six more paratroop battalions
were flown in from the delta.

The Việt-Minh force, under the leadership of
General Võ Nguyên-Giáp, consisted of 40,000 men,
the equivalent of four full divisions, equipped
with 105mm Chinese artillery pieces and 37mm
anti-aircraft guns. These 105mm and 37mm guns
were brought forward dismantled, carried by men
to caves and dug out emplacements on the hills
surrounding the garrison. The battle started on
the night of March 13, 1954 and continued until
the garrison fell to the Việt-Minh on May 7, 1954.
The principal determining factor of the outcome
of the battle was the ability of the Việt-Minh to
transport the heavy artillery pieces to such advantageous positions. They were so well camou-
flaged and protected with anti-aircraft guns that
they were impervious to French fire power. The
artillery barrages, coupled with the human wave
attacks by the infantry and poor weather conditions which limited the use of aircraft led to
the total defeat of the French forces by the Việt-
Minh. It is generally agreed that the battle of
Điện-Biên-Phủ provided the final crushing blow that
forced the French to abandon their efforts to maintain control of Indochina.

ĐIỂN-CỐ. The literary style in which reference is made
to historical events or personages. This is
accomplished by referring directly to an historical event or by using words or phrases from other
works which in turn, allude to the event.

DIỂN-KHÁNH. A small district town in Khánh-Hòa Province. It is situated on highway number one
about eleven kilometers (seven miles) west of
Nha-Trang. A citadel was built there around
1893 and still remains standing.

DIKE. (Đê). The Red River Delta in north Vietnam is
interlocked with a system of about 4,800 kilometers (3,000 miles) of dikes which protect the
population and the rice fields from the ravaging
flood waters of the Red River during the monsoon
season. This system of primary, secondary and
tertiary dikes was started back before the dawn
of the Christian era. The Chinese, upon their
arrival in the second century A.D. began to
strengthen and tend the dikes. Systematic and
large scale construction of the dikes began in

the thirteenth century under the Trần Dynasty
(1225-1400). In 1248 the Đinh-Nhi network was
begun. In 1255 the Emperor appointed a mandarin
to be in charge of the dikes. At the end of each
harvest, the army was also employed to work on
the dike system. Subsequent dynasties gave similar attention to the construction and maintenance of the dikes. During the flood season,
villages in the delta would station guards along
the dikes who would keep close watch to make sure
that the dikes were holding. In case of a weak
spot or an imminent break, a relay alarm system
would warn the villagers. See RED RIVER, RED
RIVER DELTA.

ĐINH. (Đình làng). A multi-purpose communal house in
the village. The đình is the most important
institution in the life of a village. It symbolizes the very soul and lifeline of that community.
Both secular and religious functions are held in
this sacred structure. The đình is unique to
Vietnam. Above all, it is the place of worship
of the guardian spirit or patron saint (Thành-
Hoàng) of the village. It houses the statue of
the patron saint and contains a shrine dedicated
to him. The patron saint is believed to reside
in the đình. It is from here that he dispenses
rewards and punishments for the deeds committed
by the villagers. He also plays a hand in determining the good or bad fortune of the village.
The đình also serves as a meeting hall for the
council of notables as they settle local judicial
disputes and take action on administrative, financial, and electoral questions. Village ceremonies and festivals are organized here which
often include large banquets. Finally, the important historical and genealogical records together with the village charter (hương-ước) are
stored here and guarded protectively.
    It is understandable, therefore, why the đình
is given so much attention and importance. Popular belief has it that the geomantically determined position of the đình would greatly influence the future of the people. The đình is designed and built with great care. The most
capable and renowned workmen are employed and the
finest materials are used within the limits of
the resources of the community. Each village
strives to have the most elegant and majestic
đình. The villagers and especially the wealthier
ones, are called upon to maintain the đình in
good

good order. The đình usually consists of two
sections. The inner part is reserved for worship
of the guardian spirit. Besides the altar honoring the guardian spirit, the precious village
documents are kept in this section. The outer
part is where the meetings and banquets are held.
This area is less formal. The đình traditionally
has three sets of doors. The center doors are
used only on special occasions. Although the
đình is a place of worship it is quite distinct
from the village temple (đền or miếu) or Buddhist
pagoda. While there may be similarities between
the cult of the guardian spirit and the cult of
the ancestors or the cult of Buddha and his disciples, they never interfere or compete with each
other. It should also be pointed out that the
origins of the đình are purely Vietnamese. No
similar village institution can be found in China
or other nearby countries. See ĐỀN, HƯƠNG-ƯỚC,
MIẾU, NGÀY GIỖ LÀNG, THÀNH-HOÀNG, XÃ.

ĐINH BỘ-LĨNH. See ĐINH TIÊN-HOÀNG.

ĐINH ĐÌNH-BẢNG. One of the best known đình (communal
house) in Vietnam. It is located in Đình-Bảng
Village in Hà-Bắc Province in north Vietnam. It
was built in 1736 out of iron wood. The worship
hall comprises seven main compartments with a
covered corridor leading to the inner sanctuary.
The four sides are enclosed by panelled doors
which can be opened for special occasions. There
are sixty main pillars in ten rows. The pillars,
beams and shrine are lacquered in gold and bright
red. See ĐÌNH.

ĐINH DYNASTY. (968-980 A.D.). (Nhà Đinh, Triệu Đinh).
A short-lived dynasty founded by Đinh Tiên-Hoàng
in 968 A.D. He named his kingdom Đại-Cồ-Việt and
established the capital at Hoa-Lư. Đinh Tiên-
Hoàng had three sons; Đinh-Liễn, the oldest; Đinh-
Tuệ; and Đinh Hạng-Lang, the youngest. Đinh Hạng-
Lang was made the crown prince which made Đinh-Liễn
angry whereupon he had his youngest brother killed.
In 979, a minor official named Đỗ-Thích dreamed of
a falling star which he interpreted as meaning that
he was about to become king. Thus, he killed both
Đinh Tiên-Hoàng and Đinh-Liễn. Consequently, the
only remaining son of the royal family, Đinh-Tuệ,
then only six years old, was made king. However,
the Queen and Lê-Hoàn, a high mandarin, were
having an affair. When the Chinese threatened to
invade, Lê-Hoàn dethroned Đinh-Tuệ after only

seven months of rule, and proclaimed himself
emperor, thus establishing the Early Lê Dynasty
(980-1009). See ĐINH TIÊN-HOÀNG, ĐINH-TUỆ, HOA-
LƯ.

DINH POINT. (Mũi Dinh, also called Cap Padaran). A
cape or point extending into the South China Sea
south of Phan-Rang in Ninh-Thuận Province in central Vietnam.

DINH RIVER. See CÂY RIVER.

ĐINH TIÊN-HOÀNG. (Also known as Đinh Bộ-Lĩnh). The
founder and first emperor of the Đinh Dynasty
(968-980). He was the son of a mandarin who
served as Governor of Hoan-Châu District under
the Ngô Dynasty (939-965). His father died early,
so Đinh Tiên-Hoàng went with his mother to live
in the countryside where he was raised. After a
period of strife during which the country was
divided up among twelve warlords, Đinh Tiên-Hoàng
raised an army and defeated the twelve lords. He
then established his capital at Hoa-Lư and formed
an administration of civilian and military officials. Most notably, he organized the army into
symmetrical units of multiples of ten. In 979,
he was assassinated at the age of twenty-six by
a minor official, Đỗ-Thích. Đỗ-Thích, motivated
by a vision, stabbed both the Emperor and his
son the crown prince, Đinh-Liễn. Đinh Tiên-Hoàng
had ruled for twelve years. He was very popular
with the citizenry and is remembered particularly
for having taken the first steps toward organizing
the religious life of the country. He created
an administrative hierarchy of priests, founded
a number of monasteries and built several temples.
See ĐINH DYNASTY, HOA-LƯ.

ĐINH TIÊN-HOÀNG TEMPLE. (Đền Đinh Tiên-Hoàng). A
well-known temple dedicated to Emperor Đinh Tiên-
Hoàng (968-979). It is located in Trường-Yên
Village in Ninh-Bình Province in north Vietnam,
on the site of Hoa-Lư, which was the capital
during the Đinh Dynasty. The temple was built on
the actual site of the royal palace and has been
repaired or replaced several times throughout history. The present temple was built in the seventeenth century during the Lê Dynasty (1428-1788).
It is famous for its beauty and symmetry. Each
year from the fifteenth to the twentieth day of
the second lunar month, a festival is held in
the temple in memory of Emperor Đinh Tiên-Hoàng.

See ĐỀN, ĐINH TIÊN-HOÀNG, HOA-LƯ.

ĐINH-TUỆ. (Vệ-Vương Đinh-Tuệ). The second son of
    Đinh Tiên-Hoàng who took the throne at the age of
    six in 979. He ruled for only seven months after
    which Lê-Hoàn proclaimed himself emperor and found-
    ed the Early Lê Dynasty (980-1009). See ĐINH DY-
    NASTY, LÊ ĐẠI-HÀNH.

ĐINH-TƯỜNG PROVINCE. An inland Mekong Delta province
    in south Vietnam. It is located south of Long-An
    Province and north of Vĩnh-Long Province. The
    population is 478,586 (1971) and the area is
    1,550 square kilometers (598 square miles). The
    provincial capital is Mỹ-Tho. Mỹ-Tho is located
    on highway number four which runs from Sài-Gòn
    to Cà-Mau. Đinh-Tường was one of the original
    six provinces in south Vietnam as established by
    Emperor Minh-Mạng (1820-1840) in 1832. In accord-
    ance with the treaty of 1862, it was one of three
    provinces relinquished to the French. The French
    acquired the remaining three provinces in the
    south with the treaty of 1874. These six were
    then divided into twenty provinces. Đinh-Tường
    became three provinces: Mỹ-Tho, Tân-An, and Gò-
    Công. In 1956, the provinces of Gò-Công and Mỹ-
    Tho were combined to form Đinh-Tường Province.
    In 1963, Gò-Công Province was reestablished
    leaving the boundaries of Đinh-Tường as they are
    today. The chief products of the province are
    rice, coconuts, vegetables, and fruits. It is
    the highest pork producing province in the Re-
    public of Vietnam. See MỸ-THO.

DJARAI. See JARAI.

DJIRING. See DI-LINH.

DMZ. See DEMILITARIZED ZONE.

ĐỒ-CHIỂU. See NGUYỄN ĐINH-CHIỂU.

ĐỒ-SƠN. A coastal town near the city of Hải-Phòng in
    north Vietnam. It is situated 110 kilometers
    (68 miles) from Hà-Nội and is a popular seaside
    resort. It has a good beach and several temples
    and pagodas of historical interest. The town is
    situated on a cape or point of the same name
    which protrudes out into the Gulf of Tongking.

ĐOAN-NGỌ. See LỄ ĐOAN-NGỌ.

ĐOÀN THỊ ĐIỂM (1705-1746). (Also known by her pen
name; Hồng-Hà). A famous female author and teacher in north Vietnam. Born in Bắc-Ninh Province,
she gained an early reputation for her literary
talents. She was invited to teach young ladies
at the royal court after which she opened a school
of her own in Hà-Đông. She married a mandarin at
the age of thirty-seven. However, after only six
years of marriage she died on the road en route
to join her husband at his new post in Nghệ-An.
One of her best known works is Chinh-Phụ-Ngâm.
See CHINH-PHỤ-NGÂM.

ĐỘI-CẤN. (Trịnh Văn-Cấn). A revolutionary and a
leader of the Thái-Nguyên Revolt against the
French on August 31, 1917. See THÁI-NGUYÊN REVOLT.

ĐỘI-SƠN PAGODA. (Chúa Đội-Sơn). A famous pagoda located on Đội-Sơn Mountain in Nam-Hà Province in
north Vietnam. It is situated opposite Đội-Điệp
Mountain upon which another pagoda is located.
Đội-Sơn Pagoda was built during the early Lý Dynasty (544-602). Emperor Lê Đại-Hành (980-1005),
in the year 987, is said to have performed the
Rice Planting Rites (Lê Tịch-Điền) at the foot of
Đội-Sơn Mountain. When the ground was plowed, a
jar of gold and a jar of silver were found the
next year. Thereafter, the harvests were always
good. These paddy fields were Kim Ngân Điền
(Gold and Silver Fields). See LỄ TỊCH-ĐIỀN.

ĐỒN ĐIỀN. Military settlements. The đồn-điền was a
form of settlement of new lands which was used by
the government in traditional Vietnam to promote
the occupation of new land. The đồn-điền appeared
in the fifteenth century. In times of peace,
soldiers were used to clear new frontiers. Under
the Lê Dynasty (1428-1788) a particular category
of soldier was established for this purpose called
Thục Điền Binh. Lands cleared by the Thục Điền
Binh belonged to the state, but when a village was
created, a section of this land was given to the
village. This then became village-owned public
land. After the land was cleared and a new village formed, the Thục Điền Binh were moved forward to clear more land. This system of land
development accounted, in part, for the success
of the southward expansion (nam-tiến). See LÃO-
TRẠI, NAM-TIẾN, NÔNG-TRẠI.

ĐÒN GÁNH. A bamboo or wooden carrying pole used
    throughout Southeast Asia. The pole is supported
    on the shoulder with the loads attached in a hang-
    ing fashion from both ends. The carrier often
    trots along in order to make maximum utilization
    of the springing action of the pole.

ĐỒNG-BẰNG. (Also called Bình-Nguyên). Plains or delta
    area. There are three principal plains in Việt-
    nam. The northern coastal plain (đồng-bằng bắc-
    phần) which is dominated by the Red River Delta
    is the most densely populated area in Vietnam.
    The southern coastal plain (đồng-bằng nam-phần)
    is dominated by the Mekong Delta. The central
    coastal plain (đồng-bằng trung-phần) or central
    lowlands includes a string of small deltas from
    Thanh-Hóa Province to Bình-Thuận Province. The
    plains area accounts for twenty-seven percent of
    the total land mass of Vietnam. See BÌNH-TRỊ-
    THIÊN PLAINS, BÌNH-PHÚ-KHÁNH-NINH PLAINS, CENTRAL
    COASTAL PLAIN, NAM-NGÃI PLAINS, NORTHERN COASTAL
    PLAIN, SOUTHERN COASTAL PLAIN, THANH-NGHỆ-TĨNH
    PLAINS, TRUNG-NAM PLAIN.

ĐỐNG-ĐA BATTLE. (Trận Đống-Đa, also called Trận Ấp
    Thái-Hà). A decisive victory against the Chinese
    invaders in 1789. In 1788, Vietnam was divided.
    The Lê Dynasty (1428-1788) still maintained the
    throne in the north while the Tây-Sơn brothers
    controlled the south and were revolting against
    the Lê Emperor. The leader of the Tây-Sơn, Nguyễn-
    Huệ, later to become Emperor Quang-Trung (1788-
    1792) heard that the Chinese army had occupied
    Hà-Nội. He gathered 100,000 troops and several
    hundred elephants and marched directly to Hà-Nội.
    It was near to the lunar new year (Tết) and the
    intention was to catch the Chinese off guard. The
    Vietnamese troops packed their rations of cooked
    sticky rice cakes (which are still a specialty of
    Tết in remembrance of the occasion). The troops
    marched in teams of three with two carrying the
    third on a litter, allowing each to rest in turn.
    They arrived at Tam-Điệp Pass where Nguyễn-Huệ's
    generals advised him to fall back and entrench.
    He responded with resolve to oust the foreigners
    and celebrate Tết in Hà-Nội. Taking the Chinese
    by surprise, the Vietnamese first engaged the
    Chinese at the village of Ngọc-Hồi. At Đống-Đa,
    the site of the major confrontation, the Chinese
    were massacred. Over 10,000 Chinese were killed
    and their army collapsed. They fled in panic.

Thus, Nguyễn-Huệ's promise that his men would enjoy Tết in Hà-Nội was fulfilled. See NGUYỄN-HUỆ, TÂY-SƠN DYNASTY, TÂY-SƠN REBELLION.

ĐÔNG-DU MOVEMENT. (Phong-Trào Đông-Du, literally, Eastern Studies Movement). The movement led by Phan Bội-Châu to send Vietnamese students to study in Japan. The anti-colonialist movement was designed to equip future political activists with a sound education, especially in the fields of politics and military science. The movement was made to appeal to wealthy Vietnamese for financial support. Phan Bội-Châu took the first three students to Japan in 1905. See PHAN BỘI-CHÂU.

ĐÔNG-DƯƠNG. The site of Indrapura, a major city in the ancient Kimgdom of Champa. It is located in Quảng-Nam Province in central Vietnam. Archaeological explorations have yielded many vestiges of Champa. Of particular notoriety is a bronze Buddha in the gupta style dating from the fourth to fifth century A.D. and showing strong Indian influence. The Buddha, now known as the Đông-Dương Buddha, is presently located in the national museum in Sài-Gòn. Similar figures have been found in Thailand at Korat and Nakom Pathom. In the year 875 a great Mahayana monastery was founded at Đông-Dương. The encircling wall of the monastery measured about a half mile. See CHAMPA, INDRAPURA, MỸ-SƠN, TRÀ-KIỆU.

ĐÔNG-DƯƠNG CỘNG-SẢN ĐẢNG. (Indochinese Communist Party). The principal Vietnamese communist political organization during the World War II period. It was formed in 1929 in Hong Kong. In 1930 it was amalgamated with the Indochina Communist Alliance and the Annam Communist Party. The French arrested over two hundred party leaders in 1939 and drove the party underground. In 1940, under the leadership of Hồ Chí-Minh, the party agitated throughout Vietnam and staged an insurrection in Cochinchina (south Vietnam) which was rapidly suppressed by the French. The Indochinese Communist Party played a major role in the August Revolution in 1945. However, in order to minimize the Communist image and for the sake of unity, Hồ Chí-Minh officially dissolved the Indochinese Communist Party on November 11, 1945. See AUGUST REVOLUTION.

ĐÔNG-DƯƠNG TẬP-CHÍ. A literary journal which was published in Quốc-Ngữ (Romanized script) in Hà-Nội beginning in 1913. Its purpose was to establish

Quốc-Ngữ as a national language while developing the general field of literature.

ĐÔNG HỒ. (1906-1969). Pen name of Lâm Tấn-Phác, a twentieth century poen, scholar, and teacher. He was born into a family of Chinese origin in Hà-Tiên Province in south Vietnam and was closely associated with the journal, Nam-Phong. One of his most famous poems was Linh-Phượng, published in 1928. In 1952 he founded the Bốn-Phương publishing house in Sài-Gòn and published the newspaper Nhân-Loại. He also taught in the Faculty of Letters at the University of Sài-Gòn.

ĐÔNG-HỚI. The capital city of Quảng-Bình Province in central Vietnam. It is located near the coast and suffered extensive damage from United States bombing during the late 1960's and early 1970's. There have been archaeological finds near Đông-Hới relating to the neolithic (early stone age).

ĐÔNG-HỚI RIVER. (Sông Đông-Hới). See NHẬT-LỆ RIVER.

ĐÔNG-HỚI WALL. A fortified wall built in 1631 in Quảng-Bình Province by Đào Duy-Từ. The wall was twenty-four kilometers (fifteen miles) long and as high as six meters (nineteen feet). On some sections it was defended every twenty meters (sixty-five feet) by a cannon. It was situated at the mouth of the Nhật-Lệ River. On the other side of the river was located the Nhật-Lệ Wall. Together, the sea port could be closed up, as that of the ancient Byzantium, by an iron chain fastened to both walls. See ĐÀO DUY-TỪ, NHẬT-LỆ WALL.

ĐÔNG-KHÁNH (ruled 1886-1888). The ninth emperor in the Nguyễn Dynasty (1802-1945). He was placed on the throne by the French after Emperor Hàm-Nghi (1884-1885) was captured and deported to Algeria. Emperor Đông-Khanh was predictably obedient to the French. He tried unsuccessfully to win the support of Hàm-Nghi's followers. He died in January, 1888, after a reign of only two years. See HÀM-NGHI, NGUYỄN DYNASTY.

ĐÔNG-KINH NGHĨA-THỤC. (Literally, Public School of the Eastern Capital). A progressive school founded in 1907 by a number of Vietnamese patriots. The school was designed to train and educate nationalist political activists. It used non-

traditional educational techniques. The format
and style were strongly influenced by the Japanese model of Keio University. Phan Chu-Trinh was
one of the many well-known figures that was associated with the school. The French closed the
school in 1908. See PHAN CHU-TRINH.

ĐÔNG-NAI RIVER. (Sông Đông-Nai). A major river in the
northern part of south Vietnam. It originates in
the Lâm-Viên Plateau area and is formed by the
merger of two smaller rivers, the Đa-Nhim and the
Đa-Dung. The main tributaries of the Đông-Nai are
the Sài-Gòn River, Bé River (Sông Bé), Vàm-Cỏ
River and the La-Nha River. The Đông-Nai River
flows southeasterly through Lâm-Đông and Long-
Khanh provinces to Biên-Hoa Province where it is
joined by the Sông-Bé. It then flows southward
through Gia-Định Province where it meets the Sài-
Gòn River. It then breaks down into several
branches, each of which empties into the South
China Sea at different outlets. From Nha-Bé, the
Nha-Bé River empties into the sea at Cửa Soai-Rạp.
Another branch, the Long-Tào River, also flows
into the sea at Cửa Soai-Rạp. Still another main
branch, the Đông-Tranh River, flows into the sea
at the Cửa Cần-Giờ. The valley of the Đông-Nai
River was the first area in south Vietnam that
was settled by the ethnic Vietnamese.

ĐÔNG POINT. (Mũi Đông). A cape or point extending
into the Gulf of Tongking in Hà-Tĩnh Province,
central Vietnam.

ĐÔNG-QUAN HIGHLANDS. (Cao-Nguyên Đông-Quan or Đông-
Quan Plateau). A mountainous area that occupies
the entire northern tip of Vietnam, including
parts of Hà-Giang, Lạng-Sơn and Tuyên-Quang provinces. It lies between the Sông-Gâm Mountain
Range and the Chiêm-Hoa Mountain Range. Included
in the Đông-Quang Highlands area are the smaller
highlands of Binh-Lạng, Trà-Lĩnh, Bông-Sơn and
Đông-Khê.

ĐÔNG-SƠN CIVILIZATION. (Also called Đông-Sơn Culture
or Văn-Hoa Đông-Sơn). A protohistoric civilization of the Bronze Age that existed in what is
now north Vietnam and the northern part of central
Vietnam. It is named for the village of Đông-Sơn
in Thanh-Hoa Province of central Vietnam where the
most important archaeological finds of this civilization were made. The most famous discoveries
were the bronze drums which were mushroom-shaped

with flat tops and side handles and richly decorated with pictures of scenes and human figures.
They were used in funeral and burial rites.
Other vestiges of this civilization that have been
unearthed include bronze arrowheads, bracelets,
knives, containers and ornaments as well as stone
axes and tools, jade items and pottery-ware. The
people of this society were farmers whose houses
were built on stilts or pilings. They had domesticated the dog, pig and buffalo and probably
grew rice. They were excellent craftsmen in
bronze. They believed in a life after death and
that their dead sailed away in "boats of life" to
some paradise in the west. The Đông-Sơn culture
extended from Lạng-Sơn Province southward to Hà-
Tĩnh and Quảng-Bình provinces. However, the area
of distribution of the most characteristic feature
of this culture, the bronze drum, extends from
China to Indonesia. The Đông-Sơn civilization was
at its peak of development during the last three
centuries B.C. but can be traced back to the
seventh century B.C. and up to the third century
A.D. The Đông-Sơn industry can be regarded as a
mixture of Chinese, local, western European and
possibly near eastern or south European elements.
The Sa-Huỳnh archaeological site in Quảng-Ngãi
Province is believed to have been a colony of the
Đông-Sơn civilization and is dated in the first
century A.D. See SA-HUỲNH, PREHISTORY.

ĐỘNG-THỔ CELEBRATION.   See LỄ ĐỘNG-THỔ.

ĐONG-TRIỀU MOUNTAIN RANGE.   (Dãy Đông-Triều).   A chain
of mountains extending from where the Thương River
and the Lục-Nam River meet in Hà-Bắc Province to
the northeast corner of the country. The tallest
mountain in the chain is the Nam-Mẫu Mountain
(1500 meters or 4,921 feet) near the Chinese border in Lạng-Sơn Province. Other well-known
mountains include Yên-Tử Mountain (1,088 meters
or 3,569 feet) in Hà-Bắc Province and Am-Vấp
Mountain (1,049 meters or 3,441 feet). The
mountain range meets the sea at Quảng-Ninh Province
and actually continues on to form a group of islands in and around Hạ-Long Bay.

ĐỐT MÃ.   The act of burning paper articles in the
rituals of ancestral worship. This practice varies
from place to place but is usually done in connection with the death anniversary (Ngày Giỗ) of an
ancestor. The purpose is to provide the spirits
of the dead with tools, utensils, and so on for

their use in the spiritual world. These articles
are made from paper and include such things as
clothes, dishes, animals, tools and even a minia-
ture house. See CULT OF THE ANCESTORS, NGÀY-GIỖ.

DOUBLE SEVEN FESTIVAL. See LỄ THẤT-TỊCH.

DOUMER, PAUL (1857-1932). Governor General of Indochina from February, 1897 to March, 1902. He
founded the famous Ecole Francaise d'Extreme
Orient (French School of the Far East) and promoted financial reform and public works programs
in Indochina. He later became President of the
French Republic but was assassinated on May 6,
1932, a year after taking office.

DRAGON. See LONG.

DRV. See DEMOCRATIC REPUBLIC OF VIETNAM.

ĐƯA ĐÁM. (Also called Phát-Dẫn). Funeral procession.
The order and make-up of a funeral is very important. The body is carried in a hearse pulled
by horses or motorized. In traditional Vietnam
and even today in the rural areas, the coffin is
carried on a platform which is carried on two
horizontal poles by four men. An altar with the
deceased person's picture and other sacraments is
carried in like fashion. Other members of the
procession carry wreaths and banners which bear
tribute to the dead or send well wishes to the
spirit of the dead. The immediate family wear
mourning clothes and some (depending on their
relation to the deceased) carry a walking cane.
The size and fanciness of the processions vary
greatly with the financial resources and social
status of the family. See CẢI-TÁNG, HỌ-LỄ, MỘC-
DỤC, TANG-CHỦ.

DUAN. An ethno-linguistic minority group of highland
people located along the valley of the upper Sông
Thanh River in the Lao/Vietnam border area. They
are classified linguistically as Mon-khmer. They
number around 3,500.

DỤC-ĐỰC (ruled 1883). The fifth emperor in the Nguyễn
Dynasty (1802-1945). He was the nephew of Emperor Tự-Đức (1848-1883) and rightful heir to the
throne when Tự-Đức died in July, 1883. But he
was deposed by the court officials after only
several days of rule. He was replaced by Hàm-
Nghi (1884-1885). See NGUYỄN DYNASTY.

ĐƯỜNG-LUẬT. A form of poetry dating from the Đường
Dynasty (618-907) in China. This form of poetry
includes works written in the tứ-tuyệt style (four
line verse) or the bát-cú style (eight line verse).

ĐUỐNG RIVER. (Sông Đuống). A small river in north
Vietnam. It flows from the Red River to the Thái-
Bình River in Bắc-Thái Province.

DUPERRE, BARON VICTOR-AUGUST. Titulary Governor of
Cochinchina from 1874-1877 and Rear Admiral in
the French Navy. He disagreed with French expansion in Tongking. He built the Catholic
cathedral in Sài-Gòn and helped with the creation
of the Bank of Indochina.

DUPRE, JULES-MARIE. Governor of Indochina from 1871-
1874. While in office he instituted obligatory
vaccinations, commissioned a study of public
schools, started a college to train administrators
(College des Stagiaires) and established a civil
corps of administrators. He ordered Francis Garnier to come to the aid of the trader Dupuis in
Tongking which resulted in the French attack on
Hà-Nội and the battle death of Garnier.

DUY-TÂN (ruled 1907-1916). The eleventh emperor in
the Nguyễn Dynasty (1802-1945). He was the fifth
son of Emperor Thành-Thái (1889-1907). He was
placed on the throne by the French when he was
only eight years old. Duy-Tân was an intelligent
and nationalistic emperor. At the age of thirteen
he sent a letter to Paris complaining that the
French were not adhering to the treaty of 1884.
In reaction to continued oppression, he secretly
conspired with Vietnamese revolutionaries (Trần
Cao-Vân and Thái-Phiên) and planned a general uprising of the Vietnamese troops against the French.
The plan was reported to the French the day before
it was to have been implemented. The French were
thus able to disarm the Vietnamese soldiers and
prevent the uprising. Thái-Phiên and Trần Cao-Vân
were arrested and beheaded. Duy-Tân was immediately deposed and exiled to Reunion Island off
of the coast of Africa. He later joined the
Allied Forces in World War II and in 1945, with
the rank of Major, was lost in a plane crash. See
NGUYỄN DYNASTY, THÁI-PHIÊN, TRẦN CAO-VÂN.

-E-

EARLY LÊ DYNASTY (980-1009 A.D.). (Nhà Tiền Lê, Triều
    Tiền Lê). The early Lê Dynasty was founded by Lê-
    Hoàn. Lê-Hoàn dethroned the child Emperor Đinh-
    Tuệ (979-980) of the Đinh Dynasty and proclaimed
    himself Emperor under the name of Đại-Hành-Hoàng-
    Đế (Lê Đại-Hành). Diplomatic relations with China
    were attempted but failed. Instead, China in-
    vaded the country by land and sea. Lê Đại-Hành
    defeated the land army at Lạng-Sơn and the Chinese
    navy retreated. Relations were then established
    with China with Lê Đại-Hành paying tribute to
    China. After defeating the Chinese armies, Lê
    Đại-Hành invaded Chiêm-Thành (Champa), occupied
    and plundered their capital. Chiêm-Thành was
    forced to pay tribute, and in 1,000 A.D. Chiêm-
    Thành abandoned its capital in Quảng-Nam and es-
    tablished it at Vijaya in Bình-Định Province.
    Thus began the constant open conflict between the
    Vietnamese and Champa Empire.
        Lê Đại-Hành died in 1005. The crown prince,
    Lê Trung-Tông was killed by his brother Lê Long-
    Đinh only three days after coming to the throne.
    Lê Long-Đinh (Lê Ngọa-Triều) was a tyrant who
    killed and tortured for pleasure. He ruled for
    two years. His only son was still an infant when
    Lê Long-Đinh died, so the court appointed Lý Cong-
    Uẩn to serve as the Emperor. Lý Cong-Uẩn then
    became the founder of the Lý Dynasty.
        The early Lê Dynasty was not a peaceful one.
    Besides the fighting with China and Champa, there
    were many local uprisings that had to be put down.
    It is also noteworthy that the Vietnamese command
    of the Chinese literary arts (Hán Văn) had al-
    ready developed as is evidenced by the official
    communiques issued by the early Le court. See
    LÊ ĐẠI-HÀNH.

EARLY LÝ DYNASTY (544-602 A.D.). (Nhà Tiền Lý, Triều
    Tiền Lý). An early dynasty founded in 544 A.D.
    by Lý-Bôn who led a popular uprising against the
    Chinese. The Chinese returned the following year
    in an unsuccessful attempt to regain their terri-
    tory. Lý-Bôn died in 548. His chief military
    commander, Triệu Quang-Phục usurped the throne
    and assumed the royal name of Triệu Việt-Vương.
    In 557 Lý Phật-Tử, the only surviving relative
    of Lý-Bôn led an army against Triệu Việt-Vương
    to regain the throne. Evenly matched, they de-
    cided to divide the kingdom in half. However,

in 571, Lý Phật-Tử attacked and defeated Triệu
Việt-Vương. He then established the capital at
Phong-Châu in Vĩnh-Yên Province and assumed the
royal name Lý Nam-Đế (he is also known as Hậu
Lý Nam-Đế). His rule lasted until 602 when in
the face of an invading Chinese army many times
the size and quality of his own, he surrendered
to the Chinese who then proceeded to occupy the
country for the third time. See LÝ-BÔN, LÝ NAM-
ĐÊ, TRIỆU VIỆT-VƯỜNG.

ECOLE FRANCAISE D'EXTREME ORIENT (EFEO). (Literally,
French School of the Far East). A French research
institute founded in Hà-Nội in 1899 by Paul
Doumer, Governor General of Indochina. The institute had a two-fold mission: 1) to conduct
scholarly research in all the countries of the
Far and Middle East whose cultures created an influence in the countries of Indochina and 2) to
conserve and classify the French colonies' historical monuments. The EFEO sponsored research,
published the results, amassed a large library
and collected, studied, classified and preserved
many old manuscripts, relics and East Asian
antiques. It also operated a number of museums
throughout the country during the colonial period.
The EFEO continued to operate for a while in Hà-
Nội after the end of the French Indochina War in
1954 but was obliged to move its headquarters to
Paris where it still functions. See PAUL DOUMER.

EDE. See RHADE.

EDUCATION. Formal education in traditional Vietnam was
heavily influenced by Chinese Confucianism. It
stressed the teaching of moral precepts as well as
literary skills and the instruction was given
through the medium of Chinese characters. The organizational aspects of education were informal.
At the village level, a parent would send his child
to study with a teacher, usually in the same village. For higher studies, a pupil would attend
lessons given by a retired mandarin or outstanding
scholar. The teachers were greatly respected and
revered by the students and were, in turn, expected to serve as models of virtue, scholarship
and wisdom. At the national level, Emperor Lý
Nhân-Tông (1072-1127) established a national
academy (Quốc-Tử-Giám) in Hà-Nội for the education
of the mandarins' sons. In 1252 it was opened to
the common people. In the fourteenth century a
hierarchy of teacher-mandarins was established to

take charge of education in the provinces. By the
nineteenth century, each province had a government
school. A new national academy was set up at Huế
in 1803 and opened to the sons of princes and mandarins as well as the sons of the citizenry.
These public schools were established for advanced
studies while the primary education was left to
local and private initiative. The triennial examinations (mandarinal examinations) provided much
of the impetus for higher education. In accordance with the Confucian tradition education was
highly esteemed and sought after.

Democratic Republic of Vietnam: The Democratic Republic of Vietnam (DRV) has emphasized
the eradication of illiteracy, development of
vocational and higher education, and the extension of education to the highland minorities.
An extensive complementary education program
(adult education) was launched. In 1966 the
government claimed that illiteracy was basically
eliminated. The general education system with
the corresponding 1969-1970 enrollment figures
include:

-Infant classes for children
  of 6-7 years of age........ 1,771,966
-First level classes (4 forms)3,159,000
-Second level classes (3
  forms).................... 1,208,000
-Third level classes (3 forms)..156,000

The University of Hà-Nội is the oldest university
in all of Vietnam and has eleven faculties, including liberal arts, mathematics, chemistry,
physics, literature and languages, history, geography, and natural sciences. It has an enrollment of about 20,000 (1963) full time students.
In addition, the DRV has a total of thirty-six
university or college level institutions plus
192 professional schools with over 200 branches.
Republic of Vietnam: School enrollment has
increased almost five-fold in the Republic of
Vietnam since 1954. Primary schools currently
enroll more than two million students or over
eighty percent of the children aged 6-11. Secondary school enrollment was about 550,000 during the
1970-71 school year. There are seven universities
in the Republic of Vietnam: Sài-Gòn University,
Vặn-Hạnh University (Buddhist) in Sài-Gòn, Minh-
Đức University (Catholic) in Sài-Gòn, Huế University, Cần-Thơ University, Đà-Lạt University
(Catholic), and Hòa-Hảo University in Long-Xuyên.

Additionally, there are several college level institutions including a polytechnic institute, military academy, national college of agriculture and
national institute of administration. A number of
normal schools and secondary level technical schools
have been established in major cities throughout
the country. Some private schools still offer a
curriculum in Chinese, French or Khmer languages
and are supervised by the government. See LYCEE,
ÔNG ĐỒ, QUỐC-TỬ-GIÁM, THÀY, THI ĐÌNH, THI HƯỚNG,
THI HỘI, UNIVERSITY OF HÀ-NỘI.

ELY, GENERAL PAUL. Commissioner General and Commander
in Chief of French forces in Indochina from 1954-
1955.

ÉN POINT. (Mũi Én). A cape or point extending into
the South China Sea just east of Qui-Nhởn in Binh-
Định Province in central Vietnam.

ETHNO-LINGUISTIC GROUPS. The largest ethno-linguistic
group in Vietnam is formed by the ethnic Vietnamese. In the Democratic Republic of Vietnam they
constitute eighty-five percent of the total population while in the Republic of Vietnam they make
up about eighty percent of the population. The
ethnic Vietnamese are of a southern mongoloid type
with a strong admixture of Indonesian-type blood.
They are pale yellow in skin shade, with straight
black hair, well-marked cheek bones and oblique
eyes which have the mongolian fold at the inner
corner. They are generally slight of built and
the men average about 1.6 meters (5'3") in height.
     Democratic Republic of Vietnam: According to
the 1960 census, 14.8% of the population was made
up of highland (montagnard) people, the largest
groups of which are the Tày (3.1%), Mưởng (2.6%),
Thái (2.4%), and the Nùng (2%).
     Republic of Vietnam: The ethnic Chinese are
the largest minority group in the Republic of Vietnam, constituting 6.6% of the population. The
Khmers (people of Cambodian origin), concentrated
mainly in the southwestern part of the country,
account for about 4% of the population. The highland people, concentrated in the central highlands,
compose about 4-5% of the total. They are divided
into about thirty different ethno-linguistic groups,
the largest of which are the Jarai, Rhade, Hre,
Bahnar, and the Koho. See CHINESE, KHMER, TÀY,
MƯỜNG, THÁI, NÙNG, MEO, MÁN, SANZIU, CAOLAN, XA,
NHANG, LÔLÔ VAN-KIỀU, RHADE, JARAI, HRE, KOHO,
BAHNAR, BRŨ, CHÀM, SEDANG, KATU, STIENG, CIL,

MNONG, RAGLAI, CUA, CHROO, CHRU, PACOH, DIE, MỌI,
LANGUAGE.

-F-

FAI-FO. See HỘI-AN.

FAN SI PAN. See HOÀNG-LIÊN-SỜN MOUNTAIN.

FATHERLAND FRONT. See MẶT-TRẬN TỔ-QUỐC.

FEAST OF THE LEARNED. See LỄ TRẠNG-NGUYÊN.

FEAST OF THE PURE LIGHT. See LỄ THANH-MINH.

FEAST OF THE WANDERING SOULS. See LỄ VU-LAN.

FISHING. Fishing has always been a major occupation
in Vietnam. There is over 2,300 kilometers
(1,420 miles) of coastline plus 122,275 hectares
(303,019 acres) of lakes, ponds, rivers and marshes. The coastal waters are very advantageous
to fishing - the beds are accessible to the sunlight, the warm temperatures make for teaming
life in the shelf waters, and the southwest/
northeast movement of the summer currents brings
fish migrating from the Gulf of Thailand. Most
fishing is done more or less on a family basis.
The boats vary in size from one region to the
other. The fishermen use a large variety of nets
and equipment according to the kind of fish they
are after.

FONTAINEBLEAU CONFERENCE. A post World War II series
of negotiations between the French and Vietnamese
concerning the future of Vietnam and the relationship between the two countries. The conference
was held at the French city of Fontainebleau from
July 6, 1946 through September 14, 1946. The
Vietnamese delegation was headed by Hồ Chí-Minh
and was unable to extract any concessions from
the French. The only concrete achievement was
the signing of a modus vivendi which provided
for a cessation of hostilities and was generally
favorable to the French. Thereafter, the situation deteriorated rapidly and on November 23,
1946 Hải-Phòng was bombed by the French.

FOOD. Rice is the basic staple in the Vietnamese diet
as well as being the single most important econ-

omic and cultural commodity. The rest of the
Vietnamese diet is based around fish, fruits, and
vegetables, all of which exist in good supply
throughout Vietnam. Vietnamese cooking has been
heavily influenced by the Chinese tradition and,
to a much lesser degree, by Indian, Malay and
French cooking. One particular characteristic of
Vietnamese cooking is the extensive use of fish
sauce (nước-mắm). This is used for seasoning in
a way similar to the use of soysauce by the Chinese
and Japanese, but results in the food retaining a
more natural and fresher color. Individual foods
and dishes are listed under separate entries.
See BÁNH CHƯNG, BÁNH ĐA, BÁNH ĐÚC, BÁNH GIÁY, CHẢ
GIÒ, CHẢ TÔM, CHÈ, HỘT VỊT LỘN, NEM, PHỞ, RAU-
MUỐNG, SEA SWALLOW'S NEST, SEN, THỊT BÒ BẢY MÓN.

FORESTRY. The forests constitute one of the principal
natural resources of Vietnam. There are many
varieties of wood, mainly from the mangrove swamps,
that are used for local consumption. These uses
include firewood, charcoal, box making or temporary construction. The more valuable woods come
from the dry forest and include rosewood, mahogany, ebony, sandalwood, pine, lát-hoa (Churasia
tabularis) and gụ (sindora tonkinensis). By-
products of the lumber industry include resin,
rosin, turpentine and various oils. Bamboo, ratan,
cinnamon, and aloes wood are also produced in
significant quantity. The forests have suffered
devastating destruction due to the war, especially
as a result of the carpet bombing, defoliation
and artillery. See BAMBOO, TRẦM-HƯỞNG WOOD.

FRENCH INDOCHINA WAR (1946-1954). The armed conflict
between France and the Việt-Minh (short for Việt-
Nam Độc-Lập Đồng-Minh Hội). In 1945, the Japanese occupation of Vietnam ended when the Việt-Minh
under Hồ Chí-Minh, staged the August Revolution
and declared the founding of the Democratic Republic of Vietnam on September 2, 1945. It can
be said that the French Indochina War actually began on September 22, 1945 when the French took
over the city of Sài-Gòn in an effort to reestablish French colonial rule in Indochina. The
French met strong resistance south of the sixteenth parallel. In the northern part of the
country, the Việt-Minh entered a series of negotiations with the French culminating in a jointly
signed modus vivendi between Hồ Chí-Minh and
France.

Then, on November 20, 1945 the Vietnamese
fired on a French war ship that was in turn firing
on a Chinese junk running contraband into the port
city of Hải-Phòng. Fighting broke out inside the
city. The French retaliated with air bombardment
and heavy artillery - over 6,000 Vietnamese were
killed. Fighting was only sporadic until December
19, 1945 when the Việt-Minh attacked French forces
and civilians in Hải-Phòng. Within a few hours,
French strongholds throughout Vietnam were under
attack. The French Indochina War had begun in
earnest.
    For a time, the French controlled the coastal
lands, but the Việt-Minh guerrilas controlled the
highlands. From 1949-1950, the Việt-Minh gravit-
ated to the Communist camp obtaining recognition
from the Soviet Union and communist China in 1950.
The Vietnamese received arms from communist China
and waged a protracted war against the French.
They steadily wore down the French whose enthus-
iasm for Indochina was waning, both in the field
and at home. The end came at Điện-Biên-Phủ, a
valley outpost in the mountainous province of Lai-
Châu, near the Lao border. The French poured in
paratroops to hold this bastion, but the Việt-Minh
ringed the hills with heavy artillery. On May 7,
1954 the French surrendered and 10,000 Frenchmen
were taken prisoner. Some say that the war was
lost at Điện-Biên-Phủ, others say that it was lost
in Paris by French disenchantment and frustration.
See ĐÀ-LẠT CONFERENCE, ĐIỆN-BIÊN-PHỦ, FONTAINEBLEAU
CONFERENCE, HỒ CHÍ-MINH, VIỆT-NAM DÂN-CHỦ CỘNG-HÒA,
VIỆT-NAM ĐỘC-LẬP ĐỒNG-MINH HỘI, VÕ NGUYÊN-GIÁP.

FU-NAN. An Indianized Kingdom founded at the end of
    the first century A.D. in the lower Mekong Valley.
    Legend has it that the kingdom originated with
    the marriage of an Indian Brahman to the daughter
    of a local native chief. Much of what we know
    about Fu-Nan is derived from the Chinese annals,
    accounts and descriptions of Chinese travelers
    and emmisaries. During the period 225-250 A.D.
    Fu-Nan entered into relations with China and
    India. The kingdom reached the height of its
    grandeur in the late fifth century and gave rise
    to a civilization of great brilliance. The cap-
    ital, Vyadhapura (City of the Hunter) was located
    near the hill called Ba-Phnom and near the village
    of Banam in the Cambodian Province of Prei-Veng.
    The territory of Fu-Nan encompassed, at its peak,
    the central Mekong, the southern part of Vietnam,
    and a large part of the Menam Valley and the Malay

Peninsula. The principal port city was located
some 192 kilometers (120 miles) from the capital
in what is now Kien-Giang Province of the Republic
of Vietnam. The name of this city was Oc-Eo and
its site has yielded foundations of buildings and
many objects bearing witness to Fu-Nan's contact
with the West such as Roman medals and rings with
inscriptions in Indian script. In the middle of
the sixth century Fu-Nan was attacked by a Khmer
kingdom to the north of Fu-Nan called by the
Chinese, Chen-La. Fu-Nan was steadily absorbed
by the Kingdom of Chen-La until almost all of
its territory was yielded to Chen-La. However,
the Fu-Nanese kings and the royal entourage continued to exist, possibly in one of their former
dependencies in the Malay Peninsula. See OC-EO.

-G-

GẦM RIVER. (Sông Gầm). A river in north Vietnam and
a tributary of the Lô River. It originates in
China and enters Vietnam in Hà-Giang Province.
It meets the Lô River north of Tuyên-Quang City.

GARNIER, FRANCIS (1839-1873). A French naval officer,
administrator, explorer and writer. He became
the administrator of the city of Chợ-Lớn in 1863.
In 1866 he was second in command of an expedition
to determine the course of the Mekong River, which
was assumed to be a possible commercial route to
western China. The expedition returned to Sài-
Gòn via Hankow and Shanghai two years later with
the report that while the Mekong did not connect
Vietnam with China, the Red River did. Garnier
went to Paris to prepare the report of the trip.
In 1872 he resigned from the navy and went to
China as an explorer and businessman. In 1873
he was recruited by Admiral Dupre, Governor of
Cochinchina to lead an expedition to establish
control over Tongking. He arrived in Sài-Gòn in
August, 1873 and went to Hà-Nội under the pretense of seeking a negotiated access to the Red
River. However, on November 23rd, he stormed the
citadel at Hà-Nội and proceeded to attack the
towns along the Red River between Hà-Nội and the
coast. After capturing most of the towns, including Nam-Định, Garnier was killed by the Black
Flags (Cờ Đen outside Hà-Nội on December 21, 1873.
He was made a martyr among the French. He is
reputed to have been one of the most outstanding

French leaders to have served in Indochina.

GENEVA AGREEMENTS. See GENEVA CONFERENCE.

GENEVA CONFERENCE. A conference called to negotiate
the end of the nine year Indochina war between
the French and the Việt-Minh. It was also designed to devise a settlement to the Korean conflict but was not successful in that regard. The
conference was held in Geneva from April 26, 1954
to July 21, 1954. In attendance were representatives of France, Russia, China, The United States,
The United Kingdom, The Democratic Republic of
Vietnam (Việt-Minh) and the State of Vietnam (Bảo-
Đại's government). The resultant agreements provided for prisoner exchange, division of the country and free elections two years hence (1956).
Two documents were produced: the agreements on
the cessation of the hostilities and the final
declaration. The former was signed on July 20,
1954 by General Delteil, Commander-in-Chief of
the French Union forces in Indochina and Tạ Quang-
Bửu, Vice Minister of National Defense of the
Democratic Republic of Vietnam. It consisted of
forty-seven articles setting forth the terms of
the agreement. The final declaration was issued
a day later and consisted of thirteen points acknowledging the accords and discussing the political problems including elections and sovereignty.

GENOUILLY, CHARLES RIGAULT DE. Vice-Admiral in the
French navy and Commander-in-Chief of French
forces in Indochina from February to November,
1859. He was Captain of one of the warships that
bombarded Đà-Nẵng in April, 1847. He was made
Vice-Admiral in 1858 and occupied Đà-Nẵng in
September of that year. In February, 1859, in
concert with a Spanish force, he sailed up the
Sài-Gòn River and took the port of Sài-Gòn. However his troops suffered serious losses due to
the tropical climate and infectious diseases.
And, because of the French declaration of war on
Austria, reinforcements were not available. Unable to defeat the Vietnamese or force an agreement, he asked to be relieved of his command. He
returned to France where he became a Senator in
1860 and an Admiral in 1864.

GIA-ĐỊNH-BÁO. The first Vietnamese newspaper. Established by the government, the paper was first
published in 1865 in Sài-Gòn. It was written in

Romanized script (Quốc-Ngữ) and influential in promoting the use of that script. Trương Vĩnh-Ký became the editor in 1869. See TRUONG MINH-KÝ, TRƯƠNG VĨNH-KÝ, QUỐC-NGỮ.

GIA-ĐỊNH CITY. The capital city of Gia-Định Province. Population 400,109 (1971). The city is located on the west side of and adjacent to the city of Sài-Gòn. In fact, the boundaries between the two cities are indistinguishable as both urban cities completely blend into each other. Most of the economy of Gia-Định City is dependent upon providing goods and services to Sài-Gòn as well as employment in the national governmental offices. The city was established at the end of the eighteenth century by Chinese merchants who fled from Biên-Hòa as it had been destroyed by the Tây-Sơn armies. See GIA-ĐỊNH PROVINCE.

GIA-ĐỊNH PROVINCE. A province in south Vietnam. Gia-Định was one of six original provinces in south Vietnam, created by Emperor Minh-Mạng in 1832. In accordance with the treaty of 1862 it was relinquished to the French. With the treaty of 1874 the French acquired the remaining three provinces in the south, An-Giang, Vĩnh-Long and Hà-Tiên. The six provinces were then divided into twenty, one of which was Gia-Định. The province today surrounds the independent municipality of Sài-Gòn. The population of the province is 1,345,425 (1971) and the area is 1,445 square kilometers (552 square miles). The provincial capital is Gia-Định City and is located adjacent to Sài-Gòn. The heavy population is a result of the overflow of people from the city of Sài-Gòn. The province extends eastward to the coast, enveloping the outlets of the Sài-Gòn River. In addition to employment in Sài-Gòn, the province has a significant amount of light industry and commerce which provides jobs for the population. One of the most famous personalities to come from Gia-Định Province was Võ-Tanh, a leading military leader who helped Emperor Gia-Long (1802-1819) in his fight against the Tây-Sơn. Another was Nguyễn Đình-Chiểu, a famous blind poet who wrote many works for the resistance movement against the French. See GIA-ĐỊNH CITY, NGUYỄN ĐÌNH-CHIỂU, VÕ-TANH.

GIA-HUẤN-CA. A poem written by Nguyễn-Trãi (1380-1442). The work was written in lục-bát (6-8) style and in six sections. The purpose of the poem was to

teach proper manners and behavior to the population. See NGUYÊN-TRÃI.

GIA-LAI PLATEAU. (Also known as the Kontum-Pleiku
    Plateau). The plateau area extending from the
    Hải-Vân Pass near Đà-Nẵng to the Ayun River Valley
    near Phú-Bổn in the central highlands. The pla-
    teau clearly shows the presence of volcanic for-
    mations although no volcano has ever been active
    in modern times. This highland region has many
    passes such as the An-Khê Pass, which facilitate
    transportation and communication with the coastal
    area. It includes parts of Kontum, Bình-Định,
    Phú-Bổn, and Pleiku provinces.

GIA-LONG (ruled 1802-1819). (Nguyễn Phúc-Anh). The
    founder and first Emperor of the Nguyễn Dynasty
    (1802-1945). The last of the Nguyễn Lords,
    Nguyễn Phúc-Anh launched a campaign against the
    Tây-Sơn regime in 1787 which resulted in the
    collapse of that regime in 1802. He proclaimed
    himself Emperor Gia-Long in June, 1802. He
    changed the name of the country from Đại-Việt to
    Việt-Nam and established his capital at Phú-Xuân
    (Huế). Gia-Long used the French volunteers and
    material to defeat the Tây-Sơn, but once on the
    throne he gave them no role in the affairs of
    state. In fact, he refused to establish any
    official relations with the west. He did tolerate
    Catholic missionaries, possibly because his French
    benefactor was a bishop. Gia-Long made great
    strides in the area of political and administra-
    tive reforms. He retained the Lê system of the
    mandarinal corps with minor changes. New admin-
    istrative units were formed and the administra-
    tive boundaries of the provinces, districts, etc.,
    were completely revised. A census was taken
    every five years. Confucianism flourished and
    education was strongly emphasized. Several lit-
    erary epics were written during his reign includ-
    ing the famous Kim-Vân-Kiều by Nguyễn-Du. The
    literature was written in nom during this period.
    Gia-Long also ordered the writing of national his-
    torical and geographical works. One of the most
    significant achievements was the establishment
    of the Gia-Long legal code. This code was
    actually drawn from the legal code of the Chinese
    Ch'ing Dynasty. Gia-Long ruled from 1802 to 1819.
    He died at the age of fifty-nine after a reign of
    eighteen years. See BEHAINE, PIGNEAU DE, NGUYÊN
    DYNASTY, NGUYỄN PHÚC-ANH, TÂY-SƠN DYNASTY, GIA-
    LONG LEGAL CODE.

GIA-LONG LEGAL CODE. (Hoàng-Việt Hình-Luật). The set
of laws promulgated by Emperor Gia-Long (1802-
1819) in 1812. The code was closely modeled on
the Chinese legal code of the Ch'ing Dynasty. It
reflected strong Confucian influence such as
hostility towards Buddhism and Taoism and reducing
the legal status of women provided for in the Hồng-
Đức code in the late fifteenth century. The Gia-
Long Legal Code consisted of 398 articles arranged
in 22 books or volumes. See GIA-LONG, HỒNG-ĐỨC
LEGAL CODE, NGUYỄN DYNASTY.

GIA-NGHĨA. The capital city of Quảng-Đức Province in
the central highlands. Population 6,759 (1971).
Gia-Nghĩa is a small frontier-like settlement
inhabited mainly by highland people.

GIA-PHẢ. The family register or geneaology book. The
family register is usually maintained by the gia-
trưởng, head of the immediate family or, in the
case of the extended family (Họ), the records are
kept by the trưởng-tộc. Great care is taken to
keep the register current and accurate. Some of
the information recorded includes the name, birth
date, children's names and date of death for every
member of the family. Additional information
such as the occupation, outstanding achievements,
native village residence and place of death is
also usually included. It also contains the location of the tombs of each individual in the
family. See GIA-TRƯỞNG, TRƯỞNG-TỘC.

GIA-TRƯỞNG. The head of a nuclear family. The father
is the gia-trưởng until he dies at which time the
oldest son assumes the responsibility and duties
of the family head. The authority of the gia-
trưởng was greater in traditional Vietnam than it
is in modern times. It included rights of owner-
ship and management of family property as well as
the right to dispose of the property belonging to
individuals within the family. He also serve as
arbitrator for family disputes and counsel for
major decisions within the family. The head of
the family was held responsible for the actions
and behavior of all the members of the family and
was, in turn, expected to exercise strict and firm
discipline within the family. See GIA-PHẢ, HƯỚNG-
HỎA, TRƯỞNG-TỘC.

GIÁC. Cupping. A form of traditional Vietnamese medicine in which a glass cup is heated and applied
to the surface of the skin for drawing blood or

humours to the surface. This treatment is used
especially for the relief of asthma and other
respiratory diseases. See Y-DƯỢC.

GIẢN ĐỊNH-ĐẾ. See TRẦN GIẢN ĐỊNH-ĐẾ.

GIANH RIVER. (Sông Gianh, also known as Sông Linh-
Gianh or Sông Rào-Nay). A river in central Vietnam. It originates west of Hoành-Sơn Mountain
and flows southeasterly through Quảng-Bình Province. It empties into the South China Sea and
Quảng-Khê.

GIAO-CHÂU. The name of the Chinese province which
later became Vietnam. The name Giao-Châu was
used during the period of 203-544 A.D. and was
located in what is now northern Vietnam. Giao-
Châu was bordered on the south by Lâm-Ấp, a precursor state of Champa.

GIAO-CHỈ. 1. The name of the Vietnamese district of
the Chinese colony of Giao-Chỉ-Bộ during the first
period of Chinese domination (111 B.C. - 39 A.D.).
Actually, the districts of Giao-Chỉ, Cửu-Chân and
Nhật-Nam comprised the area of what is now northern central Vietnam, and north Vietnam.
2. The independent state under the rule of the
Trưng sisters (Hai Bà Trưng). The capital was
established at Mê-Linh in the province of Sơn-
Tây. The state of Giao-Chỉ lasted from 40-43
A.D.
3. The district formed by the defeated state of
Giao-Chỉ after the fall of the Trưng sisters. The
district was ruled by a Chinese governor and
marked the second period of Chinese domination
(43-544). However, in 203 the district of Giao-
Chỉ was elevated to provincial status and was renamed Giao-Châu. See HAI BÀ TRƯNG, SĨ-NHIẾP.

GIAO-THỪA. The transition hour between the old year
and the new year. It is one of the most important
times during the Tết (lunar new year) holidays.
It occurs at the midnight hour on new year's eve.
Giao-Thừa is a time when the family ushers out
the spirits of the old year and welcomes the
spirits of the new year, a ritual called Lễ Trừ-
Tịch. It is especially important to give a warm
welcome to the spirit of the hearth (Táo-Quân)
who has been to visit the Jade Emperor. Drums,
gongs and firecrackers announce the hour of
Giao-Thừa. See CÂY NÊU, TÁO-QUÂN, TẾT.

GIAY. See NHANG.

GIỖ. See NGÀY GIỖ.

GIÓ LÀO. (Literally, Winds of Laos). Excessively hot
    and dry winds which occur in the summer months in
    the plateau areas of the central highlands. They
    differ in their unusual aridity from the general
    character of the monsoon. They sometimes blow
    with extreme violence and provoke intense evap-
    oration.

GÒ-CÔNG CITY. The capital city of Gò-Công Province.
    Population 36,611 (1971). It is situated at the
    intersection of highway number five fifty-eight
    kilometers (thirty-six miles) south of Sài-Gòn
    and highway number twenty-four, thirty-six kilo-
    meters (twenty-two miles) east of Mỹ-Tho. It is
    also connected to the major water routes to Sài-
    Gòn via the Gò-Công River. It is nineteen kilo-
    meters (twelve miles) from the ocean fishing
    port of Vàm-Lang. See GÒ-CÔNG PROVINCE.

GÒ-CÔNG PROVINCE. A coastal province in south Vietnam.
    It is situated north of Kiến-Hòa Province and
    south of Gia-Định Province. The provincial cap-
    ital, Gò-Công City is connected by highway number
    five to Sài-Gòn and by highway number twenty-four
    to Mỹ-Tho. The population of the province is
    198,088 (1971), and the area is 510 square kilo-
    meters (196 square miles). It is the smallest
    province in the Republic of Vietnam. Gò-Công
    was part of Định-Tường Province which, along
    with Gia-Định and Biên-Hòa provinces, were ceded
    to the French with the treaty of 1862. After the
    French acquired the remaining three provinces of
    Vĩnh-Long, An-Giang, and Hà-Tiên, they divided
    the six into twenty separate provinces, one of
    which was Gò-Công. In 1956 it was converted into
    a district of Định-Tường Province. It was re-
    established as a separate province in 1963. The
    population is almost entirely ethnic Vietnamese
    with a small minority of Chinese. About seventy-
    five percent of the population is engaged in farm-
    ing while the rest are in fishing or commerce.
    The economy of the province is centered around
    rice production and fishing. Other products in-
    clude coconuts, vegetables, bananas, sugar cane,
    pork, poultry and fruits. See GÒ-CÔNG CITY.

GỐM. See CERAMICS.

GULF OF THAILAND. (Formerly called the Gulf of Siam).
A large inlet of the South China Sea mostly in
Thailand. Its southeast shore is formed by Cambodia and the southwest part of Vietnam. The
Bay of Rạch-Giá is located in the Gulf of Thailand off the coast of Kiên-Giang and An-Xuyên
provinces.

GULF OF TONGKING. (Vịnh-Bắc). An arm of the South
China Sea on the northeastern coast of Vietnam.
The Gulf is about 480 kilometers (300 miles) long.

GUỐC. Wooden shoes. In traditional Vietnam wooden
shoes were worn in the rainy season to walk a-
round the village without sinking into the mud.
They were handcrafted out of large bamboo roots
which, because of the curvature of the root
could readily conform to the shape desired.
These were generally made with a sole and heel of
equal size about six inches thick with an upward
curve at the front. Around 1910 a new, lower
setting style called the Guốc Sài-Gòn was introduced and gained immediate popularity. This
style was made from wood and held on the foot with
a strap or band of cloth. The guốc Sài-Gòn is
still used today by both men and women. A more
fashionable style of guốc is also popular among
the women. This style is very ornate, often
lacquered, and features a very high heel.

-H-

HÀ-BẮC PROVINCE. (Formerly Bắc-Giang and Bắc-Ninh Provinces). A province in north Vietnam located east
of Hà-Nội, south of Bắc-Thái and Lạng-Sơn provinces
and west of Quảng-Ninh Province. The estimated
population is 1,127,000 (1969) and the land mass
is 4,700 square kilometers (1814 square miles).
The capital of the province is Bắc-Ninh City.
The northern part of the province (former Bắc-
Ninh Province) is mountainous while the southern
portion is flat plains. Although most of the inhabitants are ethnic Vietnamese, there is a number of small communities of Thổ, Nùng and Mán
highland minority people. There are three large
rivers in Hà-Bắc, all of which empty into the
Thái-Bình River: the Cầu River, Thương River,
and the Lục-Nam River. Hà-Bắc Province is noted
for its folk songs and is considered to be the
cradle of the Quan-Họ, a type of village folk song.

The Bồ-Hạ orange, which is native to the area is
well-known and is considered to be an exceptionally sweet variety. See BẮC-NINH CITY, BẢO NGHIÊM
STONE TOWER.

HẠ-ĐIỀN CEREMONY. See LỄ HẠ-ĐIỀN.

HÀ-ĐÔNG CITY. The capital city of Hà-Tây Province in
    north Vietnam.

HÀ-ĐÔNG PROVINCE. See HÀ-TÂY PROVINCE.

HÀ-GIANG CITY. The capital city of Hà-Giang Province
    in north Vietnam. It is located 348 kilometers
    (215 miles) north of Hà-Nội on the Sông Lô (Lô
    River).

HÀ-GIANG PROVINCE. A mountainous province in the north-
    west part of north Vietnam. It borders on China
    and is situated between Lào-Cai and Cao-Bằng pro-
    vinces. The estimated population is 240,800 (1968).
    The land mass of the province is 7,995 square kilo-
    meters (3,086 square miles). Hà-Giang has many
    tall mountains over 2,000 meters (6,500 feet) and
    important rivers. The inhabitants of this province
    are primarily of the Thổ ethno-linguistic group.
    Also represented are the Chinese, Mèo, Mán, Nùng,
    Giay, and the Lô-Lô. Very few ethnic Vietnamese
    live in the province. Hà-Giang is connected by
    road and river to Hà-Nội, both routes going via
    Tuyên-Quang Province. Hà-Giang is historically
    linked to the Thái peoples, of which the Thổ is
    the largest group. The border district of Bảo-
    Lạc has been contested by China and Vietnam. In
    1895 China and France agreed to the present bor-
    ders. Several strategic border forts were lo-
    cated in Hà-Giang. Paddy rice and corn are the
    principal crops. Lumber is exported from the
    province. Some of the better woods used to be
    shipped to China. The province capital is the
    city of Hà-Giang and is situated on the Lô River.
    The province is presently part of the Việt-Bắc
    Autonomous Region (Khu Việt-Bắc Tự-Trị). See
    HÀ-GIANG CITY, VIỆT-BẮC AUTONOMOUS REGION.

HẠ-LÔI TEMPLE. A temple dedicated to the two Trưng
    sisters (Hai Bà Trưng). It is located in Hạ-Lôi
    Village in Vĩnh-Phú Province near the Red River.
    Hạ-Lôi is the native village of the Trưng sisters.
    Traditionally, a festival is held each year on the

fifteenth of the first lunar month. A pageant is
held which includes the participation of 150 boys
and 150 girls. See HAI BÀ TRƯNG.

HẠ-LONG BAY. (Vịnh Hạ-Long, also known as Vịnh A-Long).
A very picturesque bay along the coast of Quảng-
Ninh Province in north Vietnam. It covers an area
of over 2,000 square kilometers (722 square miles)
and is characterized by thousands of limestone
islets of various sizes. The action of the salt
water on the soft limestone over the ages has
carved the islets into unusual shapes and has
produced interesting caves and grottoes in the
rock. Legend has it that a dragon came down from
the heavens and plunged into the bay. Thus it is
that it is named Hạ-Long (Descending Dragon) Bay.

HÀ-NAM PROVINCE. See NAM-HÀ PROVINCE.

HÀ-NỘI. The capital city of the Democratic Republic of
Vietnam. Hà-Nội is administered as an autonomous
municipality. It is situated at the confluence of
the Red River and the Đuống River. The municipality is divided into four urban districts and four
suburban districts. It covers an area of 580
square kilometers (223 square miles) and has a
population of 1,100,000 (1970).
      Hà-Nội has always been a principal city of
Vietnam. In the third century the vicinity of
present day Hà-Nội was called Long-Biên and was
part of Giao-Châu. In 791 Governor Triệu-Xưởng
built a citadel on the present site of Hà-Nội
which was enlarged in the ninth century. From
980 to 1,009 it was the capital town of Giao-Chỉ
district. In the year 1010 Emperor Lý Thái-Tổ
(ruled 1010-1028) moved the imperial capital to
that city which by that time was known as Đại-La.
Lý Thái-Tổ renamed it Thăng-Long (Soaring Dragon).
Thăng-Long continued to serve as the capital until the Hồ Dynasty (1400-1407) built a new citadel in Thanh-Hóa which was named Tây-Đô (Western
Capital) and at the same time Thăng-Long was renamed Đông-Đô (Eastern Capital). When the Chinese (Ming Dynasty) took over Vietnam from 1414-
1427, Thăng-Long became the province capital of
An-Nam. Emperor Lê Thái-Tổ (1428-1433), after
expelling the Chinese, made Thăng-Long his capital and renamed it Đông-Kinh (Eastern Capital).
The Tây-Sơn armies invaded north Vietnam and captured the city in 1789. They fortified the city
and renamed it Bắc-Thanh (Northern Citadel). The
present name of Hà-Nội was given in 1831 by

Emperor Tự-Đức (1848-1883) as the capital city of
Hà-Nội Province. In 1888 the province was renamed Hà-Đông but the city remained Hà-Nội. The
French took Hà-Nội in 1882. From 1902-1954 Hà-
Nội was the central location for the French colonial regime in Indochina. With the defeat of the
French and the establishment of the Democratic
Republic of Vietnam, Hà-Nội became the national
capital once again. The city is particularly
well-known for its scenic spots (botanical gardens, lakes (Hoàn-Kiếm and Hồ-Tây) etc.), its
points of historical and cultural interest (Văn-
Miếu Pagoda, One Pillar Pagoda, etc.), and its
institutions of higher learning. Hà-Nội is also
an industrial center. It accounts for twenty-five
percent of the total industrial output of the
Democratic Republic of Vietnam. See HOÀN-KIẾM LAKE,
HỒ TÂY, MỘT-CỘT PAGODA, NGỌC-SƠN TEMPLE, VĂN-MIẾU
PAGODA, VIỆT-NAM DÂN-CHỦ CỘNG-HÒA.

HÀ-TÂY PROVINCE. (Formerly Hà-Đông and Sơn-Tây Provinces). A province in north Vietnam. It is
located in the Red River Delta south of Vĩnh-Phú
and northeast of Hoà-Bình Province. The population of the province is approximately 1,190,000
(1960) and the land mass is 2,142 square kilometers
(827 square miles). The provincial capital is the
city of Hà-Đông. Hà-Tây Province is known for its
handicrafts, particularly silk and bamboo products. There have been several new industrial
plants established in the province including a
paper mill and sugar refinery. Other products
include sweet potatoes, corn, jute and pork. The
population of Hà-Tây is mainly ethnic Vietnamese.
However, a number of Mường people are found in
the western part of the province. Under the
French there were several large plantations situated in Hà-Tây. There are also several famous
temples and landmarks in the province including
the Ngô-Quyền Temple, Thầy Pagoda and the Hương-
Tích Pagoda. The merger of the two provinces of
Sơn-Tây and Hà-Đông took place in 1964. See
HƯƠNG-TÍCH PAGODA, THẦY PAGODA.

HÀ-TIÊN. A former province and presently the name of
a town in Kiên-Giang Province in south Vietnam.
It is situated near the Cambodian border on the
coast of the Gulf of Thailand. It was part of
Cambodia until the eighteenth century when the
Thai armies harrassed the area. In 1708 the
Cambodian appointed Governor Mae Cuu, a Chinese
immigrant from Lei-Chow, Kwangtung, asked the

Nguyễn Lords for protection and help. From that
time forward, Hà-Tiên became part of Vietnam. It
was made one of six provinces comprising Vietnam
by Emperor Minh-Mạng (1820-1840). When the
French conquered the south in 1867 they divided
the six provinces into twenty smaller provinces,
one of which was Hà-Tiên. In 1956, Hà-Tiên Province was combined with Rạch-Giá Province to form
Kiên-Giang Province. The town of Hà-Tiên is connected by road to Rạch-Giá and Vĩnh-Long. There
are important limestone deposits near Hà-Tiên and
a cement factory located there.

HÀ-TIÊN/RẠCH-GIÁ CANAL. (Kinh Hà-Tiên Rạch-Giá). A
major waterway running from the Bay of Hà-Tiên to
the city of Rạch-Giá. It was built parallel to the
coast of the Gulf of Thailand.

HÀ-TĨNH PROVINCE. A coastal lowland province in central Vietnam located between Nghệ-An Province to
the north and Quảng-Bình Province to the south.
The land mass of the province is approximately
6,100 square kilometers (2,355 square miles) with
a population of 689,349 (1960). In ancient Vietnam, Hà-Tĩnh was called Bộ Cửu-Đức and approxi-
mated one of the fifteen districts (Bộ) of Văn-
Lang. Later it was called Quận Cửu-Chân, one of
nine districts of Giao-Chỉ-Bộ. The province is
known as a relatively poor province and together
with Nghệ-An Province (the two are often known
as Nghệ-Tĩnh) is reputed to be the homeland of
many of Vietnam's revolutionaries. The capital
city Hà-Tĩnh, is located on highway number one.
See HÀ-TĨNH CITY.

HÀ-TRUNG LAGOON. (Đầm Hà-Trung). A salt water lagoon
in Thừa-Thiên Province in central Vietnam. It
extends from Cửa Thuận-An southward to Cầu-Hai
Lagoon.

HẮC-GIANG RIVER. (Sông Hắc-Giang). See ĐÀ-GIANG
RIVER.

HAI BÀ TRƯNG (40-43 A.D.). (The Trưng Sisters). The
two Trưng sisters, Trưng-Trắc and Trưng-Nhị. The
husband of Trưng-Trắc, a minor feudal lord, was
slain by the Chinese who were then occupying
Vietnam (40 A.D.). In response the two Trưng
sisters raised an army and led the revolt against
the Chinese that resulted in the expulsion of the
Chinese. A new and independent country was established and the two Trưng sisters were proclaimed

Queens. The capital was established at the village of Mê-Linh in present-day Vĩnh-Phú Province.
The Chinese counter attacked under the famous
General Mã-Viện in 43 A.D. and defeated the Vietnamese. Rather than surrender to the enemy, the
two Trưng sisters chose suicide. On the sixty
day of the second lunar month in the year 43 A.D.
the Trưng sisters drowned themselves in the Hát-
Giang River. See HÀ-LÔI TEMPLE.

HẢI-DƯƠNG CITY. The capital city of Hải-Hưng Province
in north Vietnam. It is located on the Thái-Bình
River (Sông Thái-Bình) and on the road and rail
routes between Hà-Nội and Hải-Phòng. It is 53
kilometers (34 miles) from Hà-Nội and 42 kilometers (26 miles) from Hải-Phòng. Hải-Dương City
served as the provincial capital of Hải-Dương
Province from 1804 until recently when Hải-Dương
Province was merged with Hưng-Yên Province to
form Hải-Hưng Province.

HẢI-DƯƠNG PROVINCE. See HẢI-HƯNG PROVINCE.

HẢI-HƯNG PROVINCE. (Formerly Hải-Dương and Hưng-Yên
provinces). An inland delta province in north
Vietnam. It is located south of Hà-Bắc Province,
north of Thái-Bình Province and southeast of Hà-
Nội. The population of Hải-Hưng is given as
1,499,747 (1960). The land mass is 2,300 square
kilometers (1,235 square miles). The capital of
the province is the city of Hải-Dương. Hai-Hung
is mountainous only in the northern-most part.
Otherwise it is flat delta land. The Thái-Bình
River system runs through the province. The
capital, Hải-Dương, is located on highway number
five which connects Hà-Nội with Hải-Phòng, and
on the rail route which runs between these two
major cities. Rice is the principal agricultural crop. Secondary crops include tea, coffee,
and silk. Although most of the population is
ethnic Vietnamese Buddhist, there is a pocket of
Catholicism at Kẻ-Sạt which dates back to 1676.
A famous temple dedicated to Trần Hưng-Đạo is
located at Kiếp-Bạc. See KIẾP-BẠC TEMPLE.

HẢI-NINH PROVINCE. See QUẢNG-NINH PROVINCE.

HẢI-PHÒNG. The second largest city and the major port
in the Democratic Republic of Vietnam. It is
located on the bank of the Cửa-Cấm River, one of
the ocean outlets of the Thái-Bình River. Hải-
Phòng is situated 51 kilometers (32 miles) from

the sea and 100 kilometers (62 miles) from Hà-Nội.
The French took possession of Hải-Phòng in accordance with the treaty of 1874. At that time it was
just a market area. The French established themselves there and opened a consulate. The river
was dredged, the marshes were drained and the port
facilities built. The town soon became an industrial center due partly to the local supply of
coal and the direct railroad line to Hà-Nội. Hải-
Phòng is now administered as an autonomous municipality. It occupies much of what formerly was
the province of Kiến-An and has a population of
369,248 (1960). Hải-Phòng's industrial facilities
include a phosphate plant, fish cannery, cement
factory, shipyard, electric power plant and rail
yards.

HẢI-VÂN PASS. (Đèo Hải-Vân, also called Đèo Ải-Vân,
    or Hải-Vân Quan). The mountain pass on the coast
    between Quảng-Nam and Thừa-Thiên provinces in
    central Vietnam. The pass is formed by the
    Trường-Sơn Mountain Range which extends to the
    sea at that point. The northern part of the pass
    is located in Phú-Lộc District of Thừa-Thiên Pro-
    vince while the southern part of the pass is lo-
    cated in Hòa-Vang District of Quảng-Nam Province.
    National highway number one runs from Huế south-
    ward through the pass to Đà-Nẵng. The railroad
    runs around the base of the pass following the
    shore line. Đèo Hải-Vân literally means the
    "Pass of the Ocean Clouds" and is known as one
    of the most scenic spots in Vietnam. It is also
    of great strategic and commercial importance. The
    pass is located about thirty kilometers (nine-
    teen miles) north of the city of Đà-Nẵng and
    sixty-nine kilometers (forty-three miles) south of
    the city of Huế. The pass is about twenty kilo-
    meters (12.4 miles) long. At one time prior to
    the fifteenth century, the Hải-Vân Pass marked
    the traditional boundary between Vietnam and the
    Kingdom of Champa.

HALANG. An ethno-linguistic minority group of highland
    people located in southwest Kontum Province and in
    the neighboring areas of Laos. The Halang seem to
    have been migrating westward during the recent
    years, resulting in the bulk of the population now
    being located in Laos. Recent estimates place the
    total Halang population at 40,000 with only 10,000
    actually residing in Vietnam. They are a member
    of the Mon-Khmer linguistic group, speaking a
    language closely related to that of the Sedeng to

the north. The Halang society is patriarchal and
the autonomous village is the basic political unit.
Their religion is animistic spirit worship. The
Halang practice slash-and-burn rice cultivation
and grow corn as a second crop.

HALF HATCHED DUCK EGGS. See HỘT VỊT LỘN.

HÀM-NGHI (ruled 1884-1885). The eighth emperor in the
  Nguyễn Dynasty (1802-1945). He was only thirteen
  years old when he was placed on the throne in
  1884. In July, 1885, the Vietnamese troops attacked the French troops stationed in Huế. The
  next day the city fell to the French and Hàm-Nghi
  and his court fled. They went to Quảng-Trị, and
  then to Quảng-Bình in order to continue the resistance movement against the French. For three
  years he led the resistance movement. Finally
  in 1888 he was betrayed by a local village chief
  and captured by the French. Hàm-Nghi spent the
  rest of his life in forced exile in Algeria. He
  died there in 1947. One of this followers in the
  resistance movement, Phan Đình-Phùng, avenged
  his betrayal by killing the village chief who had
  reported him to the French authorities. See CẦN
  VƯƠNG MOVEMENT, CAO-THẮNG, ĐỀ-THÁM, NGUYỄN DYNASTY,
  PHAN ĐÌNH-PHÙNG.

HÀM-TÂN. The capital city of Bình-Tuy Province in
  south Vietnam. The population is 24,933. It is
  located near the coast at the mouth of the Dinh
  River.

HAMLET. See ẤP.

HÁN. (Chữ Hán, or Hán-Văn). Chinese characters. The
  word actually originated from the time of the Han
  dynasty in China and came to mean the Chinese
  written language. Chữ hán is also called chữ nho.
  In traditional Vietnam before the advent of the
  Romanized script (quốc-ngữ), the Vietnamese
  authors, scholars and mandarins used Chinese characters in all official correspondence and much of
  the literature. See NÔM, QUỐC-NGỮ.

HAN. (Also called Ngái). An ethno-linguistic minority
  group of highland people located in the provinces
  of Quảng-Ninh, Hà-Bắc, Lạng-Sơn and Hà-Giang provinces. They speak a language of the Sino-Tibetan
  language family. They numbered 174,644 in the 1960
  census.

HÀN THỰC. See LỄ HÀN THỰC.

HÀN-THUYÊN. See NGUYỄN-THUYÊN.

HANDICRAFTS. Vietnam has a wide variety of handicrafts. The highland tribal peoples have highly
   developed such skills as basketry and weaving.
   The Vietnamese handicrafts, many of which were
   imported from China, include lacquerware, pottery,
   woodcarving, sculpture, ceramics, metal working,
   embroidery and ivory and marble carving.

HARMAND AGREEMENT. See TREATY OF PROTECTORATE.

HARMAND, DR. FRANCOIS-JULES (1845-1921). Anthropolo-
   gist, diplomat, and physician. He served as
   General Commissioner in Huế from June, 1883, to
   October, 1883. He negotiated the Treaty of
   Protectorate of August, 1883, which is sometimes
   referred to as the Harmand Agreements. See
   TREATY OF PROTECTORATE.

HÁT Ả-ĐÀO. A form of singing poetry. A tradition of
   north Vietnam, hát ả-đào was probably introduced
   in the fifteenth century and enjoyed a golden age
   in the nineteenth century. However, it has since
   rapidly declined in popularity and has become
   almost extinct. This type of entertainment music
   was sung by a professional or semiprofessional
   singer (comparable to a Japanese Geisha girl),
   and accompanied by one musician playing a three-
   stringed lute (đàn-đáy). This form of music is
   quite complicated and refined. Often the perform-
   er would be obligated to sing a poem which had
   just been composed on the spot by the one being
   entertained. The hearer would sometimes express
   his pleasure, displeasure or encouragement with
   a special small drum with which he would also
   punctuate the poem. One of the most popular forms
   of hát ả-đào was the hát nói. See CÁ HUẾ, HÁT
   NÓI, MUSIC.

HÁT BÀI-CHÒI. A form of musical theater which grew out
   of festival card games in Bình-Định Province in
   central Vietnam. The dealer would sing the name
   of each card as he dealt. Eventually they became adept at telling stories in their song pattern, and at the end of their festivals they
   would go around the countryside singing love songs
   as well as moral tales celebrating the virtues of
   Confucianism. This developed into a theater form
   with instrumentation and gestures. Troupes formed

in the early 1900's and increased in popularity in
all parts of Vietnam.

HÁT BỘI. (Also called hát tuồng). The classical theater of Vietnam. Hát Bội is based primarily on
the Chinese opera. It was probably introduced
into Vietnam in the late thirteenth century during
the Mongol invasion. The Hát bội employs the use
of scenery and gestures, all of which are quite
similar to Chinese theater. The orchestra is
usually composed of six players. The predominant
role is played by the drum. Relatively few spoken parts are used, the majority of the performance being occupied with singing. Often times
the audience has a drum with which to comment on
the performance. Hát bội is presently becoming
less popular and is being preserved only in
north Vietnam.

HÁT CHÈO. A satirical and folkstyle form of Vietnamese
theater. This theater form employs instruments
and songs or poetry of 7-7 or 6-8 syllable lines
as well as spoken script. The early form of hát
chèo reflected the rural life and times. But,
beginning with the French occupation it became
more urbanized and formalized. Hát chèo is
presently performed almost exclusively in the Red
River Delta area of north Vietnam.

HÁT NÓI. A form of the musical tradition of hát a-đào.
Hát nói is the most commonly used and most appeal-
ing form of the hát a-đào. Each poem in this
style is divided into three distinct parts, each
adhering to very rigid rules of composition. See
HÁT A-ĐÀO.

HÁT QUAN-HỌ. A form of singing prevalent in north
Vietnam. This type of singing involves dialogue
songs with verses exchanged between boys and girls
and is associated with the spring and autumn festivals. Usually boys and girls stand in two lines
facing each other and answer each other's rhymes.

HÁT TRỐNG-QUÂN. (Literally, Army Drum Songs). A form
of martial singing. This unique form was started
by Nguyễn-Huệ (who later became Emperor Quang-
Trung, 1788-1792) as a stirring and inspirational
device used in recruiting his army. It was also
used for marching songs as his forces marched
northward, and for victory songs as they defeated
the invading Chinese. Hát trống-quân has been
preserved as a tradition of singing with the male
singers trading verses with the female singers.

HÁT TUỒNG. See HÁT BỘI.

HẦU. Marquis, a rank of nobility. See NOBILITY.

HẬU-BỔN. (Formerly known as Cheo-Reo). The capital
    town of Phú-Bổn Province in the central highlands.
    Population 16,752 (1971). Hậu-Bổn is a small
    frontier-like settlement inhabited primarily by
    highland people of the Jarai ethno-linguistic
    group. See JARAI, PHÚ-BỔN.

HẬU-GIANG. The area in southernmost south Vietnam which
    is dominated by the lower Mekong River (Sông Hậu-
    Giang also called the Bassac River). Included in
    the area are the provinces of Kiên-Giang, Phong-
    Dinh, Chương-Thiện, Ba-Xuyên, Bạc-Liêu and An-
    Xuyên. See COCHINCHINA, HẬU-GIANG RIVER, NAM-
    PHẦN.

HẬU-GIANG RIVER. (Sông Hậu-Giang, also known as the
    lower Mekong River or the Bassac River). The
    southern branch of the Mekong River. It flows
    from Châu-Đốc, past Long-Xuyên and Cân-Thơ to the
    South China Sea. The three outlets to the sea are
    the Cửa Định-An, Cửa Ba-Thắc (also called Cửa Hậu-
    Giang) and Cửa Cung-Hầu. See MEKONG RIVER.

HẬU LÊ DYNASTY. (Nhà Hậu Lê or Later Lê Dynasty). See
    LÊ DYNASTY.

HẬU LÝ DYNASTY. (Nhà Hậu Lý or Later Lý Dynasty). See
    LÝ DYNASTY.

HẬU LÝ NAM-ĐẾ (571-602). (Also known as Lý Phật-Tử or
    Lý Nam-Đế). The last emperor in the Early Lý Dy-
    nasty (544-602). He defeated Triệu Việt-Vương in
    571 A.D. and established his capital in Vĩnh-Yên
    Province. After the reunification of China and
    the founding of the Shin Dynasty in China, Hậu Lý
    Nam-Đế surrendered to an invading Chinese force.
    See EARLY LÝ DYNASTY.

HẬU-NGHĨA PROVINCE. An inland province in south Viet-
    nam. Bordering on Cambodia to the west it is
    situated south of Tây-Ninh Province and north of
    Long-An Province. The provincial capital, Khiêm-
    Cương, is located near the Cambodian border. The
    population is 234,756 and the area is 1,285 square
    kilometers (496 square miles). The province is
    relatively new, having been created in 1963. The
    chief products are rice and sugarcane. See KHIÊM-
    CƯƠNG.

HẬU TRẦN DYNASTY. (Nhà Hậu Trần or Post Trần Dynasty).
See POST TRAN DYNASTY.

HIẾN-LƯỜNG RIVER. See BẾN-HẢI RIVER.

HIỆP-HOÀ (ruled 1883). The sixth emperor in the
Nguyễn Dynasty (1802-1945). He was the younger
brother of Emperor Tự-Đức (ruled 1848-1883), and
placed on the throne by court officials. However,
he ruled for only four months after which the same
officials forced him to abdicate and commit suicide by taking poison on November 29, 1883. See
NGUYỄN DYNASTY.

HIẾU-GIANG RIVER. (Sông Hiếu-Giang or Sông Cam-Lộ).
A river in central Vietnam and a tributary of the
Thạch-Hãn River. It originates in the Trường-Sơn
Mountains in western Quảng-Trị Province and flows
past the towns of Cam-Lộ and Đông-Hà. It joins
the Thạch-Hãn River which empties into the South
China Sea at Cửa-Việt. See CỬA-VIỆT, QUẢNG-TRỊ
PROVINCE.

HIẾU-KINH. The classic of filial piety. A textbook
in Chinese used by students in traditional Vietnam.
This book was a compendium of Confucian teachings
on filial piety.

HIGHWAYS. The basic network of highways in Vietnam
was built under the French and was a part of the
larger network of Indochina roadways. National
highway number one was the main artery leading
from Hà-Nội southward along the coast to Sài-Gòn.
Highway number four connected Sài-Gòn with the
Mekong Delta region and extended to the Cà-Mau
Peninsula. In addition to the government sponsored roads, the village would often construct
and maintain a roadway which may or may not have
accommodated a four-wheeled vehicle.
     Democratic Republic of Vietnam: Highway
construction was given high priority during the
1960's. By 1966 there were over 9,656 kilometers
(6,000 miles) of main roads and some 70,800 kilometers (44,000 miles) of secondary roads. In
addition, almost 151,000 kilometers (94,000 miles)
of rural roads were built, widened or repaired
between 1961 and 1966. The main north-south artery, highway number one, connects the principal
cities in central Vietnam with Hà-Nội and other
points in the Red River Delta. Hà-Nội is also
linked to other outlying provinces along the
Vietnamese-Chinese border and Vietnamese-Lao

border by a recently improved network of roads.
The United States air raids between 1965 and 1973
caused heavy damage to roads and bridges in the
Democratic Republic of Vietnam.

Republic of Vietnam: Highway number one is
the major north-south artery and connects the
coastal cities in central Vietnam with Sài-Gòn.
A network of primary roads in the central highlands has been improved and upgraded since 1967.
There is a total of 18,500 kilometers (11,400
miles) of main roads and about 4,500 bridges.

HÔ.   Lake. Individual lakes are listed under separate
entries. See BA-BỂ LAKE, HỒ TÂY, HOAN-KIỂM LAKE.

HỒ CHỈ-MINH (1890-1969). (Also known as Nguyễn Ai-
Quốc, and Nguyễn Thất-Thanh). A patriot, revolutionary and first president of the Democratic
Republic of Vietnam. Born in Nghệ-An Province,
he took more than fifty aliases throughout his
career. The most popular term of address has been
Bác Hồ (Uncle Hồ). He went to Quốc-Học College
in Huế and then became a teacher in Phan-Thiết.
In 1911 he hired on a ship as a kitchen hand and
travelled to North America, Africa and Europe.
He stayed in Europe working as a gardener, snow
sweeper, waiter, photo retoucher and stoaker. It
was during this period that he began to be a political activist and to develop his communist ideology. He joined the French Socialist Party and
founded the Association of Vietnamese Patriots.
He began to write, speak and debate on the Indochina problem. It was also during this period
that he mastered numerous languages, including
French, English, Mandarin and German.

The Russian revolution is said to have had a
decisive influence on his life. In 1923 and 1924
he went to Moscow to attend the fourt and fifth
Comintern Congress. He then visited Phan Bội-Châu
in Canton where he stayed for two years. He
founded the Việt-Nam Cách-Mạng Đồng-Chi-Hội (Vietnamese Revolutionary Youth Association), lectured
at revolutionary training camps, and wrote Đường
Cách-Mạng (Revolutionary Path). After two or
three years of travel throughout Europe and Southeast Asia, Hồ went to Hong Kong where he helped to
organize the Vietnamese Communist Party. The
British police arrested him in June, 1931, and
held him for two years. After release from prison,
Hồ went to Moscow to enter Lenin University.
While in Moscow he was quite active in support of
the Vietnamese communist cause. From there he

went to China where he was assigned to the Eighth
Route Army. He finally returned to Vietnam after
thirty years absence and helped to found the Việt-
Nam Độc-Lập Đồng-Minh Hội, (Việt-Minh) on May 19,
1941, his 51st birthday. In August, 1942, he was
once again arrested and jailed, this time by the
Chinese nationalists, who held him for a year.
During World War II, the Việt-Minh was strengthened under the leadership of Võ Nguyên-Giáp, and
even enjoyed limited support from the American
OSS. With the defeat of Japan, the Việt-Minh
staged the August Revolution in 1945 and on
September 2, 1945, Hồ Chí-Minh read the Declaration
of Independence. On March 2, 1946, Hồ was elected
President of the Democratic Republic of Vietnam.

The return of the French in the same year
drove Hồ and the Việt-Minh to armed resistance
resulting in the French Indochina War (1946-1954).
The Việt-Minh defeated the French and negotiated
the Geneva Accords. The Democratic Republic of
Vietnam was given control of north Vietnam and
part of central Vietnam while the remaining parts
of the country came under the control of the non-
communist nationalists. Hồ Chí-Minh proceeded to
consolidate the Democratic Republic of Vietnam and
effect a period of socialist transformation during
which extensive land reform and economic reorgan-
ization took place along socialist lines.

Hồ Chí-Minh is undoubtedly one of the most
important figures in Vietnamese history. In the
Democratic Republic of Vietnam he is a national
hero and looked upon as the Father of that country.
He was an inspiration to all anti-colonialists
during the French Indochina War. On the morning
of September 3, 1969, Hồ Chí-Minh died of a heart
attack at the age of 79. See AUGUST REVOLUTION,
ĐẢNG LAO-ĐỘNG VIỆT-NAM, DEMOCRATIC REPUBLIC OF,
VIETNAM, VIỆT-NAM CÁCH-MẠNG THANH-NIÊN ĐỒNG-CHI-
HỘI, VIỆT-NAM ĐỘC-LẬP ĐỒNG-MINH HỘI.

HỒ DYNASTY (1400-1407). (Nhà Hồ). A short-lived dynasty which included the reign of two emperors:
Hồ Qúy-Ly (1400), and Hồ Hán-Thương (1401-1407).
Hồ Qúy-Ly (also known as Lê Qúy-Ly) usurped the
throne from the Trần Dynasty (1225-1400) but ruled
directly only one year. He then abdicated in
favor of his son, Hồ Hán-Thương. However, Qúy-Ly
retained complete control of the throne. The dynasty was overthrown by the Ming Dynasty in China
who defeated the armies of the Hồ and annexed the
country in 1407. See HỒ HÁN-THƯƠNG, HỒ QÚY-LY.

HỒ GƯƠM. See HOÀN-KIẾM LAKE.

HỒ HÁN-THƯỜNG (ruled 1401-1407). The second and last
emperor of the Hồ Dynasty (1400-1407). Hồ Hán-
Thương was on the throne only six years. Even
though his father, Hồ Quý-Ly (1400) abdicated in
his favor, all the power of the throne was retained by Hồ Quý-Ly. During the short period of reign,
progress was made in several fields. The system
of military draft was reestablished resulting in
a larger and more efficient army. The system of
taxation was reorganized and the civil service
examinations were expanded. At the same time the
armies of the Hồ invaded Champa and gained more
territory. But, the Chinese armies attacked Vietnam from the north, quickly defeating the Vietnamese and capturing both Hồ Quý-Ly and Hồ Hán-Thương.
The rest of the royal family was also captured
while the mandarins either surrendered, were captured or committed suicide. Thus, the Hồ Dynasty
was ended and there began a period of Chinese rule
during which the Chinese tried to restore the
former Trần regime. See HỒ DYNASTY, HỒ QUÝ-LY.

HỘ-LỄ. A person who has the responsibility of insuring
that all the proper procedures and rituals are
followed during the funeral and related rites.
Usually a close friend of the family assumes this
position. See CẢI-TÁNG, ĐƯA ĐÁM, MỘC-DỤC.

HỒ QUÝ-LY (ruled 1400). (Also known as Lê Quý-Ly).
The founder and first emperor of the Hồ Dynasty
(1400-1407). Hồ Quý-Ly was of Chinese ancestry.
Two of his aunts were wives of Emperor Trần Minh-
Tông (1314-1329). One gave birth to Trần Nghệ-
Tông (1370-1372) and one gave birth to Trần Duệ-
Tông (1372-1377). Emperor Trần Nghệ-Tông relied
heavily on Hồ Quý-Ly and gave him a high rank in
the court and nobility. Under Emperor Trần Duệ-
Tông he was made Chief-of-Staff of the Army. In
1380 and again in 1382 the army, under Hồ Quý-Ly,
and the naval forces repelled attacks by the Chams.
In 1383 Hồ Quý-Ly led the Vietnamese armies
against the Chams but failed. He convinced Trần
Nghệ-Tông to replace and eventually kill the Emperor Trần Hiến-Đế (1377-1388).
     After the death of Trần Nghệ-Tông in 1394,
Hồ Quý-Ly was made the regent (Phụ-Chính Thái-Sư)
and exercised an increasing amount of power. He
instituted the first issuance of paper money, reorganized the court and political administrative
structure of the country and carried out extensive
land reform. In 1397 he successfully manipulated

the overthrow of Trần Thuận-Tông and placed the
three year old crown prince on the throne. A
year later he completely overthrew the Trần Dynasty (1225-1400) and founded the Hồ Dynasty,
assuming the title of Emperor. In less than one
year, Hồ Quý-Ly abdicated in favor of his son, Hồ
Hán-Thương. Hồ Quý-Ly took the title of Thái-
Thương-Hoàng, a kind of semi-retirement position
which allowed him a strong voice in the affairs
of state. In fact, he still controlled the throne.
The Hồ Dynasty lasted only seven years, but under
Hồ Quý-Ly's leadership, many progressive and
developmental changes were instituted, especially
in the areas of land reform, military reorganiz-
ation, development of education and changes in
the civil service.
      In 1407 the Ming armies of China invaded
from the north, ostensibly in order to revive
the Trần Dynasty. The Chinese armies were too
powerful and enjoyed a quick victory. Hồ Quý-Ly
and his son, Hồ Hán-Thương were both captured and
taken to China. In spite of his cruel and ruthless trip to power, Hồ Quý-Ly is remembered as a
progressive leader who made many significant contributions toward the advancement of the country.
See HỒ DYNASTY, HỒ HÁN-THƯƠNG, TRẦN DYNASTY, TRẦN
NGHỆ-TÔNG.

HỒ TÂY. (Literally, West Lake). A lake in Hà-Nội. It
covers an area of five square kilometers (two
square miles) and is one of the beauty spots in
Hà-Nội. It is the site of the battle in which the
two Trưng sisters defeated the Chinese General Mã
Viễn in 42 A.D. The emperors of the Lý Dynasty
(1010-1225) built many Buddhist shrines, temples
and pagodas on the lake shore. See HÀ-NỘI, HAI
BÀ TRƯNG.

HỒ THÀNH. See TÂY-ĐÔ CITADEL.

HỒ XUÂN-HƯƠNG. An eighteenth century poet famous for
her provocative poems. The daughter of a concubine, she was born in the late 1700's in north
Vietnam. She was well educated and at the age
of thirty she herself became a concubine of a
district chief in Vĩnh-Yên Province. However,
two years later her husband died and she re-
married, this time to a canton chief. A few years
later he also died leaving Hồ Xuân-Hương to lead
a lonely life. She wrote in nôm. Much of her
poetry was suggestive and almost always had a
double meaning. She vented her frustration at

being merely a concubine, lamenting her unfair
treatment at the hands of fate and, most significantly, attacked such established institutions
as the court, pagoda and the sexual mores of the
times.

HOÀ-BÌNH CITY. The capital city of Hoà-Bình Province
in north Vietnam. It is located on the Hắc-Giang
River and is situated seventy-five kilometers
(forty-six miles) from Hà-Nội. See HOÀ-BÌNH
PROVINCE.

HOÀ-BÌNH CIVILIZATION. (Also called Hoa-Binhian culture). A prehistoric culture of the mesolithic
(middle stone age) era which existed in what is
now north Vietnam about 10,000 years ago. It
takes its name from the province of Hoà-Bình
where the first discoveries of the culture were
made. The characteristic implement used by these
early cave-dwellers was a stone shaped on one face
so as to produce a chopper or crusher. There are
indications that these people had domesticated
the dog.

HOÀ-BÌNH PROVINCE. A mountainous, inland province of
north Vietnam located north of Thanh-Hóa Province
and south of Vĩnh-Phú Province. Hoà-Bình Province
marks the southern limits of the highland area
(thượng-du) of north Vietnam and is the smallest
province of that area. The land mass of the province is 4,700 square kilometers (1,814 square
miles) and the population is estimated at 290,000
(1969). The provincial capital, Hoà-Bình City,
is located seventy-five kilometers (forty-six
miles) from Hà-Nội on the Hắc-Giang River (also
called the Đà-Giang River). Hoà-Bình Province
is inhabited primarily by people of the Mường
ethno-linguistic minority group. A number of
ethnic Vietnamese took refuge in the mountains
of the province to escape Chinese domination in
the fifteenth century. But, they were located
near the Thái people and actually lost their
ethnic identity. The Thái, Man and Chinese make
up the non-Mường population. The area has traditionally been governed by the Mường. Emperor
Lý Thánh-Tông (ruled 1054-1072) enlisted the
support of the Mường armies to fight the Khmers.
After their military success, many Muong leaders
were given noble titles. The French organized
the province of Hoà-Bình with the capital at Chợ-
Bờ. But, after the Mường sacked and burned the
town of Chợ-Bờ in 1891, the capital was moved to
the present site of Hoà-Bình City. The main

natural resources of the province include limestone, iron, timber and hot springs. Although
there are many lush green valleys, the province
is too mountainous to be of major agricultural
importance. See HOA-BINH CITY, MƯỜNG, THƯỢNG-DU.

HOA-HẢO. (Phật-Giáo Hòa-Hảo). A Buddhist sect which
originated in the Mekong Delta in 1939. The
founder of the sect was Huỳnh Phú-Sổ, a village
notable in Châu-Đốc Province. The seat of the
sect is Hòa-Hảo Village in Châu-Đốc Province. It
is estimated that there are one and a half million
members of the Phật-Giáo Hòa-Hảo in Vietnam today.
The Hòa-Hảo sect emphasizes simplicity in worship,
elimination of temples and intermediaries in order to better communicate with the Supreme Being.
It has also become a viable and significant political force in western south Vietnam. See HUỲNH
PHÚ-SỔ, RELIGION.

HOA-LƯ. The capital of Vietnam during the Đinh Dynasty
(968-980) and in the Early Lê Dynasty (980-1009).
Hoa-Lư is located Trường-Yên Village, Gia-Khánh
District, Ninh-Bình Province. It was built in
968 A.D. by Emperor Đinh Tiên-Hoàng (968-979).
Emperor Lý Thái-Tổ moved the capital in 1010 to
Thăng-Long, which is now called Hà-Nội. Most of
the structures of the ancient citadel have been
destroyed. Some vestiges of the capital remain.
The city covered an area of about 300 hectares
(121 acres), and wws situated between the mountains and the Hoàng-Long River. The outer citadel,
covering an area of about 140 hectares (56.6 acres),
was used for temples and shrines as well as the
place to hold the royal court. The inner citadel
was used to house the families of the royal court.
In the middle of the outer citadel is located the
temple dedicated to Đinh Tiên-Hoàng. The anniversary of his death is still celebrated in this
temple. See ĐINH DYNASTY, ĐINH TIÊN-HOÀNG, LÝ
THÁI-TỔ.

HOA-TIÊN. A classic poem written in nom in the late
eighteenth century. This epic poem was written
by Nguyễn Huy-Tự and revised by Nguyễn-Thiện. It
was based on an old Chinese story. It contains
1826 lines and was written in the style of lục-
bát (6-8). See LỤC-BÁT.

HÒA-ƯỚC GIÁP-TUẤT. See TREATY OF 1874.

HÒA-ƯỚC QUÝ-MÙI. See TREATY OF PROTECTORATE.

HỌA-VẬN. A form of poetry in which one verse is responded to by a second verse. The response matches
the original verse in both meaning and rhyme.
This form was often used to challenge someone to
demonstrate his literary skill.

HÓA VÀNG. The act of burning votive paper or imita-
tion paper money as a sacrifice or offering to an
ancestral spirit. The practice of making votive
offerings is well-known in the history of many
parts of the world. In Vietnam it is practiced
especially at the death anniversary (ngày giỗ).
Colored paper, representing silver and gold is
burned at a temple or altar for the use of the
spirit of the deceased in the afterlife. It is
said that this practice predated the arrival of
the Chinese colonists in the first century. See
NGÀY-GIỖ, RELIGION, THẮP-HƯƠNG.

HOÀN-KIẾM LAKE. (Hồ Hoàn-Kiếm, also called Hồ Gươm or
Lake of the Restored Sword). A well-known lake
in the center of Hà-Nội. Legend has it that Emperor Lê Thái-Tổ (1428-1433) was given a magical
sword which he used to defeat the Chinese invaders. After his victory over the Chinese he was
boating one day in the Hoàn-Kiếm Lake. He saw
a large tortoise swimming on the surface of the
water. When the Emperor tried to run it through
with his sword, the tortoise grabbed it and disappeared into the lake. From that time on, the
lake has been known as Hồ Hoàn-Kiếm (Lake of the
Restored Sword). See HÀ-NỘI, LÊ THÁI-TỔ.

HOÀNG-ĐẠO (1906-1948). (Nguyễn Tường-Long). A modern
author and political activist in the resistance
movement. He was a native of Quảng-Nam Province
and a brother of Nhất-Linh, a well-known author
whose career closely paralleled his own. Hoàng-
Đạo was one of the more militant members of the
Tự-Lực Văn-Đoàn (Self Reliant Literary Group)
movement. He was imprisoned by the French for
his political activities. He then went to China,
returning briefly to Vietnam in 1946 to participate in the resistance coalition government. He
died in China in 1948. See NHẤT-LINH, TỰ-LỰC VĂN-
ĐOÀN.

HOÀNG HOA-THÁM. See ĐỀ-THÁM.

HOÀNG-LIÊN-SƠN MOUNTAIN. (Also known as Fansipan). The
tallest mountain in all of Vietnam. It is located
in Lào-Cai Province and stands 3,142 meters (10,308
feet) high. It is part of the mountain range of

the same name.

HOÀNG-LIÊN-SƠN MOUNTAIN RANGE. A chain of mountains
    located between the Red River and the Đà-Giang
    River and extending from the Chinese border to
    Hoà-Bình Province. This large mountain range is
    divided into several minor chains by passes such
    as the Keo-Co Pass. The tallest peak in Vietnam
    is located in this range in Lào-Cai Province. It
    is named Hoàng-Liên-Sơn Mountain and is 3,142
    meters (10,249 feet) high.

HOÀNG VĂN-HOAN (1905-   ). Vice Chairman of the
    National Assembly Standing Committee and member
    of the Lao-Động Party Politburo of the Democratic
    Republic of Vietnam. He was born in Nghệ-An Pro-
    vince and was one of the founders of the Indochina
    Communist Party in 1930. He continued to be active
    with the Việt-Minh and has held several high rank-
    ing positions, both domestic and foreign with the
    Democratic Republic of Vietnam.

HOÀNG-VIỆT HINH-LUẬT. See GIA-LONG LEGAL CODE.

HOÀNG-XA ARCHIPELAGO (Quần-Đảo Hoàng-Xa). See PARACELS
    ISLANDS.

HOÀNH-SƠN MOUNTAIN RANGE. A chain of mountains in the
    larger Trường-Son Mountain Range. The Hoành-Son
    mountains are located in the border region between
    Quảng-Bình and Hà-Tĩnh provinces in central Viet-
    nam. They extend out to the coast where the Ngang
    Pass (Đèo Ngang) cuts through providing access for
    north-south transportation via highway number one.
    The highest peak in the chain is Phù So Mountain
    which stands 1,536 meters (5,128 feet) high. See
    NGAN PASS.

HỘI-AN. (Fai-Fo). The capital city of Quảng-Nam Pro-
    vince. The city of Hội-An was originally called
    Fai-Fo by early Western traders. The town gained
    prominence after the Nguyễn Lord Nguyễn-Hoàng
    formed the Province of Quảng-Nam (Quảng-Nam-Dinh)
    in 1601. Hội-An was an established port of for-
    eign trade in the early seventeenth century
    accommodating Chinese and Japanese commercial junks
    as well as Portuguese and Dutch trading vessels.
    It was almost totally destroyed in the fighting
    during the Tây-Sơn rebellion (1771-1788). The city
    recovered and continued to serve as a major port
    until the end of the nineteenth century. As the
    channel in the river became more shallow due to
    the alluvial deposits Hội-An gradually gave way

to Đà-Nẵng as the main port in central Vietnam.
The city is located on the left bank of the
Thu-Bồn River (also called the Cái River). It
has a population of 50,272 (1971) and is situated
about thirty kilometers (eighteen miles) south of
Đà-Nẵng. Hội-An has several noteworthy historical
sites including a small wooden covered bridge
called Cầu Nhật-Bản (Japanese Bridge) or Lai-Viên-
Kiều. It was built in the seventeenth century and
is commonly believed to have been built by the
Japanese. Other points of interest include several
temples that served as the Hội-Quan (assembly hall)
of Chinese congregations and various pagodas which
date back as far as the seventeenth century. See
QUẢNG-NAM PROVINCE.

HỘI-ĐỒNG KỲ-MỤC. (Also known as the Hội-Đồng Hoa-Mục
   or Hội-Đồng Xã). The village council of notables,
   the decision making body in the administration of
   the village in traditional Vietnam. The council
   of notables was composed of members of the village
   who had acquired academic degrees, who had served
   as mandarins or who were endowed with official
   titles. Although each village had its own requirements for eligibility, the membership on the council was usually unlimited and the term of office
   undefinite. The council was headed by the first
   notable (Tiên-Chỉ) who was assisted by the second
   notable (Thứ-Chỉ). The council met in the village
   communal hall (Đình) to discuss such village affairs as taxation, distribution of village farm
   land and public works projects. The council was
   also responsible for maintaining a high moral
   level among the population by encouraging public
   ceremonies, insuring proper upkeep of the village
   shrines and temples and by overseeing the village
   chief (Xã-Trưởng) and his assistants. See ĐÌNH,
   TIÊN-CHỈ, XÃ, XÃ-TRƯỞNG, XÃ-QUAN.

HỘI TAO-ĐÀN. (The Tao-Đàn Literary Club). A group of
   literati organized by Emperor Lê Thánh-Tông (1460-
   1497). The club had twenty-eight members who were
   known as the twenty-eight stars (28 vị sao). The
   club was indicative of Lê Thánh-Tông's emphasis
   on developing and encouraging Vietnamese literature. See LÊ THÁNH-TÔNG, LITERATURE.

HOLIDAYS AND FESTIVALS. Most of the traditional holidays and celebrations are of a religious nature
   and have their roots in the Chinese (and infrequently in the Indian) culture. There are also
   a number of commemorative holidays of an historical or patriotic nature. The main traditional

festivals are listed below in chronological order, according to the lunar calendar.

1. Tết Nguyên-Đan - New Year's Day
2. Lễ Trạng-Nguyên - Feast of the Learned
3. Lễ Han-Thực - Cold Food Festival
4. Lễ Thanh-Minh - Feast of the Pure Light
5. Tết Đoan-Ngọ - Double Five Festival
6. Lễ Thất-Tịch - Double Seven Festival
7. Lễ Vu-Lan - Feast of the Wondering Souls
8. Tết Trung-Thu - Mid-autumn Festival
9. Lễ Trùng-Cửu - Double Nine Festival
10. Lễ Tao-Quân - Feast of the Household Gods

Individual holidays mentioned above are listed as separate entries. See NGAY GIỖ, LỄ HÔN-NHÂN.

HON-GAY. (Also known as Hồng-Gay). The capital city of Quảng-Ninh Province in north Vietnam. It is situated on the Hạ-Long Bay and serves as a coal port, on-loading coal from nearby mines for export and for coastal shipping to domestic destinations. See QUẢNG-NINH PROVINCE.

HÔN-NHÂN. See LỄ HÔN-NHÂN.

HỒNG-BẰNG DYNASTY. The legendary dynasty which ruled over the kingdom of Văn-Lang from 2,879-258 B.C., a total of 2,600 years. There were said to have been eighteen kings in this dynasty, all of which were named Hùng-Vương (Hùng-Vương I, Hùng-Vương II, etc.). According to legend, the Hồng-Bàng Dynasty is a descendant of the Emperor Thần-Nông. King Đế-Minh, the third generation offspring of Thần-Nông wandered south and met a female fairy. They married and gave birth to Kinh Dương-Vương. Kinh Dương-Vương was made king of the southland, which was called Xích-Quỷ. Kinh Dương-Vương married a dragon's daughter who gave birth to Lạc Long-Quân. Lạc Long-Quân then married the fairy named Âu-Cơ who gave birth to one hundred eggs which hatched out one hundred boys. Fifty followed the mother to the mountains and the other fifty went with the father to the seaside. The oldest son of Âu-Cơ became the first king of the Hồng-Bàng Dynasty. This dynasty is considered to be the first genuinely Vietnamese dynasty. This legend is also used to explain the origins of the Vietnamese people. See ÂU-CƠ, KINH DƯƠNG-VƯƠNG, VĂN-LANG, XÍCH-QUỶ.

HỒNG-ĐỨC LEGAL CODE. (Circa 1475). The extensive set of laws promulgated by Emperor Lê Thánh-Tông

(1460-1497). This legal code was a significant
step in establishing a system of law and resultant
social and cultural features which were distinct
from the Chinese model. The code encompassed many
facets of Vietnamese life, including provisions
for the proper care of dykes, an elevation of the
status of women, especially in the area of inheritance, and domestic rights. However, actors
and slaves were specifically excluded from full
civil rights. This extended to the families of
actors as well. See GIA-LONG LEGAL CODE, LÊ DY-
NASTY, LÊ THÀNH-TÔNG.

HỒNG-HÀ NỮ-SĨ. See ĐOÀN THỊ ĐIỂM.

HỒNG-HÀ RIVER. See RED RIVER.

HỘT VỊT LỘN. (Also called Trung Vit Lon). Half-hatched
    duck eggs. Same as the Philippine Balut. Half-
    hatched duck eggs are most commonly sold by street
    vendors. They are served hard-boiled and are eaten
    while still warm with salt, pepper and a few sweet
    smelling herbs.

HOUSING. The types of housing found in Vietnam vary
    widely according to locale and social class. Trad-
    itional rural houses are usually made from bamboo,
    thatch, straw, reed and mud. They are built on
    the ground with a dirt floor. The yard is some-
    times fenced but always with a gateway (Cổng-Ngõ).
    The wealthier homes are sometimes made of brick
    and mortar with tile roofs. Concrete block con-
    struction is also quite common. Urban dwellings
    are often made of concrete construction with
    ceramic tile floors, various types of roofing and
    a stucco type exterior which is whitewashed.
    Electrification is mainly limited to the urban
    and suburban areas. Drinking water is taken from
    communal or household wells except in the larger
    population centers where city water systems have
    been installed. In some areas, families live on
    the rivers and canals in houseboats or sampans.
    In the highlands, most of the tribal people live
    in thatched huts built off the ground on piles.
    Certain tribes, such as the Rhade and Jarai,
    construct long houses which accommodate an extend-
    ed family. See ARCHITECTURE, CỔNG-NGÕ.

HRE. (Also known as Kre or Kare). An ethno-linguistic
    minority group of highland people located in the
    river valleys and highland areas of Quảng-Ngãi
    Province. Official estimates in 1965 placed the
    Hre population at 43,051. The Hre society is

patriarchal, lineage and inheritance is passed
along the male line. Hre law and custom sanction
polygyny and divorce is recognized. Their religion is animistic and involves belief in good
and evil spirits which dwell in both persons and
the natural environment. Animal sacrifices to
these spirits are common. Many Hre are seden-
tary and practice wet-rice agriculture. Others
are semi-nomadic and practice slash-and-burn
agriculture. In addition to rice, the Hre also
grow cash crops such as tobacco, coconuts, ramie,
hemp, tea and fruit. While the Hre are known as
a peaceful group, they offered stiff resistance
to the ethnic Vietnamese in their southward expansion and to the French in their conquest of
Vietnam.

HROI. See HROY.

HROY. (Also called Hroi). An ethno-linguistic minority of highland people located in Phú-Yên and
western Phú-Bổn provinces. There seems to be a
controversy as to which language grouping the
Hroy belong. Some place the Hroy in the Chamic
group of the Austronesian language family. Others
consider it in the Bahnaric group of the Mon-Khmer
family. In any case, there are two distinct dialects: a northern one showing strong Bahnaric influence, and a southern dialect which exhibits
strong Rhade and Chamic influence. The Hroy
social structure is based on the nuclear family
and the village. Village chiefs are male, and
men and women share authority in the family.
However, the kinship system is matrilineal, descent being reckoned through the female line. They
have a slash-and-burn method of upland rice cultivation which is the basis for their subsistence
economy. Rice growing is supplemented by vegetable gardens, fishing, hunting, and basket weaving. It is estimated that the Hroy number around
8,000 (1965).

HUÉ. The imperial capital during the Nguyễn Dynasty
(1802-1945) and the principal city in central
Vietnam. Huế was established by Emperor Gia-Long
(1802-1819) who constructed a citadel two kilometers (1.2 miles) northeast of Phú-Xuân, the
capital during much of the Nguyễn Lords period
(1687-1778). It is situated 680 kilometers (422
miles) south of Hà-Nội and 1080 kilometers (670
miles) north of Sài-Gòn and is the capital city
of Thừa-Thiên Province. Both the north-south
railroad and highway number one pass through the
city of Huế. It is served by an airport at Phú-

Bài which was enlarged by the Americans in the late
1960's and used as a military base. The Perfume
River (Sông Hương) runs through the center of the
city separating the citadel and commercial area on
the left bank from the administrative section on
the right bank. In the middle of the city there
are two large islands: Giã-Viên Island and Hên
Island. There are two man-made canals - the An-
Cựu and Đông-Ba canals. The large, main market
(Chợ Đông-Ba) and the nearby bridge (Cầu Đông-Ba)
are well-known throughout Vietnam. Equally well-
known is the picturesque six-span Tràng-Tiền Bridge.
The city is administered as an autonomous municipality and has a population of 199,893 (1971). It
covers an area of sixteen square kilometers (six
square miles). The many tourist sights in Hue
include the citadel and throne room, the tombs of
the various emperors, Thiên-Mụ Pagoda, National
Museum and the Ngọ-Môn Gateway. A modern hospital
and a public university are also located in Huế.
The city suffered severe damage and destruction in
during the fighting on the Tết holidays in 1968,
commonly referred to as the Tết Mậu-Thân. The city
of Huế is known as a cultural center of Vietnam
and exerts a significant amount of political influence, especially among the Buddhists. See
NGUYỄN DYNASTY, PERFUME RIVER, PHÚ-XUÂN, THIÊN-MỤ
PAGODA.

HƯNG-ĐẠO-VƯƠNG. See TRẦN HƯNG-ĐẠO.

HÙNG-VƯƠNG. The regal name assumed by all eighteen
kings of the legendary Hồng-Bàng Dynasty (2897-
258 B.C.). The Hùng-Vương kings are considered
to be the founders of the Vietnamese ethnic stock.
Thus, the cult of Hùng-Vương is widely honored
and celebrated by all Vietnamese. Some scholars
argue that the word Hùng is derived or mistaken
from the Chinese character Lạc (as is Lạc-Việt).
See HỒNG-BÀNG, NGÀY GIỖ TỔ HÙNG-VƯƠNG.

HƯNG-YÊN PROVINCE. See HẢI-HƯNG PROVINCE.

HƯƠNG-HỎA. Patrimonial land. That land which is inherited down through the extended family. The
land is managed and actually owned by the Trưởng-
Tộc or head of the extended family (họ). The
income from the land is used to defray the cost
of maintaining the graves of the ancestors and
holding the rituals and festivities which honor
the common ancestors. See CULT OF THE ANCESTORS,
NGÀY GIỖ HỌ, TRƯỞNG-TỘC.

HƯƠNG RIVER. (Sông Hương). 1. The Perfume River in
    Thừa-Thiên Province which runs through the city
    of Huế. See PERFUME RIVER.
    2. A small river in north Vietnam, actually a
    part of the Văn-Úc River. See VĂN-ÚC RIVER.

HƯƠNG-TÍCH PAGODA. (Chùa Hương-Tích, also called the
    Chùa Hương). One of the most beautiful pagodas
    in north Vietnam. It is located on Hương-Tích
    Mountain in the village of Yên-Vĩ in Hà-Tây Pro-
    vince. Emperor Lê Thánh-Tông (1460-1497) honored
    the pagoda by describing it with the five char-
    acters: Nam Thiên Đệ Nhất Động (Foremost cave
    under the Vietnamese sky). The temple is dedi-
    cated to the Chinese deity, Bà-Quan-Âm (Goddess
    of Mercy). Each year from the tenth to the last
    day of the first lunar month a celebration is held
    at the pagoda. Thousands of people visit the
    pagoda during this period.

HƯƠNG-ƯỚC. Village charter. The traditions and cus-
    toms of a village as well as the moral and spirit-
    ual foundations of a village were recorded in the
    village charter. These covered such subjects as
    the traditions in determining the hierarchy of
    the council of notables, the customs followed in
    village celebrations, the granting of allowances
    for the village chief and the worship of the vil-
    lage guardian spirit. The charter also contained
    procedures for distribution of public farm land
    and for imposing fines on the villagers for acts
    considered detrimental to the moral life of the
    village. These traditions varied widely from one
    village to the other and were, sometimes, contrary
    to the law of the imperial court. The Hương-Ước
    was kept in the Đình (village communal hall). See
    ĐÌNH, HỘI-ĐỒNG KỲ-MỤC, XÃ, XÃ-TRƯỞNG.

HUYỆN. District or sub-prefecture. An administrative
    unit first used under Emperor Lê Thái-Tổ (1428-
    1433). Several Huyện comprised a Trấn or Lộ (Pro-
    vince). One Huyện was divided into smaller vil-
    lages (Xã). In some cases, the province was div-
    ided into prefectures (Phủ) which were in turn
    divided into sub-prefectures (Huyện). Huyện is
    still used to designate a district in the Demo-
    cratic Republic of Vietnam. See ADMINISTRATIVE
    DIVISIONS, QUẬN.

HUỲNH PHÚ-SỔ. (Huỳnh Giáo-Chủ). The founder of the
    Hòa-Hảo Buddhist sect (Phật-Giáo Hòa-Hảo). He
    was born in Hòa-Hảo Village of Châu-Đốc Province
    where he became a village notable. He studied
    under a hermit of the Tra-Sơn Pagoda where he was
    cured of a previously hopeless illness. When the
    hermit died, Huỳnh Phú-Sổ returned to his village.
    One stormy night he began to speak for several
    hours as though possessed by spirits. He talked
    of a new doctrine of Buddha and proclaimed him-
    self to be a prophet and founder of "Phật-Giáo
    Hòa-Hảo". He preached a doctrine that emphasized
    simplicity in worship and practicality in every-
    day life. He advocated the elimination of tem-
    ples, ornate symbols and expensive trappings of
    religion. He also abolished intermediaries in
    order to communicate directly with the Supreme
    Being.
        He travelled widely in south Vietnam preaching
    his new religion. He was well-known for his pro-
    phecies, many of which have been fulfilled. He
    also healed a number of people almost miraculously.
    In April, 1947, in Đốc-Vàng (Kiến-Phong Province)
    he was caught in an ambush, captured and dis-
    appeared. Each year on the eighteenth day of the
    fifth lunar month the followers of Phật-Giáo Hòa-
    Hảo honor that event with memorial services for
    Huỳnh Phú-Sổ. See HÒA-HẢO, RELIGION.

HUỲNH TẤN-PHÁT (1913-   ). President of the Provision-
    al Revolutionary Government of the Republic of
    South Vietnam (PRG). He was born near Mỹ-Tho,
    studied at Hà-Nội University and was graduated as
    an architect. He was active in the anti-French
    movements in north Vietnam and was jailed twice
    by the French. He became active with the National
    Front for the Liberation of South Vietnam (NLF)
    during the Diệm regime and was named Secretary
    General of the NLF central committee in mid-1964.
    He was elected President of the PRG during the
    South Vietnam's People's Representatives Congress
    which was held in south Vietnam from June 6-8,
    1969. See CHINH-PHỦ CÁCH-MẠNG LÂM-THỜI CỘNG-HÒA
    MIỀN NAM VIỆT-NAM, MẶT-TRẬN DÂN-TỘC GIẢI-PHÓNG
    MIỀN NAM.

-I-

INDOCHINA. (Also referred to as French Indochina or Former French Indochina). The term applied to designate that area of mainland Southeast Asia that was colonized by France. It includes what is now Laos, Cambodia and Vietnam.

INDOCHINESE COMMUNIST PARTY. See ĐÔNG-DƯƠNG CỘNG-SẢN ĐẢNG.

INDOCHINESE PENINSULA. That part of mainland Southeast Asia that presently includes Burma, Thailand, Laos, Cambodia, Vietnam and Malaysia.

INDOCHINESE UNIVERSITY. See UNIVERSITY OF HÀ-NỘI.

INDRAPURA. The capital of the Kingdom of Champa from the beginnings of the kingdom up to the eleventh century. The capital was moved to Vijaya in present-day Bình-Định Province around the year 1000 because Indrapura was too vulnerable to attacks from the Vietnamese and Chinese. In 1402 it was ceded to the Vietnamese. Indrapura was located around Đồng-Dương in Quảng-Nam Province in central Vietnam.

INDUSTRY. Most of Vietnam's industrial resources are located in north Vietnam while the richest agricultural potential is in south Vietnam. Central Vietnam is not well endowed in either respect. Except for a cement factory at Hà-Tiên near Cambodia, the bulk of south Vietnam's industry is centered around the Sài-Gòn/Biên-Hòa area, the majority of which is categorized as light industry. Manufactured goods produced in south Vietnam include pottery, paper, glassware, cigarettes, soap, leather goods, textile products and a few industrial chemicals. Agricultural industries include sugar refining, rice processing, fish sauce (nước mắm) production and fiber production. In central Vietnam there are small deposits of limestone around Huế and a coal field at the An-Hòa/Nông-Sơn complex near Đà-Nẵng. Brick and tile kilns are scattered throughout central Vietnam and a modest textile industry has been developed in Đà-Nẵng. Most recently, an automobile factory has been established at Đà-Lạt which produces a car by the same name as the city. Hà-Nội, Hải-Phòng, Việt-Trì, Thanh-Hóa, and Nam-Định are the industrial centers of north Vietnam. The largest industrial establishment is the Thái-

Nguyễn iron and steel works. Việt-Trì produces
sugar, wood products and industrial and agricultural chemicals. Cement, brick and tile are produced in Hà-Nội, Hải-Phòng, and Thanh-Hoá. Nam-
Định has long been the center of the textile industry. Coal, with the reserves estimated at
twenty million tons, is the most important mineral
product of north Vietnam. The major coal fields
are located at Quảng-Yên north of Hải-Phòng and
at Phan-Mê and Tuyên-Quang, 112 kilometers (70
miles) northwest of Hà-Nội. Much of the industry,
especially the light industry, was dispersed and
decentralized because of the American bombing.
See AGRICULTURE, HANDICRAFTS, MINERALS.

-J-

JARAI. (Also called Djarai or Charai). One of the
    larger ethno-linguistic minority groups of high-
    land people in central Vietnam. They occupy an
    extensive area which includes most of the pro-
    vinces of Pleiku and Phú-Bổn, the southwestern
    corner of Kontum Province and parts of Cambodia.
    The Jarai population was placed at 150,000 in
    1972. They can be divided into seven distinct
    subgroups. The Jarai language is a Chamic lan-
    guage of the Austronesian stock and is related to
    Rhade. The Jarai have historically played a
    dominant role among the highland tribes. The two
    mystical leaders of the Jarai, the King of Fire
    (Hỏa-Xa) and the King of Water (Thủy-Xa) were
    recognized by other tribes as well as by the
    courts of Laos, Cambodia, and Vietnam. It has
    been speculated that they were at one time in
    early history under Chàm domination. As early as
    the reign of Lê Thanh-Tông (1460-1497) the two
    leaders, Hỏa-Xá and Thủy-Xá were acknowledged as
    ruling the land of Nam-Bàn. In 1558, Hỏa-Xá and
    Thủy-Xá submitted themselves to the overlordship
    of the Nguyễn Lords. In the early twentieth
    century, the Vietnamese court even bestowed the
    title of Phiên-Vương (Vassal King) on the two
    leaders. The Jarai have a reputation of being
    fierce fighters and very belligerent. They fought
    strongly against the French, forcing the French to
    mass a force of 1,200 tribesmen against them which
    resulted in a disastrous defeat of the Jarai in
    1897. The Jarai are a matrilineal group and live
    in villages which, individually, are traditionally
    the highest political unit. The basic social unit
    is the extended family. A number of extended fam-

ilies are organized into clans and share a common
family name. A village is formed by several clans
for common defense and mutual aid. The Jarai religion is based on spirit worship. Their principal crop is upland rice cultivated by slash-and-
burn methods. Secondary crops include corn, beans,
fruit, and tobacco. Livestock are domesticated,
mainly for religious sacrifices.

JEH. See DIE.

-K-

KARÊ. See HRÉ.

KATU. (Also known as K'Tu and Ka-Tu). An ethno-linguistic minority group of highland people who inhabit the mountainous area along the Lao/Vietnam-
ese border in the provinces of Quảng-Nam and Quảng-
Tín. The Katu are divided into two groups: the
highland Katu found in the higher mountains near
the Laotian border and the lowland Katu who are
located in the lower mountains toward the coast.
They are generally considered as one of the most
technologically primitive tribes in Vietnam.
Their social organization is patriarchal, the
key unit of which is the extended family. The
eldest male is the head of the extended family.
He owns all family property and makes all major
decisions. The Katu language is of the Mon-Khmer
language family and has several distinct subgroups or dialects. It was estimated in 1972 that
there were around 30,000 Katu living in the mountains around the Lao/Vietnamese border area. The
Katu still practice slash-and-burn agriculture.

KHẢI-ĐỊNH (ruled 1916-1925). The twelfth emperor in
the Nguyễn Dynasty. He was the son of Emperor
Đồng-Khánh (1885-1889) and was known for his
gambling and his debts. Khải-Định was a weak emperor and easily manipulated by the French.
During the entire period of his reign the French
exercised all the power of the throne. He visited France briefly in 1922 and left Prince Vĩnh-
Thuy, the heir apparent, in Paris to be educated.
Khải-Định died in 1925 after a reign of only nine
years.

KHẢI-HƯNG (1896-1947). (Trần Khánh-Giư). A modern
author famous for his novels and short stories.
A native of Hải-Dương Province, he contributed

to several periodicals as well as producing numerous works of fiction. Among his most well-
known works are Nửa Chừng Xuân, and Hồn Bướm Mơ
Tiên. He also collaborated with another contemporary author, Nhất-Linh, to produce several works
including Anh Phải Sống and Đời Mưa Gió. In 1939
he became active in politics, specifically with
other nationalists against the French. Finally
in 1947 he was killed by the Việt-Minh for his
affiliation with the Đại-Việt Party.

KHAI-TÂM. See LỄ KHAI-TÂM.

KHÂM-ĐỊNH VIỆT SỬ THÔNG-GIÁM CƯƠNG-MỤC. (Literally,
Imperial Historical Mirror of Đại-Việt). A
fifty-three volume history of Vietnam written by
the court historians during the reign of Emperor
Tự-Đức (1847-1883). The preliminary section
consists of five volumes and the main section
contains forty-seven volumes. The work covered
the period from the Hồng-Bàng Dynasty (2,897-258
B.C.) to the reign of Emperor Lê-Mẫn-Đế (1787-1788).
It was written during the years 1856-1859, edited
in 1871-1884 and printed in 1884.

KHÁNH-HÒA PROVINCE. A coastal province in central
Vietnam. Khánh-Hòa Province is located south of
Phú-Yên and north of Ninh-Thuận Province. It has
a population of 250,000 (1971) and covers an area
of 5,937 square kilometers (2,292 square miles).
The province is best known for its capital city,
Nha-Trang. Nha-Trang is a very popular seaside
resort situated at the mouth of the Cái River.
Also located in Nha-Trang is a Protestant seminary, an oceanographic institute, a naval academy
and a Pasteur medical institute. Khánh-Hòa was
once a part of Champa. Well-known Chàm temples
can still be seen in Nha-Trang. Eleven kilometers (seven miles) to the west of Nha-Trang is
the citadel at Diên-Khánh, built in 1893. Highway number one and the national railroad runs
from north to south through the province. Highway number twenty-one connects Ninh-Hòa district
of Khánh-Hòa with Ban-Mê-Thuột and Đà-Lạt. The
largest river in the province is the Cái River
which empties into the South China Sea at Nha-
Trang. The western part of the province is mountainous although none of the peaks are very high.
The main products of the province are rice, fish,
salt, coconuts, tobacco, charcoal and wood. The
province is known for its sea food, especially
shrimp, lobster, and squid. The deep-water port
of Cam-Ranh was part of Khánh-Hòa Province until

1966, at which time it was made an autonomous
municipality. Located near Cam-Ranh is a settlement of Nùng refugees. Other ethnic minority
groups in the province include the Rhade and Roglai. See NHA-TRANG.

KHÁNH-HƯNG. The capital city of Ba-Xuyên Province.
Population 70,436. It is located on highway number four which runs from Sài-Gòn to Cà-Mau. It
is also known as Sóc-Trăng and has a large Khmer
population. See BA-XUYÊN PROVINCE.

KHAO-VỌNG. Celebrations. In addition to holidays and
festivals traditional Vietnamese villages would
often organize a celebration to honor the accomplishments or deeds of a living member of the
village. These accomplishments included the
successful passing of the triennial examinations
(khao thi đỗ), outstanding performance of official
duties (khao chức việc), receiving an appointment
as mandarin (khao đi làm quan), receiving royal
recognition for service (khao phẩm-hàm), and
reaching a certain old age (khao thượng thọ). The
details of the khao-vọng varied from village to
village. The decision as to whether or not an
individual warranted a celebration was usually
made by the village council. The celebrations
included a feast and a small contribution to the
village fund. But the real significance was the
public honor and recognition bestowed upon the
individual involved. See XÃ.

KHÊ-SANH. A small mountain town in Quảng-Trị Province.
It is situated on highway number nine which runs
from Đông-Hà to Tchepone in Laos. Several coffee
plantations were located nearby. The town became famous in early 1968 when the American air
base located three kilometers (1.8 miles) from
Khê-Sanh was held under seige for several weeks
during which constant heavy artillery attacks
were launched against the base.

KHIÊM-CƯỜNG. The capital city of Hậu-Nghĩa Province
in south Vietnam. It has a population of 30,975
and is located near the Cambodian border, west of
highway number one. See HẬU-NGHĨA PROVINCE.

KHMER. 1. The term referring to the ancient kingdom
which centered in what is now Cambodia. This
kingdom, also called Chen-La by the Chinese existed from the sixth to the end of the eighth centuries.

2. The term used to designate the ethnic group of
people known more commonly as Cambodians and people
of Cambodian origin. The Khmers constitute the
third largest ethno-linguistic group in the Republic of Vietnam. They number about 700,000 (4%
of the total population) and are concentrated in
the southwestern part of the country. The Khmers
are Theravada Buddhists in contrast to the ethnic
Vietnamese, most of whom are adherents of Mahayana Buddhism.

KHOA-CỬ. Triennial examinations or civil service exam-
    inations. In the Confucianist tradition, man-
    darins of the court were chosen on the basis of
    competitive examinations. These examinations
    date back to 1075 during the reign of Emperor Lý
    Nhân-Tông (1072-1127). There have been three
    principal levels of examinations: (1) thi-hương
    (regional examinations or second degree examin-
    ations) for the lower level Cử-Nhân degree or Tú-
    Tài degree; (2) thi-hội (general examinations or
    first degree examinations) for eligibility for
    taking the court examinations, and; (3) thi-đình
    (court examinations) for the Tiến-Sĩ or doctor's
    degree. See THI-ĐÌNH, THI-HỘI, THI-HƯƠNG, THI-
    KHOA.

KHỞI-NGHĨA LAM-SƠN (1418-1428). See LAM-SƠN UPRISING.

KHỞI-NGHĨA THÁI-NGUYÊN (1917). See THÁI-NGUYÊN REVOLT.

KHÓM. A subdivision of a hamlet, similar to a ward.
    The term Khóm is commonly used in urban commun-
    ities to indicate a grouping of houses.

KHỔNG-GIÁO. See CONFUCIANISM.

KHỔNG-TỬ. Confucius. See CONFUCIANISM.

KHU TÂY-BẮC TỰ-TRỊ. See TÂY-BẮC AUTONOMOUS REGION.

KHU VIỆT-BẮC TỰ-TRỊ. See VIỆT-BẮC AUTONOMOUS REGION.

KHUA. See CUA.

KIẾN-AN PROVINCE. See HẢI-PHÒNG.

KIẾN-GIANG PROVINCE. A province on the southwestern
    tip of south Vietnam. It borders on the Gulf of
    Thailand and Cambodia, and includes the island
    of Phù-Quốc. The population is 386,094 (1971)
    and the area of the province is 5,189 square
    kilometers (2,000 square miles). The provincial

capital is the port city of Rạch-Giá. Kiên-Giang
was originally part of Hà-Tiên Province which was
created in 1734. Under the French it was known
as Rạch-Giá Province. In 1956 it became Kiên-
Giang and the following year it was expanded to
include the Province of Hà-Tiên and the island
of Phù-Quốc. The chief products of the province
include rice, fish, sea food, coconuts, vegetables, pineapples, and sweet potatoes. See
PHÙ-QUỐC ISLAND, RẠCH-GIÁ.

KIÊN-HÒA PROVINCE. A coastal province in south Vietnam. It is located north of Vĩnh-Bình Province
and south of Gò-Công Province. Population is
618,870. It covers an area of 2,084 square kilometers (804 square miles). The Bến-Tre Province.
In 1956 it was renamed Kiên-Hòa. The provincial
capital is Trúc-Giang. The principal products
include rice, fish, pineapples, bananas, and
coconuts. See TRÚC-GIANG.

KIÊN-PHONG PROVINCE. A Mekong Delta province in south
Vietnam. It borders on Cambodia to the west and
is located north of Châu-Đốc and An-Giang provinces and south of Kiên-Tường Province. Kiên-
Phong Province was created in 1956. It has a
population of 407,729 and covers an area of 2,393
square kilometers (923 square miles). The provincial capital is the city of Cao-Lãnh. The main
crops include rice, corn, tobacco and coconuts.
See CAO-LÃNH.

KIÊN-PHÚC (ruled 1883-1884). The seventh emperor in
the Nguyễn Dynasty (1802-1945). He was only fifteen years old when he was placed on the throne
in 1883 to replace the deposed emperor Hiệp-Hòa
(1883). He held the title for only seven months
when he was replaced by the thirteen year old
Hàm-Nghi (1884-1885). See NGUYỄN DYNASTY.

KIÊN-TƯỜNG PROVINCE. A province in the Mekong Delta
area of south Vietnam. It borders on Cambodia
to the north and is located north of Định-Tường
Province, east of Kiên-Phong Province and west of
Long-An and Hậu-Nghĩa provinces. The province
was created in 1956. The provincial capital is
Mộc-Hóa which is located on the western Vàm-Cỏ
River near the Cambodian border. The entire
province is situated in the Plain of Reeds. There
is only one major road, highway number twenty-nine,
plus a system of canals that provides the principal mode of transportation. The chief products
of the province are rice, bamboo and fish. See

MỘC-HOA, PLAIN OF REEDS.

KIẾP-BẠC TEMPLE.   (Đền Kiếp-Bạc).   A famous temple
    dedicated to Trần Hưng-Đạo, a national hero who
    successfully drove the invading armies of China
    out of Vietnam three times between 1257 and 1288.
    The temple was built in 1300 in the village of Van-
    Yên in Hải-Hưng Province in north Vietnam. The
    temple faces the Lục-Đầu-Thường River and is
    surrounded on three sides by mountains. In the
    surrounding mountains are located two pagodas,
    the Nam-Tào and the Bắc-Đầu Pagodas which are
    dedicated to his generals, Phạm Ngũ-Lão and others.
    At Kiếp-Bạc Trần Hưng-Đạo had many fortifications
    built and large plantations established for the
    production of medicinal plants to be used in
    treating the wounded and sick soldiers. Kiếp-Bạc
    was also Trần Hưng Đạo's old-age retreat. He
    died there on September 4, 1300. See BACH-ĐẰNG
    BATTLE, ĐỀN, TRẦN HƯNG-ĐẠO.

KIỀU-LỬU-TI MOUNTAIN.   (Núi Kiều-Lửu-Ti).   A mountain
    in Hà-Giang Province in north Vietnam. It has an
    elevation of over 2400 meters (7,897 feet).

KIL.   See CIL.

KIM-LONG.   A town on the Perfume River (Sồng Hương)
    three kilometers (1 1/2 miles) north of the Huế
    citadel.   During the seventeenth and eighteenth
    centuries, Kim-Long developed into the trading
    port and commercial center of the capital at Phú-
    Xuân.   See HUẾ, PHÚ-XUÂN.

KIM-VÂN-KIỀU.   (Also known as Đoạn Trường Tân-Thanh).
    A narrative poem written in nôm by Nguyễn-Du in
    the early nineteenth century.   The poem is a lit-
    erary masterpiece and often referred to as the
    national poem of Vietnam.   There are 3,250 verses
    or lines with a total of 22,778 words in the Kim-
    Vân-Kiều.   It was written in the lục-bát form,
    i.e., the verses are composed alternately of
    six words and eight words.   The poem is based on
    a popular Chinese novel and takes place in north-
    eastern China.   The story concerns a girl named
    Thúy-Kiều who, out of filial piety, sold herself
    into bondage.   The cruel hand of fate led her
    into a life of several marriages, two houses of
    prostitution and an attempted suicide.   Her boy-
    friend and true lover, who had remained loyal
    to her throughout, searched for her for fifteen
    years.   Finally they met again and were united,
    but only in a chaste relationship so as to honor
    their pure love.   See LỤC-BÁT, NGUYỄN-DU.

KINH DỊCH. The Book of Changes. One of the famous
     Chinese Five Classics (Ngũ Kinh). Kinh Dịch deals
     with the principles of cosmic and social evolution
     as interpreted and preserved by the Confucian
     school. It is built up around the eight trigrams
     and sixty-four hexagrams (three or six line com-
     binations of broken and solid lines) and serves
     as a kind of reference for divining or advising
     about certain courses of action. Like the other
     Chinese classics, this book played an important
     role in the educational process in traditional
     Vietnam. It was used in the triennial or man-
     darinal examinations. See NGŨ KINH.

KINH DƯƠNG-VƯƠNG. One of the legendary ancestors of
     the Vietnamese ethnic stock. Kinh Dương-Vương
     was the son of a King Đế-Minh and a female fairy.
     He ruled over a kingdom somewhere in southern
     China called Xích-Quỷ around 2,879 B.C. For more
     complete details see HỒNG-BÀNG DYNASTY. See
     LẠC-LONG-QUÂN, XÍCH-QUỶ.

KINH LỄ. Book of Rites. One of the famous Chinese
     Five Classics (Ngũ Kinh). Also known as the
     record of rituals, the Kinh Lễ is a compilation
     made in the second century B.C. of various cere-
     monial observances in ancient China. These rit-
     uals were a key element in the whole Confucian
     concept of social order. This work, along with
     other Chinese classics, was studied by scholars
     and students in traditional Vietnam and was used
     in the mandarinal examinations for entrance into
     the civil service or mandarinal corps. See NGŨ
     KINH.

KINH-THẦY RIVER. (Sông Kinh-Thầy). A river in north
     Vietnam. It is actually a branch of the Thái-
     Bình River. It flows from the Thái-Bình near Phú-
     Lại to Phú-Nam-Sách where it splits temporarily
     into two branches, one of which is called the Kinh-
     Môn River. It empties out into the South China
     Sea at Cửa-Cấm. See THÁI-BÌNH RIVER.

KINH THI. Book of Poetry. One of the famous Chinese
     Five Classics (Ngũ Kinh). Kinh Thi is a collec-
     tion of 305 songs or poems in various meters and
     dating from about the tenth to the seventh cen-
     tury B.C. Many are simple love poems, others are
     political poems and ritual hymns of greater
     length. It contains valuable information about
     the customs, traditions, usages, mores, govern-

mental machinery, etc., in ancient times. It was
used by scholars and students in traditional Vietnam. The mandarinal examinations were based, in
part, on this and similar works. It is also
indicative of the important role that poetry
played in traditional Vietnam. The ability to
recite and compose poetry was the mark of an
educated man in Vietnam. See NGŨ KINH.

KINH THU. Book of Records. One of the famous Chinese
Five Classics (Ngũ Kinh). Kinh Thu is a collection of historical documents and speeches from
the early Chou period in China (1100 B.C.). It
is also known as the Book of Documents or the
Book of History. Like the other Chinese classics,
this collection was studied by scholars and
students in traditional Vietnam, especially those
preparing for the civil service (triennial) examinations. See NGŨ KINH.

KINH XUÂN THU. The Annals of Spring and Autumn. One
of the famous Chinese Five Classics (Ngũ Kinh).
Kinh Xuân Thu is a brief and factual chronological record of major events at the court of the
ancient Chinese State of Lu between the years
722-481 B.C. It was studied by scholars and
students in traditional Vietnam. The triennial
or mandarinal examinations for entrance into the
civil service were based in part on this and similar works. See NGŨ KINH.

KINSHIP SYSTEM. The Vietnamese kinship system is
patrilineal and is traced to the fifth generation,
both ascending and descending. The patrilineage
is the most important aspect of the kinship and
descent system. The head of the patrilineage
(Trưởng-tộc) is the most influential and pivotal
person in the family. Emphasis is placed on
classified relative age. In the case of siblings
distinctions are made on the basis of age differences among them. In more distant relationships
such as cousins, the age distinction is made
relative to ones father's age. Many of the highland ethnic groups have matrilineal kinship systems, particularly those classified as Malayo-
Polynesian (Austronesian) including the Rhade,
Jarai and Cham. See CULT OF THE ANCESTORS,
HƯƠNG-HỎA, TRƯỞNG-TỘC.

KLOBUKOWSKI, ANTONI-WLADISLAS. Governor General of
Indochina from September, 1908, to February, 1911.
He also served in several high positions in the
colonial administration between 1880 and 1889.

KOHO. An ethno-linguistic group of highland people
    located in the mountainous area between Sài-Gòn
    and Khánh-Hòa Province, including primarily the
    provinces of Lâm-Đồng and Tuyên-Đức. The Koho
    group is composed of several distinct groups -
    the Cil, Chroo, Maa, Lat, Nop and Tring - each
    of which speak a dialect of Koho. The Koho lan-
    guage stems from the Bahnaric subgroup of the
    Mon-Khmer language stock. With the exception of
    the Maa, the Koho groups are matrilineal and
    matrilocal, with the extended family and the vil-
    lage as the two most important social units.
    Most of the Koho groups still use the slash-and-
    burn method of agriculture. Upland rice is the
    main crop supplemented by corn, beans, yams, and
    other vegetables as well as wild game and fish.
    Official estimates in 1965 placed the Koho pop-
    ulation at around 65,000. See CIL, CHROO, MAA,
    LAT, NOP, TRING.

KOL. See CUA.

KONTUM CITY. The capital city of Kontum Province.
    Population 33,554. See KONTUM PROVINCE.

KONTUM PROVINCE. A mountainous province in the cen-
    tral highlands. Kontum borders on Cambodia and
    Laos to the west and lies south of Quảng-Ngãi
    and north of Pleiku Province. The provincial
    capital, Kontum City, is situated on highway
    number fourteen which runs to Pleiku. The pop-
    ulation of the province is 117,046 (1971) and it
    covers an area of 10,181 square kilometers (3,930
    square miles). The province is inhabited prim-
    arily by highland ethnic minority groups including
    the Jarai, Bahnar, Sedeng and Rengao.

KOR. See CUA.

KRANTZ, JULES-FRANCOIS-EMILE. Interim Governor of Co-
    chinchina from March, 1874 to December, 1874 and
    Rear Admiral in the French Navy. He later be-
    came Minister of the Navy in 1888.

KRE. See HRE.

K'TU. See KATU.

KY-CUNG RIVER. (Sông Kỳ-Cùng). A river in north Viet-
    nam. It originates in the Đông-Triều Highlands
    near the Chinese border. It flows northwesterly
    past Lạng-Sơn to Thất-Khê where it empties into
    the Tây-Giang River.

KỲ-LÂN. See LY.

KỲ-MỤC. Village notables. Usually elders of high
       stature in the village. The Kỳ-Mục served as a
       high council (Hội-Đồng Kỳ-Mục or Ban Kỳ-Mục) on
       village affairs in traditional Vietnam. See HỘI-
       ĐỒNG KỲ-MỤC, XÃ.

KỴ NHẬT. See NGÀY GIỖ.

                         -L-

LA-VANG BASILICA. A well-known Catholic Church in
     Quảng-Trị Province about six kilometers (four
     miles) from Quảng-Trị City. During the reign of
     Cảnh-Thịnh (1792-1802) reprisals were carried out
     against the Catholics because Bishop de Behaine
     was assisting Nguyễn Anh in his efforts to over-
     throw the throne of the Tây-Sơn Dynasty. The
     Catholic community in and around Quảng-Trị were
     forced out of their villages and took refuge at
     what is now the La-Vang Basilica. Legend has it
     that in 1798 the Catholic refugees were praying
     to the Virgin Mary when she appeared to them
     saying that she heard their prayers and would
     grant them their requests. Since then there have
     been numerous reports of the appearance of the
     Virgin Mary. The purge of the Catholics continued
     with the reign of Emperor Minh-Mạng (1820-1840)
     and lasted over fifty years. Finally, in 1886
     plans were made and material purchased for the
     construction of a church. It was completed in
     1900 with a capacity for 400 people. The first
     Catholic convention at the La-Vang Church was
     held in 1901. It was soon found to be too small
     a church. In 1924 construction was started on a
     new and larger church which was completed in 1928.
     That structure remained intact throughout the
     French Indochina War (1946-1954). Additional
     buildings were built for living quarters, school
     rooms, etc., around the church. Frequent pil-
     grimages were made to the Basilica by people from
     all parts of Vietnam as well as Vietnamese and
     foreign dignitaries. The La-Vang Basilica was
     completely destroyed in the spring of 1972 by
     the fierce bombing and artillery which also des-
     troyed the city of Quảng-Trị. See QUẢNG-TRỊ CITY.

LẠC-LONG-QUÂN. One of the legendary ancestors of the
     Vietnamese ethnic stock. Lạc-Long-Quân was the
     son of Kinh Dương-Vương. He married the fairy
     Âu-Cơ who gave birth to the famous 100 sons (or

eggs that hatched into sons). For more complete
details see HỒNG-BÀNG DYNASTY. See also ÂU-CƠ,
KINH DƯƠNG-VƯƠNG.

LẠC-VIỆT. The ethnic name applied to the peoples of
Âu-Lạc (257-208 B.C.). There were reportedly
fifteen tribes of Lạc-Việt who together with the
numerous tribes of Âu-Việt united together to
form the kingdom of Âu-Lạc. See ÂU-LẠC, VĂN-LANG.

LẠCH-TRÂY RIVER. (Sông Lạch-Trây). A small river
which originates from the Tam-Bạc River (between
Kiến-An and Hải-Phòng) and empties into the South
China Sea at Cửa Lạch-Trây.

LACQUERWARE. (Sơn Mai). The Vietnamese have known
the techniques of making lacquer since ancient
times. Prior to the fifteenth century it was
used only for waterproofing boats or for export
to China. Emperor Lê Nhân-Tông (1443-1459) sent
a mandarin of the court, Trần Thưởng-Công to
China in search of a new industry. He learned
the art of making lacquerware and brought it back
to Vietnam. Lacquer is a resin extracted from
the Sơn Tree (cây sơn, rhus succedanea or rhus
vernicifera). It is creamy white in raw form,
but can be made black by mixing it for forty
hours in an iron container and adding rosin.
Items to be lacquered are usually made from teak,
or French okume plywood, although metal, leather,
and porcelain are also being used. The lacquer-
ing process begins after the wood has been pre-
treated with a fixative coating, filled and sanded. Ten coats of lacquer are then applied, each
of which must be dried for one week and then
thoroughly sanded before the next coat can be
applied. For the eleventh and final coat, a
specially prepared lacquer is used. One week
later it is sanded with a fine coal powder and
whitewash. Several methods of embellishment are
used, including an engraved low relief, inlayed
material (gold, silver, mother-of-pearl, or egg
shell), and painted designs. The techniques
have been improved throughout the centuries. In
the 1930's the Beaux Arts School in Hà-Nội employed
several Japanese teachers who introduced new methods of production and style variations. This
accounts for the sometimes noticeable Japanese
influence in Vietnamese lacquerware, especially
in that which was made in north Vietnam.

LAFONT, COUNT LOUIS-CHARLES. Governor of Cochinchina
from 1877-1879. He was a Rear Admiral in the

French Navy and the last military Governor of Cochinchina. He attempted to bring about tax reforms, including an export tax on rice. He resigned because of a disagreement with his superior
over the export tax issue.

LAI-CHÂU CITY. The capital city of Lai-Châu Province
in north Vietnam. It is located 468 kilometers
(290 miles) from Hà-Nội via road and 300 kilometers (186 miles) via river. It is situated
on the Hắc-Giang River (Sông Hắc-Giang, also
called the Black River). See LAI-CHÂU PROVINCE.

LAI-CHÂU PROVINCE. A mountainous province in the
northwestern corner of north Vietnam. With a
land mass of 19,800 square kilometers (7,644
square miles), Lai-Châu is the largest province
in the Democratic Republic of Vietnam. It borders on China to the north, Laos to the west and
Sơn-La, Nghĩa-Lo, and Lào-Cai provinces to the
east. Lai-Châu is all jungle and mountains with
breathtaking valleys and high mountain peaks.
The principal river passing through the province
is the Hắc-Giang River (also called the Black
River) which comes out of southern China and is
the main route for water transportation. Other
rivers include the Nam-Hà, Nam-Nhia, and Nam-Tia
Rivers. There are hot springs located at Ngọc-
Chén, Bản-Ni-Hà and Mường-Lợi. The province is
populated almost exclusively by non-ethnic Vietnamese. The most numerous are the Thái and the
Mèo, but also represented are the Xa, Hu-Ni, Dao
and the Lao. The Thái include the White Thái to
the north of the Hắc-Giang River and the Black
Thái to the south of the river.
    This area has historically been ruled by the
Thái tribal chiefs. Because of the disputes a-
mong the three countries, the Thái chiefs allied
themselves at various times with the Chinese,
Lao and Vietnamese. Điện-Biên-Phủ, the site of
the decisive battle in which the Việt-Minh defeated the French, is located in Lai-Châu. The
province is presently part of the Tây-Bắc Autonomous Region. See ĐIỆN-BIÊN-PHỦ, MÈO, LAI-CHÂU
CITY, TÂY-BẮC AUTONOMOUS REGION, THÁI.

LAI-GIANG RIVER. (Sông Lại-Giang). A river in Bình-
Định Province in central Vietnam. It flows past
Bồng-Sơn and is a tributary of the Kim-Sơn River.

LÂM-ẤP. The Chinese name given to the first kingdom
of the Chàm people. It could be regarded as the
precursor state of Champa. Lâm-Ấp (also called

Lin-Yi) was founded around 190-193 A.D. It was
an Indianized state with its capital near Huế.
This state was in constant conflict with the
Vietnamese to the north. See CHAMPA.

LÂM-ĐỒNG PROVINCE. A mountainous province at the
southern end of the central highlands. Lâm-Đồng
is situated south of Tuyên-Đức Province, north
of Long-Khánh Province and west of Bình-Thuận
Province. The population of the province is
reported at 89,106 (1971) and the land mass at
5,504 square kilometers (2,125 square miles). The
province is inhabited chiefly by highland minority
groups and north Vietnamese who settled there after the partition of Vietnam in 1954. The main
highland group is the Koho (over 25,000). Highway number twenty, which runs from Đà-Lạt to Sài-
Gòn passes through the province. The two principal towns are Bảo-Lộc, the provincial capital,
and Di-Linh. The climate is mild and comfortable.
The province has large areas of plateau which are
suited for agricultural production. The French
maintained several large coffee and tea plantations in Lâm-Đồng. A large modern tea factory
has recently been built at Bảo-Lộc. Other products include rice, avocados, bamboo, and silk.
A College of Agriculture was established at Bảo-
Lộc which has since become an agricultural high
school. See BẢO-LỘC, DI-LINH, KOHO.

LÀM RẪY. Swidden agriculture or slash-and-burn agriculture. This type of farming is practiced by
the highland tribal people (montagnards). All
the vegetation is cut down from the land that is
to be planted, often the entire side of a mountain. After it is dried out it is burned. The
land is then clear to plant and is rich in potash
from the ashes. The productivity of the land de-
creases rapidly so that after three to five years
another piece of land is cleared and planted in
the same way and the original fields are abandoned.
Crops cultivated in this fashion include up-land
rice, sweet potatoes, corn, and small vegetables.
The slash-and-burn process is destructive because
it destroys forest areas which do not return to
woodlands but revert to dense grass and under-
brush. See AGRICULTURE, RICE CULTURE.

LÀM RỂ. (Also called ở rể). The custom of a bride-
groom-to-be living with and working for the parents of the bride-to-be before the marriage could

take place. This provided an opportunity for the
girl's family to become familiar with their prospective son-in-law. Such a period of service
could also substitute for the brideprice. This
custom was practiced frequently in traditional
Vietnam but is no longer common in modern times.
See ĂN-HỎI, HÔN-NHÂN, THÁCH-CƯỚI.

LAM-SỒN. A village in Thanh-Hóa Province of central
Vietnam. This village was the location of the
famous resistance movement of the same name (Khởi-
Nghĩa Lam-Sồn) which was led by Lê-Lợi against the
Chinese (1418-1428). It was this revolt that drove
out the Chinese troops of the Ming Dynasty and
established Lê-Lợi as Emperor Lê Thái-Tổ (1428-
1433). See LAM-SỒN UPRISING, LÊ-LỢI, LÊ THÁI-TỔ.

LAM-SỒN UPRISING (1418-1428). A resistance movement
which resulted in the expulsion of the Chinese
troops of the Ming Dynasty who were occupying
Vietnam and the establishment of independence
for the Vietnamese. The revolt was led by Lê-Lợi
and his chief lieutenant, Nguyễn-Trãi. The Chinese
defeated the Vietnamese forces of the Hồ Dynasty
(1400-1407) and created a cruel and exacting rule
over the Vietnamese. The period between 1407 and
1418 was marked by many local uprisings. Lê-Lợi
began to raise an army of resisters using his
native village of Lam-Sồn as a center of operations. He started with eighteen comrades in 1416
all of whom pledged their life to overthrow the
Chinese invaders. The first battles took place
in 1418 in the mountainous region of Chí-Linh in
Thanh-Hóa Province. In 1419 Lê-Lợi asked for and
received help from Laos. But shortly thereafter
the Laotions cut off their aid and helped the
Chinese. In 1422 Lê-Lợi's forces suffered a
serious defeat cuusing him to withdraw into the
mountains. His troops were forced to eat rice
and grass as well as slaughtering their war horses
and elephants for food. Lê-Lợi sued for peace but
the armistice lasted only two years. When the
fighting resumed, Lê-Lợi soon gained control of
Nghệ-An and Thanh-Hóa provinces. In 1426 he led
a three pronged attack northward. After a series
of disastrous defeats the Chinese offered to withdraw in favor of the assumption of power by a
descendant of the Trần Dynasty. Lê-Lợi accepted
and placed Trần-Cao on the throne. The Chinese
General Vương-Thông continued to conspire against
the Vietnamese but was discovered when Lê-Lợi
intercepted a message in which Vương-Thông sent
for help from China. Lê-Lợi resumed the fighting

resulting in numerous victories over the Chinese.
In 1427 he outmaneuvered the 100,000 reinforcements coming from China and killed or captured
most of the Chinese Generals. The Chinese army
was disarmed and returned to China. Prisoners
were exchanged and a new era of peaceful relations
between China and Vietnam began. Lê-Lợi then came
to the throne under the royal name of Lê Thái-Tổ
and founded the Lê Dynasty (1428-1788). See BINH-
NGÔ ĐẠI-CÁO, LÊ DYNASTY, LÊ-LỢI, LÊ THÁI-TỔ,
NGUYỄN-TRÃI.

LÂM TẤN-PHÁC. See ĐÔNG HỒ.

LÂM-VIÊN PLATEAU. A plateau area north of the Di-Linh
Plateau and centering around the city of Đà-Lạt
in the central highlands. It covers Tuyên-Đức
Province and parts of Ninh-Thuận and Bình-Thuận
provinces. The area is most famous for the resort
city of Đà-Lạt. The Lâm-Viên Plateau is characterized by thick forests, cool comfortable climate
and fertile soil. The two important rivers, the
Đa-Nhim and the Đa-Đồng, originate here. The large
Đa-Nhim Dam and hydroelectric power plant are located southeast of Đà-Lạt. The plateau area is
inhabited primarily by highland people, most of
whom are of the Koho ethno-linguistic group. See
ĐA-NHIM RIVER DAM, ĐÀ-LẠT, KOHO.

LÀNG. The popular term for village. See XÃ.

LANG-BIÊN MOUNTAIN. A mountain in the central highlands. It is located in Tuyên-Đức Province just
north of Đà-Lạt and has an elevation of 2,163
meters (7,380 feet).

LANG-CUNG MOUNTAIN. (Núi Lang-Cung or Núi Lang-Tân).
A mountain Lào-Cai Province near the border of
Yên-Báy Province in north Vietnam. It has an
elevation of 2,913 meters (9,557 feet).

LẠNG-SƠN CITY. The capital city of Lạng-Sơn Province
in north Vietnam. It is located 147 kilometers
(91 miles) from Hà-Nội. It lies on the road from
Hà-Nội to Cao-Bằng and is also connected to Hà-Nội
via railroad. The city is only fourteen kilometers
(nine miles) from the Chinese border at Đồng-Đăng.
See LẠNG-SƠN PROVINCE.

LẠNG-SƠN PROVINCE. A mountain province in north Vietnam.
It borders on China to the northeast. The population is approximately 332,000 (1968) and the area
is 7,000 square kilometers (2,702 square miles).

The province is inhabited primarily by highland
tribal people, the largest group of which is the
Thổ.   Other ethno-linguistic groups include Nùng,
Mán, and Dao as well as a small number of ethnic
Vietnamese.   Lạng-Sơn City is the provincial capital and is on the road from Hà-Nội to Cao-Bằng.
The province is also connected by railroad to Hà-
Nội.   The natural resources include coal, lumber
and a small amount of phosphorous.   Beef is
raised for shipment to the lowlands and small
amounts of millet, tea, and silk are produced.
A specialty of the province is mẫu-sơn tea.   The
area is also known for its scenic beauty and the
famous Tam-Thanh Grottoes which were destroyed in
World War II.   Lạng-Sơn has been an historical
gateway into and out of China.   The province is
presently part of the Việt-Bắc Autonomous Region.
See ẢI-NAM-QUAN, LẠNG-SƠN CITY, THỔ.

LANGUAGE.   The official language in both the Democratic
Republic of Vietnam and the Republic of Vietnam is
Vietnamese.   The written language (Quốc-Ngữ) is a
Latinized script and used throughout the country.
Many other languages are spoken by the numerous
minority groups as well as English and French.
The languages of Vietnam can be divided into five
major or super families:

   1.   Kadai or Thai/Kadai - spoken only by
   north Vietnamese highland groups, mainly
   the Thái, Thổ, and Nùng.

   2.   Sino-Tibetan or Tibeto-Burman - spoken
   only by groups native to north Vietnam including the Lô-Lô.

   3.   Miao-Yao - spoken by the Mèo and Mán
   of north Vietnam.

   4.   Austronesian (or Malayo-Polynesian) -
   spoken by groups in central Vietnam including the Chàm, Rhade and Jarai.

   5.   Austroasiatic - includes the Mon-Khmer
   languages of the highland people of north
   and central Vietnam.   Also included in
   this grouping is the Việt-Mường language
   family which in turn, includes Vietnamese
   as spoken by the ethnic Vietnamese.

There has been great progress made in both the
Democratic Republic of Vietnam and the Republic
of Vietnam toward providing many of the minority

languages with a written script and extending
educational facilities and programs to the minority peoples. See ETHNO-LINGUISTIC GROUPS, NÔM,
QUỐC-NGỮ, VIETNAMESE LANGUAGE.

LÀO-CAI CITY. The capital city of Lào-Cai Province.
It is located 296 kilometers (183 miles) from Hà-
Nội on the Red River (Sông Hồng-Hà) at the junc-
ture of the Nam-Ti River (Sông Nam-Ti). It is
situated on the Vietnamese/Chinese border, and
therefore, has always been in a strategic and
precarious position vis-a-vis China. See LÀO-
CAI PROVINCE.

LÀO-CAI MOUNTAIN RANGE. A chain of mountains in north
Vietnam extending from the Chinese border to the
Lô-Qui-Hồ Pass. This chain of mountains is often
classified as part of the larger Hoàng-Liên-Sơn
Mountain Range.

LÀO-CAI PROVINCE. (Also spelled Lào-Cay). A mountainous province in the northwestern part of north
Vietnam. It borders China to the north and is
situated between Lai-Châu and Hà-Giang provinces
to the west and east respectively. The estimated
population is 130,200 (1969) and the land mass of
the province is 4,154 square kilometers (1,603
square miles). There are two main rivers in the
province: the Chẩy River (Sông Chẩy) in the eastern part of the province and the Red River (Sông
Hồng-Hà) in the center. Although scarcely populated the province has several ethno-linguistic
groups including the Thổ, Thái, Nùng, Mèo and Mán
plus a small number of ethnic Vietnamese.
    Lào-Cai was originally part of Giao-Châu and
frequently occupied by the Chinese. The Thai lords
later laid claim to the territory continually.
Lào-Cai has always been a strategic border province with border outposts in several locations.
The most important resource of the province is the
wide variety of precious woods. There are also
small deposits of copper and iron. There are
several large markets in such towns as Lào-Cai,
Cốc-Liêu, Cam-Đường, and Bắc-Kha, but the province is limited by the lack of transportation
facilities. There is one mountain resort at Sa-Pa.
For wild game hunting there are large numbers of
tigers, panthers and bears. The capital of the
province is Lào-Cai City which is located 296
kilometers (183 miles) from Hà-Nội on the Red
River. See HOÀNG-LIÊN-SƠN MOUNTAIN, LÀO-CAI CITY.

LAO-ĐỘNG PARTY. See ĐẢNG LAO-ĐỘNG VIỆT-NAM.

LÃO-GIÁO. See TAOISM.

LÃO TRẠI. Penal settlements. The Lão Trại was a form
    of homesteading which was used by the Vietnamese
    government in traditional Vietnam to promote the
    occupation of newly opened lands. The prisoners
    and their families were sent to the frontier to
    clear new land. After a period of time these
    settlements were established as villages and the
    prisoners were absolved of any further obligation
    to society and became the villagers in the new
    village. This form of land development accounted,
    in part, for the success of the southward expan-
    sion (nam-tiến). See ĐỒN ĐIỀN, NAM-TIẾN, NÔNG
    TRẠI.

LÃO-TỬ. Lao Tzu, the founder of Taoism. See TAOISM.

LAT. An ethno-linguistic minority group of highland
    people located in the Đà-Lạt/Di-Linh area of the
    central highlands. The Lat are a subgroup of the
    Koho and speak a Mon-Khmer language. Their pop-
    ulation is estimated at approximately 10,000.

LỄ. Festival, celebration or ritual. Individual
    festivals are listed under separate entries. See
    ĂN HỎI, ĂN-GIẠM, CHẠM-NGỎ, GIAO-THỪA, KHAO-VỌNG,
    LỄ ĐỘNG-THỔ, LỄ HẠ-ĐIỀN, LỄ HÀN-THỰC, LỄ THẤT-
    TỊCH, LỄ THƯỢNG-ĐIỀN, LỄ TỊCH-ĐIỀN, LỄ TÁO-QUÂN,
    LỄ TRẠNG-NGUYÊN, LỄ TRÙNG-CỬU, LỄ VU-LAN, NAM-
    GIAO, TẾT ĐOAN-NGỌ, TẾT NGUYÊN-ĐÁN, TẾT TRUNG-THU,
    YÊN-LÃO, LỄ KHAI-TÂM, LỄ NGHINH-XUÂN, LỄ THƯỜNG-
    TÂN.

LỄ ĂN HỎI. See ĂN HỎI.

LÊ ANH-TÔNG (ruled 1556-1573). The third emperor of
    the Restored Lê Dynasty (1533-1788). Emperor Lê-
    Trung-Tông died childless in 1556. Le Anh-Tong
    was one of the only surviving relatives of the Le
    Emperors. He was the great-great-grandchild of
    Lê-Trừ, the older brother of Emperor Lê Thái-Tổ
    (1428-1433). When the power passed from Trịnh-
    Kiểm (first of the Trịnh Lords) to Trịnh-Tùng
    (son of Trịnh-Kiểm), Lê Anh-Tông was forced to
    flee to Nghệ-An. But he was pursued and killed
    by Trịnh-Tùng. He was emperor for sixteen years
    and was killed in 1573 at the age of forty-two.
    See RESTORED LÊ DYNASTY, TRỊNH-KIỂM, TRỊNH-TÙNG.

LÊ CHÂN-TÔNG (ruled 1643-1649). The seventh emperor

in the Restored Lê Dynasty (1533-1788). He was
the son of Emperor Lê Thân-Tông (1619-1643). He
died childless in 1649 at the age of twenty. See
RESTORED LÊ DYNASTY.

LÊ CHIÊU-TÔNG (ruled 1516-1524). The ninth emperor in
the Lê Dynasty (1428-1788). He was the great-
grandsom of Emperor Lê Thánh-Tông (1460-1497).
During his reign he successfully put down a revolt
led by Trân-Cao. However, the dynasty was in the
process of rapid decline. His court fell into a
state of anarchy. In order to achieve unity in
the court, Lê Chiêu-Tông called on Mạc Đăng-Dung
who soon had designs on the throne for himself.
In 1524, realizing that Mạc Đăng-Dung was preparing to usurp the throne, Lê Chiêu-Tông made
ready to fight Mạc Đăng-Dung. He ordered the
army to leave the capital while he himself travelled
to Sơn-Tây to prepare for the battle. However,
Mạc Đăng-Dung responded by placing Lê Cung-Hoàng
on the throne. Finally, before the year was up
his forces captured and killed Lê Chiêu-Tông in
Thanh-Hóa Province. He ruled for eleven years
and was twenty-six years old when he died. See
LÊ CUNG-HOÀNG, LÊ DYNASTY, MẠC ĐĂNG-DUNG.

LÊ CUNG-HOÀNG (ruled 1524-1527). (Also known as Lê
Cung-Hoàng-Đế). The tenth and last emperor of
the Lê Dynasty (1428-1788) before the throne was
usurped by the Mạc. He was placed on the throne
by Mạc Đăng-Dung after the overthrow of Lê Chiêu-
Tông in 1524. All the actual power during his
reign was held by Mạc Đăng-Dung. In 1527 Lê Cung-
Hoàng and his mother were both killed by Mạc Đăng-
Dung who usurped the throne and established the
Mạc Dynasty (1527-1592). See LÊ CHIÊU-HOÀNG, LÊ
DYNASTY, MẠC ĐĂNG-DUNG.

LÊ ĐẠI-HÀNH (ruled 980-1005). (Also known as Lê Hoàn).
The founder and first emperor of the Early Lê Dynasty (1010-1225). He ruled for twenty-four years.
A native of Hà-Nam Province, he served as Command-
ing General (Thập-Đạo Tướng-Quân) under Emperor
Đinh Tiên-Hoàng (968-979). After the death of Đinh
Tiên-Hoàng he had an affair with the Queen. In
980 he usurped the throne from the six-year old
crown prince and founded the Early Lê Dynasty (Nhà
Tiền Lê). Lê Hoàn took the royal name of Lê Đại-
Hành. He defeated the invading Chinese in 981, but
also realizing that his small country was no match
for China, he established tributary relations with
China. Since China was occupied defending her borders on other fronts, she welcomed this arrangement. He then proceeded to carry out a successful

campaign against Chiêm-Thành (Champa) to the
south. At the same time he put down numerous local insurrections.
    Lê Đại-Hành is credited with maintaining
statehood and independence during a very precarious time. He was also the first Vietnamese monarch to replace Chinese currency with Vietnamese
money. On the other hand, he is strongly crit-
icized for plotting against the Đinh rulers and
for having an illicit affair with the Queen.
See EARLY LÊ DYNASTY.

LÊ ĐẾ-DUY-PHƯỜNG (ruled 1729-1732). The twelfth emperor in the Restored Lê Dynasty (1533-1788). He
ruled only three years. In 1732 he was said to
have committed adultery with the wife of the
Trịnh Lord Trịnh Cường. He was thus forced to
abdicate the throne and assume a lesser title
(Hôn-Đức-Công), shortly after which he was assassinated. See RESTORED LE DYNASTY.

LỄ ĐOAN-NGỌ. See TẾT ĐOAN-NGỌ.

LỄ ĐỘNG-THỔ. (Động-Thổ Celebration). The ritual of
the first ground stirring, and one of the most
important agricultural ceremonies in traditional
Vietnam. This ritual was usually held during the
first week of the lunar new year. This ceremony,
during which offerings were made to the spirits
of the soil, was held at both the village level
and by the royal court. Later it was performed
only by villagers, since the emperor made his
Nam-Giao celebrations. See LỄ HẠ-ĐIỀN, LỄ THƯỢNG-
ĐIỀN, LỄ TỊCH-ĐIỀN, NAM-GIAO.

LÊ DỤ-TÔNG (ruled 1705-1729). The eleventh emperor in
the Restored Lê Dynasty (1533-1788). He ruled for
twenty-four years. In 1729 he was forced by the
Trịnh Lord Trịnh-Cường to abdicate in favor of
his son. He died in 1731 at the age of fifty-two.
See RESTORED LÊ DYNASTY.

LÊ DUẨN (1908-   ). First Secretary of the Lao-Động
Party Central Committee, member of the Lao-Động
Party Secretariat and member of the Lao-Động Politburo of the Democratic Republic of Vietnam. He
was born in 1908 in Quảng-Trị Province and became
active in the early communist movement in the 1930's
and with the Việt-Minh in the 1940's. He was imprisoned twice for his political activities (1931-
1936 and 1940-1945). Many consider him to be the
most influential personality in the Democratic Republic of Vietnam. He has written extensively on

political strategy. See DEMOCRATIC REPUBLIC OF
VIETNAM, ĐẢNG LAO-ĐỘNG VIỆT-NAM, VIỆT-MINH.

LÊ ĐỨC-THO (1910-   ). Member of the Lao-Động Party
Politburo and Secretariat, and Director of the
Party Training School of the Democratic Republic
of Vietnam. He was born in Nam-Hà Province in
north Vietnam. He was one of the founding members
of the Indochina Communist Party. He has served
in many high-level positions and has made many
other contributions to party organization and
ideology. In 1968 he was appointed special advisor to the north Vietnamese at the Paris peace
talks and later became the principle spokesman
for the delegation. See DEMOCRATIC REPUBLIC OF
VIETNAM, ĐỒNG-DƯỜNG CỘNG-SẢN ĐẢNG, ĐẢNG LAO-ĐỘNG
VIỆT-NAM, VIỆT-MINH.

LÊ DYNASTY (1428-1788). (Nhà Lê, also called Nhà Hậu
Lê or Later Lê Dynasty). The Lê Dynasty was
founded by Lê-Lợi after he drove the occupying
Chinese (Ming) out of the country. The two outstanding emperors of the dynasty were Lê-Lợi, who
came to the throne under the name of Lê Thái-Tổ
(1428-1433) and Lê Thánh-Tông (1460-1497). The
first seventy years of the dynasty comprised a
period of great achievements in many fields. The
civil service was developed, the triennial examinations were refined and the territory expanded
with the acquisition of land from Champa. The Le
period is often referred to as the Golden Age of
Sino-Vietnamese Literature. Outstanding literary
figures of the dynasty include Nguyễn-Trãi, Ngô
Sĩ-Liên, Vũ-Quỳnh, Lê Quý-Đôn, Nguyễn Bỉnh-Khiêm,
Đặng Trần-Côn and Emperor Lê Thánh-Tông. Vietnamese art also flourished as attested to by the
remains of tombs and other buildings dating to
that period. The famous Hồng-Đức Legal Code was
compiled in 1483. The Lê Dynasty was usurped by
the Mạc (Mạc Đăng-Dung) in 1527 but was later restored in 1533. Some refer to the dynasty from
1533 to 1788 as the Restored Lê Dynasty (Nhà Lê
Trung-Hưng). See HỒNG-ĐỨC LEGAL CODE, LÊ THÁI-
TỔ, LÊ THÁNH-TÔNG, LITERATURE, RESTORED LÊ DYNASTY.

LÊ GIA-TÔNG (ruled 1672-1675). The ninth emperor in
the Restored Lê Dynasty (1533-1788). He was the
third son of Emperor Lê Thần-Tông (1619-1643).
When he was two years old his father died. He
was taken in and raised by the powerful Trịnh
Lord, Trịnh-Tạc. In 1672, when Lê Gia-Tông's
brother Lê Huyền-Tông (1663-1671) died childless,
Trịnh-Tạc placed Lê Gia-Tông on the throne. He

ruled only four years. He died in 1675 at the age
of fifteen. See RESTORED LÊ DYNASTY, TRỊNH-TẠC.

LỄ HẠ-ĐIỀN. (Also known as Lễ Xuống-Đồng). An annual
ceremony held at rice transplanting time. The
ceremony was of Vietnamese origin and performed
at the village level by a notable or group of
notables in the village. The ritual consisted of
sacrifices, invocations and symbolic transplanting
of rice.

LỄ HÀN-THỰC. (Also known as Tết Hàn-Thực). The Cold
Food Festival. A holiday which commemorates the
anniversary of the death of Giới-Chi-Thôi who,
according to legend, was a general under an exiled Chinese Lord of the Tấn State, i.e., Prince
Vấn Hậu, around the year 654 B.C. The exiles had
to keep on the move constantly for nineteen years.
Conditions were so harsh at times that the king
and his followers suffered terribly. At one
point, Giới-Chi-Thôi sliced some of his own flesh
to provide food for the king. The king was
eventually reinstated to his throne, but when he
distributed rewards to his loyal troops he over-
looked Giới-Chi-Thôi. The General was not angry
because he had only done his duty. He took his
mother to live in the mountains.
     When the king realized his oversight, he
offered a high position to his former loyal general. Giới-Chi-Thôi refused whereupon the king
ordered the mountain burned with the intention of
forcing the two people out of seclusion. But
Giới-Chi-Thôi did not give in. Both he and his
mother perished in the flames. The king was
filled with remorse and shame. He erected a temple to honor Giới-Chi-Thôi and in order not to
remind the spirit of the general of the sufferings
he had endured in the flames, only cold foods were
placed on the altar. Hence, the Festival of Cold
Foods. The holiday falls on the third day of the
third lunar month. The Vietnamese traditionally
eat two special kinds of rice cake on this holiday-
bánh trôi and bánh chay.

LÊ HI-TÔNG (ruled 1676-1705). The tenth emperor in the
Restored Lê Dynasty (1533-1788). He was the fourth
son of Emperor Lê Thần-Tông (1619-1643 and 1649-
1662). Lê Hi-Tông was emperor for twenty-eight
years after which he abdicated in favor of his son.
He then assumed the position of Thái-Thượng-Hoàng,
a semi-retirement status with a strong voice in
the affairs of state. See RESTORED LÊ DYNASTY.

LÊ HIÊN-TÔNG (ruled 1497-1504). The fifth emperor in
    the Lê Dynasty (1428-1788). He attempted to
    carry on in the same tradition as his father,
    Lê Thanh-Tông (1460-1497). He is considered an
    intelligent and charitable emperor. His reign
    was peaceful and he placed great emphasis on
    agriculture and literature. Lê Hiên-Tông ruled
    for only seven years. He died in 1504 at the
    age of forty-four. See LÊ DYNASTY, LÊ THANH-TÔNG.

LÊ HIÊN-TÔNG (ruled 1740-1786). The fifteenth em-
    peror of the Restored Lê Dynasty (1533-1788).
    He was the son of the Emperor Lê Thuận-Tông and
    ruled for forty-six years. He died in 1786 at
    the age of seventy. See RESTORED LÊ DYNASTY.

LÊ HOÀN. See LÊ ĐẠI-HÀNH.

LÊ HÔN-NHÂN. The wedding ceremony. The Lễ Hôn-Nhân
    is held after the Lễ Ăn Hỏi (engagement ceremony)
    and, in traditional Vietnam, after the bride price
    has been paid. The wedding procession starts
    from the house of the groom and is led by an el-
    derly man of high stature, and preferably, with
    many children. As the procession nears the house
    of the bride firecrackers are lit. It is the
    custom for children to block the path at the
    gateway of the yard of the bride's house. The
    groom's family must give them a small amount of
    money before they will clear the way. Inside
    the bride's house the groom's family present
    offerings to the bride's family after which the
    bride and groom pay homage to the ancestors of
    the bride at the family altar. Both the bride
    and groom bow to the parents of the bride. The
    groom is then led to the main temple or shrine
    of the bride's extended family (Họ) where he
    makes an offering. The family of the bride then
    invites the groom's family to have tea and chew
    betel. At an appropriate time, a representative
    of the groom's family stands and asks permission
    to take the bride back to the groom's house.
    The procession which takes the bride to the
    groom's house (Đám Rước Dâu) includes both fam-
    ilies and friends of the bride except the bride's
    mother and father, who never accompany their
    daughter to her new husband's house. The pro-
    cession is led by the same elder who carries
    burning incense. The procession arrives at the
    groom's house. The bride is resplendent in her
    bridal gown and is preceded by the bridesmaids.
    Upon arrival at the groom's home both bride and
    groom make offerings to the groom's ancestors

and bow to the groom's parents and grandparents.
The couple then join the guests in the yard for
the official marriage ceremony (Lễ Tơ-Hồng). The
couple stand next to a prepared altar while someone reads the marriage eulogy which offers thanks
to the God of Marriage (Nguyệt-Lão) and asks his
blessings. The couple then shares one cup of tea
and chews betel to indicate that they now are one.
The two families and the guests join in a feast
prepared by the groom's family. The bride's
family returns home but she stays at her husband's
house. See ĂN HỎI, ĂN-GIAM, BÀ MAI, CHAM-NGÕ,
CHEO, NGUYỆT-LÃO, THÁCH-CƯỚI.

LỄ HUYỀN-TÔNG (ruled 1663-1671). The eighth emperor
in the Restored Lê Dynasty (1533-1788). He was
the second son of Emperor Lê Thần-Tông (1619-1643
and 1649-1662). He died at the age of eighteen
in 1671 after a reign of nine years. See RESTORED
LÊ DYNASTY.

LỄ KHAI-TÂM. Ceremony of the opening of the heart or
mind. A ceremony in traditional Vietnam which
marked the beginning of a child's formal education.
It was held on the student's first day of class.
After a short ritual at home, the father would
take his son (both in their very best dress) to
the teacher's house where the teacher would be
given an offering to be sacrificed to the spirit
of Confucius. This might consist of glutinous
rice, wine, or a chicken according to the means
of the family. The teacher would in turn, perform a ritual at the altar of Confucius and his
own ancestoral altar, thus accepting the child
as his pupil. By this means, the child's mind
was believed to be opened and he was prepared
to be taught. See EDUCATION, ÔNG ĐỒ, THẦY.

LỄ KINH-TÔNG (ruled 1600-1619). The fifth emperor of
the Restored Lê Dynasty (1533-1788) and the son
of Emperor Lê Thế-Tông (1573-1599). He was made
the emperor in 1600 by the Trịnh Lord, Trinh-Tung.
The Trịnh held most of the power and became repressive causing unrest and revolts throughout
the land. Emperor Lê Kinh-Tông plotted against
Trịnh-Tung, enlisting the cooperation of his son,
Trịnh-Xuân. But Trịnh-Tung discovered the plot
and killed both his son and Lê Kinh-Tông. Lê
Kinh-Tông ruled for twenty years and was thirty-
two years old when he died. See RESTORED LÊ
DYNASTY, TRỊNH-TÙNG.

LE MYRE DE VILERS, CHARLES-MARIE. The first civilian
Governor of Indochina. He served as governor
from 1879-1883. While in office he instituted a
number of innovations designed to improve local
conditions, including the first railroad (Sài-
Gòn/Mỹ-Tho), a court of appeals and numerous surveys in Laos and Cambodia.

Although he sent Captain Henri Riviere to
Tongking to protect French interests, de Vilers
later resigned over his insistance that Riviere
be restrained from attempting to conquer all of
Tongking. His resignation was in vain. Even
though Riviere was later killed in battle, the
French went on to conquer Tongking and concluded
the Treaty of Protectorate on August 25, 1883,
which established north and central Vietnam as
French Protectorates.

LÊ-LAI. An officer and martyr under Lê-Lợi. He was a
native of the Lam-Sơn area of Thanh-Hóa Province.
In 1419 Lê-Lợi was surrounded by the Ming armies
of China. Lê-Lai dressed in the royal color of
yellow and rode an elephant into battle with the
Chinese. Thinking that he was Lê-Lợi, the Chinese
captured and killed him, then withdrew. Lê-Lai's
sacrifice enabled Lê-Lợi to escape and carry the
fight for national sovereignty to a successful
conclusion. See LAM-SƠN UPRISING, LÊ-LỢI.

LÊ-LỢI. (Also known as Bình-Định Vương (Pacification
King) and Lê Thái-Tổ). Lê-Lợi was the leader of
the resistance movement against the Chinese (Ming
Dynasty) occupying armies and later, the founder
of the Lê Dynasty (1428-1788). He is one of the
most celebrated Vietnamese national heroes. Born
into a large and rich family in the village of
Lam-Sơn, Thanh-Hóa Province, he was noted for
using his wealth to aid the poor. He was invited
by the ruling Chinese to become a mandarin but
he refused.

In 1418 he started to raise troops in the
mountains around Lam-Sơn. He took the name of
Bình-Định Vương (The Pacification King) and went
about the country to rally the people against the
Chinese. At first the resistance movement was
weak - inexperienced soldiers, too few officers,
sparce supplies, and a small number of troops.
His forces had to retreat to the Chí-Linh Mountains near Lam-Sơn three times. Eventually they
took Nghệ-An Province and from there they marched

northward against the Chinese occupying army. He
defeated the Chinese forces in 1428, after which
he supplied the Chinese soldiers with junks to
return to China. Lê-Lợi had placed Trần-Cao on
the throne to placate the Chinese who, ostensibly,
conquered Vietnam to restore the Trần Dynasty.
But after his victory over the Chinese, Lê-Lợi
had Trần-Cao killed and seated himself on the
throne, thus founding the Lê Dynasty. He then
assumed the royal name of Thuận-Thiên, but is
known today by his posthumous name of Lê Thái-Tổ.
See LAM-SƠN UPRISING, LÊ DYNASTY, LÊ-LAI, LÊ THÁI-
TỔ, NGUYỄN-TRÃI.

LÊ MẪN-ĐẾ (ruled 1787-1788). The sixteenth and last
emperor in the Restored Lê Dynasty (1533-1788).
He was the grandson of Emperor Lê Hiển-Tông (1740-
1786). Lê Mẫn-Đế ruled Vietnam only two years.
In 1788 the armies of the Tây-Sơn defeated him
and he fled to China where he tried to keep the
Lê Dynasty alive. He requested and received help
from the Chinese to fight the Tây-Sơn. However,
he was defeated again and was forced once more
to flee to China. He was dishonored by the
Chinese mandarins and died in Yen-Kinh Province
(Pekin). See RESTORED LÊ DYNASTY, TÂY-SƠN RE-
BELLION.

LỄ NGÂU. See LỄ THẤT-TỊCH.

LỄ NGHINH XUÂN. An annual ceremony held at the imperial court to welcome the arrival of spring.

LÊ NHÂN-TÔNG (ruled 1443-1459). The third emperor in
the Lê Dynasty (1428-1788). Lê Nhân-Tông was
only two years of age when his father, Emperor
Lê Thái-Tông (1434-1442) died. The Queen Mother
held the power of the throne for several years.
At the age of thirteen he began to assert himself. He gave land to outstanding officials and
commissioned Phan Phù-Tiên to write a ten volume
national history covering the period from the
Trần Dynasty (1225-1400) to the Chinese (Ming)
domination (1414-1427). In 1459 Lê Nhân-Tông was
killed at the age of nineteen by his jealous
brother, Nghi-Dân. See LÊ DYNASTY.

LÊ QUÝ-ĐÔN (1726-1784). A scholar, author and mandarin under the Restored Lê Dynasty (1533-1788).
Born in Thái-Bình Province, he was known for his
unusually keen memory and intellect. He held
various posts as mandarin, including a mission to
China in 1760. He is best known for his literary

and historical achievements which were written in
Sino-Vietnamese as well as classical Chinese.

LÊ QUÝ-LY (ruled 1400). (Better known as Hồ Quý-Ly).
The founder and first emperor of the Hồ Dynasty
(1400-1407). Hồ Quý-Ly actually reigned only
one year (1400) after he gained the throne by
usurping the Trần Dynasty (1225-1400). See Hồ
QUÝ-LY, HỒ DYNASTY.

LÊ TẮC. A scholar and author during the thirteenth
century. He was a descendant of Nguyễn-Phủ,
Governor of Giao-Châu (317-419). Lê Tắc fled to
China during the war with the Mongols. While
there he wrote An-Nam Chí-Lược. See AN-NAM CHÍ-
LƯỢC.

LÊ TÁO-QUÂN. (Also called Tết Táo-Quân). Feast of
the Household Gods. A holiday which falls on
the twenty-third of the twelfth month of the
lunar year. The holiday marks the day on which
the chief guardian spirit of the kitchen (Thổ-
Công) returns to heaven to report on the activities of the family. A new spirit is then assigned
to the household for the coming year to replace
the previous one. On the day of the Lễ Táo-Quân,
each family pays tribute to the kitchen god.
This includes burning sacrificial gold paper, and
offering a fish (carp) for Thổ-Công to ride on
his journey to heaven. See TÁO-QUÂN.

LÊ THÁI-TỔ (ruled 1428-1433). (Also known as Lê-Lợi).
The first emperor and founder of the Lê Dynasty
(1428-1788). Lê-Lợi was born into a family of
rich farmers in the province of Thanh-Hóa, the
village of Lam-Sơn. In 1418 under the name of
Bình-Định Vương (Pacification King), he led the
Lam-Sơn Uprising, a resistance movement against
the Chinese (Ming Dynasty) occupational forces.
In 1428 after the expulsion of the Chinese, he
became Emperor Lê Thái-Tổ. Although he defeated
the Chinese, he still requested recognition for
the country as a tributary state of China. This
was granted and every three years an envoy from
Vietnam presented tribute to the Chinese court.
    Lê Thái-Tổ named is closest lieutenant
during the resistance movement, Nguyễn-Trãi, as
the chief civilian mandarin and Lê-Van as head of
the military. During his reign, Lê Thái-Tổ reorganized the triennial examination system for
entry into the civil service. Buddhist and Taoist
priests were also required to take an examination
in order to lead their congregations. He also

refined the penal code, carried out extensive
land reform and established a system of rotating
military duty so that one fifth of the army was
always on duty, while the other four-fifths
farmed their land. When Lê Thái-Tổ became emperor he became overly suspicious and, consequently, had many people of import killed, including
many skilled and talented individuals. Lê Thái-
Tổ died in 1433 at the age of forty-nine after a
reign of six years. See LAM-SƠN UPRISING, LÊ
DYNASTY, LÊ-LAI, LÊ-LỢI, NGUYỄN-TRÃI.

LÊ THÁI-TÔNG (ruled 1433-1442). The second emperor in
the Lê Dynasty (1428-1788). Lê Thái-Tông was
only eleven years old when he became emperor. So,
all of the power of the throne was in the hands
of the chief mandarin (Quan-Phụ-Chính) Lê-Sát.
Lê-Sát proved to be a ruthless leader. When Lê-
Thái-Tông was a few years older he had Lê-Sát
killed. Supposedly because he was young and
without trusted advisors Lê Thái-Tông fell victim
to wine and women. For the same reason he is not
considered to have been an effective monarch. To
make matters worse, the country was plagued by
droughts, floods and locust attacks causing crop
failures. However, progress was made in several
areas. The civil service examinations were revised, the nation's currency was reorganized and
new standards of measurements were introduced.
In 1442 he took a concubine of Nguyễn-Trãi by the
name of Nguyễn Thị Lộ. After one night with her
Lê Thái-Tông died. It was assumed that she killed
the emperor. Blame was placed on Nguyễn-Trãi and
all of his family were ordered executed. Lê Thái-
Tông died at the age of twenty after a reign of
nine years. See LÊ DYNASTY, NGUYỄN-TRÃI.

LÊ THẦN-TÔNG (ruled 1619-1643 and 1649-1662). The sixth
emperor in the Restored Lê Dynasty (1533-1788).
He was the son of Lê Kính-Tông (1600-1619). He
ruled as emperor from 1619-1643 at which time he
abdicated in favor of his son, Lê Chân-Tông (1643-
1649) and assumed the position of Thái-Thượng-
Hoàng, a semi-retirement status with a strong
voice in the affairs of state. When his son died
childless, the powerful Trịnh Lords placed Lê
Thần-Tông on the throne again where he ruled from
1649 until his death at the age of fifty-six in
1662. See RESTORED LÊ DYNASTY.

LỄ THANH-MINH. Feast of the Pure Light. A holiday
so-called because it occurs on April 5th, fifteen
days after the vernal equinox (first day of spring).
It is the practice, on this day, for people to

stroll outdoors to evoke the spirit of the dead.
It is usually a clear and sunny spring day.
Family graves are decorated and otherwise attend-
ed to. The mood is festive.

LÊ THANH-NGHỊ (1911-   ). Deputy Prime Minister and
member of the Lao-Động Party Politburo of the
Democratic Republic of Vietnam. A native of
north Vietnam, he has served in several high
ranking positions in the Democratic Republic of
Vietnam, including Minister of the Interior. See
ĐẢNG LAO-ĐỘNG VIỆT-NAM, DEMOCRATIC REPUBLIC OF
VIETNAM.

LÊ THÁNH-TÔNG (ruled 1460-1497). The fourth emperor
of the Lê Dynasty (1428-1788). He was placed on
the throne in 1460 when the usurper Nghi-Dân was
deposed. Nghi-Dân had reigned only eight months.
Lê Thánh-Tông ruled for thirty-eight years and
along with Lê Thái-Tô (1428-1433), is considered
to be one of the greatest rulers - if not the
greatest - in the Lê Dynasty (1428-1788). The
country was certainly greatly developed and
strengthened under his rule. He reorganized the
administrative divisions of the country, revised
the tax system, instituted a periodic census, and
commissioned the now famous Ngô Sĩ-Liên to write
a national history (Đại-Việt Sử-Ký). Under his
reign the province of Quảng-Nam was won from
Champa by force. The Chăm capital was taken which
led to the final collapse of Champa. Successful
military action was taken against Laos in retaliation for the Lao led armed insurrections in the
western part of Vietnam. Diplomatic relations
with China continued as before with Vietnam paying
tribute to China.
     The famous Hồng-Đức Legal Code was promul-
gated in 1470-1497. Lê Thánh-Tông himself showed
great concern for the society and his subjects.
He provided medical aid for epidemics, founded
homes for the aged, and encouraged farmers to
cultivate abandoned lands. He considered the
construction of new pagodas as a waste of the
people's money and forbade all such construction.
He set forth twenty-four articles concerning
moral behavior and had them read at public
gatherings.
     Lê Thánh-Tông was also a writer and poet.
He established the Hội Tao-Đàn literary circle
which met together to recite verses. The arts
flourished under his reign. He also placed a
great deal of emphasis on education in the Confucianist tradition, especially on the official

examinations. The Great Emperor Lê Thánh-Tông
died in 1497 at the age of fifty-six. The Lê Dynasty slowly began to decline after his death.
See ĐẠI-VIỆT SỬ-KÝ, HỘI TAO-ĐÀN, HỒNG-ĐỨC LEGAL
CODE, LÊ DYNASTY, NGÔ SĨ-LIÊN.

LỄ THẤT-TỊCH. (Also called Lễ Ngâu). The Double
Seven Festival. A holiday that takes place on the
evening of the seventh day of the seventh lunar
month. It commemorates the love affair between a
lowly ox driver, Ngưu-Lang and the daughter of
the Jade Emperor, Chức-Nữ, who was also a talented spinning girl. According to the legend, the
ox driver and the princess fell in love. The
disparity between their social classes and status
would normally have made it impossible for them
to marry. However, with permission from the Jade
Emperor the two were wed.
    Ngưu-Lang was a poet at heart. The two lovers
were so enamored in married life that each neglected their duties. The Jade Emperor was so angered
that he ordered the separation of the two lovers
by stationing them at opposite ends of the Milky
Way in order that they would never see each
other again. But, by a special act of grace he
allowed them to come together briefly once a year
on the night of the seventh day of the seventh
month. To enable the two to unite the black
crows built a bridge; the span was built from
stones carried on the heads of the crows. This
accounts for the fact that the crows of Vietnam
are bald.
    The holiday falls during the rainy season,
where especially in the north it rains constantly
from one day to the other. This rain is said to
be the tears of the two lovers and is called Mưa
Ngâu (Ngâu Rain).

LÊ THẾ-TÔNG (ruled 1573-1599). The fourth emperor of
the Restored Lê Dynasty (1533-1788). He was the
fifth son of Emperor Lê Anh-Tông (1556-1573). By
1573 the Trịnh Lord Trịnh-Tùng held all the power
of the throne. He killed Lê Anh-Tông and en-
throned Lê Thế-Tông who was then only seven years
old. During the period of his reign, Trịnh-Tùng
brought an effective end to the Mạc Dynasty (1527-
1592). Lê Thế-Tông died in 1599 at the age of
thirty-three. See RESTORED LÊ DYNASTY, TRỊNH-TÙNG.

LÊ THUẬN-TÔNG (ruled 1732-1735). The thirteenth emperor in the Restored Lê Dynasty (1533-1788). He
was the son of Emperor Lê Dụ-Tông (1705-1729),
and originally designated as the crown prince.

However, the powerful Trịnh Lord Trịnh-Cương made
Lê Duy-Phường crown prince and eventually emperor
(1729-1732). But in 1732 Trịnh-Cương deposed Lê
Duy-Phường and placed Lê Thuận-Tông on the throne.
He had ruled for only three years when he died in
1735 at the age of thirty-seven. See RESTORED LÊ
DYNASTY.

LỄ THƯỢNG-ĐIỀN. (Also known as Lễ Lên-Đồng). An
annual ceremony held at the time the rice plants
were in bloom. The ceremony included a sacrifice
followed by a feast. It was held at the village
level in traditional Vietnam and officiated at by
a notable of the village. See LỄ HẠ-ĐIỀN.

LỄ THƯỜNG-TÂN. An annual celebration in traditional
Vietnam during which the first fruits of the harvest are sampled. At the village level, the
ceremony included a feast and sacrifices to the
guardian spirit of the village. It was also a
time when the emperor received the special products of each province such as oranges from Hải-
Dương and Thanh-Hóa provinces, litchis from Hà-
Nội, coconuts from Định-Tường Province and mangoes from Bình-Định, Quảng-Nam and Phú-Yên provinces. The Thường-Tân also offered an opportunity for presenting gifts to one's superiors
and benefactors as a token of deference or gratitude. These gifts usually consisted of the first
fruits of various trees as well as new rice. It
was also customary to make an offering of first
fruits to the spirits of the ancestors and to
the guardian spirit and the god of the soil.

LỄ TỊCH-ĐIỀN. Plowing Ceremony. An annual ceremony
of Chinese origin in which the emperor personally
plows a number of furrows beginning the ground
breaking season for the country. The ritual was
first performed by Emperor Lê Đại-Hành (980-1005)
near Đội-Sơn Mountain. Legend has it that when
he began to plow, a jar of gold was unearthed.
Similarly, a jar of silver was found the following year. Each successive dynasty has treated
this ceremony differently. The Lý Dynasty (1010-
1225) for example, attached great importance to
it while the Trần Dynasty (1225-1400) entirely
neglected it. It was last performed under the
Nguyễn Dynasty (1802-1945). See ĐỘI-SƠN PAGODA.

LỄ TRẠNG-NGUYÊN. The Feast of the Learned. A holiday
which commemorates the practice started by one
of the emperors in which he would call together
the scholars on the first full moon of the year.

He would give them a feast and they, in turn,
would compose poetry on subjects chosen by him.
The holiday falls on the fifteenth day of the
first lunar month.

LÊ TRANG-TÔNG (ruled 1533-1548). The first emperor of
the Restored Lê Dynasty (1533-1788). He was the
last son of Emperor Lê Chiêu-Tông (1516-1524).
During the early years of the Mạc Dynasty (1527-
1592), the patriot Nguyễn-Kim fought to reinstate
the Lê Dynasty. He took Lê Trang-Tông to Laos
where he proclaimed him emperor. Later, when by
1543 Nguyễn-Kim had gained a foothold in central
Vietnam, he brought Lê Trang-Tông to Thanh-Hóa
Province where they controlled Thanh-Hóa and Nghệ-
An. Lê Trang-Tông died in 1548 at the age of
thirty-one. He was succeeded by his son, Lê
Trung-Tông (1548-1556) who together with Nguyễn-
Kim and his following, continued the fight against
the Mạc. See RESTORED LÊ DYNASTY, NGUYỄN-KIM.

LỄ TRÙNG-CỬU. (Also known as Tết Trùng-Cửu or Tết
Trùng-Dương). The Double Nine Festival. A holiday which falls on the ninth day of the ninth
lunar month. Legend has it that during the Han
Dynasty in China, a student named Hoàn-Cảnh was
told by his teacher, Phí Tràng-Phồng, of an im-
pending disaster and that he and each person in
his house should make a purse, and fill it with
a special flower. On the ninth day of the ninth
month they were to take it to the highest place
they could find and sip wine. Hoàn-Cảnh did as he
was advised and no misfortune befell him. But
when he and his family returned home all the domestic animals in the house were dead.
     The holiday also marks the near end of au-
tumn. Poets and romantics have traditionally
sought the inspiration and seclusion of a high
mountain on this day. Consequently, there is the
proverb that says, "On the double nine day, we
climb mountains" (Trùng-Cửu Đăng Cao).

LÊ TRUNG-HƯNG. (Nhà Lê Trung-Hưng). See RESTORED LÊ
DYNASTY.

LÊ TRUNG-TÔNG (ruled 1005). The second emperor of the
Early Lê Dynasty (980-1009). He was the son of
Emperor Lê Đại-Hành. Only three days after he
took the throne he was assassinated by assassins
hired by the royal family. See EARLY LÊ DYNASTY.

LÊ TRUNG-TÔNG (ruled 1548-1556). The twelfth emperor
of the Restored Lê Dynasty (1533-1788). He was

emperor for eight years when he died childless in
1556 at the age of twenty-eight. See RESTORED LÊ
DYNASTY.

LÊ TÚC-TÔNG (ruled 1504). The sixth emperor of the Lê
Dynasty (1428-1788). Lê Túc-Tông was the third
son of Lê Hiến-Tông (1497-1504). He died in 1504
only six months after coming to the throne. See
LÊ DYNASTY.

LÊ TƯỚNG-DỰC (ruled 1510-1516). The eighth emperor of
the Lê Dynasty (1428-1788). He was the second
cousin of Emperor Lê Uy-Mục whom he killed in
1509 in order to take the throne. However, he
proved to be just as cruel and corrupt as his
predecessor. He ruled for seven years until 1516
when at the age of twenty-four he was overthrown
and killed by a court official, Trịnh Duy-Sản.
See LÊ DYNASTY.

LÊ UY-MỤC (ruled 1505-1509). The seventh emperor of
the Lê Dynasty (1428-1788). He was called by the
Chinese the "Diabolical King" (Qủi-Vương). As
soon as he was made emperor, he had his grand-
mother and two of his ministers killed. He was
so ruthless and treacherous that many officials,
both civilian and military, were either dismissed
or resigned. In 1509 he was overthrown by his
cousin. Lê Uy-Mục was responsible, in large part,
for the decline of the Lê Dynasty. See LÊ DYNASTY.

LÊ VĂN-DUYỆT (1763-1832). A famous general and patriot
under the early Nguyễn Dynasty (1802-1945). Although a native of Quảng-Ngãi Province he grew up
in the delta near Mỹ-Tho. He was one of Nguyễn-
Anh's (later to become Emperor Gia-Long 1802-1819)
earliest and most faithful lieutenants. He went
with Nguyễn-Anh to Thailand and returned to
fight with him against the Tây-Sơn. After Nguyễn-
Anh was proclaimed emperor in 1802, Lê Văn-Duyệt
served in various posts and was instrumental in
subduing several local uprisings. In 1820, under
Emperor Minh-Mạng (1820-1840), he was made govern-
or of Gia-Định Province. He served in that position for twelve years. On July 30, 1832 he
died. Emperor Minh-Mạng had his tomb destroyed
a few years later because Lê Văn-Duyệt was accused
of eleven counts of treason. His followers were
brought to trial, including his adopted son, Lê
Văn-Khôi, who had led a revolt against the court.
Emperor Tự-Đức (1848-1883) reinstated Lê Văn-
Duyệt's posthumous title and restored his tomb.
See GIA-LONG, NGUYỄN-ANH.

LÊ VĂN-HỮU. A scholar and historian during the Trần
    Dynasty (1225-1400). Born in Thanh-Hóa Province,
    he passed his civil service examination when he
    was only eighteen years old. He was commissioned
    by Emperor Trần Thái-Tông (1225-1258) to write a
    national history. In 1272 he completed Đai-Việt
    Sử-Ký. This major work was comprised of thirty
    volumes and chronicled the events from the time
    of Triệu Việt-Vừơng (207 B.C.) to the end of the
    Lý Dynasty (1224). See ĐẠI-VIỆT SỬ-KÝ.

LÊ VU-LAN. See VU LAN.

LÊ XUỐNG-ĐỐNG. See LỄ HẠ-ĐIỀN.

LÊ Ý-TÔNG (ruled 1735-1740). The fourteenth emperor
    of the Restored Lê Dynasty (1533-1788). He was
    the son of Emperor Lê Dụ-Tông (1705-1729). The
    powerful Trịnh Lord, Trịnh-Giang placed Lê Ý-Tông
    on the throne rather than the son of Lê Thuận-
    Tông (1732-1735), the preceeding emperor. How-
    ever, in 1740 after five years of rule he was
    forced to abdicate by the Trịnh Lord, Trịnh-Doanh.
    He then assumed the title of Thái-Thừơng-Hoàng,
    a semi-retirement type of status with a strong
    voice in the affairs of state. He died in 1759
    at the age of forty-one. See RESTORED LÊ DYNASTY.

LEAGUE FOR THE INDEPENDENCE OF VIETNAM. See VIỆT-NAM
    ĐỘC-LẬP ĐỒNG-MINH HỘI.

LEAGUE FOR THE RESTORATION OF VIETNAM. See VIỆT-NAM
    PHỤC-QUỐC ĐỒNG-MINH HỘI.

LETOURNEAU, JEAN. High Commissioner to Indochina from
    April, 1952 to June, 1953.

LỊCH-TRIỀU HIỀN-CHỪƠNG LOẠI-CHÍ. (Literally, Classified
    Description of the Traditional Institutions of
    Vietnam). A forty-nine volume history of Viet-
    nam written by Phan Huy-Chú. This major histor-
    ical work covers the policies, rites, personal-
    ities, and achievements of the various dynasties
    prior to the Nguyễn Dynasty (1802-1945). This
    is considered one of the most valuable resource
    documents because of its organization and compre-
    hensive coverage. Written during the reign of
    Minh-Mạng, the contents are divided into ten
    sections or monographs (Chí), each of which has
    as its reference ancient Chinese and Vietnamese
    historical works.

LIÊN-HOÀN. A form of poetry in which the last line of
    one verse is the same as the first line of the

next verse.

LIÊN-NGÂM. (Also called Liên-Cú). A form of poetry
in which two or more people would alternately
compose one or two lines.

LINH-GIANH RIVER. (Sông Linh-Gianh). See GIANH RIVER.

LITERATURE. Vietnamese literature is divided into
three categories:

1. Oral literature (Truyền-Khẩu), which
pre-dates recorded history and continues
today. Forms included in this classif-
ication include proverbs, folk songs and
legends.

2. Sino-Vietnamese Literature (Hán-Việt)
which includes those works which were recorded in Chinese. This type dates from
the establishment of the first Vietnamese
independent kingdom in 939.

3. Vietnamese literature (Quốc-Âm) which
was recorded in nôm or Quốc-Ngữ. This
category began in the thirteenth century
with the invention of nôm (Chữ-Nôm).

Sino-Vietnamese literature (Vietnamese literature
written in Chinese characters) was dominated by
Buddhist texts and prose written by Confucian
scholars and members of the imperial family and
court. Quite understandably, this literature
was marked by an extremely heavy Chinese influence.
For example, the strict rules of meter and verse
that governed Chinese poetry were also adopted
and applied to Vietnamese poetry. Some of the
more prominent literary figures in the Sino-Vietnamese literature were Emperors Lý Thái-Tông
(1028-1054) and Lý Nhân-Tông (1072-1127), General
Lý Thường-Kiệt (1015-1105), Nguyễn-Trãi and Emperor Lê Thánh-Tông (1460-1497).
    The first text written in Chữ-Nôm was written
in the late thirteenth century, Văn-Tế Cá Sấu
(Ode to an Alligator), by Hàn-Thuyên. The great
Vietnamese classics including Kim-Vân-Kiều by
Nguyễn-Du, Hoa Tiên by Nguyễn Huy-Tự, Chinh-Phu-
Ngâm by Đoàn Thị Điểm and Cung-Oán Ngâm Khúc by
Nguyễn Gia-Thiều are but a few of the master-
pieces that represent the achievements of Vietnamese literature (Quốc-Âm). Chữ-Nôm was never
accepted as the official language but always
limited to popular or common literature forms.

The modern novel and poem is written in Quốc-Ngữ. Literature in this Romanized script has played an important role in the nationalistic literary movements such as those that were spearheaded by Nguyễn Văn-Vĩnh and Phạm-Quỳnh. See BÍCH-CÂU KỲ-NGỘ, CHINH-PHỤ-NGÂM, CUNG-OÁN NGÂM KHÚC, HỘI TAO-ĐÀN, KIM-VÂN-KIỀU, NHO, NÔM, LỤC-BÁT, QUỐC-NGỮ, SÔNG-THẤT LỤC-BÁT, TỰ-LỰC VĂN-ĐOÀN, VIETNAMESE LANGUAGE.

LIVESTOCK. The most prominent domesticated animal in Vietnam is the water buffalo. It was estimated that there were 1,535,000 water buffalo in the Democratic Republic of Vietnam in 1965 and 733,000 in the Republic of Vietnam in the same year. The buffalo are used as draft animals by the ethnic Vietnamese while the highland people also use them as a sign of prestige and for ceremonial sacrifices. Oxen are also used as draft animals. The small breed of horses which is native to Vietnam is commonly used for pulling small two-wheeled carts. Pigs are the chief meat animal and were grown for export during peacetime. Beef cows are slaughtered throughout Vietnam. One of the largest cattle markets is located in Châu-Đốc Province. Ducks have been grown widely in the Mekong Delta, a convenient arrangement because they feed on the small fish and insects in the rice paddy. They are grown for their feathers as well as for the meat. Chickens are popular for meat and eggs. Sheep and goats are not too numerous but can be found in some locales, especially around Phan-Rang. Two factors that tend to discourage the consumption of meat are: (1) some of the religious sects such as the Hoa-Hảo Buddhist as well as the more devout Buddhist in general, abstain from eating meat; and (2) fish and fish products are more available and less expensive than meat and have traditionally been the main source for animal protein in the Vietnamese diet. See AGRICULTURE.

LỘ. Province. The term Lộ was used during various periods of Vietnamese history to designate a province. It is no longer in use. See ADMINISTRATIVE DIVISIONS, TỈNH.

LÔ-GIANG RIVER. See LÔ RIVER.

LÔ-LÔ. An ethno-linguistic group of highland people located in Hà-Giang and Lào-Cai provinces in north Vietnam and extending on into Laos, northern Thailand and Burma. They speak a Tibeto-Burmese language of the Sino-Tibetan language family.

According to the 1960 census there were 6,898 LÔ-
LÔ living in Vietnam. The group found in Laos
and Vietnam is often referred to as the Indochina
LÔ-LÔ. They practice swidden agriculture with
maize, rice, tobacco and opium poppies as the
main crops.

LÔ POINT. (Mũi Lô). A cape or point extending into
the Gulf of Tonking north of Hà-Tĩnh City in Hà-
Tĩnh Province in central Vietnam.

LÔ RIVER. (Sông Lô, also known as Sông Lô-Giang, Sông
Thao, or Sông Thanh-Gianh). A large river in
north Vietnam and a tributary of the Red River.
It originates in China and flows through Hà-Giang,
Tuyên-Quang Provinces and meets the Red River at
Việt-Trì. The Lô River has two major tributaries:
the Gâm River and the Chây River. It is 360 kilometers (223 miles) long although only 250 kilometers (155 miles) is located in Vietnam.

LOA-THÀNH. See CÔ-LOA.

LOCUST REVOLT 1854. A revolt during the reign of
Emperor Tự-Đức (1848-1883) led by an alleged descendant of the Lê Dynasty (1428-1788), named Lê
Duy-Cụ and a famous scholar, Cao Bá-Quát. The
revolt started in Sơn-Tây Province and met with
temporary success as it spread to Bắc-Ninh and
Hải-Dương. However, before long, the armies of
Tự-Đức put down the revolt and captured the leaders. The revolt derives its name from the fact
that locusts were ravaging the area of Sơn-Tây
and Bắc-Ninh at the time of the revolt. See
CAO BÁ-QUÁT.

LONG. (Also called Rong). Dragon. The dragon is a
principal character in Vietnamese mythology and
one of the four sacred animals (Tứ-Linh). It
represents power, strength, nobility, and was
used as a special symbol of the emperor. Unlike
the western concept of the dragon as evil and
ferocious, the dragon in Vietnamese folklore is
a benevolent and revered animal. It has the
head of a camel, horns of a deer, eyes of a fish,
ears of a buffalo, body and neck of a snake,
scales of a carp, claws of an eagle and feet of
a tiger. A long barb hangs on each side of its
mouth and a precious stone shines brilliantly on
its tongue. It has a crest of eighty-one scales
running the entire length of its backbone. It
can breathe smoke, fire, or water at will. It
is immortal. The five-clawed dragon was used on

the official dress of the Emperor. Vietnamese legend has it that the dragon was the procreator of the ethnic Vietnamese stock. The mighty Mekong River is named in Vietnamese Sông Cửu-Long (River of Nine Dragons). See TỨ-LINH.

LONG-AN PROVINCE. A delta province in south Vietnam. Formerly the provinces of Tân-An and Chợ-Lớn. The province is situated south of Sài-Gòn and north of Định-Tường Province. The provincial capital is Tân-An and is located on highway number four which connects Sài-Gòn with Cần-Thơ and Cà-Mau. The population of Long-An Province is 381,861 (1971) and the area is 1,639 square kilometers (632 square miles). The chief products are rice, pineapple, mango, sugarcane and pork. See TÂN-AN.

LONG-KHÁNH PROVINCE. An inland province at the northern edge of south Vietnam. The province was created in 1956 from the former district of Xuân-Lộc in Biên-Hòa Province. The population is 161,605 and the area is 4,464 square kilometers (1,723 square miles). The provincial capital, Xuân-Lộc, is located on highway number one which runs the length of Vietnam. The Đồng-Nai River runs through the province. Several large French rubber plantations were located in Long-Khánh. Other major products include mung bean, corn, pineapple and sugar cane. See XUÂN-LỘC.

LONG, MAURICE. Governor General of Indochina from February, 1920 to January, 1923.

LONG-SÔNG RIVER. (Sông Long-Sông). A river in northern Bình-Thuận Province in central Vietnam. It empties into the South China Sea at Long-Hương near Tủy-Phong.

LONG-XUYÊN. The capital city of An-Giang Province. Population 101,505 (1971). The city is located on the west bank of the lower Mekong River (Bassac River). It is connected by road to Cần-Thơ and Châu-Đốc. See AN-GIANG PROVINCE.

LONG-XUYÊN/RẠCH-GIÁ CANAL. (Kinh Long-Xuyên/Rạch-Giá, also called Kinh Cái-Sắn). A canal which runs from the lower Mekong River (Bassac River or Hậu-Giang River) near Long-Xuyên to Rạch-Giá on the Gulf of Thailand. The canal is a major transportation artery in the Mekong Delta.

LOTUS. See SEN.

LUẬN-NGŨ. The Analects. One of the four famous
   Chinese Books (Tứ-Thư) dealing with the philosophy and doctrine of Confucius. Luan-Ngũ is a
   work of twenty short chapters condensing the say-
   ings of Confucius and some of his disciples. This
   book was used by scholars and students in traditional Vietnam. It was particularly important
   because the mandarinal examinations were based,
   in part, on it. See TỨ-THƯ.

LỤC-BÁT. A form of poetry in which the lines of the
   poem are alternately composed of six words and
   eight words. The length of the poem may vary but
   must always end with an eight word line. This
   form is very popular, especially for the Truyện
   (narrative verse or epic poem) written in nôm.
   A related form, Biến-Thể Lục-Bát was used for the
   Truyện of a less classical and less formal nature.
   See KIM-VÂN-KIỀU, NÔM.

LỤC-ĐỨC. The six virtues. The six important virtues
   were based on the Chinese classics and repeatedly
   referred to in Vietnamese literature. These include Trí (wisdom or intellect), Nhân (benevol-
   ence), Tín (sincerity), Nghĩa (righteousness),
   Trung (moderation) and Hòa (harmony).

LỤC-HẠNH. The six obligations of conduct. In classical Chinese Confucian tradition, the guidelines
   for behavior were clearly prescribed in traditional Vietnam. The six obligations of conduct include Hiếu (filial piety), Hữu (friendship), Mục
   (kindness), Uyên (love of kin), Nhiệm (tolerance),
   and Tuất (charity).

LỤC-NAM RIVER. (Sông Lục-Nam). A river in north Viet-
   nam. It originates near the Chinese border in the
   Đồng-Triều Mountain Range and flows through Hà-
   Bắc Province, past Phủ-Lục-Nam and meets the Thái-
   Bình River at Phả-Lại.

LỤC-NGHỆ. The six arts in traditional Vietnam. These
   include Lễ (propriety or politeness), Nhạc (music),
   Xạ (archery), Ngự (chariot riding), Thư (writing),
   and Số (mathematics).

LỤC-NGÔN-THỂ. A form of the Thất-Ngôn style of poetry
   (seven word lines) into which is inserted a pair
   of six word lines. This form was used frequently
   under the Trần Dynasty (1225-1400) and the Lê Dynasty (1428-1788).

LỤC-VÂN-TIÊN. An epic poem written in the nineteenth
   century by Nguyễn Đình-Chiểu. Written in nôm,
   the poem has 2,076 lines and is considered a
   masterpiece of the same caliber as Kim-Vân-Kiều.
   See NGUYỄN ĐÌNH-CHIỂU.

LUNAR CALENDAR. See ÂM-LỊCH.

LUỘC RIVER. (Sông Luộc). A small river in north Vietnam. It flows from the Red River to the Thái-
   Bình River in Thái-Bình Province.

LƯƠNG NGỌC-QUYẾN (1885-1917). The patriot who inspired
   the Thái-Nguyên Revolt of 1917. Born in Hà-Nội,
   he was one of the first Vietnamese students to
   study in Japan. There he met and was strongly
   influenced by Phan Bội-Châu. He graduated in
   1911 and went to China, then on to Vietnam. He
   was continually active in the National Restoration
   Movement. In 1916 he was captured by the British
   in Hong-Kong and turned over to the French. The
   French tried to buy him off but failed. He was
   imprisoned in a garrison at Thái-Nguyên. While
   in prison he provoked the Thái-Nguyên Revolt.
   Lương Ngọc-Quyến was a cripple and rather than
   slow the escape of his comrades, he committed
   suicide on September 5, 1917. See THÁI-NGUYÊN
   REVOLT.

LƯU VĨNH-PHÚC. Political exile from China and leader
   of the Black Flags (Cờ Đen) in north Vietnam in
   the late nineteenth century. He fled to north
   Vietnam in 1863. In 1865 he joined the pirate
   band called the Black Flags. After making peace
   with the Vietnamese emperor the Black Flags
   fought against the French in their efforts to
   conquer Vietnam. It was the Black Flags under
   Lưu Vĩnh-Phúc who killed the French Captain
   Francis Garnier in 1873 and Captain Henri Riviere
   in 1883. He also joined the resistance against
   the Japanese occupation of Taiwan in 1895 and
   then returned to China where he showed support
   for various Vietnamese revolutionaries who went
   to China. See BLACK FLAGS.

LŨY RIVER. (Sông Lũy). A river in Bình-Thuận Province in central Vietnam. It has two tributaries,
   the Sông Mao and the Sông Cà-Tốt. It flows past
   Hải-Ninh and empties into the South China Sea at
   Phan-Rí Cửa.

LŨY THẦY. See NHẬT-LỆ WALL.

LY. (Also called Lân or Kỳ-Lân). Unicorn. The unicorn is an important character in Vietnamese mythology and one of the four sacred animals (Tứ-
Linh). It symbolizes intelligence and goodness
and is extremely gentle. It appears only on rare
and special occasions. For example, when Confucius was born in 481 B.C. it is said to have
appeared. The Vietnamese unicorn is somewhat
similar to the English griffin. It has the body
of an antelope, the feet of a horse, the tail of
a buffalo and a single horn on the head. See
TỨ-LINH.

LÝ ANH-TÔNG (ruled 1138-1175). The sixth emperor in
the Lý Dynasty (1010-1225). He was only three
years old when he took the throne. The Queen
Mother acted as regent but was having an affair
with a courtier Đỗ Anh-Vũ. All the power, therefore, was in the hands of Đỗ Anh-Vũ. Several
mandarins in the court plotted to assassinate him
but they were all exposed and killed. General Tô
Hiến-Thành was largely responsible for the peace
and stability of this period. He put down
several rebellions by small local bands.
    In 1171 Lý Anh-Tông toured the country to
learn about the life of the people, the lay of
the land, roadways and communications. He also
kept a journal which contained geographical descriptions of the country. The journal unfortunately, has been lost. Significantly, in 1164,
the Chinese changed their name for the country
from Giao-Châu-Quận (Giao-Châu District) to An-
Nam Quốc (An-Nam Nation). This represented the
first time that the Chinese recognized the country as a nation-state. Lý Anh-Tông became ill
in 1175 and gave responsibility for the affairs
of state to Tô Hiến-Thành, including entrusting
him with the regency of the crown prince, who
at that time was only two years old. The following year in 1176, Lý Anh-Tông died at the age
of forty after a reign of thirty-seven years.
See LÝ DYNASTY, TÔ HIẾN-THÀNH.

LÝ BÔN (ruled 544-548). (Also known as Lý Bí, Lý Nam-
Đế). The founder of the Early Lý Dynasty (544-
602). Although of royal Chinese lineage, Lý-Bôn's
family had lived in Giao-Châu for seven genera-
tions. In 542 A.D. at a time when Giao-Châu
was being harassed by Champa from the south and
increasingly oppressed by the Chinese, Lý-Bôn
led a popular revolt against the Chinese which
resulted in independence in 544. Lý-Bôn assumed
the royal name of Lý Nam-Đế and proclaimed his

kingdom to be Vạn-Xuân (10,000 Springs). Lý-
Bôn was credited with being gifted both as an
intellectual and as a military leader. But his
victory was short-lived as the Chinese returned
in force and reoccupied the territory of Giao-
Châu a few years later. Conflicting reports
state that he was assassinated or that he died
of malaria. His successor, Triệu Quang-Phục
(i.e., Triệu Việt-Vương) continued to resist the
Chinese and finally succeeded in driving them
out. The dynasty that he founded lasted until
602. See EARLY LÝ DYNASTY. TRIỆU VIỆT-VƯƠNG.

LÝ CAO-TÔNG (ruled 1176-1210). The seventh emperor
in the Lý Dynasty (1010-1225). Lý Cao-Tông was
only three years old when he took the throne
under the regency of Tô Hiến-Thành. However, the
queen wanted to put her first son on the throne
and offered a large bribe to Tô Hiến-Thành's wife
which was refused. Lý Cao-Tông grew up to be
corrupt and oppressive, taking his pleasure at
the expense of the people. One of his excesses
was the construction of temples. As a result of
an uprising in Nghệ-An Province led by Phạm-Du,
Lý Cao-Tông and the crown prince had to seek
refuge in a fishing village in Phú-Thọ. However,
they did return to the palace. Lý Cao-Tông died
in 1210 at the age of thirty-eight after a reign
of thirty-five years. His reign is considered
to mark the beginning of the decline of the Lý
Dynasty. See LÝ DYNASTY, LÝ HUỆ-TÔNG.

LÝ CHIÊU-HOÀNG (ruled 1224-1225). (Also known as Công-
Chúa Chiêu-Thánh or Princess Chiêu-Thanh). The
ninth and last monarch in the Lý Dynasty (1010-
1225). She was only seven years old when her
father, Lý Huệ-Tông (1211-1224) turned the rule
over to her. The Trần family had been in effective control of the throne for some time, but now
plotted to end the Lý Dynasty.
    Trần Thu-Độ was having an affair with the
Queen Mother and was the one with the most power
in the court. He arranged with the Queen Mother
to have Lý Chiêu-Hoàng marry his eight year old
nephew, Trần-Cảnh, who was later proclaimed Emperor, thus marking the end of the Lý Dynasty
and the beginning of the Trần Dynasty (1225-1400).
See LÝ DYNASTY, TRẦN DYNASTY, TRẦN THÁI-TÔNG,
TRẦN THỦ-ĐỘ.

LÝ ĐẠO-THÀNH. A high-ranking official under two emperors, Lý Thánh-Tông (1054-1072), and Lý Nhân-
Tông (1072-1127). The Emperor Lý Nhân-Tông took

the throne when he was only seven years old. It
was Lý Đạo-Thành who looked after the affairs of
state until the emperor came of age. He was a
member of the Lý family, but very conscientious
and dedicated to the welfare of the country and
of the people. He was a civilian mandarin known
for his loyalty. See LÝ NHÂN-TÔNG.

LÝ DYNASTY (ruled 1010-1225). (Nhà Lý, sometimes referred to as the Nhà Hậu Lý or Post Lý Dynasty).
The Lý Dynasty was the first of the great dynasties of Vietnam. It lasted continuously over
two hundred years, maintaining its sovereignty
and independence from China. At the same time,
it prospered and developed internally. The first
major system of dams was constructed to protect
the rice fields from the flooding of the Red River.
The army was reorganized, the civil service was
developed including the first triennial examinations which were held in 1075. Classical Chinese
studies were encouraged and a temple dedicated to
the cult of Confucius was built in 1070. A
national college (Quôc-Tu-Giám) was created in
1076. The Lý Dynasty produced some outstanding
national figures such as Lý Thường-Kiệt, Tô Hiến-
Thành and Lý Đạo-Thành. See LÝ ĐẠO-THÀNH, LÝ
THƯỜNG-KIỆT, TÔ HIẾN-THÀNH, QUÔC-TU-GIÁM, VĂN-
MIẾU PAGODA.

LÝ HUỆ-TÔNG (ruled 1211-1224). The eighth emperor in
the Lý Dynasty (1010-1225). The son of Lý Cao-
Tông, he was forced to flee with his father from
the armies of one of the generals. The emperor
fled to Qui-Hóa (Phú-Thọ) while the crown prince
went to Hải-Âp in Nam-Định Province. There, Lý
Huệ-Tông stayed at the house of Trần-Lý and fell
in love with one of his daughters, Trần-Thị.
Members of the Trần family helped to put down the
rebellion and the emperor and his son returned
to the capital. On the death of Lý Cao-Tông he
took the throne. He sent for Trần-Thị who became his first wife. He also gave high rank to
members of the Trần family who quickly came to
have a disproportionate amount of influence in
the affairs of state. This caused the Queen
Mother to object and eventually try to poison
Trần-Thị. Lý Huệ-Tông turned more and more
power over to the Trần family until he himself
effectively had no power. He became sickly and
often had periods of insanity and drunkeness.
Since he had no sons, he gave the throne over to
his daughter, Princess Lý Chiêu-Hoàng in 1224 and
entered the pagoda where he lived out the rest of

his life. He reigned for fourteen years. See LÝ
CHIÊU-HOÀNG.

LÝ NGUYÊN-CÁT. A Chinese actor in the thirteenth century who is said to have introduced Chinese classical theater to Vietnam. According to legend,
Trần Hưng-Đạo captured a Chinese theatrical troup
led by Lý Nguyên-Cát. The troup not only performed in the court, but Lý Nguyên-Cát also
trained the Vietnamese dancers of the imperial
court.

LÝ NHÂN-TÔNG (ruled 1072-1127). The fourth emperor in
the Lý Dynasty (1010-1225). He was only seven
years old when his father Lý Thánh-Tông (1054-
1072) died. He ruled at first under the regency
of a high court mandarin, Lý Đạo-Thành. His
reign began in 1072. The first civil service
examinations in Vietnam were held in 1075. The
following year the national college (Quốc-Tử-Giám)
was established. Also in 1075, the Chinese were
preparing to invade Vietnam when General Lý
Thường-Kiệt forestalled the attack by attacking
first. He took his armies against the Chinese
in Kwang-Tung and Kwang-Si provinces. He layed
seige to and pillaged the city of Nam-Ninh. The
Chinese managed to retaliate by taking three districts. These districts, however, were returned
to Vietnam in return for prisoners taken by Lý
Thường-Kiệt's army. The negotiations for prisoner release between Vietnam and China indicated
that the Vietnamese were dealing with the Chinese
on an equal footing.
    Meanwhile, Champa continued to harass Vietnam
from the south. Lý Nhân-Tông sent General Lý
Thường-Kiệt against Champa in 1075 (before he engaged the Chinese) and again in 1103, resulting
in a Vietnamese victory over the Chams. Lý Nhân-
Tông died in 1127 at the age of sixty-three. His
reign lasted fifty-six years. See LÝ ĐẠO-THÀNH,
LÝ DYNASTY, LÝ THƯỜNG-KIỆT, QUỐC-TỬ-GIÁM.

LÝ THÁI-TỔ (ruled 1010-1028). (Lý Công-Uẩn). The
founder of the Lý Dynasty (1010-1225). Lý Công-
Uẩn was born in Bắc-Ninh Province and raised in
a pagoda. He served as a mandarin under the Early
Lê Dynasty (980-1009). At the death of Emperor
Lê Long-Đinh (1005-1009), the court officials
plotted to place Lý Công-Uẩn on the throne. He
was proclaimed Emperor Lý Thái-Tổ in 1010 at the
age of thirty-five. He moved the capital from
Hoa-Lư to Đại-La Thành which he renamed Thăng-
Long, just west of present-day Hà-Nội.

Lý Thái-Tô appointed a new court. He supported the development of agriculture and was
responsible for the construction of the Cơ-Xá Dike
that afforded protection against the flooding
tidal waters. He established new regulations
concerning taxation and importation of goods.
Under his reign classical education was encouraged.
A temple was built to honor the three predominant
religions or tam-giao (Buddhism, Confucianism
and Taoism). Lý Thái-Tô died in 1028 at the age
of fifty-five. His reign seems to have been a
peaceful and progressive one. See LÊ LONG-ĐỈNH,
LÝ DYNASTY, LÝ CÔNG-UÂN.

LÝ THÁI-TÔNG (ruled 1028-1054). The second emperor
in the Lý Dynasty (1010-1225). Lý Thái-Tông was
designated crown prince by his father but he had
to fight his three brothers for access to the
throne. He reign was filled with small local rebellions as well as armed incursions from Laos
and Champa. He also successfully quelled a sec-
cession from his empire by the Nùng people near
Lạng-Sơn in 1038 and again in 1041. The third
attempt to establish a separate Nùng kingdom in
1048 ended in defeat of the Lý armies. However,
the Chinese did succeed in defeating the Nùng
King, Trí-Cao.
     Lý Thái-Tông led a sea expedition against
Champa which ended in the capture of 5,000 Chams,
thirty elephants, and the royal harem. Of great
importance during his reign was the promulgation
in 1042 of a new penal code, creation of a relay
postal system, distribution of rice in times of
famine and the creation of special dispensations
for returned soldiers such as tax exemptions. He
also concerned himself with the religious and
educational well-being of the people. Lý Thái-
Tông died in 1054 at the age of fifty-five. See
LÝ DYNASTY.

LÝ THÁNH-TÔNG (ruled 1054-1072). The third emperor in
the Lý Dynasty (1010-1225). Lý Thánh-Tông was
noted for his concern and compassion for his subjects. He also reorganized the army and gained
a reputation as a strategist. In fact, the Sung
Dynasty in China copied his methods of military
organization, a point of pride for the Vietnamese.
Upon coming to power he changed the name of the
country from Đại-Cô-Việt to Đại-Việt. Under his
reign, Confucianism thrived as he ordered the
repair and construction of temples dedicated to
Confucius.
     In 1060, during a border incursion, one of

Lý Thánh-Tông's generals captured a Chinese general and his officers. The Chinese court demanded
their release but the Vietnamese refused. This
reflects the military strength and diplomatic
stature of Vietnam at the time. In 1068 in response to repeated attacks from Champa, Lý Thánh-
Tông led an expedition against Champa and captured the king. The Chàm king was released in
exchange for three provinces (located in present-
day Quảng-Bình and Quảng-Trị provinces). Lý
Thánh-Tông died in 1072 at the age of fifty. See
LÝ DYNASTY.

LÝ THẦN-TÔNG (ruled 1128-1138). The fifth emperor in
the Lý Dynasty (1010-1225). Lý Nhân-Tông (1072-
1127) died childless so his adopted son, Sung
Hiên-Hầu was made crown prince and succeeded him
as Emperor Lý Thần-Tông. (Some sources refer to
Sung Hiên-Hầu as the nephew of Lý Nhân-Tông).
His ten year reign was generally peaceful. Border
incursions by Cambodia and Champa did occur but
were effectively dealt with. Under the reign of
Lý Thần-Tông amnesty was granted to prisoners,
all confiscated land was returned to the populace
and the army was allowed to rotate duty every six
months to permit the soldiers to work in their
fields. General Lý Công-Bình was commander of
the army and responsible for repelling the
attacks from Cambodia and Champa as well as maintaining domestic order. Lý Thần-Tông died in
1138 at the age of twenty-three. See LÝ DYNASTY.

LÝ THƯỜNG-KIỆT (1030-1105). A military mandarin of
royal blood during the Lý Dynasty (1010-1225).
He was born in or around 1030 in what is now Hà-
Nội. Lý Thường-Kiệt served as military commander
under the Emperor Lý Nhân-Tông (1072-1127) in the
campaigns against China and Champa. He became a
noted strategist and tactician. He conducted
several successful expeditions into Kwang-Tung
and Kwang-Si provinces of China. He died in
1105, at over seventy years of age. He is still
considered one of Vietnam's national heroes. See
LÝ DYNASTY, LÝ NHÂN-TÔNG.

LÝ-TIẾN. The first native of Giao-Chỉ (a Chinese province which included much of what is now north
Vietnam) to become a mandarin administrator. He
was named Governor (Thứ-Sử) of Giao-Chỉ in 187
A.D. during the Chinese Han Dynasty. This was
indicative of the advanced stage of Chinese
assimilation in that a native of Giao-Chỉ would
meet the requirements for such a position. It

also marked the first concession to local or
ethnic feeling after the assimilation of Chinese
culture and served to draw the Vietnamese people
together. See GIAO-CHỈ.

LÝ TRƯỞNG. See XÃ TRƯỞNG.

LYCEE. A type of high school established in the early
    1900's by the French aimed primarily at training
    those Vietnamese who were expected to serve in
    government positions or go on for college studies.
    Originally, three such schools were established,
    one each in Huế, Hà-Nội and Sài-Gòn. The Lycee
    included both higher-primary and secondary cycles
    of studies. They were administered by the French
    using French as the basic language of instruction.
    See EDUCATION.

                          -M-

MA. See MAA.

MAA. (Also known as the Ma or Cau Ma). An ethno-
    linguistic minority group of highland people
    located principally in southern Quảng-Đức Province.
    The Maa are actually a subgroup of the Koho lin-
    guistic group and, as such, speak a dialect of
    Koho, a Mon-Khmer language. It was reported in
    1972 that there were around 15,000 Maa people
    living in Vietnam. The Maa are the only Koho
    subgroup that have a patriarchal, patrilineal and
    patrilocal society. It is recorded that there
    once was a small Maa nation, a kind of buffer
    state between Champa and Cambodia. It was apparent-
    ly destroyed as the two larger states expanded to
    share a common border. The Maa were known as a
    restless, belligerent people and not pacified by
    the French until 1937. They engage in slash-and-
    burn agriculture, and, in most respects, share
    the same lifestyle and culture with the other
    subgroups of the Koho. See KOHO.

MÃ RIVER (Sông Mã). A river in central Vietnam. It
    originates in Sơn-La Province and flows through
    Laos. It then enters Thanh-Hóa Province where
    it empties into the South China Sea near the
    province capital. It is about 360 kilometers
    (223 miles) in length almost all of which is
    through mountainous terrain. It is extremely
    rapid in the upper part. The famous Đồng-Sơn
    archaeological site is located at the lower

reaches of the river. See ĐÔNG-SƠN.

MẠC ĐĂNG-DOANH (ruled 1530-1540). The second emperor
    in the Mạc Dynasty (1527-1592). He came to
    power when his father, Mạc Đăng-Dung abdicated in
    1530. However, he died in 1540 after ruling only
    ten years. See MẠC DYNASTY.

MẠC ĐĂNG-DUNG (ruled 1527-1530). The first emperor
    and founder of the Mạc Dynasty (1527-1592). He
    was reportedly a descendant of the famous scholar
    Mạc Đinh-Chi of the Trần Dynasty (1225-1400) and
    the son of a fisherman. Under the reign of Em-
    peror Lê Uy-Mục (1505-1509), Mạc Đăng-Dung was
    given a military rank and advanced to the point
    where under Emperor Lê Chiêu-Tông (1516-1524) he
    was in effective control of the throne. In 1524
    he overthrew the emperor and put the deposed
    emperor's brother (Lê Cung-Hoàng (1524-1527)) on
    the throne. Finally, after killing all of his
    enemies and rivals in the court, Mạc Đăng-Dung
    usurped the throne and established the Mạc Dynasty.
        Three years later he abdicated in favor of
    his son and assumed the title of Thái-Thượng-
    Hoàng, a semi-retirement type of position that
    provided for a strong voice in the affairs of
    state. Mạc Đăng-Dung was never able to rally
    the support of the followers of the former Le
    Dynasty. He died in 1540. See LÊ CHIÊU-TÔNG,
    MẠC DYNASTY.

MẠC ĐINH-CHI. A famous scholar, poet, and mandarin
    during the Trần Dynasty (1225-1400). He was a
    small, homely man but very intelligent. He was
    known especially for his ability to compose poems
    extemporaneously. He was also reportedly the
    ancestor of Mạc Đăng-Dung, the founder of the
    Mạc Dynasty (1527-1592).

MẠC DYNASTY (1527-1592). (Nhà Mạc). The key figure
    and founder of the Mạc Dynasty was Mạc Đăng-Dung
    who usurped the throne from the Lê. Although
    he actually ruled only three years, he retained
    control and power of the throne after his ab-
    dication in favor of his son. After the estab-
    lishment of the Mạc Dynasty the supporters of
    the deposed Lê emperors gathered forces and
    initiated a military campaign against the Mạc.
    By 1554 the country was partitioned with the Lê
    in control of the area from Thanh-Hóa southward
    and the Mạc ruling over the area from Sơn-Nam to
    the north. The campaign against the Mạc was led
    by Nguyễn-Kim until his death in 1554. He was

succeeded by General Trịnh-Kiềm. Mạc Kinh-Điền
commanded the forces of the Mạc. Constant attacks and counterattacks took place until 1591.
It was in that year that Trịnh-Tùng (Trịnh-Kiềm's
son) attacked the Mạc capital Thăng-Long (present
day Hà-Nội) and captured the Mạc Emperor and the
Queen Mother. That marked the effective end of
the Mạc Dynasty although the Mạc family retained
autonomous rule in Cao-Bằng Province which was
the result of a special arrangement with the
Chinese court. This lasted until 1667 when Trịnh-
Tùng's son, Trịnh-Tráng, took possession of Cao-
Bằng. See MẠC ĐĂNG-DUNG.

MẠC MẬU-HỢP (ruled 1562-1592). The fifth and last
emperor in the Mạc Dynasty (1527-1592). He took
the throne in 1561 during the struggle with the
Lê Dynasty to the south. Taking advantage of a
weak leader (Trịnh-Cối), Mạc Mậu-Hợp attacked
and almost captured the capital in Thanh-Hóa in
1570. The confrontation between the Mạc and the
Lê became a stand-off until 1592 when the Lê
supporters led by Trịnh-Tùng advanced northward
and finally took the Mac capital at Thăng-Long
(present-day Hà-Nội) in 1592. That marked the
end of the effective rule of the Mạc. Mạc Mậu-
Hợp was later captured. He was tortured in
public for three days and then beheaded. See
MẠC DYNASTY.

MẠC PHÚC-HẢI (ruled 1540-1546). The third emperor in
the Mạc Dynasty (1527-1592). He ruled only six
years until his father's death in 1546. It was
during his reign that Nguyễn-Kim began the long
campaign to restore the rule of the country to
the Lê Emperors. The country was partitioned in
1545 between the Lê (from Thanh-Hóa southward)
and the Mạc (from Sơn-Nam northward). Mạc Phúc-
Hải was succeeded by his son, Mạc Phúc-Nguyên.
See MẠC DYNASTY.

MẠC PHÚC-NGUYÊN (ruled 1546-1561). The fourth emperor
in the Mạc Dynasty (1527-1592). Mạc Phúc-Nguyên
ruled during a period of conflict with the supporters of the Lê Dynasty. The country was
partitioned with the northern part controlled by
the Mạc and the southern part controlled by the
Lê. Mạc Phúc-Nguyên died in 1561 after a reign
of fifteen years. See MẠC DYNASTY.

MÁN. (Also known as Dao, Yao or Zao). An ethno-
linguistic group of highland people in north
Vietnam. The largest concentrations of Mán are

found in Hà-Giang, Yên-Báy, Tuyên-Quang and Bắc-
Thái provinces. The total population of Mán was
placed at about 200,000 in 1967. The Mán peoples
originated in China and have migrated to Vietnam
over the past seven centuries. There are many
subgroups within the Mán, the largest of which
are the Mán-Tiền and the Mán-Đỏ. The Mán live in
the lower altitudes in the highlands. They have
a Chinese-derived written language and possess a
spoken language that belongs to the Sino-Tibetan
language family.

MANDARIN. See QUAN.

MANDARIN ROAD. (Quan-Lộ). A term used primarily by
westerners to refer to highway number one which
runs along the coast from Hà-Nội through Huế to
Sài-Gòn. It was so named because it was the
official route of the Nguyễn Dynasty (1802-1945)
and therefore, it was used by couriers and mandarins of the court.

MẠNH-TỬ. The Book of Mencius. One of the famous four
Chinese books (Tử-Thư) dealing with the philosophy
and doctrine of Confucius. Mạnh-Tử is a collection of the writings of Mencius, one of the
earlier Confucian thinkers. It represents one of
the first attempts to systematize Confucian philosophy. This book was used by scholars and students in traditional Vietnam. It was particularly
important because the mandarinal or triennial
examinations were based, in part, on it. See TỬ-
THƯ.

MARBLE MOUNTAIN. See NGŨ HÀNH-SƠN.

MARRIAGE. See LỄ HÔN-NHÂN.

MAT MAKING. The craft of mat making is traced back to
the reign of Lê Đại-Hành (980-1005). A mandarin
named Lê Thiên-Phước was sent on a mission to
China. While there he was impressed by the prosperity of a village in Quế-Lâm District, Kwang-Si
Province, brought about by the chief occupation of
mat weaving. He returned to Vietnam and retired
in Hải-Thiên Village of Ninh-Bình Province. One
year, the rice fields were flooded leaving people
with no income. He taught the villagers to make
mats, thus he brought prosperity to the village.
When he died, a temple was erected in the village
in his memory by order of the emperor. The area
is still known for its mat weaving industry.
See HANDICRAFTS.

MẶT-TRẬN DÂN-TỘC GIAI-PHÓNG MIỀN NAM. (National Front
for the Liberation of South Vietnam, also known
as the NLF, National Liberation Front or NFL).
A military/political organization established in
Ha-Noi on December 20, 1960. The original purpose of the organization was to create a general
uprising in the Republic of Vietnam in order to
bring about a communist revolution in south Vietnam and reunification of the two Vietnams. Although it continues to function as a front organization, it was succeeded as the official communist governing body of the Republic of Vietnam by
the Provisional Revolutionary Government of the
Republic of South Vietnam. The chairman of the
NFL is Nguyễn Hữu-Thọ, a southern lawyer. He
was named chairman at the organizing congress in
1960. See CHÍNH-PHỦ CÁCH-MẠNG LÂM-THỜI CỘNG-HÒA
MIỀN NAM VIỆT-NAM, NGUYỄN HỮU-THỌ.

MẶT-TRẬN TỔ-QUỐC. (Fatherland Front). A political
front organization in the Democratic Republic of
Vietnam. It is an outgrowth of the Mặt-Trận
Liên-Hiệp Quốc-Dân Việt-Nam (United Vietnam
Nationalist Front) and was established in 1955.

MATHEMATICS. The official study of mathematics was
introduced into Vietnam from China. A mandarin
named Lường Thế-Vinh, a native of Nam-Định Province was recognized for his intelligence and
industriousness. He was sent to China by Emperor Lê Thánh-Tông (1460-1497) where he studied
mathematics and various systems of measurement.
He translated a Chinese book on mathematics entitled Khải-Minh Toán-Học and wrote several others.
It was he who introduced the abacus from China.
A temple was built and dedicated to him in his
native village of Cao-Hương.

MẪU. (Hectare). A unit of area equal to 2.471 acres.
Land is measured by various units, sometimes
varying with the locale. However, the standard
European measurement, the hectare, has been
adopted and is used as the official unit of land
measurement throughout Vietnam.

MEKONG RIVER. (Sông Cửu-Long - literally the River of
Nine Dragons). One of the twelve great rivers of
the world. The Mekong River is 4,500 kilometers
(2,800 miles) long and originates in the high
plateau of Tibet. It flows through Tibet and China
southward where it separates Burma from Laos and,
further downstream, Thailand from Laos. It flows
through Cambodia and Vietnam where it empties

into the South China Sea. The mighty Mekong splits
at Phnom-Penh into two main branches: the Hậu-Giang
(Lower River, or sometimes referred to as the
Bassac River); and the Tiền-Giang (Upper River).
The Hậu-Giang flows directly into the sea while
the larger Tiền-Giang splits at Vĩnh-Long into
several branches and empties into the South China
Sea at six locations. The difference between
high and low tides varies from three feet on the
Hậu-Giang to six feet on the Tiền-Giang.
     A tributary which empties into the Mekong at
Phnom-Penh drains the Ton-Le-Sap Lake in Cambodia.
When the Mekong is in flood stage, the river backs
up into the Ton-Le-Sap. When the flood subsides,
the water flow reverses and flows back into the
sea. The dangers of serious flooding in the
Mekong Delta area are thus sharply reduced due
to this stabilizing effect on the water level.
The River starts to rise around the end of May.
By September it is at its highest point. It then
starts to subside until it reaches its lowest
point in April. The Mekong River deposits rich,
fertile silt in the delta which accounts for the
very high rice producing capacity of the delta.
It is estimated that the coastline is advancing
as much as seventy-nine meters (250 feet) per
year in some places due to the sediment brought
to the sea by the Mekong. In fact, the entire
Mekong Delta area was formed over time by sediment deposits from the Mekong.
     An intricate system of canals, and rivers
throughout the delta coupled with the Mekong
River itself, provides an effective network of
waterways for transportation. Navigation is fac-
ilitated by dredging and constant improvement of
the canals and riverbeds. Sampans, junks and
other shallow draft vessels are most common although larger craft can be accommodated in the
lower reaches of the rivers. See MEKONG RIVER
DELTA, MEKONG RIVER PROJECT, NAM-PHẦN, WATERWAYS.

MEKONG RIVER DELTA. The area in south Vietnam formed
     by the sediment deposits of the Mekong River and
     its five branches. Although the delta areas of
     the Vàm-Cỏ, Sài-Gòn and Đồng-Nai Rivers are often
     included in the Mekong Delta (which makes it a
     total of 67,340 square kilometers or 26,000 square
     miles), the Mekong Delta proper only extends as
     far north on the coast as Gò-Công Province. The
     larger delta area extends about three hundred
     miles in length, including the delta areas of the
     three smaller rivers. About twenty-three thousand
     square kilometers (nine thousand square miles) are

under cultivation. Drainage is effected chiefly
by tidal action. The southern tip of the delta,
the Cà-Mau Peninsula, is covered with dense
jungles. The entire delta area is characterized
by an extensive and complicated network of rivers
and canals which are used for transportation as
well as for water control.
     The Mekong Delta is best known for its rich
rice land. The land, formed by silt deposits, is
very fertile and extends to the immediate shore
line. Sediment is continually being deposited
at the mouths of the rivers resulting in the
extension of the shore line as much as 79 meters
(250 feet) per year. The delta is inhabited
mainly by ethnic Vietnamese. But there is also a
significant minority of Cambodians (Khmers),
mainly in the western and southern regions. The
people are prosperous and rely heavily on the rice-
production based economy. The delta produces
enough rice to supply both south and central Vietnam as well as much of north Vietnam. Other
products of the delta include coconut, pineapple,
sugar cane, fish and some vegetables.
     The Mekong Delta was the last part of Vietnam
to be settled by the ethnic Vietnamese in their
southward expansion (nam-tiến). See MEKONG RIVER,
MEKONG RIVER PROJECT, NAM-PHẦN, WATERWAYS.

MEKONG RIVER PROJECT. (Mekong River Basin Development
     Project). A project for developing the irrigation,
     hydroelectric, and navigational potentials of the
     Mekong River. In 1957 the United Nations Economic
     Commission for Asia and the Far East (ECAFE)
     issued a report entitled "Development of Water
     Resources in the Lower Mekong Basin." In response
     to this report four of the six countries included
     in the Mekong Basin area (Laos, Cambodia, Thailand,
     and the Republic of Vietnam) formed the Committee
     for Coordination of Investigations of the Lower
     Mekong Basin. Burma and the Democratic Republic
     of Vietnam declined to join the effort. Pre-
     liminary surveys were initiated and in 1959 the
     committee appointed its own Executive Agent and
     Secretariat with funds made available from the
     United Nations Development Program (UNDP). A
     permanent office is maintained in Bangkok and
     staffed by United Nations technicians. The
     committee holds several meetings a year in the
     capitals of the four participating countries.
     By 1970, twenty-six nations outside the basin
     area as well as some United Nations agencies and
     private organizations (such as Ford Foundation
     and World Bank) had supplied funds or technical

assistance to the project. Three multi-purpose
dams have been completed while several more are
under way. It is estimated that the total Mekong
Basin could supply over 40 billion kw/h. In
addition to developing hydroelectric power,
several experimental agricultural farms have been
established, and surveys have been undertaken in
such fields as forestry, fishing, transportation
and communications. See MEKONG RIVER, MEKONG
RIVER DELTA.

MEÒ. (Also called Miao). An ethno-linguistic group
of highland people in north Vietnam. They are
located in the highest altitudes of the provinces
of Hà-Giang and Lào-Cai and extend over the border to China and Laos. The population of those
in Vietnam was placed at 219,514 in the 1960 census. The Meo speak a Sino-Tibetan language.
They are divided into five distinct groups: White
Meò, Black Meò, Red Meò, Flowered Meò and the
Meò Mong-Sua. The Meò came to Vietnam relatively
recently. The migration into north Vietnam began in the early nineteenth century. Then
around 1860, concurrent with the T'ai Ping Rebellion in China, a second migration took place.
They swept across north Vietnam and were finally
repelled by the Vietnamese. The Meò have led or
participated in numerous uprisings and rebellions
against the central government over the years.
The Vietnamese as well as the French were in constant conflict with them. A writing system based
on the Vietnamese national script (Quôc-Ngũ) has
recently been developed for the Meò by the Democratic Republic of Vietnam government. The Meò
houses are built on the ground similar to the
ethnic Vietnamese. Maize is the main crop and
is cultivated primarily by swidden agriculture.
Some Meo settlements plant paddy rice. Secondary crops include beans, peas, pumpkin, eggplant,
cucumbers, sorghum, turnips, squash and tobacco.
The kinship is patrilineal, residence after
marriage is either patrilocal or neolocal. The
principal religion is animism, although some
Buddhist deities are venerated.

MERLIN, MARTIAL-HENRI. Governor General of Indochina
from August, 1923 to July, 1925. Although highly
successful as a governor in French Africa, he
became very unpopular in Indochina and had to be
recalled.

MIAO. See MÈO.

MID-AUTUMN FESTIVAL. See TẾT TRUNG-THU.

MIỀN BẮC. See BẮC-PHẦN.

MIỀN NAM. See NAM-PHẦN.

MIỀN TRUNG. See TRUNG-PHAN.

MIẾU. A small village temple used to honor and wor-
    ship a spirit. The Miếu is smaller than a Đền
    and is usually dedicated to a specific spirit or
    saint. There is usually only one or two build-
    ings in a Miếu. Because it is considered to be
    a place where the spirits reside, it is usually
    located in a peaceful location away from the
    residential center such as on a river bank, on a
    hill, or at the edge of the village. Unlike the
    Đình and Đền, the Miếu is maintained by the
    villagers who live closest to the Miếu. There
    is no full time custodian to oversee the temple.
    See ĐỀN, ĐÌNH, MIẾU.

MIỄU. A small shrine or altar used for the worship of
    spirits. It is often found in grottoes, hollow
    trees, thickets or other places where spirits
    are believed to reside.

MINERALS. The most important mineral deposits are
    located in north Vietnam. Coal, with reserves
    estimated at twenty million tons, is by far the
    most important mineral product. Major coal
    fields are located at Quảng-Yên, north of Hải-
    Phòng and at Phan-Me and Tuyên-Quang, northwest
    of Hà-Nội. Iron ore is mined near Thái-Nguyên,
    Vĩnh, and Hà-Tĩnh. Other mineral deposits in-
    clude gold, zinc, chromite, tin, copper, lead,
    phosphate, and limestone. The white sands all
    along the coast contain a high amount of silica
    which is used as a raw material for making glass.
    Salt is manufactured from the sea water, part-
    icularly in central Vietnam. See INDUSTRY.

MINH-ĐẠO GIA-HUẤN. (Minh-Đạo's Book of Family Educa-
    tion). A textbook used by students in tradition-
    al Vietnam. This book contained five hundred
    four-word verses composed by Minh-Đạo, a Chinese
    scholar living in the eleventh century.

MINH-MẠNG (ruled 1820-1840). (Also spelled Minh-Mệnh).
    The second emperor in the Nguyễn Dynasty (1802-
    1945). Minh-Mạng was an accomplished intellectual

who stressed Confucianism and education even more
than his predecessor, Emperor Gia-Long (1802-
1819). He reestablished the national college
(Quốc-Tử-Giám) and refined the civil service
examination system. Although literature thrived
during his reign, he specifically discouraged the
use of nôm, preferring instead to use the traditional Chinese characters. He outlawed Christianity and persecuted the missionaries and their
followers. He resisted the influence of western
cultures and, in fact, feared its effect on
Vietnamese culture. His concern for the Vietnamese traditional society and way of life is attested to by his issuance of the ten moral maxims
which were aimed at preserving the Confucianist
style of cultural stability. His reign was
marked by minor political unrest. Minh-Mạng became suspicious of two national figures, Lê Văn-
Duyệt and Lê-Chất. Both were charged, post-
humously, with treason and their graves destroyed.
Minh-Mạng died in 1840 at the age of fifty after
a reign of twenty years. See LÊ VĂN-DUYỆT, NGUYỄN
DYNASTY, NÔM.

MINH-TÂM BẢO-GIÁM. The Precious Mirror of the Heart.
A compilation of various moral precepts taken
from the Chinese classics. This textbook, written
in Chinese, was used by students and scholars in
traditional Vietnam.

M'NONG. An ethno-linguistic minority group of highland people located in the central highlands.
The M'nong population was estimated to be around
36,000 in 1972, most of whom lived in the western
part of the plateau area of Quảng-Đức Province,
but also extending into Cambodia. They speak a
Mon-Khmer language and can be divided into five
distinct subgroups each with its own dialect.
The M'nong society is matrilineal, descent is
traced through the female line. The family name
is that of the wife and the children are considered as members of the mother's family. The
extended family, or clan, is the basic social
unit. The village is the highest level of political organization. The M'nong have a subsistence economy based primarily on the slash-and-
burn technique of upland rice cultivation, although some villages grow paddy rice. Secondary
crops include fruits, vegetables, sugar cane
and tobacco. The M'nong have an animistic religion. They are known as a fiercely belligerent
people and have historically been hostile to
surrounding tribes as well as to the ethnic Viet-

namese and French. In the early twentieth century, the French explorer and ethnographer, Henri
Matre, and his escort of soldiers were attacked,
killed and beheaded by the M'nong. The French
eventually pacified them and even used them as
militiamen and in local administrative positions.

M'NONG PLATEAU. A plateau southwest of the Ðạc-Lắc
Plateau in the central highlands. The area is
situated in Quảng-Ðức and Phước-Long provinces.

MỘC-DỤC. (Lễ Mộc-Dục). The ceremony of bathing the
body of a deceased person prior to the funeral
rites. The washing of the body includes special
prayers, shampooing the hair, trimming the toe-
nails and fingernails. The ceremony is performed
by the deceased man's son or the deceased woman's
daughter. See CẢI-TÁNG, ĐƯA-ĐÁM.

MỘC-HÓA. The capital city of Kiến-Tường Province.
Population 14,490. The city is situated near
the Cambodian border. See KIẾN-TƯỜNG PROVINCE.

MỌI. A pejorative term meaning "Savage" and used to
refer to the highland ethnic minority peoples.
The term is not commonly used anymore but has
been replaced by the terms montagnard (French),
người thượng-du (meaning highland people) or
người thiểu-số (meaning minority people).

MONOM. (Also called Bonom). An ethno-linguistic
group of people located northeast of the town of
Kontum. They speak a Mon-Khmer language and
have an estimated population of 2,100 (1968).

MONTAGNARD. A French term meaning highlander or
mountain people. It is used to refer to the
ethnic minority people of the Vietnamese highlands.

MỘT CỘT PAGODA. (Chùa Một Cột or One Pillar Pagoda).
A famous wooden pagoda built in Hà-Nội in the
year 1049 by Emperor Lý Thái-Tổng (1028-1054).
It is the oldest existing example of architectural
work in Hà-Nội. According to the annals, the
Emperor met the Buddha in a dream and had the
pagoda erected in honor of the event. The pagoda is built to resemble a lotus flower and rests
on a single wooden pillar in the middle of a pond
to symbolize a "pure" lotus rising from the sea
of sorrow. The architectural lines and carvings
are simple and harmonious. In 1954 before leaving
Hà-Nội, the French blew up the pagoda. It was
then rebuilt by the government of the Democratic

Republic of Vietnam.   See LÝ THÁI-TÔNG.

MỤ-GIA PASS. (Đèo Mụ-Gia). A strategic mountain pass
located in the Trường-Sơn Mountain Range on the
Lao/Vietnam border in Quảng-Bình Province of
central Vietnam. The pass was heavily bombed by
the Americans in the 1960's in an effort to block
the flow of supplies to the south. Highway number fifteen travels through the pass.

MŨI. Cape or point. Individual capes or points are
listed under separate entries. See BÃI-BÙN POINT,
ĐÁ POINT, ĐỒ-SƠN, ĐỒNG POINT, EN POINT, NẠY POINT,
LỒ POINT, NGA-SƠN POINT, RỌN POINT.

MƯỜNG. The second largest ethno-linguistic minority
group in Vietnam (second to the Tày). They are
located in the mountainous area southwest of
the Red River in the provinces of Thanh-Hóa, Sơn-
La, Hà-Tây, Nghĩa-Lộ and Hòa-Bình. There is also
a grouping of Mường in Nghệ-An Province. The
Mường population was recorded as 515,658 in the
1960 census. This represents 2.6% of the total
population of the Democratic Republic of Vietnam
at the time. The historical and cultural relationship between the ethnic Vietnamese and the
Mường is still unclear, although it seems certain
that they both derived from a common stock. The
Mường language is more closely related to Vietnamese than to any of the other minority languages.
There are also similarities in culture, religion,
and physical appearance. It seems that prior to
the first period of Chinese domination, the Mường
and Vietnamese coexisted in what is now north
Vietnam and south China. However, the Vietnamese
were gradually, but strongly influenced by the
Chinese culture while the Mường resisted it. The
Vietnamese abandoned their feudal system around
the eleventh century, i.e., with the establishment of the Lý Dynasty (1010-1225) but the Mường
still retain traces of it. The French began to
extend their influence into the north Vietnamese
highlands in 1802. The Mường rebelled against
Vietnamese control in 1822, 1826-27, 1833 and
again in the 1880's. Each time the rebellions
were quelled.
     The Mường social system is patrilineal and
based on a strong extended family structure.
Males have the exclusive right to own property.
There are traces of an ancient feudal system in
which the village chiefs and the elite class
enjoyed special privileges and authority over
the peasant class. Their economy is agrarian

and is based around the cultivation of dry rice
and a variety of other crops. They also raise
animals and engage in numerous crafts. Their
religion includes the worship of ancestral spirits
and a large pantheon of supernatural beings,
many of which are also found in the oral tradition
of Vietnamese religions. The Mường lacquer their
teeth black when they are about sixteen years old.
Vietnamese and Mường are similar enough that most
Mường can speak Vietnamese. Public education is
conducted in Vietnamese. The Vietnamese and
Mường languages constitute a sub-branch of the
Mon-Khmer language group which is part of the
Austroasiatic language family.

MƯỜNG-MẪN RIVER. (Sông Mường-Mẫn). A river in Bình-
Thuận Province in central Vietnam. The river
flows southeasterly and empties into the South
China Sea at Phan-Thiết, the provincial capital
of Bình-Thuận.

MUSEUMS. The first museum and library was set up in
the eleventh century when Emperor Lý Thái-Tông
(1028-1054), a fervent Buddhist, sent for the
Buddhist scriptures from China and kept them in
the Đại-Hưng Treasury. There are presently five
principal museums in Vietnam. These are located
at Hà-Nội, Thanh-Hóa, Huế, Đà-Nẵng, and Sài-Gòn.
The museum in Huế was heavily damaged in the
fighting during the 1968 Tet holidays. The Đà-
Nẵng museum houses vestiges of the Chàm civilization.

MUSIC. The predominant influence on Vietnamese music
comes from China. Many of the instruments are
derived from Chinese sources, the five-note
(pentatonic) scale and the system of musical
notation are of Chinese origin. The Vietnamese
theater is also closely related to the Chinese
theater. Traces of Indian influence, which came
to Vietnam via Cambodia and Champa are also
noticeable, especially in south Vietnam. However,
Vietnamese music still retains a large degree of
originality in both instrumentation and style.
One particularly unique aspect of Vietnamese
vocal music is the requirement that the melody
conform to the language tones - in other words,
the melody may not go downwards on a word that
has a rising tone.
    Folk music, theater music and classical
music comprise the three broad categories of
traditional Vietnamese music. Folk music takes
the form of work songs (hò), festival songs

(hát quan-họ and hát trống-quân), love songs,
lamentations, childrens' songs, lullabies and songs
for special occasions such as funeral songs. These
folk songs are usually sung by individuals or
groups without instrumentation and, like folk
music the world over, are popular among all classes
of people.

Classical music is much more formal and rigid
than folk music. Often called "learned music",
it includes the official music of the old imperial
court and the chamber music for the entertainment
of the aristocracy. The court music has not been
used since the end of the monarchy (1945). It
was presented with an orchestra of more than
forty musicians. The chamber music of Vietnam
falls into two major categories: hát ả-đào (or-
iginating in north Vietnam) and the ca-Huế (from
central Vietnam).

All theater music of Vietnam is musical and
includes singing, dancing, and instrumentation.
The older forms (hát bội, hát tuồng, and hát chèo)
are native to north Vietnam while the newer forms
(hát bài-chòi and cải-lương) are associated with
the south.

In addition to the musics of the ethnic Vietnamese described above, the various ethnic minorities such as the Chàm, the various highland
peoples and the people of Khmer, Chinese or Indian
ancestry all possess their own unique musical
traditions. See CA HUẾ, CA-DAO, CẢI-LƯƠNG, ĐÀN
BẦU, ĐÀN ĐÁY, ĐÀN NGUYỆT, DÀN TRANH, HÁT Ả-ĐÀO,
HÁT BÀI-CHÒI, HÁT BỘI, HÁT NÓI, HÁT QUAN-HỌ, HÁT
TRỐNG-QUÂN, THEATER, VỌNG-CỔ.

MỸ-SƠN. A village in Quảng-Nam Province in central
Vietnam. It is an important archaeological site
which has yielded many vestiges of the kingdom
of Champa dating back to the fourth century A.D.
Mỹ-Sơn was a religious city at the time when the
heart of the Chàm empire was located in Quảng-Nam
Province, (from the fourth to the eighth century).
A temple dedicated to the worship of Shiva Bhad-
reshvara was built at Mỹ-Son around the middle
of the fourth century but was later destroyed by
fire. See CHAMPA, ĐỒNG-DƯƠNG, TRÀ-KIỆU.

MỸ-THO. The capital city of Định-Tường Province in
south Vietnam. Population 92,891. The city is
located south of Sài-Gòn on highway number four
which runs from Sài-Gòn to Cà-Mau. It was
originally founded in the 1680's by Chinese
refugees who fled from Taiwan for political

reasons, Mỹ-Tho was also the name of what is now
Đinh-Tường Province under the French. On September 30, 1970, Mỹ-Tho was established as an autonomous municipality. See ĐINH-TƯỜNG PROVINCE.

-N-

NAM. Baron, a rank of nobility. See NOBILITY.

NAM-BẮC TRIỀU. The periods in Vietnamese history when
the country was divided into two parts and there
were two dynasties simultaneously claiming sovereignty over the entire country. The first was
from 1527-1592 when the area from Thanh-Hóa southward was under control of the Lê Dynasty (1428-
1788) while the northern part was ruled by the
Mạc Dynasty (1527-1592). The second period was
from 1600 to 1788 when the Trịnh Lords controlled
the area from the Hoành-Sơn Mountains northward
and the Nguyễn Lords occupied the southern part.

NAM-BỘ. See NAM-PHẦN.

NAM-ĐỊNH CITY. The capital city of Nam-Hà Province
in north Vietnam. It is known as a center of
the textile industry. Population 175,000 (1972).
See NAM-HÀ PROVINCE.

NAM-ĐỊNH PROVINCE. See NAM-HÀ PROVINCE.

NAM-GIAO. (Tế Nam-Giao). A ceremony in honor of the
God of heaven and earth. The Tế Nam-Giao was
probably the most important religious ceremony
performed in Vietnam. The rites were performed
and presided over by the Emperor. The ceremony
is Confucian in origin but is certainly compatible
with the other major religions in Vietnam. It
was originally performed annually. However,
since the third year of the reign of Emperor
Đồng-Khánh (1885-1889) the ritual was held every
three years. The last emperor to perform the
Tế Nam-Giao was Emperor Bảo-Đại (1925-1945) on
March 29, 1942 in the city of Huế.
     The large outdoor altar was constructed in
the village of An-Cựu, about three kilometers
(less than two miles) from the imperial citadel
at Huế. Preparations actually started a year
before with the selection of the several hundred animals to be used for sacrifice. These
were all raised separately from the other stock.
A procession took the Emperor and his entourage

from the palace to the site of the ritual. Many
of the rites performed by the Emperor were open
for only a select few to observe. No women were
permitted to watch. After many hours of ceremony,
the royal party would return to the palace grounds.
His procession would be greeted by the citizenry.

NAM-HÀ PROVINCE. (Formerly Hà-Nam and Nam-Định provinces). A coastal lowland province in north
Vietnam. It is situated north of Ninh-Bình Province and borders on Thái-Bình, Hải-Hưng, and Hà-
Tây provinces to the north and northeast. The
population of the province is estimated at
1,507,397 (1969) and the land mass is given at
2,335 square kilometers (901 square miles). The
city of Nam-Định (population 175,000) is the third
largest city in the Democratic Republic of Vietnam and serves as the capital of Nam-Hà Province.
The city is located about thirty-two kilometers
(twenty miles) inland from the sea and is a major
industrial center. The Nam-Định textile mill,
built under the French in 1899-1900, is one of
the largest and oldest textile factories in Vietnam. The city is linked to many other population
and industrial centers via railroad, waterway,
and highway which facilitates its industrial
utility.
     Nam-Hà Province has about seventy-five kilo-
meters (forty-six miles) of coastline. With the
exception of a small concentration of Mường in
the Lạc-Thủy area, there are no ethnic minorities
native to Nam-Hà. The majority of the inhabitants
are Buddhist although the province has a strong
following of Catholics. This area was one of the
first to be evangelized by Catholic missionaries.
Portuguese priests arrived here in 1627. At Kẻ-
Sở, near the town of Phủ-Lý, there stands a famous church built by Bishop Puginier between
1879 and 1894. This became a center for the
propagation of the Catholic church, complete with
schools and printing presses.
     There are many well-known pagodas and churches
throughout the province. Especially well-known
are the pagodas built on the two mountains - Núi
Đội-Sơn and Núi Đội-Điệp. These were built at
the direction of Emperor Gia-Long (1802-1819).
Nam-Hà is also the native province of the Trần
Emperors (1225-1400). A temple (Đền Thiên-Trường)
built in 1238 and dedicated to the ancestors of
the Trần rulers is located at the village of Tức-
Mạc. See ĐỘI-SƠN PAGODA, NAM-ĐỊNH.

NAM-HẢI. South China Sea. The entire eastern coastline of Vietnam borders on the South China Sea.

NAM-KIM MOUNTAIN RANGE. A chain of mountains in north
Vietnam. It is actually a minor chain belonging
to the larger Hoàng-Liên-Sơn Mountain Range. The
tallest mountain in the chain is Lam-Cung Mountain which stands 2,917 meters (9,570 feet). The
chain extends from the Keo-Co Pass to the Khao-
Kim Pass. See HOÀNG-LIÊN-SƠN MOUNTAIN RANGE.

NAM-KỲ. See NAM-PHẦN.

NAM-NGÃI PLAINS. (Đồng-Bằng Nam-Ngãi). That part of
the central coastal plains extending from the
Hải-Vân Pass southward to the Én Point in Quảng-
Ngãi Province and including the lowland areas of
Quảng-Nam, Quảng-Tín and Quảng-Ngãi provinces.
It measures about 3,250 square kilometers (1,245
square miles). There are two main rivers in this
area - the Cái (or Thú-Bồn) and the Trà-Bồng
Rivers. The region is characterized by a narrow
sandy strip on the coast which is dotted with
fishing villages and a larger parallel strip of
farm land. The soil is poor and subject to
drought, flooding and, in certain places, saltwater intrusion. See CENTRAL COASTAL PLAINS.

NAM-PHẦN. (Also known as Nam-Bộ, Nam-Kỳ or Miền-Nam).
South Vietnam. That portion of Vietnam which
lies south of the Trường-Sơn Mountain Range. The
northern limits of the area are the northern borders of the provinces of Bình-Tuy, Long-Khánh,
and Phước-Long. The region is dominated by the
Mekong River Delta and also includes the delta
areas of the Đồng-Nai, Vàm-Cỏ and Sài-Gòn rivers.
The area is characterized by rich rice land, a
vast system of waterways, rubber plantations in
the northern part and an absence of high mountains and highland tribal minorities. There are,
however, a significant number of ethnic Cambodians
(Khmer), especially in the western and southern
parts, and ethnic Chinese, mainly in the Sài-Gòn/
Chợ-Lớn area. The people of south Vietnam exhibit
a distinct cultural individuality with strong influences from Cambodia. The southern dialect of
Vietnamese is also clearly distinguishable from
the central and northern dialects. See MEKONG
RIVER, MEKONG RIVER DELTA, SOUTHERN COASTAL
PLAINS.

NAM-PHONG. (Tập-Chí Nam-Phong). A popular intellectual journal published in Hà-Nội from July, 1917
to December, 1934 for a total of 210 issues.
Phạm-Quỳnh was Editor-in-Chief and publisher. The
magazine included translations, social science

research and collections of old literary works
in both sino-Vietnamese and nôm.

NAM-TIẾN. (Also called "the march to the south").
The process by which the ethnic Vietnamese expanded their territory southward from the Red
River Delta to include all of what is now referred to as Vietnam (north, central and south
Vietnam). Although this process of southward
expansion actually began sometime in the period
of ancient history (257 B.C. - 938 A.D.), most
historians consider the establishment of independence from China (939 A.D.) as marking the
beginning of the nam-tiến.
The reasons or causes of the march to the
south are many and complicated. Among the chief
reasons usually cited are population pressure,
political instability, Chinese military power,
and available land. The process was slow and,
for the most part, peaceful, only occasionally
was it consolidated or advanced by a large military push. The direction of expansion was
predetermined by the Vietnamese requirement for
land suitable for paddy rice cultivation and by
a lack of other alternatives (they were faced
with mountains to the west, the sea to the east
and the powerful Chinese to the north). The
eastern coast of Vietnam is composed of a series
of small deltas providing outlets to the sea for
the waterways of the Trường-Sơn Mountain Range.
The Vietnamese went southward from one delta to
another, continually advancing their frontier
at the expense of the southern neighbor, Champa,
and later, Cambodia. The nam-tiến finally ended in 1834 when Cambodia ceded the regions of
Sà-Đéc and Châu-Đốc.
The march to the south was not just a hap-
hazard spillover of population. It was directly
supported and directed by the Vietnamese government. Settlers were recruited and promised land
and protection in return for moving to the frontier. These people were often prisoners, adventurers or other soldiers of fortune who were
promised a parcel of land and an honorable status in the new village in return for opening the
frontier. These people were expected to clear
and till the land, and always be ready to revert
to being a soldier whenever an enemy threatened.
The regular Vietnamese armies also provided a
pool of manpower - usually eager to settle down
after a war or battle was over - for settline
the frontier. See LÃO-TRẠI, NÔNG-TRẠI.

NAM-VIỆT. (Chinese - Nan-Yüeh). A kingdom founded
    in 207 B.C. by a Chinese General, Triệu-Đà. The
    kingdom was formed from the three Chinese Command-
    aries (Canton, Siun-Chou and Nan-Ninh) plus the
    lands to the south which now form the provinces
    of Thanh-Hóa, Nghệ-An and Hà-Tĩnh. The capital
    of Nam-Việt was Phiên-Ngu (Canton). Although
    Sinization was not forced, the founding of Nam-
    Việt was significant in that it represented the
    introduction of the first elements of Chinese
    civilization. Nam-Việt accepted Chinese suzer-
    ainty in 196 B.C. but renounced it again in 112
    B.C. This resulted in the invasion and occupation
    of the kingdom by China in 111 B.C. and conse-
    quently the end of Nam-Việt. See TRIỆU-ĐÀ,
    TRIỆU DYNASTY.

NÀNG-HẦU. Concubine. In traditional Vietnam, if a
    man's first wife did not bear a male child, or if
    the male child died, he might take a concubine.
    Most often the concubine would be a young girl
    from a poor family. A price would be paid for
    the girl. Any children born by the concubine
    would be considered as the children of the man's
    wife.

NẠP-TỆ. See ĂN HỎI.

NATIONAL FRONT FOR THE LIBERATION OF SOUTH VIETNAM.
    See MẶT-TRẬN DÂN-TỘC GIẢI-PHÓNG MIỀN NAM.

NẠY POINT. (Mũi Nạy, also called Cape Varella). A
    cape or point extending into the South China Sea
    about forty kilometers (twenty-five miles) south-
    east of Tuy-Hòa in Phú-Yên Province.

NEM. A sausage-type of pork dish. The lean meat is
    pounded fine in a mortar, mixed with a powder
    made of grilled rice and spices then tightly
    packed in banana leaves. It is allowed to stand
    for a few days until it becomes a little acid.

NEW VIETNAM REVOLUTIONARY FRONT. See TÂN-VIỆT CÁCH-
    MỆNH ĐẢNG.

NGA-SƠN POINT. (Mũi Nga-Sơn). A cape or point ex-
    tending into the South China Sea. It is located
    on the border between Ninh-Bình and Thanh-Hóa
    provinces. Nga-Sơn is also the name of a district
    in Thanh-Hóa Province.

NGÂM. (1) A form of poetry written in the style of

Sông-Thất Lục-Bát (two seven-word lines followed
by one six-word line and one eight-word line) and
used to express sadness.
(2) An art form of reciting poetry in a chanting
voice. It is a popular folk tradition enjoyed by
all classes of society and not just reserved for
the literati. It is used to express the emotions
of a poem, such as sorrow, pain, love, etc.

NGANG PASS. (Đèo Ngang, also historically called An-
    Nam-Quan meaning Gateway to An-Nam). A pass in
    the Trường-Sơn Mountain Range along the coast
    in Quảng-Bình Province in central Vietnam. The
    pass is situated at the point where the Hoành-
    Sơn Mountain Chain extends out to the sea coast
    forming a natural barrier for north/south travel.
    This pass served as a natural boundary between
    Vietnam and Champa, and later between the terri-
    tory controlled by the Trịnh Lords and that con-
    trolled by the Nguyễn Lords in the seventeenth
    and eighteenth centuries.

NGÂN-SƠN MOUNTAIN RANGE. (Dãy Ngân-Sơn). A chain
    of mountains located in northern Bắc-Thái and Cao-
    Bằng provinces in north Vietnam. The highest
    peak in the chain is Pia-Ouac (1,931 meters or
    6,340 feet) in Cao-Bằng Province.

NGÀY GIỖ. (Also called Ngay Kỵ-Nhạt). The anniver-
    sary of the death of someone. The most important
    holiday in the practice of ancestor worship. The
    death anniversary day is observed by Vietnamese
    of all religions, but only those who believe in
    ancestor worship will actually make ceremonial
    offerings. The head of the immediate family
    (Gia-Trưởng) presides over the celebration. The
    observance can be modest or large according to
    the resources of the family, and according to the
    relationship of the dead to the person who has
    organized the affair. Usually in the observance
    of the death anniversary of a parent or grand-
    parent, all members of the extended family are
    invited to attend as well as close friends in the
    village. The guests usually bring an offering
    such as tea, wine, etc. Each guest usually per-
    forms the ritual of making an offering and pray-
    ing to the spirit of the dead person being honored.
    The guests are then invited to chew betel and
    have tea.
        The banquet is then served. The older men
    sit separately as do the older women. The head
    of the family must take care to seat people of
    the same social status together. After the

guests have left, the head of the family burns
ceremonial golden leaves or simulated paper money
for the use of the spirit of the deceased. With
this ritual, the celebration of the anniversary
of the death day is complete.

The first anniversary of one's death is
called the ngày giỗ đầu or ngày tiểu-tường. The
second anniversary is called ngày giỗ hết or ngày
đại-tường. Each observance of the death day after the second year is called ngày giỗ thường or
ngày cát-kỵ. Similar celebrations are also held
in honor of the head of an extended family (ngày
giỗ họ), the patron saint of a village (ngày giỗ
làng) the patron saint of a profession or trade
(ngày giỗ phường), and in honor of the Đống-Đa
Battle (ngày giỗ Đống-Đa). See CULT OF THE
ANCESTORS, ĐẠI-TƯỜNG, ĐỐT MÃ, HÓA VÀNG, NGÀY GIỖ
HỌ, NGÀY GIỖ LÀNG, NGÀY GIỖ TỔ HÙNG-VƯỜNG, TIÊN-
SỬ, TIỂU-TƯỜNG.

NGÀY GIỖ ĐỐNG-ĐA. An annual celebration in memory of
the famous Đống-Đa battle in which Nguyễn-Huệ defeated the Chinese invaders outside Hà-Nội in
1789. The celebration is held on the fifth day
of the first lunar month in the village of Đống-
Quang in the municipality of Hà-Nội. Normally,
a ngày giỗ is a holiday commemorating the death
of someone. The Ngày Giỗ Đống-Đa is held on the
anniversary of a battle, but can be said to be in
commemoration of the thousands of troops who
died there. See ĐỐNG-ĐA BATTLE, NGÀY GIỖ, NGUYỄN-
HUỆ.

NGÀY GIỖ HỌ. (Also called Ngày Giỗ Tổ). The celebration of the anniversary of the death of the
founder of an extended family or clan (Họ). The
head of the extended family (Trưởng-Tộc) presides
over the celebration. He is also responsible
for the patrimony (Hưởng-Hỏa) which is used in
part, to pay for the costs involved in celebrating
the Ngày Giỗ Họ. Even so, all members of the clan
must also contribute. There are no outside guests
invited to the observance. All the heads of the
immediate families within the clan must attend.
After the rituals and banquet, the affairs of the
clan are discussed. See NGÀY GIỖ, HỌ.

NGÀY GIỖ LÀNG. (Also called Ngày Thần-Kỵ). The anniversary of the death of the founding fathers or
the patron saints of a village. While the
actual rituals are performed in one day, the holiday often lasts for several days or a week, depending on the traditions of the locale. The

mood is festive, especially if it falls in the
spring or fall. The celebration starts with a
ceremony to officially open the center doors of
the village communal house (Đình) which otherwise
are closed. A ritual is held in which the statue
of the patron saint is cleaned. The main memorial
ceremony (Tế-Lễ) is then begun. This includes
the reading of a eulogy which recounts the life
and good deeds of the patron saint. After it is
read the eulogy is burned as a part of the ritual
in order that the words of tribute will rise to
follow the spirit of the saint. Finally, the
people go in a procession from the Đình to the
pagoda and back to the Đình. The procession includes standard bearers, musicians and the village elders and leaders in full regalia. An
important part of the ngay gio lang is the theatrical presentation which depicts the key events
in the life of the patron saint. See ĐÌNH, NGÀY
GIỖ, THÀNH-HOÀNG, XÃ.

NGÀY GIỖ TỔ HÙNG-VƯƠNG. The annual celebration in
honor of the eighteen emperors of the semi-legend-
ary dynasty of Hồng-Bàng, all of whom took the
name of Hùng-Vương. The Hồng-Bàng Dynasty (2879-
258 B.C.) is considered to be the founding dynasty of what is now known as Vietnam and the
common ancestors of the ethnic Vietnamese people.
Consequently, the cult of Hùng-Vương is celebrated widely. The holiday falls on the tenth
day of the third lunar month. The main temple
dedicated to the Hùng-Vương rulers is located in
Cổ-Tích Village in Phú-Thọ Province (now part of
Vinh-Phu Province). It is here that the principal celebration has traditionally been held.
The emperor used to send a representative to
preside over the ceremony. See HỒNG-BÀNG DYNASTY,
HÙNG-VƯƠNG, NGÀY GIỖ.

NGÀY RẰM. See RẰM.

NGHỆ-AN PROVINCE. A coastal province in central Vietnam. It is situated north of Hà-Tĩnh Province
and south of Thanh-Hóa Province. The population
of Nghệ-An is estimated at 1,221,842 (1960). The
provincial capital is the city of Vinh. Nghệ-An
is perhaps best known for its revolutionary spirit.
Among the more famous revolutionaries who were
native to Nghệ-An are Hồ Chí-Minh and Phan Bội-
Châu.

NGHỆ-SƯ. (Also called Tiên-Sư or Thánh-Su). The
patron saint of a trade or profession. See TIÊN-
SƯ.

NGHỆ-TĨNH UPRISING. (1893-1895). A revolt against
the French which was led by the famous scholar,
Phan Đình-Phùng, in Nghệ-An and Hà-Tĩnh provinces.
The rebels finally broke up their organization
in response to the Nguyễn Court and after the
death of Phan Đình-Phùng. See PHAN ĐÌNH-PHÙNG.

NGHỆ-TĨNH UPRISING. (1930-1931). A general uprising
against the French led by the Indochinese Communist Party. Public demonstrations began in May,
1930 and continued until September 12, 1930 when
French aircraft fired on a crowd of six thousand
demonstrators. From then on the uprising became
clandestine and took the form of assassinations
and terror. The French ended the revolt by capturing the communist leaders and by taking firm
administrative control of the area. The uprising
was also known as the Nghệ-Tĩnh Soviet Movement.

NGHĨA-LỘ CITY. The capital city of Nghĩa-Lộ Province
in north Vietnam. The city is located on the
Ngòi Tre River.

NGHĨA-LỘ PROVINCE. A mountainous province in north
Vietnam. It is bordered on the north by Lai-Châu,
Lào-Cai and Yên-Bảy provinces, on the south by
Sơn-La Province and on the east by Vĩnh-Phú Province. The provincial capital, Nghĩa Lộ City is
located on the Ngòi Tre River. The province is
inhabited predominantly by highland people of
the Thổ and Mán ethno-linguistic groups. Nghĩa-
Lộ Province was established after the partition
of Vietnam in 1954 and is a part of the Tây-Bắc
Autonomous Zone.

NGHINH XUÂN CEREMONY. See LỄ NGHINH XUÂN.

NGÔ ĐÌNH-CẨN. The younger brother of former President
Ngô Đình-Diệm. Less educated than his brothers,
Ngô Đình-Cẩn played a role similar to that of a
feudal lord during Ngô Đình-Diệm's presidency.
He ruled central Vietnam with an extensive intelligence and police network, almost independent
of the central government. He was shot by a
firing squad in Sài-Gòn after Diệm was overthrown
in November, 1963. See NGÔ ĐÌNH-DIỆM.

NGÔ ĐÌNH-DIỆM (1901-1963). First President of the Republic of Vietnam. He was born in central Vietnam into a Catholic aristocratic family. He
attended a French Catholic school in Huế and then
went on to study at Quốc-Học College, which was
founded by his father. In 1921 he graduated from

the School for Law and Administration in Hà-Nội.
Diệm entered the mandarin corps under Emperor
Khải-Định (1916-1925) and was made governor of
Phan-Thiết in 1929. At this early stage in his
career he was already fighting the Communist
Revolutionary Youth.

Emperor Bảo-Đại (1925-1945) appointed him
Minister of the Interior in 1933. However, he
became frustrated over his inability to bring
about legislative reforms and resigned his post
the same year and relinquished his titles and
decorations. For the next ten years he lived a
quiet life in Huế, keeping in contact with other
anti-French nationalists, including Phan Bội-Châu.

When the Japanese occupied Vietnam in 1940,
Ngô Đinh-Diệm tried to collaborate with them for
an independent Vietnam. He was offered a position as Premier under Bảo-Đại (the first of
many such offers) but he did not accept. After
the August Revolution in 1945 he was kidnapped
by the Việt-Minh and taken to the mountains in
north Vietnam. It is reported that Hồ Chí-Minh
offered him a position but Diệm walked out on
him. He was later released in accordance with
the release of political prisoner clause of the
March 8, 1946 accords between the French and Việt-
Minh.

In 1949, Diệm and his brother, Monsignor Ngô
Đinh-Thục, visited Japan (to see Cường-Để), the
United States and Europe. Diệm returned to the
United States in 1951 and stayed for two years
at a seminary in New Jersey. He toured the country speaking at American universities advocating
an anti-communist, anti-French, nationalism.
After returning to Europe in 1953 he was invited
again by Emperor Bảo-Đại to serve in the Vietnamese government. Finally, after the fall of
Điện-Biên-Phủ, he accepted the post of Prime
Minister with full dictatorial powers. On July 7,
1954 Diệm announced his first cabinet. Although
the Geneva Accords called for elections in 1956
for the unification of the country, Diệm refused.
He did, however, call for a national referendum
on October 23, 1955 to decide between himself or
Bảo-Đại as Chief of State. Diệm won with 98%
of the votes. On October 27, 1955 he proclaimed
the southern half of Vietnam to be the Republic
of Vietnam. He formed a commission to draft a
constitution which guaranteed his position
through a five-year period. In April, 1961,
presidential elections were held in which Diệm
received 88% of the votes.

Finally on November 1, 1963, Ngô Đinh-Diệm
and his brother Ngô Đinh-Nhu were killed in a
coup that was engineered by his army. Diệm was,
above all, a Catholic, Confucianist, and an un-
compromising anti-communist. During the first
few years of his presidency, he successfully
consolidated his power through manipulation,
bribery, and force. However, he became increasingly heavy handed and isolated from the people.
He concentrated all the power as well as all his
trust and confidence, in his immediate family -
specifically Mr. Ngô Đinh-Nhu, Madam Ngô Đinh-Nhu
and Mr. Ngô Đinh-Cẩn. In 1963, the situation
deteriorated rapidly until November when after
six months of violent political confrontation
between the Buddhists and the President (complicated by the growing communist insurgency) Diệm
was toppled. See NGÔ ĐINH-CẨN, NGÔ ĐINH-NHU
(MADAM), NGÔ ĐINH-NHU (MR.), NGÔ ĐINH-THỤC, VIỆT-
NAM CỘNG-HÒA. CẦN-LAO NHÂN-VỊ CÁCH-MẠNG ĐẢNG.

NGÔ ĐINH-NHU (MADAM). (Trần Lệ-Xuân, usually referred
to as Madam Nhu). Daughter of Trần Văn-Chương,
lawyer and ambassador to the United States under
President Ngô Đinh-Diệm, wife of Counselor Ngô
Đinh-Nhu and sister-in-law of President Ngô Đinh-
Diệm. She was the official hostess under President Diệm (1955-1963). She was an aggressive,
showy, controversial, and influential member of
the ruling family. She organized the Women's
Solidarity Movement and the women's paramilitary
corps. Her moralistic decrees that, among other
things, outlawed dancing, contraceptives, gambling and divorce, caused her to be highly unpopular. She was out of the country at the time of
the 1963 coup and has never returned to Vietnam
since then. See NGÔ ĐINH-DIỆM, NGÔ ĐINH-NHU (MR.).

NGÔ ĐINH-NHU (MR.). The younger brother of President
Ngô Đinh-Diệm. He was an ardent Catholic, shrewd
political strategist, and a key figure in the
regime of Ngô Đinh-Diệm. He was trained in
French schools. In 1945 he became political ad-
visor to Ngô Đinh-Diệm and probably his most
trusted counselor. In 1955 he formed the Cần-Lao
Nhân-Vị Cách-Mạng Đảng (Revolutionary Personalist
Worker's Party). Ngô Đinh-Nhu was killed on
November 1, 1963 together with his brother Diệm
in a coup that was engineered by the army generals.
See CẦN-LAO NHÂN-VỊ CÁCH-MẠNG ĐẢNG, NGÔ ĐINH-DIỆM,
NGÔ ĐINH-NHU (MADAM), VIỆT-NAM CỘNG-HÒA.

NGÔ ĐINH-THỤC (BISHOP). The older brother of President
Ngô Đinh-Diệm. He became the Archbishop of Huế
and extremely influential in both church and
government. He founded the Catholic University
of Đà-Lạt. He was abroad when his brothers were
killed in the coup of November 1, 1963 and has
remained in exile in Europe. See NGÔ ĐINH-DIỆM.

NGÔ DYNASTY (939-965). (Nhà Ngô, Triều Ngô). The
dynasty founded by Ngô-Quyền in 939 A.D. which
marked the end of one thousand years of Chinese
domination. The dynasty was characterized by
turbulence and internal fighting. Ngô-Quyền
ruled until his death in 944 A.D. after which his
brother-in-law, Dương Tam-Kha, usurped the throne
and remained in power for five years. In 951
the two rightful heirs to the throne (Ngô Xương-
Văn and Ngô Xương-Ngập) replaced the usurper and
ruled jointly until 964. The capital was established at Cổ-Loa in present day Vĩnh-Phú Province.
        Ngô-Quyền is known as Tiền Ngô-Vương (Earlier
Ngô King) and Ngô Xương-Văn and Ngô Xương-Ngập
are jointly known as Hậu Ngô-Vương (Later Ngô
Kings). The Ngô Dynasty was also marked by a
feudalistic character that developed more fully
after the death of Ngô-Quyền. Twelve warlords
divided the country among themselves and enjoyed
almost complete independence. See NGÔ-QUYỀN.

NGÔ-QUYỀN (ruled 939-944). The founder and first ruler
in the Ngô Dynasty (939-965). Ngô-Quyền served
as a general under one of the feudal lords of the
Chinese Protectorate of An-Nam. In 938 he led
his armies against the occupying forces of the
Chinese in reprisal for the death of his lord
at the hands of the Chinese. His final victory,
the famous battle on the Bạch-Đằng River, ended
the thousand years of Chinese domination. With
his capital at Cổ-Loa in present day Vĩnh-Phú
Province, he founded the first independent Vietnamese dynasty. His reign lasted only six years
ending with his death at forty-seven years of age.
        In addition to establishing independence
from China which was to last nine hundred years,
he also reorganized the court, established standards of measurement and reorganized the political
life of the country. Unfortunately, the dynasty
that he founded was marked by feudalism, internal
instability and the rise of local warlords. See
BẠCH-ĐẰNG BATTLE, CỔ-LOA, NGÔ DYNASTY.

NGÔ SĨ-LIÊN. An historian and scholar, he authored
the fifteen volume national history, Đại-Việt
Sử-Ký Toàn-Thư. This work was commissioned by
Emperor Lê Thánh-Tông (1460-1497) and was completed in 1479. See ĐẠI-VIỆT SỬ-KÝ TOÀN-THƯ.

NGÔ VĂN-CHIÊU (1878-1932). The founder of the Cao-Đài
Religious sect. He was born in Chợ-Lớn on February 28, 1878. He became a civil servant and
was assigned to Phú-Quốc Island. He was known as
a fervent spiritualist and holy man. While on
Phú-Quốc in 1919, Ngô Văn-Chiêu experienced a
major divine revelation which led him to form-
ulate the Cao-Đài doctrine. After he was transferred back to Sài-Gòn in 1924 he began to travel
and preach his new faith. In 1926, with the
assistance of Lê Văn-Trung, the Colonial Counsellor, he founded the Cao-Đài religion (Đại-Đạo
Tam-Kỳ Phổ-Độ). He died on April 18, 1932 in
the Tiên-Giang area but the Cao-Đài church continued to grow into a major religious organization
in the Tây-Ninh Province area with a significant
number of followers throughout south and central
Vietnam. See CAO-ĐÀI, TÂY-NINH.

NGỌC-KRINH MOUNTAIN. (Núi Ngọc-Krinh, also known as
Núi No-Ko-Rin). A mountain north of Kontum City
in the central highlands. It has an elevation
of 2,025 meters (6,644 feet).

NGỌC-LINH MOUNTAIN. (Núi Ngọc-Linh). The tallest
mountain in the Trường-Sơn Mountain Range. It
is located in Kontum Province about 128 kilometers (75 miles) inland from the coast. It
stands 2,598 meters (8,521 feet) high.

NGỌC-PAN MOUNTAIN. (Núi Ngọc-Pan). A mountain in
Kontum Province. It has an elevation of 2,251
meters (7,385 feet).

NGỌC-SƠN TEMPLE. (Đền Ngọc-Sơn). A temple built in
the eighteenth century on a green islet in the
middle of the Lake of the Restored Sword (Hồ
Hoàn-Kiếm). It is linked with the bank of the
lake by a wooden bridge called Cầu Thê-Húc which
was built in 1885. See HOÀN-KIẾM LAKE.

NGŨ HÀNH SƠN. (Also known as Núi Non-Nước or Marble
Mountain). An outcropping of marble near the
coast in Quảng-Nam Province in central Vietnam.
There are five mounds in all. The name Ngũ Hành
Sơn was given by Emperor Minh-Mạng (1820-1840).
There are numerous temples and pagodas which are

located in the grottoes which have been formed in
the mounds as well as on the surface in and around
the area. Craftsmen use the marble to fashion
artifacts at the foot of the hills which are then
marketed in surrounding towns.

NGŨ KINH. The Five Classics. Five of the earliest
Chinese books dating from the second century B.C.
These famous five classics are venerated works
and include Kinh Thi (The Book of Poetry); Kinh
Thư (The Book of Records); Kinh Xuân Thu (The
Annals of Spring and Autumn); Kinh Dich (The Book
of Changes), and Kinh-Lễ (The Book of Rites).
These were used by scholars and students in traditional Vietnam. They were particularly important for those who were preparing for the mandarinal (civil service) examinations which were
based, in part, on these five works. See KINH
DỊCH, KINH LỄ, KINH THI, KINH THƯ, KINH XUÂN THU.

NGŨ-NGÔN. A form of poetry in which each line of
poetry contains five words.

NGŨ THIÊN TỰ. The Book of Five-thousand Characters.
A compilation of 5,000 Chinese characters and
their meaning in Vietnamese arranged under head-
ings such as astrology, politics, and morals.
This vocabulary book was used to teach Chinese
characters to Vietnamese students in traditional
Vietnam.

NGŨ THƯỜNG. The five basic or cardinal virtues.
These are based on the Confucianist teachings
of the Chinese classics and include: nhân (bene-
volence), nghĩa (righteousness), lễ (propriety),
trí (wisdom), and tín (sincerity).

NGUYỄN AN-NINH. A revolutionary who was active
against the French in the early 1900's. Born in
Hóc-Môn District of Gia-Định Province in south
Vietnam, he received his bachelor degree in law
from France. Upon returning to Vietnam he refused a high position in the French colonial
administration and chose instead to publish a
newspaper. Because he was constantly critical
of the French his paper was closed and he was
imprisoned for sentences ranging from eighteen
months to five years. He died in July, 1943.

NGUYỄN-ANH. (Also known as Nguyễn Phúc-Anh, Nguyễn
Vương and later Emperor Gia-Long). The nephew
of the Nguyễn Lord Nguyễn Phúc-Thuần. He proclaimed himself King in 1780 but was driven
from Vietnam by the Tây-Sơn in 1783. He solicit-

ed reinforcements from Thailand which were again
routed in 1784.

Nguyễn-Anh sought refuge in Thailand where
he prepared to return to Vietnam. He requested
military assistance from France. The French
agreed but later dropped the agreement. However,
a French missionary, Pigneau de Behaine, (Bishop
of Adran), did manage to raise troops and supplies which were delivered in 1789. Meanwhile,
taking advantage of the disunity of the Tây-Sơn
brothers Nguyễn-Anh invaded the southern part
of the Tây-Sơn territory and managed to capture
Gia-Định in 1788. Using Gia-Định as a base, he
proceeded to attack the Tây-Sơn capital of Qui-
Nhơn which he captured from Nguyễn-Nhạc in 1793.
But, he was quickly routed by Tây-Sơn troops
from the north. He attacked Qui-Nhơn again in
1797 and a third time in 1799 at which time the
city fell and was occupied. He then went on to
capture the central capital of Phú-Xuân.

In 1802 Nguyễn-Anh proclaimed himself Em-
peror Gia-Long and marched north to capture
Thăng-Long and unify the country under the name
of Vietnam with the capital at Huế (near Phú-
Xuân). See GIA-LONG, HUẾ, NGUYỄN DYNASTY, NGUYỄN-
NHẠC, TÂY-SƠN REBELLION, PIGNEAU DE BEHAINE,
BISHOP.

NGUYỄN BỈNH-KHIÊM (1491-1585). (Also known as Trạng-
Trình). A scholar and prophet under the Mạc Dynasty (1527-1592). Born in Hải-Dương Province,
he passed the civil service examinations at the
age of forty-four. However, he served at the
court only eight years. He resigned when he
could not convince the emperor to execute eighteen other mandarins. He retired to a village
life where he taught such pupils as Phùng Khắc-
Khoan. His poems often praised the virtues of
a quiet life, and were written in Sino-Vietnamese.
Many of his prophecies have materialized, including the end of the French domination and the
downfall of the Diệm regime.

NGUYỄN CAO-KỲ (1930-   ). General officer in the
Vietnamese air force and Vice-President of the
Republic of Vietnam from 1967-1971. He was born
in Sơn-Tây Province in north Vietnam. His father
was a professor. He graduated from high school
in 1948 and started his military career. He
received training from the French and later from
the United States. In 1955 he served in his
first command position. Nine years later in 1964
he was made Commander of the air force, a position

which he retained until November, 1967. Nguyễn Cao-Kỳ served as Prime Minister of the government of the Republic of Vietnam from June 19, 1965 until September, 1967 at which time he became Vice President to President Nguyễn Văn-Thiệu. However, he broke with the President in 1971 and tried to oppose him in the 1971 presidential elections. The supreme court disqualified his candidacy. When it later reversed its decision, Kỳ refused to run.

NGUYỄN CÔNG-TRỨ (1778-1859). A scholar and statesman during the early Nguyễn Dynasty (1802-1945). Born in Hà-Tĩnh Province, he did not pass the civil service examinations until he was forty years old. He served as Governor of north Vietnam's coastal provinces where he carried out extensive land development and put down several local revolts. His career was filled with both promotions and demotions, resulting at one point in his serving in the army as a private. He retired at the age of seventy when he was Governor of Thừa-Thiên Province. Ten years later he died in the village of his birth. Nguyễn Công-Trứ wrote in nôm. His poems often expressed the Confucian ethic. Although he was a literary master, he was known for his pursuit of the more earthly pleasures as well, including gambling and women.

NGUYỄN ĐINH-CHIỂU (1822-1888). A poet, scholar and teacher. He was born in Gia-Định Province where he graduated from high school in 1843. He went to Huế to prepare for the provincial examinations. In 1849 he received word that his mother died and cried until he was blind. The following year he opened a school in Gia-Định where he became known as Đồ-Chiểu (Teacher Chiểu). When the French took Gia-Định in 1858 he fled to the countryside. Members of the anti-French resistance as well as the French authorities tried to enlist his services but he always refused, although many of his works were in support of the resistance movement. His most famous poem was Lục-Vân-Tiên but he wrote many others, mainly in nom in the luc-bat (6-8) style. Đồ-Chiểu died on July 3, 1888 in Bến-Tre Province. See LỤC-BÁT, LỤC-VÂN-TIÊN, NÔM.

NGUYỄN-DU (1765-1820). (Pen name: Tố-Như). A famous poet, scholar, diplomat and mandarin during the early Nguyễn Dynasty (1802-1945). Nguyễn-Du was

born into an aristocratic family in Hà-Tĩnh Province in north Vietnam. Like his family before
him, he remained loyal to the Lê Dynasty (1428-
1788) even after the Tây-Sơn Rebellion (1771-
1788). When Emperor Gia-Long (1802-1819) came to
power, Nguyễn-Du was forced to accept a post as
a mandarin. He served the Emperor in Hà-Đông,
Huế and Quảng-Bình. He was selected three times
to head an embassy to Peking.

His writings are in both nom and Chinese.
But, his most famous poem, indeed, Vietnam's most
famous poem, is Kim-Vân-Kiều. See KIM-VÂN-KIỀU.

NGUYỄN DUY-TRINH (1910-   ). Member of the Lao-Động
Party Politburo and former Foreign Minister of
the Democratic Republic of Vietnam. He was born
in Nghệ-An Province in central Vietnam. He
joined Hồ Chí-Minh's Indochina Communist Party
in 1930 and has remained an active leader in the
communist party ever since. He has held a variety of high level positions and has travelled
extensively.

NGUYỄN DYNASTY (1802-1945). (Nhà Nguyễn, Triều Nguyễn).
The last imperial dynasty in Vietnam. The dynasty
was founded by Nguyễn-Anh (also known as Nguyễn
Phúc-Anh) who was a descendant of the Nguyễn Lords
(1558-1778). He overthrew the Tây-Sơn regime and
was proclaimed Emperor Gia-Long (1802-1819). The
first fifty years of the dynasty was a time of
consolidation and reconstruction. The first
four emperors (Gia-Long, Minh-Mạng, Thiệu-Trị and
Tự-Đức) were dictatorial but able monarchs in the
Confucianist tradition. Emperor Gia-Long toler-
ated Catholic missionaries since he used a
missionary's help to gain the throne. However,
his successors turned more and more against
Christianity culminating in the mass persecution
of Christians. This gave the French and Spanish
reason to engage the Vietnamese army. Gradually,
the Nguyễn lost control of the country as the
French began their campaign to conquer all of
Indochina.

The early Nguyễn period was also a time of
great literary activity. The classic poem, Kim-
Vân-Kiều, by Nguyễn-Du, was a product of this
era. The mandarinate and civil service was well
organized and functioned effectively. The Emperor ruled through a cabinet of ministers called
"Cơ-Mật". The governmental system was highly
centralized and reached down to the level of the
district. Education was strongly emphasized and,
in accordance with Confucianist ethic, was the

only means to power and influence. Emperor Gia-
Long reestablished the Quốc-Tử-Giám (National
College) in Huế. The government encouraged and
promoted education at the provincial and district levels.

The French conquest of Indochina and the
decline of the Nguyễn Dynasty began during the
reign of Tự-Đức (1848-1883). All relations with
the west were broken, Christianity was outlawed
and the French shelled Đà-Nẵng in 1847. By 1883,
after several treaties and agreements, the French
captured Hà-Nội and established their rule over
all of Vietnam. Tonking (north Vietnam) and An-
Nam (central Vietnam) were made French protectorates while Cochinchina (south Vietnam) was placed
under the direct control of the French colonial
administration. The French developed and exploited the country by establishing rubber, coffee, tea and other plantations and opening up
new ricelands in the south. Railroads were built,
coal mines opened and new industries started. At
the same time, radical social changes took place,
usually in spite of the conservative nature of
the court, and catalyzed by the establishment of
an extensive system of French education, the
adoption of the new Romanized script (Quốc-Ngữ)
and a growing impotence of the imperial court at
Huế. Numerous nationalistic movements came into
being and added to the internal unrest and instability.

In 1940, Japan took advantage of the weakened French government and established control
over the entire Indochinese Peninsula but left
the French administration in place until March,
1945, when it granted independence to Vietnam
under Bảo-Đại while maintaining a protectorate
role. Bảo-Đại, unable to form an effective
government, was forced by the Việt-Minh after the
August Revolution to abdicate the throne. On
August 25, 1945, he turned over his imperial seal
and other symbols of his office to Hồ Chí-Minh
and thus ended the 143 year old Nguyễn Dynasty.
See AUGUST REVOLUTION, GIA-LONG, HUẾ, MINH-MẠNG,
NGUYỄN-ANH, TỰ-ĐỨC.

NGUYỄN GIA-THIỀU (1741-1798). A mandarin and author
during the Restored Lê Dynasty (1533-1788). A
native of Bắc-Ninh Province, he served as successfully in military affairs as he did in civilian
assignment. When the Tây-Sơn brothers took over
he refused to work with them. His most well-
known work is the epic poem, Cung-Oán Ngâm-Khúc.
See CUNG-OÁN NGÂM-KHÚC.

NGUYỄN-HOÀNG (ruled 1558-1613). The second son of
   Nguyễn-Kim, the patriot who led the fight against
   the Mạc Dynasty (1527-1592) to reestablish the
   Lê Dynasty. His brother was killed by the Trịnh
   Lord Trịnh-Kiểm. Fearing the same fate he settled
   in Quảng-Trị Province. He applied for and was
   granted in 1558 the governorship of Thuận-Hóa
   (Quảng-Trị and Thừa-Thiên) and Quảng-Nam Provinces. In 1572, the Mạc forces invaded Quảng-
   Trị from the ocean. Nguyễn-Hoàng succeeded in
   capturing the commander and ousting the Mạc forces.
   In 1593, he took his army to the north and fought
   for eight years with the Trịnh against the Mạc.
   In 1600 he obtained permission to return to the
   south to put down a local rebellion. Although
   he never returned to the north, he gave his
   daughter's hand to the Trịnh Lord Trịnh-Tràng to
   maintain good relations. Later in 1613 Nguyễn-
   Hoàng captured Phú-Yên from Champa, thus expand-
   ing the country's frontier. He died in 1613 at
   the age of 89. See NGUYỄN LORDS, TRỊNH-NGUYỄN
   INTERNECINE WAR.

NGUYỄN-HUỆ. (Later to become Emperor Quang-Trung
   1788-1792). The second of the Tây-Sơn brothers
   who led the Tây-Sơn Rebellion (1771-1788) and
   who proclaimed himself Emperor Quang-Trung in
   1788. Nguyễn-Huệ, together with his brothers
   fought and defeated the Nguyễn Lords in the south
   and then marched north against the Trịnh.
   Nguyễn-Huệ professed allegiance to the Lê Emperor
   and returned to the south, leaving the court in
   the hands of the Lê. The Tây-Sơn brothers then
   divided the south into three kingdoms with
   Nguyễn-Huệ controlling the northern part from
   Thuận-Hóa, Nguyễn-Nhạc controlling the center
   from Qui-Nhơn and Nguyễn-Lữ ruling the south
   with Gia-Định as its center. When the Trịnh tried
   to take over again in the north, the Tây-Sơn again
   interceeded in the capital to ensure the contin-
   uance of the Lê Dynasty. However, the Lê reacted
   by asking the Chinese to assist the Lê against
   the Tây-Sơn. Nguyễn-Huệ then proclaimed himself
   Emperor and initiated the campaign that soon
   drove the Chinese out of the country. He is
   celebrated today as a national hero and is known
   as both Nguyễn-Huệ and Quang-Trung. See NGUYỄN-
   NHẠC, TÂY-SƠN DYNASTY, TÂY-SƠN REBELLION, QUANG-
   TRUNG.

NGUYỄN KHẮC-HIẾU. See TẢN-ĐÀ.

NGUYỄN-KIM. A patriot, military mandarin and general under the Lê Dynasty (1428-1788). Nguyễn-Kim remained loyal to the royal Lê family in 1527 when the throne was usurped by Mạc Đăng-Dung. He took refuge in the mountains and in 1533 he proclaimed the youngest son of former Emperor Lê Chiêu-Tông (1516-1524) as Emperor Lê Trang-Tông. From that time forward he led the fight to reinstate the Lê Dynasty. In 1540, after long preparation under Nguyễn-Kim's leadership, the forces of the Lê moved against the Mạc. He attacked Nghệ-An and by 1543 he controlled Thanh-Hóa and Nghệ-An provinces. In 1545 he had advanced his army to Sơn-Nam when he was poisoned by a surrendered enemy officer.

Nguyễn-Kim was a native of Thanh-Hóa province. He was the ancestor of the Nguyễn Lords who vied for seventy-five years with the Trịnh in the north for control of Vietnam. See LÊ TRANG-TÔNG, MẠC ĐĂNG-DUNG, NGUYỄN LORDS, TRỊNH-NGUYỄN INTERNECINE WAR.

NGUYỄN LORDS (1558-1778). (Chúa Nguyễn). The family or clan that governed the southern part of the country during the period of the Restored Lê Dynasty. They professed loyalty to the Lê emperors (as did their rivals, the Trịnh in the north), so the Nguyễn rulers took the title of lord (Chúa). This title was inherited as the crown would be in a royal family.

The Nguyễn clan was founded by Nguyễn-Kim who led the fight against the Mạc to restore the Lê Dynasty. The Nguyễn were actually the ancestors of the Nguyễn Dynasty founded by Gia-Long in 1802. The Nguyễn Lords fought the Trịnh in the forty-five year internecine war. They also engaged the Chams and the Cambodians as they sought to expand their territory. The empire of Champa finally submitted to the Nguyễn Lords in 1697 which marked the end of Champa as a nation. The Nguyễn then took the rest of the southern part of Vietnam by subversion and open attacks against Cambodia (Chân-Lạp). The reign of the Nguyễn Lords was brought to a close by the Tây-Sơn Rebellion (1771-1788) when the last Nguyễn Lord, Nguyễn Phúc-Thuần (Đinh-Vương) was driven out of the country. Although significant achievements were made in such areas as taxation, exploitation of natural resources, trade and the military, the period of the Nguyễn Lords is best known for the southward expansion of the Vietnamese territory. See NGUYỄN-KIM, TÂY-SƠN REBELLION, TRỊNH LORDS, TRỊNH-NGUYỄN INTERNECINE WAR.

NGUYỄN-LŨ. The youngest of the Tây-Sơn brothers who
led the Tây-Sơn Rebellion (1771-1788). He fought
against the Nguyễn in the south and later proclaimed himself King of the South (Đông-Định-
Vương) ruling from Gia-Định (1786). However, he
lost control of the area when Nguyễn-Anh returned
from exile and attacked his forces, capturing
his capital in 1788. See NGUYỄN-ANH, NGUYỄN-HUỆ,
NGUYỄN-NHẠC, TÂY-SƠN DYNASTY, TÂY-SƠN REBELLION.

NGUYỄN LƯƠNG-BẰNG (1904-   ). Vice President of the
Democratic Republic of Vietnam. He was born in
Hải-Hưng Province and became a seaman. He
joined Hồ Chí-Minh's Revolutionary Youth League
in 1925 and was one of the founding members of
the Indochinese Communist Party in 1930. In 1931
he was arrested by the French and sentenced to
twenty years in jail. The next year he escaped
but was arrested again in 1933. From 1933-1943
he was imprisoned in Sơn-La Province. After his
excape in 1943 he fled to China to join Hồ Chí-
Minh. From 1952-1956 he served as Ambassador
to the Soviet Union. He became Vice President
in 1969.

NGUYỄN-NHẠC. The eldest of the Tây-Sơn brothers who
led the Tây-Sơn Rebellion (1771-1788). Nguyễn-
Nhạc started the campaign against the Nguyễn
Lords in 1771 by first taking Qui-Nhơn City then
all of Quảng-Nam, Quảng-Ngãi and Bình-Định provinces. He then proclaimed himself Tây-Sơn
Vương (Tây-Sơn King), and appointed his brothers
as Princes. The Tây-Sơn then attacked Gia-Định
and drove the Nguyễn out of the country. Turning northward they fought and defeated the Trịnh.
However, they pledged support to keep the Lê on
the throne and returned to Qui-Nhơn. Nguyễn-Nhạc
then proclaimed himself king of the center and
ruled from Qui-Nhơn. However, in 1793 Nguyễn-
Anh attacked Qui-Nhơn forcing Nguyễn-Nhạc to send
for help from Nguyễn Quang-Toản, his brother
Quang-Trung's successor. The reinforcements repelled the attack but they took control of the
city and confiscated the treasury. It is said
that Nguyễn-Nhạc became so enraged that he died.
See NGUYỄN-HUỆ, QUANG-TRUNG, TÂY-SƠN DYNASTY,
TÂY-SƠN REBELLION.

NGUYỄN PHÚC-ANH. See NGUYỄN-ANH.

NGUYỄN PHÚC-CHU (ruled 1691-1725). (Also known as
    Quốc-Chúa). The sixth lord of the Nguyễn faction
    during the Restored Lê Dynasty (1533-1788). He
    acquired Bình-Thuận Province from Champa and also
    added Gia-Định and Hà-Tiên to his territory. He
    sent an envoy to China to ask recognition as an
    independent kingdom but was refused. He died in
    1725 at the age of fifty-one after thirty-three
    years of rule. It is said that he had 146 child-
    ren. See NGUYỄN LORDS, TRỊNH-NGUYỄN INTERNECINE
    WAR.

NGUYỄN PHÚC-KHOÁT (ruled 1738-1765). (Also known as
    Võ-Vương). The eighth Lord of the Nguyễn fac-
    tion during the period of the Restored Lê Dy-
    nasty (1533-1788). He fought Chân-Lạp (Cambodia)
    and acquired more land in the area of Gia-Định.
    In 1744 he organized a true court and proclaimed
    the establishment of a kingdom. He died in 1765.
    See NGUYỄN LORDS, TRỊNH-NGUYỄN INTERNECINE WAR.

NGUYỄN PHÚC-LÂN (ruled 1635-1648). (Also known as
    Chúa Thượng). The fourth Lord of the Nguyễn fac-
    tion during the period of the Restored Lê Dynasty
    (1533-1788), and the son of the Nguyễn Lord,
    Nguyễn Phúc-Nguyễn (1613-1635). He ruled for
    thirteen years during which the Trịnh attacked
    twice. He was forty-eight years of age when he
    died in 1648. See NGUYỄN LORDS, TRỊNH-NGUYỄN
    INTERNECINE WAR.

NGUYỄN PHÚC-NGUYỄN (ruled 1613-1635). (Also known as
    Chúa Sãi). The second Lord of the Nguyễn faction
    during the period of the Restored Lê Dynasty
    (1533-1788). He was the son of Nguyễn-Hoàng whom
    he succeeded in 1613 as Governor of Thuận-Hóa and
    Quảng-Nam provinces. In 1620 he sent troops to
    occupy the area around the Gianh River in Quảng-
    Bình and Hà-Tĩnh provinces. Seven years later
    Trịnh-Tùng attacked Nguyễn-Phúc-Nguyễn's forces
    thus marking the beginning of the Trịnh-Nguyễn
    war. Trịnh-Tùng was unsuccessful in his attempt.
    Nguyễn Phúc-Nguyễn died in 1635 at the age of
    seventy-three. See NGUYỄN LORDS, TRỊNH-NGUYỄN
    INTERNECINE WAR.

NGUYỄN PHÚC-TẦN (ruled 1648-1687). (Also known as
    Chúa Hiền). The fourth Lord of the Nguyễn fac-
    tion during the period of the Restored Lê Dynasty
    (1533-1788). The period of his rule was consumed
    by the constant attacks and counterattacks by the
    Nguyễn and Trịnh forces. He also conquered more
    land from Champa and established districts at
    Ninh-Hòa and Diên-Khánh in what is presently

Khánh-Hòa Province in central Vietnam. Nguyễn
Phúc-Tần died in 1687 at the age of sixty-eight.
See NGUYỄN LORDS, TRỊNH-NGUYỄN INTERNECINE WAR.

NGUYỄN PHÚC-THUẦN (ruled 1765-1777). (Also known as
Định Vương). The ninth Lord of the Nguyễn faction during the period of the Restored Lê Dynasty
(1533-1788). He was put on the throne by Trương
Phúc-Loan, the strongest official in the Nguyễn
court. During his reign most of the power remained with Trương Phúc-Loan. It was during this
period that the Tây-Sơn Rebellion (1771-1788)
started. Taking advantage of the Nguyễn pre-
occupation with fighting the Tây-Sơn, the Trịnh
attacked Quảng-Trị and Thừa-Thiên and succeeded
in taking the capital, Phú-Xuân. Nguyễn Phúc-
Thuần fled to Gia-Định and was captured and killed
by the Tây-Sơn rebels. He was twenty-four years
old when he died. See NGUYỄN LORDS, TÂY-SƠN RE-
BELLION, TRỊNH-NGUYỄN INTERNECINE WAR.

NGUYỄN PHÚC-TRĂN (ruled 1687-1691). (Also known as
Chúa Nghĩã). The fifth Lord of the Nguyễn faction during the period of the Restored Lê Dynasty (1533-1788). He established the Nguyễn
capital at Phú-Xuân (Huế). He died in 1691 at the
age of forty-three. See NGUYỄN LORDS, TRỊNH-
NGUYỄN INTERNECINE WAR.

NGUYỄN PHÚC-TRÚ (ruled 1725-1738). The seventh Lord
of the Nguyễn faction during the period of the
Restored Lê Dynasty (1533-1788). He established
a protectorate over Chân-Lạp (Cambodia). He died
in 1738 at the age of forty-three. See NGUYỄN
LORDS, TRỊNH-NGUYỄN INTERNECINE WAR.

NGUYỄN THÁI-HỌC (1902-1930). The leader of the Việt-
Nam Quốc-Dân Đảng political party and the mar-
tyred leader of the Yên-Báy uprising. He was
born in Vĩnh-Yên Province and studied in the
school of pedagogy in Hà-Nội and later in the
advanced school of commerce. He petitioned the
French several times for Vietnamese rights and
privileges always without success. In 1927, the
Vietnamese nationalist party (VNQDD) was formed
and Nguyễn Thái-Học was elected chairman. In
1930, he played a key role in the Yên-Báy uprising. He was captured by the French and executed on the guillotine on June 17, 1930 together
with twelve of his comrades. Before his death
he wrote an open letter to the French authorities
warning them to end their cruel oppression.

Nguyễn Thái-Học's girlfriend and fellow revolutionary Nguyễn Thị Giang, watched his execu-
tion then returned to his native village and
committed suicide. She left behind a very moving
letter and equally inspiring poem. Nguyễn Thái-
Học is now considered a national hero and martyr,
especially within the ranks of the VNQDD. See
VIỆT-NAM QUỐC-DÂN ĐẢNG, YÊN-BÁY UPRISING.

NGUYỄN-THIẾP (1723-1804). (Also known as the Scholar
   of La-Sơn). An influential intellectual during
   the Tây-Sơn period (1788-1802). He studied in
   order to become a mandarin until he was twenty
   one. After that he abandoned his career in
   favor of a leisurely life of private studies.
   Emperor Quang-Trung (1788-1792) solicited his
   services and made him responsible for national
   education and the completion of works in the nôm
   script. When Quang-Trung died in 1792 he returned to his native village of Nghệ-An.

NGUYỄN THUYEN. (Also known as Hàn Thuyên). A mandarin and poet during the Trần Dynasty (1225-
   1400). He is credited with composing the first
   poems in nôm. During the reign of Trần Nhân-
   Tông (1278-1293) he gained the reputation of
   being as gifted as the famous poet Hàn-Du in
   China. The Emperor, therefore, changed his name
   to Hàn-Thuyên. One of his most famous poems is
   Văn-Tế Cá-Sấu, (Ode to an Alligator). Legend
   has it that in the Phú-Lương River there lived
   a man-eating alligator who frightened the population. The Emperor called on Hàn-Thuyên who
   wrote the Văn-Tế Cá-Sấu. When the poem was
   read and the paper dropped into the river, the
   alligator disappeared. See NÔM.

NGUYỄN-TRÃI (1380-1442). A famous scholar and strategist associated with Lê-Lợi. His mother was
   one of the royal Trần family. His father, Nguyễn
   Phi-Khanh was mandarin and renowned man of letters
   who was captured by the Chinese (Ming) and taken
   to China. Nguyễn-Trãi accompanied him to the
   border whereupon they separated. This tragic
   scene is described in a poem, Ức-Trai-Tập. His
   father's last words to him were to seek out
   other brave and courageous men.
       Nguyễn-Trãi returned and joined up with Lê-
   Lợi. Both men were the two key figures in the
   Lam-Sơn Uprising (1418-1428). In order to enlist the support of the people it is said that
   these men went about the villages painting the
   slogan "Lê-Lợi for King, Nguyễn-Trãi for Minister"

on the leaves of the trees so the people would
think that this was a supernatural message.
     After Lê-Lợi became Emperor Lê Thái-Tổ
(1428-1433). Nguyễn-Trãi was made the chief civilian mandarin. But Lê Thái-Tổ's successor, Lê
Thái-Tông did not use him. Nguyễn-Trãi retired
to his mountain retreat at Côn-Sơn Mountain in
Hải-Hưng Province in 1439. In 1442, Lê Thái-
Tông visited him and took one of his concubines,
Nguyễn Thị-Lộ. Shortly thereafter, Lê Thái-Tông
died. It was assumed that his death was caused
by Nguyễn Thị-Lộ. Blame was then laid on Nguyễn-
Trãi and he and his entire family were ordered
killed. Twenty-two years later, he was exon-
erated by Emperor Lê Thanh-Tông (1460-1497).
     Nguyễn-Trãi enjoys as much fame as a scholar
as he does as a patriot. He was awarded a doctoral degree in 1400. His written works were in
Chinese (Hán-Văn) and nôm. His works in nôm are
the first products in the national or demotic
script that were recorded and still survive. Included in his writings are a chronicle of the
Lam-Sơn insurrection (Lam-Sơn Thực-Luc), an an-
thology of poems (Quốc-Âm Thi Tập), and guidelines for moral behavior, advice on raising and
teaching children (Gia Huấn Ca). One of his
most famous poems is the proclamation of victory
(Bình-Ngô Đại-Cáo).

NGUYỄN TRUNG-NGẠN (1289-1370). A famous scholar during
     the Trần Dynasty (1225-1400). Born in Hưng-Yên
     Province, he was talented at politics and debat-
     ing. He authored several books including a his-
     tory of the Trần, Hoàng Triều Đại-Điện.

NGUYỄN TRUNG-TRỰC. (Also known as Quản-Chơn or Quản-
     Lịch). A patriot and a prominent figure in the
     resistance movement against the French during
     the 1860's. In 1861 he became active in guerilla
     actions against the French forces in the area
     of Tân-An in Cochinchina. He led the raid that
     resulted in the burning of the French war-ship,
     "Esperance". He moved to Hà-Tiên where he con-
     tinued his activities against the French. When
     the three southern provinces fell to the French,
     he established himself on Hòn-Chồng Island and
     then on Phú-Quốc Island. Although he was be-
     trayed by Vietnamese informants, the French
     could not penetrate his defenses. Finally, the
     French captured his mother and a number of civ-
     ilians and threatened to kill them all if he
     did not surrender. He gave himself up and on
     October 27, 1868 he was executed by the French
     in the market place of Rạch-Giá.

NGUYỄN TRƯỜNG-TỘ (1828-1871). A Catholic reformist
    mandarin and scholar during the early Nguyễn Dy-
    nasty (1802-1945). Born in Nghệ-An Province he
    travelled throughout Asia and Europe. He returned
    to Vietnam and accepted a position in the court
    under Emperor Tự-Đức (1848-1883). He petitioned
    the Emperor on many subjects. He advocated es-
    tablishing relations with other countries, the
    use of nôm rather than Chinese as the official
    language, and the modernization of the education
    and examination systems. He also proposed moves
    towards industrialization.

NGUYỄN VĂN-THIỆU (1923-   ). The second President
    of the Republic of Vietnam. He was born in Tri-
    Thủy Village in Ninh-Thuận Province into a farm-
    ing and fishing family. In 1945 he joined the
    Việt-Minh and served as youth leader and district
    chief. He soon broke with the Việt-Minh and
    joined the Merchant Marines. In 1948 he joined
    the national army of Vietnam under the French and
    volunteered for the first class at the military
    academy of Huế. He graduated from the officer
    class in 1949 and received his second lieutenant
    commission. For the next five years he served
    as an officer in combat against the Việt-Minh.
    During this time he married Miss Nguyễn Thị Mai-
    Anh of Mỹ-Tho in Định-Tường Province. As a
    lieutenant colonel in 1956 he was appointed to
    the post of superintendent of the National Mil-
    itary Academy in Đà-Lạt. He advanced in rank
    and position, including taking command of the
    fifth infantry division. After the overthrow
    of President Ngô Đình-Diệm in 1963, General
    Nguyễn Văn-Thiệu was successively assigned to a
    number of posts, including Chief of Staff of the
    Army, Vice-Minister of Defense and Secretary-
    General of the Armed Forces Council, and then
    Commander of the Fourth Army Corps (1964). Sub-
    sequently he became Deputy Prime Minister and
    concurrently held the post of Minister of Defense.
    In June, 1965, the Armed Forces Council over-
    threw the civilian government and named Lieu-
    tenant General Nguyễn Văn-Thiệu as Chairman of
    the National Leadership Committee, which was in
    effect, the Chief of State. After the election
    of a constituent assembly in 1966 and the form-
    ation of a new constitution presidential elections
    were held in September, 1967. Thiệu was elected
    President of the Republic and, in 1971 he was
    reelected to a second four-year term. He was a
    Buddhist until his marriage, after which he be-
    came a Catholic. He has one daughter and a

younger son.

NGUYỄN VĂN-TỐ. (1889-1947). Pen name: Ứng Hòe.
Early twentieth century literary critic, author
and scholar. He published in both French and
Vietnamese and was associated with the Ecole
Francaise d'Extreme-Orient in Hà-Nội. Nguyễn Văn-
Tố wrote on various subjects ranging from literature and philosophy to sociology. Much of his
work was aimed at bringing an understanding of
Vietnamese culture to the French. He served as
the Minister of Social Relief in the government
of the Democratic Republic of Vietnam from 1945
until 1947 when he was killed by the French.

NGUYỄN VĂN-VĨNH (1882-1936). An author and journalist.
He was a leading figure in the popularization of
Quốc-Ngữ (the Romanized script). Born in Hà-Đông
Province, he went to college in Hà-Nội. He
travelled to Europe, and was editor of several
newspapers and journals in Hà-Nội and Sài-Gòn.
He wrote on contemporary social and political
issues and translated several nom and Chinese
classics into Quốc-Ngữ and several Vietnamese and
Chinese works into French.

NGUYỆT-LÃO. (The God of Marriages, also referred to as
the old man in the moon). Nguyệt-Lão is the Vietnamese version of Cupid. He resides on the moon
and, according to legend, he spends most of his
time tying lovers together with strands of scarlet
silk.

NHA-TRANG. A seaside resort town and the capital city
of Khánh-Hòa Province in central Vietnam. Population 194,969. It is located just off highway
number one, 448 kilometers (278 miles) north of
Sài-Gòn. Nha-Trang was once a part of the Kingdom of Champa (Chiêm-Thành or Campa-pura).
Vestiges of the Chàm culture are still to be seen
in and around the town. Especially well-known
are the Chàm towers on the north side of the city.
Also located in Nha-Trang is the oceanographic
institute, the Pasteur Medical Institute, a naval
academy, a Protestant seminary and commercial
port facilities. There is also some light industry located in the city. On October 22, 1970,
Nha-Trang was made an autonomous municipality.
See KHÁNH-HÒA PROVINCE.

NHA-TRANG RIVER. (Sông Nha-Trang, also known as Sông
Cái or Cái River). A river in Khánh-Hòa Province

in central Vietnam. It originates in the mountains in the western part of the province and flows through the city of Nha-Trang where it empties into the South China Sea.

NHÂM-DIÊN. The Chinese Governor who governed the district of Cửu-Chân in the Chinese protectorate of Giao-Chỉ-Bộ during the first period of Chinese domination (111 B.C. - 938 A.D.). He is credited with teaching the Việt people to use a plow and improving their agriculture to the point of being self-sufficient. He also instigated a system of contributions by which the rich gave assistance to the poor.

NHÂN-DÂN. (Literally, The People). The leading daily newspaper in the Democratic Republic of Vietnam. It is the official organ of the Lao-Động (Worker's) Party and has a circulation of about 75,000.

NHANG. (Also called Giay). An ethno-linguistic minority group of highland people located in Lào-Cai and Hà-Giang provinces and the Northwest Autonomous Zone of north Vietnam. They speak a Sino-Thai language of the Sino-Tibetan language family. They numbered 16,429 in the 1960 census.

NHANG. Joss sticks or incense sticks. Nhang are used in the ritual of worship in the belief that the dragrant smoke will please the spirits of the departed dead or will curry the favor of the Gods. They are handmade from a thin stick of bamboo rolled in a putty-like substance made from the sawdust of incense woods. Usually about a foot in length, they are lit and placed in a sand-filled container on the altar or in the temple. Some joss sticks are circular or spiral and will burn for many weeks. The act of burning the joss sticks is called thắp-hưởng. See HÓA-VÀNG, RE-LIGION, THẮP-HƯỞNG.

NHẬT-LỆ RIVER. (Sông Nhật-Lệ or Sông Đồng-Hới). A river in central Vietnam. It flows through Quảng-Bình Province and empties into the South China Sea at Đồng-Hới. See ĐỒNG-HỚI, NHẬT-LỆ WALL.

NHẬT-LỆ WALL. (Also called Lũy-Thày). A fortified wall built in Quảng-Bình Province by Đào Duy-Từ, a military strategist under the Nguyễn Lords (1558-1778). It is thirty-six kilometers (twenty miles) long and is situated at the mouth of the Nhật-Lệ River. On the opposite side of the river was located the Đồng-Hới Wall. Together the

seaport could be closed up as that of the ancient
Byzantium, by an iron chain fastened to the two
walls. See ĐÀO DUY-TỪ, ĐỒNG-HỚI WALL, NHẬT-LỆ
RIVER.

NHẤT-LINH (1906-1963). (Nguyễn Tường-Tam). A modern
author and political activist most famous for
his topical novels. He was born in Quảng-Nam
Province and was educated in Hà-Nội and Paris.
He taught school in Hà-Nội and started to publish
a paper. He joined with other authors to found
the literary movement called Tự-Lực Văn-Đoàn,
(Self Reliant Literary Group). In 1939 he became active in the resistance movement against
the French. Nhất-Linh went to China in 1942
where he spent most of the next ten years, except
for a brief stay in Vietnam when he accepted a
post in the short-lived resistance coalition
government. He returned to Vietnam in 1951 and
moved to Sài-Gòn after the partition of the country in 1954. He continued his literary career
but was arrested in 1960 for opposing the Diệm
regime. On July 7, 1963 he committed suicide by
taking poison and left behind a note reiterating
his opposition to the Diệm government. Among his
more famous works are Tối-Tăm, Lanh-Lùng, and
Đoạn-Tuyệt. See TỰ-LỰC VĂN-ĐOÀN.

NHẤT TIÊN TỰ. The Book of One Thousand Characters. A
compilation of 1,015 Chinese characters and their
meanings in Vietnamese so arranged as to produce
rhythmical effects without any meaningful sequence.
This vocabulary book served as a primer to teach
Chinese characters in traditional Vietnam.

NHỊ ĐỘ MAI. A classic epic poem written in nom by an
unknown author. It is based on a Chinese novel.
The poem is simplistic and popular. It encourages
people to adhere to their moral principles and to
choose the path of filial piety, virtue, loyalty,
and justice.

NHỊ-HÀ RIVER. See RED RIVER.

NHO. (Chữ Nho). Chinese characters. Much of the
early literature was written in classical Chinese.
Chữ Nho was also used to educate Vietnamese scholars until the general acceptance of Quốc-Ngữ
(Romanized script). During the imperial dynastic
period Chữ Nho was the official language of the
court. The study of Chữ Nho also entailed the
study of the Confucian ethic.

NHO-GIÁO. See CONFUCIANISM.

NHUỘM RĂNG. The blackening of teeth. The custom of
blackening the teeth is not unique to Vietnam nor
is it common today. However, in traditional
Vietnam, both boys and girls blackened their
teeth at the age of thirteen or fourteen. Blackened teeth were considered much more attractive
than natural teeth. The dye was made from the
sap of a particular tree and was sold only in
the cool season. The dye was mixed with lemon
and placed next to the teeth before going to
sleep at night. The reaction of the dye caused
the mouth to swell to such an extent that only
soft or liquid foods could be eaten. The first
treatment would turn the teeth red, the second
treatment would turn them black. A good and
careful treatment would last a lifetime.

NIÊN HIỆU. Reign title. A name or title by which an
emperor was known during a certain period of his
reign. One emperor would actually have three
names. For example, before becoming emperor Lê
Thái-Tô (1428-1433) was named Lê-Lợi. During the
time of his rule he was known by his niên-hiệu
(reign title), Thuận-Thiên. The dynastic name,
Lê Thái-Tô is a posthumous title. In some cases
it was considered auspicious to change the reign
title of an emperor during his lifetime. Thus,
it is not uncommon for one emperor to have two
or more reign titles. The niên-hiệu was always
used in fixing a date, i.e., 1431 would be known
as the fourth year of the reign of Thuận-Thiên.

NINH-BÌNH CITY. The capital city of Ninh-Bình Province
in north Vietnam. It is situated on the Đáy River.
It is ninety-one kilometers (fifty-six miles) from
Hà-Nội by road and 114 kilometers (69 miles) by
rail. See NINH-BÌNH PROVINCE.

NINH-BÌNH PROVINCE. A small, heavily populated coastal
province in north Vietnam. It is situated north
of Thanh-Hoá Province, east of Hoà-Bình Province
and south of Hải-Hưng and Thái-Bình provinces.
Ninh-Bình marks the southernmost reaches of the
region of north Vietnam (Bắc-Việt). The land
mass of Ninh-Bình is 1,218 square kilometers
(470 square miles) and the population is estimated
at 506,100 (1969). The inhabitants are almost
all ethnic Vietnamese except for a few thousand
Mường. There are two distinct regions of the
province: the flat delta area around Yên-Khánh
District; and the mountainous area to the south

and west in the Nho-Quan District. National
highway number one and the national railroad pass
through the province from northeast to southwest.
The province capital is situated on both highway
and railroad.

Ninh-Bình has two important landmarks: Hoa-
Lư and Phát-Diệm. Hoa-Lư was the capital of
Đại-Cổ-Việt, founded by Đinh Tiên-Hoàng (968-979).
There are still some vestiges remaining of the
capital plus a shrine dedicated to the Đinh Dynasty (968-980). Phát-Diệm is well-known as a
center of Catholicism in north Vietnam. The
settlement was established in 1901 and a monastery was founded in 1913.

The main agricultural products of the province are rice, coffee, tea, and an especially
good variety of reed used for weaving mats.
Under the French there were many plantations
established. Salt and fish are also among the
chief products of the province. The famous Non-
Nước Pagoda is located in Ninh-Bình Province.
See HOA-LƯ, MAT MAKING, NON-NƯỚC PAGODA, PHÁT-
DIỆM.

NINH-THUẬN PROVINCE. A coastal province in central
Vietnam located south of Khánh-Hòa Province and
north of Bình-Thuận Province. Ninh-Thuận has a
land mass of 3,431 square kilometers (1324 square
miles) and a population of 203,404 (1971). The
provincial capital, Phan-Rang, is located on highway number one 320 kilometers (198 miles) north
of Sài-Gòn and 760 kilometers (472 miles) south
of Hue. It is situated only seven kilometers
(4.7 miles) from the coast.

Ninh-Thuận is best known for its Chàm population and vestiges of the Chàm empire and culture. The Chàm represent about ten percent of
the population. The Roglai make up the remainder
of the minority groups. Phan-Rang (Panduranga)
was once the capital of the kingdom of Champa.
Among the historical structures that remain are
the Hòa-Lai shrine, located in Đức-Nhơn Village
and built in 1307; the Po-Rome shrine located in
An-Xuân Village; and the three Cham towers (Tháp-
Chàm) near An-Phước.

Highway number eleven and the railroad connect Phan-Rang with Đà-Lạt. The main river is
the Cây River, the many branches of which originate in the mountains of Tuyên-Đức and Khánh-Hòa
provinces. The province also receives water via
an irrigation canal from the Đa-Nhim hydroelectric
project in Tuyên-Đức Province. The weather is

usually warm all year. Ninh-Thuận has the least
amount of rainfall in alloof Vietnam. The salt
fields at Thưởng-Diêm (Cà-Na) are the largest in
Vietnam. The salt from this area is exported to
Japan. Other products of the province include
rice, banana, tobacco, and nước mắm. Ninh-Thuận
produces more goats than any other province in
central or south Vietnam. See CHAM, CHAMPA,
PANDURANGA, PHAN-RANG.

NLF. National Liberation Front. See MẶT-TRẬN DÂN-TỘC
GIẢI-PHONG MIỀN NAM.

NOBILITY. (Tước). There were several classes or
titles of nobility in traditional Vietnam. These
titles were conferred by the emperor on members
of the royal family or on mandarins who had
rendered extraordinary service. They served as
symbols of respect but included no advantage or
prerogatives in the administrative hierarchy,
nor were they passed on through inheritance.
These titles in descending order, included Vương
(Prince), Công (Duke), Hầu (Marquis), Bá (Count),
Tử (Viscount), and Nam (Baron).

NÔM. (Chữ Nôm, also called Chữ Nam). The writing
system devised by the Vietnamese following the
pattern of Chinese characters. The date of the
origins of this demotic script has not yet been
determined, but the earliest inscription in nom
is from the early fourteenth century, although
it was in use as early as the late twelfth century. Nôm was probably necessitated by the need
to record Vietnamese words which were not of
Chinese origin or words that only sounded like
Chinese. The words in this system are derived
by combining Chinese characters or using other
characters for their Vietnamese pronunciation
rather than for their original meaning. Many of
the great Vietnamese classics were written in
nôm, including the Kim-Vân-Kiều. However, the
imperial court adhered to the use of classical
Chinese, thus witholding official sanction from
the use of nôm. Nôm is no longer used.

NÓN. Conical hat. The conical (cone-shaped) hat is
worn by Vietnamese of all social and economic
classes and, in this particular style, is unique
to Vietnam. It is light and usually made from
special latania leaves. A particularly famous
type is made in Huế and called the Nón Bài Thơ
(Poetic Hat). It is made so that, when looking

at the inside of the hat as it is held up to the
light, a verse of poetry, proverb, or design is
visible. The nón is worn by men and women alike.

NON-NƯỚC MOUNTAIN. See NGŨ HÀNH SƠN.

NON-NƯỚC PAGODA. (Chùa Non-Nước). A well-known pagoda
in Ninh-Bình Province in north Vietnam. It is
situated on the Dục-Thuý Mountain along the Vân-
Sang River. When the water is high, the only
access to the pagoda is by boat. The pagoda and
surroundings are known for their scenic beauty.

NÔNG TRẠI. Agricultural settlement. The nông trại
was a form of settlement of new lands which was
used by the government in traditional Vietnam to
promote the occupation of newly opened land.
People were encouraged to homestead on these new
lands under the general direction of the government. Certain elements in the society, usually
adventurers and other ambitious men would be
attracted to this scheme. The nông trại system
accounted for much of the success of the southward expansion (nam-tiến) of the ethnic Vietnamese. See ĐỒN ĐIỀN, LÃO TRẠI, NAM-TIẾN.

NORTH VIETNAM. See BẮC-PHẦN.

NORTHERN COASTAL PLAIN. (Đồng-Bằng Bắc-Phần). The
coastal plains area of north Vietnam which is
dominated by the Red River Delta and the smaller
delta of the Thái-Bình River. The area extends
from Phát-Diệm in Ninh-Bình Province to Đồ-Sơn,
near Hải-Phòng on the coast and inland as far
west as Việt-Trì (sixty-four kilometers or forty
miles west of Hà-Nội). The area covers only
twelve percent of north Vietnam, but accounts for
the majority of the ethnic Vietnamese population.
The northern coastal plain can be separated into
three distinct regions: the northern and western
higher regions, which although it never exceeds
fourteen meters (forty-five feet), does border
on the foothills of the highland region; the
coastal area which is flat and near sea level;
and the inland region which is composed of many
smaller river basins and exhibits large deposits
of silt along the river banks. The northern
coastal plain is considered the cradle of Vietnamese civilization. It is an industrial center as
well as the center of rice production in the
north. See RED RIVER DELTA, THÁI-BÌNH RIVER, BẮC-
PHẦN.

NÚI. Mountain. Individual mountains are listed under
separate entries. See BA-ĐEN MOUNTAIN, BA-THẾ
MOUNTAIN, CÔN-SƠN MOUNTAIN, HOÀNG-LIÊN-SƠN MOUN-
TAIN, KIÊU-LƯU-TI MOUNTAIN, NGỌC-PAN MOUNTAIN,
NGŨ HÀNH SƠN, PHU-KIÊU-HAN MOUNTAIN, PHU-LƯỜNG
MOUNTAIN, PHU-NAM-MAN MOUNTAIN, PHU-SI-LONG MOUN-
TAIN, PIA-OAC MOUNTAIN, PIA-YA MOUNTAIN, POU-THẠ-
CA MOUNTAIN, SAM MOUNTAIN, TA-DUNG MOUNTAIN, TÂN-
VIÊN MOUNTAIN, THẤT-SƠN MOUNTAINS, VỌNG-PHU MOUN-
TAIN, YANG-SIN MOUNTAIN, YÊN-TỬ MOUNTAIN, LANG-
BIÊN MOUNTAIN, LANG-CUNG MOUNTAIN, NGỌC-KRINH
MOUNTAIN, NGỌC-LINH MOUNTAIN.

NÚI DỘ CIVILIZATION. A stone age culture which existed
in what is now north and north-central Vietnam.
This important archaeological site represents the
second stage of the paleolithic age in Vietnam.
It is named for the Núi Dộ Mountain in Thanh-Hoa
Province which was the site where the paleolithic
stone artifacts representing this civilization
were found. These included hand axes, chopping
and scraping tools and cleavers, almost all made
from basalt. See PREHISTORY.

NÙNG. An ethno-linguistic minority group of highland
people located in the provinces of Lạng-Sơn, Bắc-
Thái, Cao-Bằng, Hà-Giang and Hà-Bắc in north Vietnam. The Nùng population was placed at 313,998
in the 1960 census. Most of the Nùng settlements
are located at high altitudes near the Chinese
border. They speak a Thái language which belongs
to the Kadai language family. They, like the
Tay, display strong Vietnamese and Chinese cultural influence. The kinship system is patrilineal. Polygyny is practiced among the well to
do. The eldest son resides patrilocally after
marriage, while the other sons live nearby. He
also inherits the bulk of the family property.
Maize is the staple crop. Secondary crops include
buckwheat, cotton, tobacco, millet, beans, sweet
potatoes, and poppies. Their religion consists
of animism with influences of Buddhism, Confucianism and Taoism.
    A smaller group, also called Nùng, is located
in southern China and northern Vietnam around Quảng-
Ninh Province. These people speak a dialect of
Chinese (Cantonese). They are renowned as fighters
and often serve as mercenaries. Unofficial sources
estimated this group at 100,000 in population.

NƯỚC MẮM. Fermented fish sauce used extensively in Vietnamese cooking.

-o-

Ờ RẺ. See LÂM RẺ.

OC-EO. The port city of the ancient kingdom of Funan.
    It was located about eleven kilometers (six miles)
    from the sea on the maritime fringe of the Mekong
    Delta in what is now Kiên-Giang Province. The
    city dates from the first to the sixth centuries.
    The site upon which the city of Oc-Eo was located
    has been excavated by archaeologists who have
    made many important finds. Most of the buildings
    were on piles. An elaborate system of canals
    was constructed for both irrigation and trans-
    portation. These canals were so designed as to
    link up a series of lakes and rivers with the
    sea causing Chinese travelers to write about
    "sailing across Funan", on their way to the
    Malay Peninsula. Oc-Eo was a center of industry
    and commerce. There is evidence of maritime
    relations with the coast of the Gulf of Siam,
    Malaya, Indonesia, India, Persia, and even the
    Mediterranean area. It was situated on the
    great maritime route between China and the west.
    Although no sculpture has been discovered at Oc-
    Eo, the pieces of ornate architecture point to
    the high degree of refinement of Funanese art.
    One of the most interesting finds was a Roman
    gold medallion bearing the likeness of Antoninus
    Pius dated 152 A.D. This and other items indi-
    cate that Funan had extensive contact with the
    west. See FUNAN.

OHIER, MARIE-GUSTAVE-HECTOR. Governor of Cochinchina
    from 1868-1869 and Rear Admiral of the French
    Navy.

ONE-PILLAR PAGODA. See MỘT CỘT PAGODA.

ÔNG ĐẠO DỪA. (1909-   ). Coconut Monk. He was born
    in Kiên-Hòa Province and educated in France. In
    1935 he returned to Vietnam, married and had a
    daughter. In 1945 he left his family and went
    to the Thất-Sơn area of Châu-Đốc to enter a mon-
    astic life. For three years he sat on a stone
    slab beneath the flag pole meditating day and
    night. In 1948 he went to Định-Tường Province.
    Ten years later he wrote a letter to President
    Ngô Đình-Diệm after which he was jailed two or
    three times. In 1964 he went to an island in
    the middle of the Mekong River. There he built
    a tower eighteen meters (sixty feet) high. He

gathered a following and through the practice of
his religious philosophy, sought to bring about
peace in a unified Vietnam. He travelled to
Phnom Penh where he was arrested and held for
a short time. He demonstrated outside the Presidential palace in Sài-Gòn. It is said that he
was named the coconut monk because for three
years he ate nothing but coconut.

ÔNG ĐỒ. A teacher of young children in traditional
Vietnam. Often he had taken the civil service
examinations and had either failed them or had
passed them and declined a civil service position.
Sometimes, a person with a reputation of being
skilled in Chinese characters and literature was
asked by the villagers to open a class. He had
no official status and received no financial aid
from the government. His class was either held
in his own house or he was hired as a private
tutor. Frequently, an entire village joined together to support a teacher. See EDUCATION, THẦY.

ÔNG-ĐỐC RIVER. (Sông Ông-Đốc). A small river in An-
Xuyên Province on the Cà-Mau Peninsula. It empties into the Gulf of Thailand.

ÔNG LANG. See THẦY THUỐC.

ÔNG MAI. (Also called Ông Mối). A matchmaker in
traditional Vietnam. See BÀ MAI.

-P-

PACOH. An ethno-linguistic group of highland people
located in western Thừa-Thiên Province in central
Vietnam and extending into Laos. The Pacoh speak
a language belonging to the Katuic group of the
Mon-Khmer stock. They belong to a larger grouping called the Van-Kiều. In 1965 official estimates placed the Pacoh at 6,500. See VAN-KIỀU.

PAGE, THEOGENE-FRANCOIS. Rear Admiral in the French
Navy and Commander-in-Chief of the French forces
in Indochina from November, 1859-April, 1860. He
opened Sài-Gòn to western commerce. He was made
Vice-Admiral in 1861 and returned to France in
1862.

PAGODA. (Chùa). A Buddhist temple, a place of worship
and study. This is not to be confused with the

village communal hall (Đình), the temple for
spirit worship (Đền), or the shrine (Miếu). The
Vietnamese pagoda is very similar to the Chinese
pagoda. The Vietnamese pagoda usually has three
large main doors (Tam-Quan) which are opened only
on special holidays. Most pagodas also have a
bell tower, yard and a sacred pond. The living
quarters for the monks or nuns are in the back,
oft times with a garden for flowers and vegetables.
The pagoda proper consists of several sections
including the front hall, center hall, and main
altar hall. These various parts of the temple
would sometimes be terraced in ascending sequence
with the three main doors on the lowest level.
Certain pagodas would be served by nuns and others
by monks, but never do both sexes serve as clergy
in the same temple. Smaller pagodas that could
not support a full time clergy would be maintained by laymen and laywomen and would be used
only for worship. Many pagodas celebrate the
death anniversary of the founder of the temple.
See ĐINH, ĐỘI-SƠN PAGODA, HẠ-LÔI TEMPLE, HƯƠNG-
TÍCH PAGODA, KIẾP-BẠC PAGODA, MIẾU, MỘT-CỘT PAGODA,
THIÊN-MỤ PAGODA, VĂN-MIẾU PAGODA.

PAKHA HIGHLANDS. (Cao-Nguyên Pakha). An area that
occupies most of Hà-Giang Province and has an
elevation of about 2,000 meters (6,500 feet).
It is inhabited mainly by the Man people.

PANDURANGA. The Chàm name for Phan-Rang. Panduranga
was the center of the Chàm empire during the
eighth and ninth centuries after which time the
capital moved to Indrapura (Quảng-Nam Province).
Then, again after the Vietnamese pushed south and
captured Vijaya (Bình-Định Province) in the fifteenth century. the Chàms were reduced to an area
centering around Panduranga where the largest
concentration of Chams remain. See CHAMPA, INDRA-
PURA, VIJAYA.

PARACELS ISLAND. (Quần-Đảo Hoàng-Xa, or Hoàng-Xa
Archipelago). A group of islands in the South
China Sea about 300 kilometers (187 miles) west
of Đà-Nẵng. The islands have long been a source
of tortoises and other marine life, and, more
recently, rich beds of phosphates have been
discovered and exploited. Dominion over the
Paracels has been claimed by nationalist China,
Republic of Vietnam, and the Chinese People's
Republic. The issue has not yet been settled.

PASQUIER, PIERRE. Governor General of Indochina from
December, 1928 to January, 1934. He spent his
entire overseas career in Indochina. He was
killed in a plane crash on January 15, 1934.

PATENOTRE TREATY (1884). A treaty which established
An-Nam and Tongking as protectorates of France.
This treaty actually replaced the Treaty of
Protectorate (Harmand Agreement) of 1883. Under
the terms of the treaty, the national independence of Vietnam was abolished, France was to
represent Vietnam in all external relations and
was to supervise the local administration. The
treaty was signed in Huế on June 6, 1884. It
was the last treaty to be signed by France and
Vietnam during this period. See TREATY OF PRO-
TECTORATE.

PERFUME RIVER. (Sông Hương). A river in central
Vietnam. It originates in Nam-Hòa District of
Thừa-Thiên Province where its two tributaries
(the Tả-Trạch and Hữu-Trạch Rivers) join together.
It flows through the city of Huế to Cửa Thuận-An
where it empties into the South China Sea. The
Perfume River is famous for its scenic beauty.
See HUẾ.

PETRUS KY. See TRƯỜNG VĨNH-KÝ.

PHẠM HỒNG-THÁI (1896-1924). (Phạm Thanh-Tích). A
revolutionary and martyr during the anti-colonial
resistance movement. Born in central Vietnam he
became a laborer in Hà-Nội where he joined the
Việt-Nam Quang-Phục Hội (The Association for the
Restoration of Vietnam). He later went to Canton
in China for revolutionary training and later to
Shanghai, Hong-Kong and Japan. On June 18, 1924
he was on a mission to assassinate French Governor
General Martial Merlin. When he threw a bomb at
Merlin he only injured him. But, Phạm Hồng-Thái,
unable to escape, committed suicide by drowning.
Although unsuccessful, his deed was highly pub-
licized and drew the attention of the world to
the Vietnamese revolutionary cause. See MERLIN
MARTIAL-HENRY, VIỆT-NAM QUANG-PHỤC HỘI.

PHẠM-HÙNG (1912-   ). Member of the Lao-Động Party
Politburo and Deputy Prime Minister of the Demo-
cratic Republic of Vietnam. He was born in Vĩnh-
Long Province in south Vietnam. He joined Hồ
Chí-Min's Revolutionary Youth League in the 1920's
and the Indochinese Communist Party in 1930. He

was active in the Việt-Minh and has held several
high leadership positions in the Democratic Republic of Vietnam.

PHẠM NGŨ-LÃO (1225-1320). A general and scholar during
the Trần Dynasty (1225-1400). He was born in Hải-
Dương Province. He fought under Trần Hùng-Đạo
against the invading Mongols. In 1285, together
with Trần Quốc-Toản and Trần Quang-Khải, he led
the Vietnamese in the Battle of Chương-Dương
Warf which drove the Mongols out of the capital
and led eventually to the expulsion of the Mongols in the same year. After the final victory
over the invaders from the north, he fought in
minor battles against Laos and Champa. He was
known for his expert military leadership and was
an inspiration for his men. He was equally
skilled with his pen. See TRẦN HÙNG-ĐẠO, TRẦN
NHÂN-TÔNG, TRẦN QUANG-KHẢI, TRẦN QUỐC-TOẢN.

PHẠM VĂN-ĐỒNG (1908-   ). Prime Minister, Vice-
Chairman of the National Defense Council, and
member of the Politburo of the Lao-Động Party of
the Democratic Republic of Vietnam. He was born
in Quảng-Ngãi Province in central Vietnam. His
father was a mandarin and private secretary to
Emperor Duy-Tân. Đồng was educated in Huế and
Hà-Nội. In 1925 he joined Hồ Chí-Minh's Revolutionary Youth League. He continued his activities with the Vietnamese communist movement
and was forced into exile to southern China in
1939. He was involved in the founding of the
Việt-Minh in 1941. During the Indochina War from
1946-1954 he served in leadership positions with
the Việt-Minh. In July, 1954, he headed the
communist delegation to the Geneva Conference
which ended the Indochina War. In September, 1955
he was appointed Prime Minister, a post which he
has help up to the present.

PHẠM-QUỲNH (1892-1945). Influential reformist journalist in north Vietnam during the first half of
the twentieth century. Born in Hải-Dương Province, he graduated from interpreter's school in
Hà-Nội in 1908. From 1917-1932 he served as
editor-in-chief and publisher of the intellectual
journal, Nam-Phong. From this vantage point he
had a strong influence on the Vietnamese intelligentsia both as a writer and publisher. Although
he had contacts with revolutionaries, he himself
was a reformist. Such was the emphasis of his
writings as he sought to popularize western literature and philosophy. In 1932 he was invited

to serve in an official capacity by Emperor Bảo-
Đại (1925-1945). He quit his work with <u>Nam-Phong</u>
and moved to Huế and served as Secretary General
of the Bảo-Đại government until 1945 when he was
killed by the Việt-Minh near Huế. See NAM-PHONG.

PHAN BỘI-CHÂU (1867-1940). A scholar and revolutionary who played a key role in the resistance movement against the French. He was born in Nghệ-An
Province and was schooled in the Confucian tradition. When he was just nineteen years old he
organized fellow students to join the fight
against the French in response to Emperor Duy-
Tân's (1907-1916) Cần-Vương edict. The group
was disbanded but his anti-French fervor did not
lessen. After having failed the regional examinations for several years, he finally passed
them with highest honors in 1900. For the next
five years he travelled throughout the country
with official status, while also contacting other
anti-colonialists. It was during this period
that he and his comrades formulated plans for the
Đông-Du Movement and the Duy-Tân Hội. In 1905
he went secretly to Japan where he met with
Chinese and Japanese revolutionaries. He returned
to Vietnam and took Prince Cường-Đề back to
Japan together with three students. In 1908 the
Việt-Nam Công-Hiến Hội (Vietnam Public Offering
Society) was formed in Japan with Cường-Đề as
President. The society's primary mission was to
provide cohesion for the group of Vietnamese
students in Japan, numbering at that time around
100. In 1912, Phan Bội-Châu, Cường-Đề and Nguyễn
Thượng-Hiền organized the Việt-Nam Quang-Phục Hội
(the Association for the Restoration of Vietnam)
in Canton. The Quang-Phục Hội sent armed cadre
to aid the anti-French factions inside Vietnam.
Assassination squads were also sent against the
French and some Vietnamese collaborators also.
The French soon realized the involvement of the
Quang-Phục Hội and issued orders for Phan Bội-
Châu's arrest. He was captured in 1925 in
Shanghai and returned to Vietnam. In November
of that year he was sentenced to life imprison-
ment. Responding to public pressure for grant-
inh him amnesty, he was pardoned and offered a
position in the government. He refused, and
instead agreed to "retire" under a loose guard.
He moved to Huế where he lived a leisurely and
quiet life in Bến-Ngụ Hamlet on the Perfume River.
He died on September 29, 1940 at the age of
seventy-four. See CƯỜNG-ĐỀ, CẦN-VƯƠNG MOVEMENT,

PHAN CHU-TRINH (1872-1926). (Sometimes referred to as
     Phan Châu-Trinh). A scholar and political activ-
     ist during the anti-colonial resistance movement
     in the early 1900's. He was born into a wealthy
     family in Quảng-Nam Province in central Vietnam.
     He passed the regional examinations in 1900 and
     the general examinations (thi-hội) the following
     year. He rebelled against the mandarinal system
     and finally broke with it completely in 1905.
     He then went south with several of his comrades
     including Trần Quý-Cáp and Huỳnh Thúc-Kháng in
     order to generate support for the reform move-
     ment. He made contact with many of the revol-
     utionaries of this period in both the north and
     south. In 1906, he secretly went to Japan to
     meet Phan Bội-Châu. It became evident at this
     meeting that there were basic differences between
     the two. Phan Bội-Châu advocated armed resistance
     while Phan Chu-Trinh preached reform. In 1907 he
     lectured several times at the Đông-Kinh Nghĩa-
     Thục. After the school was closed in 1908 he was
     arrested in connection with the general unrest
     in Quảng-Nam Province. He was sentenced to life
     imprisonment and was taken to Côn-Đảo Island.
     However, in 1910, in response to public pressure,
     the French released him from prison. The follow-
     ing year he went to Paris where he continued his
     writings. In 1914 the French jailed him again,
     this time as a draft resister and possible sympa-
     thizer with Germany. He was released in 1915 and
     returned to Vietnam in 1925 where he toured the
     country to promote his reformist cause. He died
     quietly in a hospital in Sài-Gòn on March 24,
     1926 at the age of fifty-four years. See ĐÔNG-
     KINH NGHĨA-THỤC, PHAN BỘI-CHÂU, TRẦN QÚY-CÁP.

PHAN ĐINH-PHÙNG (1847-1895). A scholar, Mandarin,
     and patriot. Born in Hà-Tĩnh Province in cen-
     tral Vietnam, he received his doctoral degree in
     1877. The following year he was made the Grand
     Imperial Censor at the royal court. When Emperor
     Tự-Đức (1848-1883) died he willed his adopted son
     to succeed him. Phan Đình-Phùng was dismissed
     when he objected to Tự-Đức's choice. When Em-
     peror Hàm-Nghi (1884-1885) fled the capital in
     1885, Phan Đình-Phùng organized a resistance
     army to support the deposed emperor. He set up
     headquarters in Vụ-Quang, Hà-Tĩnh Province, and
     operated in the provinces of Thanh-Hóa, Nghệ-An,
     Hà-Tĩnh, and Quảng-Bình. An unusual feature of
     the resistance army was the arms production de-
     vised by another famous patriot, Cao-Thắng.

The French applied increasingly strong
pressure against him, including digging up and
exhibiting the remains of his ancestors and
arresting members of his family. As the French
army moved in, Phan Đình-Phùng had to move his
base. Cao-Thắng was killed in a desparate
attempt to take the town of Nghệ-An. After ten
years of resistance, Phan Đình-Phùng died of
dysentery in December, 1895. His army accepted
the French offer of pardon and surrendered only
to discover that they had been tricked. All
were beheaded except Phan Đình-Phùng's wife and
son. See CAO-THẮNG, HÀM-NGHI.

PHAN-RANG. The capital city of Ninh-Thuận Province.
Population 38,023. It is located 320 kilometers
(123 miles) north of Sai-Gon on highway number
one. Phan-Rang was once part of the Kingdom of
Champa and served as its capital under the name
of Panduranga. The Nguyễn Lord Nguyễn Phúc-Chu
captured the province in 1697. Today it is
best known for the heavy Chàm population which
is centered in nearby An-Phước and Tháp-Chàm.
Phan-Rang is also the former name of the Province
of Ninh-Thuận. See NINH-THUẬN PROVINCE, PANDUR-
ANGA.

PHAN-RANG RIVER. (Sông Phan-Rang). See CÂY RIVER.

PHAN THANH-GIẢN (1796-1867). A scholar, diplomat
and anti-colonialist during the early Nguyễn
Dynasty (1802-1945). Born in what is now Kiến-
Hòa Province in south Vietnam, he passed his
doctoral examinations in 1826. He then served
in several administrative positions in central
Vietnam. In 1832 he went with a delegation to
China. After returning home he resumed his
administrative career experiencing many ups and
downs as a result of taking unpopular stands.
In 1851, he was sent to the south with Nguyễn
Tri-Phương where he carried out a great many
public improvement projects in his capacity as
Viceroy. When the French invaded in 1862, Phan
Thanh-Giản was sent to negotiate a settlement,
resulting in the concession of three eastern
provinces to the French. The following year he
was sent to Paris as ambassador to negotiate a
new treaty. He was received by Napoleon III but
did not meet with success. He continued his
negotiations with the French after his return
to Vietnam. The negotiations were again unsuccessful and in June, 1867, the French forces took the
remaining three provinces in the south. Unable

to negotiate an honorable peace and unable to
convince the court to lead a national resistance,
Phan Thanh-Giản went on a hunger strike for
seventeen days. On August 4, 1867, he took poison to complete his suicide. See TREATY OF SÀI-
GÒN.

PHAN-THIẾT. The capital city of Bình-Thuận Province
in central Vietnam. Population 76,652 (1971).
The city is a coastal town located on highway
number one, 200 kilometers (124 miles) north of
Sài-Gòn. Phan-Thiết is best known for its nước
mam production (fish sauce). It is basically a
fishing town and has a fish canning industry.
See BÌNH-THUẬN PROVINCE, NƯỚC MẮM.

PHAN TRẦN. A classic epic poem written in nôm by an
unknown author. The story was based on a Chinese
story and concerns the predestined love of two
people, Phan-Sinh and Trần Kiều-Liên.

PHÁT DẪN. See ĐƯA ĐÁM.

PHÁT-DIỆM. A city in Ninh-Bình Province in north
Vietnam. It is best known as a center of Catholicism. As early as 1901 the Catholic diocese
of Phát-Diệm was established and in 1913 a monastery was founded to train Vietnamese clergy.
The Catholic cathedral at Phát-Diệm was built in
the early twentieth century and is particularly
well-known as a blend of eastern and western
architecture. See NINH-BÌNH PROVINCE.

PHẬT-GIÁO. (Đạo Phật-Giáo). Buddhism. See BUDDHISM.

PHẬT-GIÁO HÒA-HẢO. See HÒA-HẢO.

PHILASTRE, PAUL-LOUIS-FELIX. The second French Charge
d'Affairs to be stationed in Huế. He served in
that post from 1877-1879. He came to Indochina
in 1881 as a naval officer. It was he who made
the preliminary arrangements for the treaty of
1874, which is sometimes referred to as the
Philastre Treaty. He was an expert on the Chinese
language and translated the Annamite Code and
Commentaries which earned him the Stanislas Julien
Prize in 1877. See TREATY OF 1874.

PHỞ. A consomme type of soup prepared with beef and
noodles. The bouillon or broth is prepared
separately with the beef and noodles added at the
last minute with onion and spices. Phở is a
north Vietnamese dish.

PHOENIX. See PHƯỢNG.

PHONG-DINH PROVINCE. An inland Mekong Delta province
in south Vietnam. It is located southeast of
An-Giang Province, northeast of Chương-Thiện
Province, northwest of Ba-Xuyên Province and
southwest of Vĩnh-Long Province. The provincial
capital is the city of Cần-Thơ which is located
on highway number four, and on the lower Mekong
River (Sông Hậu-Giang). Highway number four runs
from Sài-Gòn to the Cà-Mau Peninsula. The population of the province is 337,159 (1971) and the
land mass is 1597 square kilometers (616 square
miles). Present-day Phong-Dinh Province was
originally a part of An-Giang Province. The
French divided An-Giang into six smaller provinces: Châu-Đốc, Long-Xuyên, Sa-Đéc, Cần-Thơ,
Sốc-Trăng and Bạc-Liêu. In 1957, Cần-Thơ Province was changed to Phong-Dinh Province. Rice
is the major crop. The province also produces
banana and pork. The city of Cần-Thơ plays a
major role in the transportation and commerce of
the Mekong Delta. It has also served as the
headquarters for the IV military region or corps
area. The University of Cần-Thơ was established
in 1966. See CẦN-THƠ.

PHÚ. A form of poetic essay used to describe nature,
traditions, or human sentiment. This form is
actually of Chinese origin.

PHỦ. Prefecture. Phủ is an administrative unit first
used under Emperor Lê Thái-Tổ (1428-1433). A
province (Lộ or Trấn) was divided into several
prefectures (Phủ). Each Phủ was governed by a
Tri-Phủ and was, in turn, divided into smaller
districts or sub-prefectures (Huyện). The term
Phủ is no longer used in this connection.

PHÚ-BỔN PROVINCE. An inland, mountainous province in
the central highlands. The province borders on
Pleiku Province to the northwest, Bình-Định Province to the northeast, Phú-Yên Province to the
east and Darlac Province to the south. The population of the province is 69,765 (1971) and the
land mass is 4,785 square kilometers (1,847 square
miles). The provincial capital is Cheo-Reo (Hậu-
Bổn). The province is inhabited mainly by highland people of the Jarai and Bahnar ethno-linguistic groups. The chief products are upland
rice, timber and some sesame. See HẬU-BỔN.

PHÚ-CƯỜNG. The capital city of Bình-Dương Province
in south Vietnam. Population 34,438. The city
is best known for its lacquerware factories.

PHU KIÊU HAN MOUNTAIN. (Núi Phu Kiêu Han). A mountain in Lai-Châu Province in north Vietnam. It
is near the Chinese border and just east of the
Black River (Sông Đà-Giang). It has an elevation
of 1,980 meters (6,409 feet).

PHU LƯỞNG MOUNTAIN. (Núi Phu Lưởng). A mountain in
Nghiã-Lộ Province in north Vietnam. It has an
elevation of 2,983 meters (9,787 feet).

PHU NAM MAN MOUNTAIN. (Núi Phu Nam Man). A mountain
in Lai-Châu Province in north Vietnam. It has
an elevation of 2,124 meters (6,969 feet).

PHÚ-QUỐC ISLAND. An island in the Gulf of Thailand.
It is triangular in shape with an area of about
66,000 hectares (26,700 acres). It is administered as a district of Kiên-Giang Province. Phú-
Quốc is best known for the production of nước
mắm (fish sauce) of excellent quality. See KIÊN-
GIANG PROVINCE.

PHU SI LUNG MOUNTAIN. (Núi Phu Si Lung). A mountain
on the Chinese/Vietnamese border in Lai-Châu
Province. It has an elevation of 3,076 meters
(10,092 feet).

PHÚ-THỌ CITY. The capital city of Vĩnh-Phú Province
in north Vietnam. It is located 100 kilometers
(62 miles) northwest of Hà-Nội. See VĨNH-PHÚ
PROVINCE.

PHÚ-VINH. The capital city of Vĩnh-Bình Province in
south Vietnam. Population 51,535. See VĨNH-
BÌNH PROVINCE.

PHÚ-XUÂN. A former city near Huế in central Vietnam.
The Nguyễn Lords (1600-1778) maintained their
court at Phú-Xuân from 1687-1778. It then be-
came the capital city of Emperor Quang-Trung
(1788-1792). In 1802, Nguyễn-Anh defeated the
Tây-Sơn regime and established his capital at
Huế, two kilometers (1.2 miles) northeast of
Phú-Xuân. See HUẾ.

PHÚ-YÊN PROVINCE. A coastal province in central Vietnam. It is located south of Bình-Định Province
and north of Khánh-Hòa Province. Phú-Yên has a

land mass of 5,233 square kilometers (2,020 square miles) and has a population of 334,184 (1971). The capital, Tuy-Hòa, is situated on the coast. Phú-Yên was a part of Champa until 1578 when it was captured by the Lê Dynasty (1428-1788) and made into a prefecture. It remained under the control of Champa until Nguyễn-Hoàng defeated the Chams in 1611 and made it part of Quảng-Nam. It became a separate province in 1802 under Gia-Long. Farming and fishing are the most important occupations. The main crops are rice, sugar, tobacco, wood, and mangoes. The mangoes of Đá-Trắng are well-known for their sweet taste.

The two main rivers are the Đá-Rang and the Hà-Bường Rivers. Highway number one and the railroad run from north to south through the province. Tuy-Hòa is also connected with Pleiku by road via Cheo-Reo in Phú-Bồn Province. The Trường-Sơn Mountain range occupies the western part of the province and extends to the sea coast at the very southern extreme of the province forming the Cả Pass (Đèo Cả). The lowland coastal region is inhabited by ethnic Vietnamese while the highland people of the Hroy and Rhade ethno-linguistic groups live in the mountains. See TUY-HOÀ.

PHÚC-YÊN PROVINCE. Former province in north Vietnam the capital city of which was Phúc-Yên City. The province was merged with Vĩnh-Yên to form the province of Vĩnh-Phúc. Vĩnh-Phúc was later merged with Phú-Thọ to form the province of Vĩnh-Phú. See VĨNH-PHÚ PROVINCE.

PHỤNG. See PHƯỢNG.

PHỤNG-HIỆP CANAL. (Kinh Phụng-Hiệp). A canal connecting Quản-Long (capital of An-Xuyên Province) with Phụng-Hiệp in Phong-Dinh Province.

PHƯỚC-LỄ. See PHƯỚC-TUY CITY.

PHƯỚC-LONG CITY. The capital city of Phước-Long Province. Population 21,960 (1971). It was founded in 1924 under the name of Sông-Bé but was later changed to Phước-Long city. It is also known as Phước-Binh. The city is located about 125 air kilometers (77 miles) north of Sài-Gòn by the Sông-Bé River and at the foot of the 915 meter (3,000 feet) Bà-Rá Mountain. See PHƯỚC-LONG PROVINCE.

PHƯỚC-LONG PROVINCE. A mountainous province in south
Vietnam. It borders on Cambodia to the northwest
and is situated south of Quảng-Đức Province, and
north of Long-Khánh and Bình-Dương Provinces. The
provincial capital is Phước-Long City which is
also sometimes referred to as Phước-Bình or Sông-
Bé. The population of Phước-Long Province is
47,210 of which 22,606 are highland tribal people,
mainly of the Stieng ethno-linguistic group (1971).
The land mass of the province is 5,299 square
kilometers (2,045 square miles). The province is
not heavily populated or well developed. Highway
number fourteen, which connects Sài-Gòn with Ban-
Mê-Thuột, runs through the province. Phước-Long
was once the district of Bà-Rá in Biên-Hòa Province under the French. It was known as a place
where political prisoners were sent. In March,
1954 Bà-Rá District became Phước-Long Province.
The province has one major river, the Sông-Bé.
About eighty percent of the province is covered
with jungle and forest. There are some rubber
plantations and fruit groves located in Phước-
Long. Rubber, fruit, timber, and coffee are
the major products. Native woods include teak,
mahogany, bamboo, and rattan. The province was
also known for its wild game, which included
elephant, tiger, leopard, bear, wild boar, peacock and pheasant. The war, however, disrupted
both the wild game and the crop production. See
PHƯỚC-LONG CITY.

PHƯỚC-THÀNH PROVINCE. A former province in south
Vietnam. Phước-Thành Province was established
in 1957 from three districts in northern Biên-
Hòa Province. The Province capital was Phước-
Vinh. In 1965, the province was dissolved and
its territory annexed to the neighboring provinces
of Biên-Hòa, Bình-Dương, Long-Khánh and Phước-
Long. The population of Phước-Thành Province in
1964 was 47,728.

PHƯỚC-TUY CITY. The capital city of Phước-Tuy Province.
Population 21,699 (1971). The city was formerly
called Phước-Lễ.

PHƯỚC-TUY PROVINCE. A coastal province in south Vietnam. It is located south of Bình-Tuy Province
and north of Gia-Định Province. The province
was established by enlarging the former province
of Bà-Rịa. The population of the province is
124,844 and the land mass is 2,203 square kilometers (850 square miles). Phước-Tuy is probably

best known for the resort city of Vũng-Tàu, which
was part of the province until 1965 when it was
made an independent municipality. The capital
of Phước-Tuy is Phước-Tuy City (formerly Phước-Lễ)
which is located on highway number fifteen. See
PHƯỚC-TUY CITY.

PHƯỜNG. An association of merchants or craftsmen at
the village or local level in traditional Vietnam.
It was comprised of members of the same profession. The purpose of the association was
mutual aid and group action on matters of common,
professional concern. Members were often both
male and female. The Phường was headed by a
chief (Trùm). See TIÊN-SƯ.

PHƯỢNG. (Also called Phụng). Phoenix. The phoenix
is an important character in Vietnamese mythology
and one of the four sacred animals (Tứ-Linh).
It represents virtue, grace, peace and concord.
It is a symbol of womanhood and female virtue
and was used as the principal emblem of queens
and other female royalty as the dragon was used
by the emperors. The Vietnamese phoenix has a
small bill, the neck of a snake, breast of a
swallow, the back of a tortoise and tail of a
fish. It is characterized by pride, nobility,
and grace of movement. It is said that its song
includes all five notes of the traditional Vietnamese musical scale, and its feathers include
the five basic colors. The phoenix appears only
during times of peace and prosperity and hides
when there is trouble. The male phoenix (phường)
is distinguished from the female phoenix (hoang).
See TỨ-LINH.

PIA OAC MOUNTAIN. (Núi Pia Oac). A mountain in Cao-
Bằng Province in north Vietnam. It is the
tallest mountain in the Ngân-Sơn Mountain Range
and has an elevation of 1930 meters (6,335 feet).
See NGÂN-SƠN MOUNTAIN RANGE.

PIA YA MOUNTAIN. (Núi Pia Ya). A mountain in Hà-
Giang Province in north Vietnam. It has an
elevation of 1976 meters (6,486 feet).

PIGNEAU DE BEHAINE, BISHOP (1741-1799). (Also known
as the Bishop of Adran). A French Catholic
Bishop who became advisor to Emperor Gia-Long
(1802-1819). He was sent to the province of Hà-
Tiên in south Vietnam in 1767 to head a Catholic

seminary. In 1775, he saved the life of Nguyễn-Anh, nephew of the Nguyen Lord, Nguyễn Phúc-Thuần, as Nguyễn-Anh was fleeing from the Tây-Sơn army. The Bishop devoted himself to the restoration of the Nguyen family to the throne and the intervention of the French military forces to that end. In 1784, armed with Nguyễn-Anh's royal seal and his five-year old son, he went to Pondicherry, in French India, to plead Nguyễn-Anh's case. In 1786, after no success he went on to Paris. He lobbied for support and finally extracted a commitment for four ships, 1650 men plus supplies. However, after returning to French India, he discovered that the French government could not keep the commitment. Pigneau was determined in his mission. He raised money from French merchants in the Mascarene Islands and in India, acquired and equipped two ships, bought weapons and ammunition, hired volunteers and deserters from the French Navy and left Pondicherry for Vietnam with his privately organized expedition on June 19, 1789.

Although many of the French troops gradually left the struggle over the next two years, Pigneau stayed on at the side of Nguyễn-Anh until he (the Bishop) died from dysentery on October 9, 1799. Nguyễn-Anh pressed forward to total victory in 1802 and proclaimed himself Emperor Gia-Long (1802-1819). Pigneau was buried on December 16, 1799 in the presence of the crown prince, all the mandarins of the court, the King's bodyguard of 12,000 men and 40,000 mourners. Nguyễn-Anh composed a funeral oration which was read aloud. See GIA-LONG, NGUYỄN-ANH, TÂY-SƠN DYNASTY.

PIGNON, LEON. High Commissioner to Indochina from October, 1948, to December, 1950. He had previously served in various positions in Indochina in the colonial civil service.

PLAIN OF REEDS. An area of some 900,000 hectares (2,223,000 acres) located in and closely associated with the delta of the upper Mekong River (Sông Tiền Giang) in Vietnam and Cambodia. It stretches about 120 kilometers (75 miles) east/west and 80 kilometers (50 miles) north/south. It covers about 6,700 square kilometers (2,586 square miles) of land in Vietnam, including the provinces of Kiến-Phong, Kiến-Tường, and parts of Định-Tường, Long-An and Hậu-Nghĩa provinces. The Plain of Reeds is characterized by low flat,

reed-covered or brush-covered land. It retains
too much water in the wet season and too little
in the dry season. Agriculture, including livestock production is the primary economic pursuit.

PLEIKU CITY. The capital city of Pleiku Province in
the central highlands. Population 34,867 (1971).
It is situated at the intersection of highways
number fourteen and number nineteen and is thus
directly linked by road to Ban-Mê-Thuột, Kontum,
An-Khê, and Qui-Nhơn. See PLEIKU PROVINCE.

PLEIKU PROVINCE. A mountainous province in the central highlands. It borders on Cambodia to the
west and lies south of Kontum Province and north
of Darlac Province. The population is 214,912
and the land mass is 8,444 square kilometers
(3,260 square miles). The province is inhabited
primarily by highland people including the Jarai,
Bahnar, and Rhade ethno-linguistic groups, in
that order of predominance. The provincial capital is Pleiku City, which is located at the
intersection of highways number fourteen and
number nineteen. The main products of the province are tea, coffee, handicrafts and timber.
See PLEIKU CITY.

POLITICAL PARTIES. As in most other Southeast Asian
nations, the use of political parties, in the
common sense of the word, came into being in
the late 1800's and early 1900's in reaction to
the process of colonialization. Since they were
outlawed by the French they were usually secret
societies and, even today, they tend to be
secretive. The communistic Worker's Party (Đảng
Lao-Động) is the official or ruling party in the
Democratic Republic of Vietnam. The two principal parties in the Republic of Vietnam are the
Đại-Việt Party (Đảng Đại-Việt) and the Nationalist Party (Việt-Nam Quốc-Dân Đảng or VNQDD),
both of which are strongly anti-communist. There
are many other smaller parties operative in Viet-
nam, particularly in the Republic of Vietnam, but
are too minor and numerous to mention. See CẦN-
LAO NHÂN-VỊ CÁCH-MẠNG ĐẢNG, ĐẢNG ĐẠI-VIET, ĐẢNG
LAO-ĐỘNG VIỆT-NAM, ĐẢNG XÃ-HỘI VIỆT-NAM, ĐÔNG-
DƯỞNG CỘNG-SẢN ĐẢNG, VIỆT-NAM CÁCH-MỆNH ĐỒNG-
MINH HỘI, VIỆT-NAM CÁCH-MỆNH THANH-NIÊN ĐỒNG-
CHÍ HỘI, VIỆT-NAM CỨU-QUỐC HỘI, VIỆT-NAM DÂN-CHỦ
ĐẢNG, VIỆT-NAM ĐỘC-LẬP ĐỒNG-MINH HỘI, VIỆT-NAM
DUY-TÂN HỘI, VIỆT-NAM PHỤC-QUỐC ĐỒNG-MINH HỘI,
VIỆT-NAM QUANG-PHỤC HỘI, VIỆT-NAM QUỐC-DÂN ĐẢNG.

POPULATION. The total population of Vietnam was estimated at nearly 39.5 million people in 1970.
The highest concentration of people is found in
the delta areas of the Red River and Mekong
River. The ethnic Vietnamese occupy these delta
areas as well as a narrow strip of lowlands along
the coast of central Vietnam. The mountainous
areas are inhabited by highland tribal groups of
a different ethnic origin than the Vietnamese.
     Democratic Republic of Vietnam: The last
official census was taken in 1960. At that time,
the total population was placed at 15,916,955,
85% of which were ethnic Vietnamese and 15% belonged to one of the many ethno-linguistic
minority groups. The average population density
was one hundred people per square kilometer.
The coastal and delta zones had 621 persons per
square kilometer, the central zone 205 and in
the highland areas there were 33 persons per
square kilometer. The urban population was
placed at 1,518,754 (9.6% of the total) and the
rural population was 14,398,201 (90.4% of the
total). Women comprised 51.7% of the total
population while 48.3% were men. The 1970 estimate of the total population is 21,150,000 with
a density of 134 persons per square kilometer
and an annual rate of increase of 3.5%.
     Republic of Vietnam: The 1971 official
estimates place the total population at 18,300,000.
Wartime conditions make it difficult or impossible
to establish accurate figures. The average population density in the Mekong Delta area is 149
persons per square kilometer. In the central
lowlands there are 93 persons per square kilometer and in the highland areas there are 18
persons per square kilometer. The urban population was estimated at 25% of the total in 1968
and continued to increase. Metropolitan Sài-Gòn
was estimated to have a 1971 population of
nearly three million. Approximately 80% of the
population are ethnic Vietnamese. The remaining
20% is composed of the various ethnic minorities,
including Chinese, Khmer and highland people.
The average rate of population increase is 2.6%
per year.

PORTS. The first port to be used on an established
basis by foreign ships was Faifo (present-day Hội
An), in Quảng-Nam Province. The Portuguese
first used this port beginning around 1540. The
Dutch later set up a trading center at Phố-Hiến
in north Vietnam. The port of Sài-Gòn was developed under the French as was the port of Hải-

Phòng.

Democratic Republic of Vietnam: Although Hà-Nội is the center of river and canal traffic, Hải-Phòng is the leading seaport. It has facilities for oceangoing vessels up to 10,000 tons. Northeast of Hải-Phòng are the two coal ports of Hòn-Gai and Cẩm-Phả which ship anthracite from nearby mines for export and domestic use. The port of Bến-Thủy near the city of Vinh in central Vietnam can admit coastal vessels up to 400 tons.

Republic of Vietnam: The principal commercial port is Sài-Gòn. It is situated about seventy kilometers (forty-five miles) from the sea on the Sài-Gòn River. The channel varies from twenty-nine to thirty-nine feet in depth. The river front docks are designed to take ships with a draft of no more than nineteen feet, although larger ships can be accommodated on favorable tides. The best port facilities in central Vietnam are at Đà-Nẵng. It has adequate harbor facilities, although its deep anchorage is exposed to heavy winds from the northeast during the winter monsoon. South of Nha-Trang is located Cam-Ranh Bay which is rated as one of the best natural harbors in Asia. This harbor was used by the French and the Japanese, but has only recently been developed as a port of the military supply system. A large runway is also a part of the complex. The resort coastal city of Vũng-Tàu has limited harbor facilities and can accommodate oceangoing vessels. A small fishing port is located at Rạch-Giá on the Gulf of Thailand. See CAM-RANH, ĐÀ-NẴNG, HẢI-PHÒNG, HỘI-AN, RẠCH-GIÁ, SÀI-GÒN.

POST TRẦN DYNASTY (1407-1413). (Nhà Hậu Trần or Hậu Trần Dynasty). The dynasty of the royal Trần family during the period of the Chinese (Ming) domination (1407-1427). After defeating the armies of the Hồ in 1407, China annexed the country. Actually, the Chinese invasion was originally under the pretense of restoring the throne to the rightful rulers - the Trần. However, China now claimed that no descendants of the Trần existed and gradually turned the country back into a Chinese colony. The Post Trần Dynasty represented the Vietnamese resistance movement against the Chinese. One of the younger sons of Emperor Trần Nghệ-Tông (1370-1372), Trần Giản-Định-Đế proclaimed himself emperor and raised an army to go against the Chinese. The effort enjoyed initial success but in 1913 when

the forces of the Trần were defeated and Trần
Gian-Đinh-Đế successor, Trần Qúi-Khoách was
captured. The permanent restoration of the Trần
dynasty was bound to fail because the forces were
weak and the support of the people was divided.
See TRẦN GIAN-ĐINH-ĐẾ, TRẦN QÚI-KHOÁCH.

POU THA CA MOUNTAIN. (Núi Pou Tha Ca). A mountain
in Hà-Giang Province in north Vietnam. It has an
elevation of 2,274 meters (7,641 feet).

PREHISTORY (? - 300 B.C.). Most of the archaeological
investigations into the period have been carried
on in north Vietnam and northern central Vietnam.
Discoveries relating to the Pleistocene Era
indicate close relationships in the fauna of
Indonesia to that of Vietnam, and specifically
that the fauna in Vietnam at the time was characteristic of that in the corresponding epochs
in which Java Man (Pithecanthropus) lived as well
as the famous Peking Man (Sinanthropus). The
earliest signs of man were found at Núi Độ (Độ
Mountain) in Thanh-Hóa Province and are dated as
belonging to the lower Paleolithic (early stone
age). Other early stone age finds were made at
Sơn-Vi in Vĩnh-Phú Province and Bình-Gia in Lạng-
Sơn Province. The stone age settlements in Vietnam were characterized by cliff dwellings in the
limestone massifs, which exists only in the
northern half of Vietnam. Paleolithic tools were
made of Basalt in Vietnam, rather than flint as
in other Paleolithic cultures in other parts of
the world. Bamboo and seashells were also used
extensively instead of other stone implements
such as arrowheads, which further distinguishes
the Vietnamese Paleolithic period from others.
    The well-known Hòa-Bình culture is class-
ified as Mesolithic or middle stone age and is
a cave dwelling culture that is characteristic
of archaeological finds extending from southern
China to Sumatra. It is marked by a refinement
in stone implements, although there is a complete absence of ground stone tools. The Neolithic or later stone age is typified by the
Bắc-Sơn culture in the mountains of Hòa-Bình Province and the Quỳnh-Văn culture on the coast of
Nghệ-An Province. The Bắc-Sơn culture is particularly characterized by a type of hand axe
with polished edges which is known as the Bac-
Sonian axe. Generally, however, it is similar
to the earlier Hòa-Bình culture. The Quỳnh-Văn
culture marks the beginnings of man's settlement

in the lowlands. The most distinguishing feature
of these finds are the shell mounds, which in
addition to the shells of edible molluscs, have
yielded fragments of stone and pottery, bones of
animals and fish, charcoal and ash. These shell
mounds are also called kitchen middens.

The Bronze Age is best represented by the
well-known Đông-Sơn civilization which dated
around 700 B.C. - 300 A.D. This civilization
showed definite Chinese influence and was quite
widespread. See BẮC-SƠN CIVILIZATION, BÌNH-GIA
CIVILIZATION, HÒA-BÌNH CIVILIZATION, NÚI ĐỘ,
QUỲNH-VĂN CIVILIZATION, SƠN-VỊ CIVILIZATION, SA-
HUỲNH, ĐÔNG-SƠN CIVILIZATION.

PRINTING. The art of printing was introduced from
China during the fifteenth century. Prior to
that time, all books were imported from China.
A mandarin named Lương Nhữ-Học was irritated
by this state of affairs and obtained the Emperor's
permission to go to China to learn printing and
pottery making. But because he was dressed as an
ambassador, all the print shops were closed to him.
So, he disguised himself as a trader in pottery
and set up shop next door to a printing house.
After he had learned the art of printing by ob-
servation, he returned home. All the people in
his village of Hồng-Liễu in Hải-Hưng Province
became skilled printers and made fortunes through
their monopoly of printing books. At the death of
Lương Nhữ-Học, the villagers built a temple in
his honor in token of their appreciation.

PROVISIONAL REVOLUTIONARY GOVERNMENT OF THE REPUBLIC
OF SOUTH VIETNAM. See CHÍNH-PHỦ CÁCH-MẠNG LÂM-
THỜI CỘNG-HÒA MIỀN NAM VIỆT-NAM.

-Q-

QUAN. Mandarin. The use of mandarins in Vietnam is
as old as Vietnamese history. However, the mandarin corps was first solidified and refined
under the Lý Dynasty (1010-1225) and further
developed under subsequent dynasties, particularly
the Lê (1428-1788). Selection of mandarins was
on the basis of the competitive mandarinal examinations (also called triennial or civil service
examinations). Originally Buddhism and Buddhist
monks exerted heavy influence on the selection
process. Later, Taoist and Confucianist materials were used for the examination. Finally,

Confucianism prevailed as the dominant influence
in the selection and philosophy of the civil
service.
     The hierarchy of the Vietnamese mandarinate
was patterned after that of China. The military
mandarins (Võ Quan) were separate from the civil
hierarchy (Kinh Quan) but were ultimately under
the authority of the civilian mandarinate. At
the central level a stratified organization of
civilian and military mandarins made up the imperial court. At the lower levels mandarins
served in local administrative positions such as
governor (Tri-Phủ), district chief (Tri-Huyện),
or village mandarin (Xã-Quan). The ranking system established a scale for prestige, status
and salary. There was a great deal of mobility
within the system. However, there was no priv-
ilege attached to the individual himself. If
a person was demoted to a lesser position, his
salary and title were changed accordingly. This
should not be confused with the system of titles
of nobility which were strictly honorific. See
NOBILITY, THI ĐÌNH, THI HỘI, THI HƯỜNG, THI KHOA,
XÃ-QUAN.

QUẬN. District. An administrative subdivision of a
     province. The district has traditionally been
     considered as the lowest territorial echelon of
     the central government. The chief of the dis-
     trict was the nearest representative of the im-
     perial court to the village. The district was
     sometimes divided into cantons (tổng) but more
     often it was directly divided into villages. To-
     day the term quận is used only in the Republic
     of Vietnam. The term huyện (and sometimes châu
     in the highlands) is used in the Democratic Re-
     public of Vietnam. See ADMINISTRATIVE DIVISIONS,
     HUYỆN.

QUẦN-ĐẢO HOÀNG-XA. See PARACELS ISLANDS.

QUẦN-ĐẢO TRƯỜNG-XA. See SPRATLEY ISLANDS.

QUAN-LỘ. See MANDARIN ROAD.

QUẨN-LONG. The capital city of An-Xuyên Province.
     Population 69,983. The city is also sometimes
     known as Cà-Mau. It is located on highway num-
     ber four which connects it with Cần-Thơ and Sài-
     Gòn. See AN-XUYÊN, CÀ-MAU PENINSULA.

QUẢNG-BINH PROVINCE. A coastal province in central
     Vietnam. Quảng-Bình is located south of Hà-Tĩnh

Province and north of the Vĩnh-Linh Special Zone
(formerly part of Quảng-Trị Province). The population of Quảng-Bình is estimated at 400,000
(1968). The province covers an area of 8,730
square kilometers (3,370 square miles). The
capital of Quảng-Bình is the city of Đồng-Hới.
The Hoành-Sơn Mountains separate the province
from Hà-Tĩnh to the north. The Trường-Sơn Mountain Range occupies the western part of the
province. The two tallest mountains in Quảng-
Bình are the Ca Ta Roun Mountain (Núi Ca Ta Roun)
which stands 1,674 meters (5,328 feet) and is located on the Lao border and the Ma Ma Mountain
(Núi Ma Ma) which stands 715 meters (2,346 feet).
The two main rivers are the Gianh River (Sông
Gianh) which flows southeasterly out of the
Hoành-Sơn Mountains and the Đài-Giang River (Sông
Đài-Giang) which empties into the sea at Đồng-Hới.
See ĐÀI-GIANG RIVER, ĐỒNG-HỚI, GIANH RIVER, NHẬT-
LỆ WALL.

QUẢNG-ĐỨC PROVINCE. A mountainous province in the
central highlands. The province was created in
1959 from parts of Darlac, Phước-Long and Lâm-
Đồng provinces, all of which now border on Quảng-
Đức Province. The provincial capital is Gia-
Nghĩa. The population is 38,305 (1971) and the
land mass is 5,958 square kilometers (2,300
square miles). The province is inhabited almost
entirely by highland people of the Rhade, Stieng,
Koho, and Mnong ethno-linguistic groups. The
province is not well developed. The major crops
are upland rice, timber, and sweet potatoes. See
GIA-NGHĨA.

QUẢNG-NAM PROVINCE. A coastal province in central
Vietnam. It is situated south of Thừa-Thiên Province and north of Quảng-Tín Province. Quảng-Nam
is mountainous to the west and has low flatlands
along the coast. The province is 6,547 square
kilometers (2,527 square miles) in area and has
a population of 575,686 (1971). The provincial
capital, Hội-An, was founded by the Nguyễn Lords
at the end of the sixteenth century. It was
originally called Faifo by the westerners. As
the major port of central Vietnam during the
seventeenth, eighteenth, and nineteenth centuries
it flourished due to the foreign trade with the
Chinese, Japanese, and Portuguese. The province
has many mountains, including Ba-Nà Mountain,
1,460 meters (4,790 feet) high and a popular
resort when security permits.

That area now occupied by Quảng-Nam played
an important role in the ancient kingdom of Champa.
Archaeological sites have been discovered at Trà-
Kiệu, Mỹ-Sơn and Đông-Dương. The province was
then known as Chiêm-Động. Hồ Quý-Lý captured it
in 1402. The citadel which still remains, was
built under the reign of Minh-Mạng (1820-1840).
    Most of the population of the province is
ethnic Vietnamese. The mountainous districts
in the western part of the province are inhabited
by highland people of the Katu and Takua ethno-
linguistic groups. The province is mainly an
agricultural province, but has developed some
light industry. Among the products of the province are textiles, cinnamon, brick, tile and
timber. Coal mining was started at Nông-Sơn and
an effort was made to develop an industrial center at An-Hòa/Nông-Sơn. However, these plans
were all but abandoned because of the war.
Another famous site, Núi Non-Nước (Marble Mountain)
is located near Đà-Nẵng. Temples and shrines
are built into the caves and grottoes of this outcropping of marble and it has become a popular
tourist attraction. See HỘI-AN, NGŨ HÀNH SƠN.

QUẢNG-NGÃI CITY. The capital city of Quảng-Ngãi Pro-
    vince. Population 46,714. It is located on
    highway number one on the west bank of the Trà-
    Khúc River. See QUẢNG-NGÃI PROVINCE.

QUẢNG-NGÃI PROVINCE. (Sometimes referred to as Quảng-
    Nghĩa). A coastal province in central Vietnam
    located south of Quảng-Nam and north of Bình-Định
    Province. The province has a land mass of 5,718
    square kilometers (2,207 square miles) and a
    population of 731,471 (1971). The Trường-Sơn
    Mountain Range runs north/south through the west-
    ern part of the province. The eastern side of
    the province is flat, near sea level and largely
    in rice production. The area presently occupied
    by Quảng-Ngãi was part of the kingdom of Champa.
    Hồ Quý-Lý built two forts there in 1402 and named
    them Châu-Tư and Châu-Nghĩa. The Lê Dynasty
    (1428-1788) established the prefecture of Tư-Nghia
    and divided it into three districts: Bình-Sơn, Mộ-
    Đức, and Nghĩa-Giang. The Tây-Sơn changed the
    name to Hòa-Nghĩa. Emperor Gia-Long (1802-1819)
    changed the name back to Quảng-Nghĩa and finally
    in 1831 it was named Quảng-Ngãi.
    The provincial capital, Quảng-Ngãi City, is
    located on the south bank of the Trà-Khúc River,
    the point at which the railroad and highway num-
    ber one crosses the river. There is a citadel

built during the reign of Emperor Gia-Long (1802-
1819) located in the capital. Quảng Ngãi is
noted for the picturesque and unusually large
bamboo and wooden water wheels used for irrigation.
Among the main products of the province are
sugarcane, peanuts, corn, and cinnamon. A large
sugar mill has recently been constructed. Salt
fields are found in the area of Sa-Huỳnh. The
three main rivers are the Trà-Bong, Trà-Khúc,
and the Trà-Câu. The province is inhabited mainly by ethnic Vietnamese. However, the western
districts are populated by highland people of the
Cua and Hre ethno-linguistic groups. See QUẢNG-
NGÃI CITY, SA-HUỲNH.

QUẢNG-NINH PROVINCE. (Formerly Quảng-Yên and Hải-Ninh
provinces). A coastal province in the northeast
corner of north Vietnam. It borders on China to
the north, the South China Sea to the east, Hải-
Hưng and Hà-Bắc provinces to the west and Hải-
Phòng to the south. The population is estimated
at 483,400 (1969) and the land mass is given at
7,076 square kilometers (2,732 square miles).
The capital city of Quảng-Ninh Province is Hồng-
Gai, a railroad town on the bay of Hạ-Long. The
province is best known for its coal mines. The
deposits at Quảng-Yên, the largest in Southeast
Asia and with reserves estimated at some 200
million tons, produce a high quality of anthracite. The coal is shipped by rail and coastal
vessels to all parts of the country and is exported by seagoing craft from Hồng-Gai. The
province is also known for the picturesque and
unusual Hạ-Long Bay. Most of the inhabitants
are ethnic Vietnamese although the northern part
of the province contains a significant number of
Thái people as well as a large number of Nùng
and Chinese. The main economic activities besides coal mining are rice farming and fishing.
The smaller industries include nước mắm (fish
sauce) and pottery production. See HẠ-LONG BAY,
HON-GAY, NƯỚC-NẮM.

QUẢNG-TÍN PROVINCE. A coastal province in central
Vietnam situated south of Quảng-Nam and north of
Quảng-Ngãi. The province was originally part
of Quảng-Nam Province until it was declared a
separate province in 1962. The province has a
population of 405,421 and covers an area of 4,861
square kilometers (1,876 square miles). The provincial capital is Tam-Kỳ. National highway number one and the railway run through the province.
Quang-Tín is quite mountainous to the west where

it borders on Laos and Kontum Province. It is
not as rich in natural resources or population
as its mother province of Quảng-Nam. See TAM-KY.

QUẢNG-TRỊ CITY. The capital city of Quảng-Trị Province. The city is located on highway number one
  sixty kilometers northwest of Huế. It is situated
  on the right bank of the Thạch-Hãn River (sometimes called the Quảng-Trị River). The city was
  completely destroyed by the war in 1972, with
  most of the inhabitants taking refuge in Huế or
  Đà-Nẵng. The population in 1971 was reported to
  be 16,906. The famous La Vang Basilica is located nearby. It was built around 1900 by a
  Catholic priest after a reported appearance of
  the Virgin Mary. Many pilgrimages were traditionally made to the site every year. The basilica
  was also completely destroyed in 1972. See LA
  VANG BASILICA, QUẢNG-TRỊ PROVINCE.

QUẢNG-TRỊ PROVINCE. A coastal province in central
  Vietnam and the northernmost province in the Republic of Vietnam. Quảng-Trị Province was actually
  divided with the partition of the country into
  north and south Vietnam. That portion of Quảng-Trị
  remaining in the southern half of Vietnam (i.e.,
  south of the Bến-Hải River) is about 4,100 square
  kilometers (1,583 square miles). The mass upheaval of population due to the war makes it
  difficult to estimate the population. However,
  in 1965, the province had a total 282,000 inhabitants, including 10,000 highland people of the
  Brũ ethno-linguistic group. The province is
  mountainous to the west and has flat lowlands to
  the east. Highway number one and the north/south
  railroad pass through the province. Highway number nine originates at the province's second major
  city, Đồng-Hà where it connects highway number one
  with Tchepone in Laos. There are two main rivers
  in Quảng-Trị: the Bến-Hải (also called the Hiền-
  Lương) River, important because, in accordance
  with the Geneva Accords, it served as the demarcation line between the Republic of Vietnam to the
  south and the Democratic Republic of Vietnam to
  the north; and the Thạch-Hãn River which runs
  by the provincial capital. The mountain areas of
  Quảng-Trị, especially the district of Hướng-Hóa,
  were the site of several productive coffee plantations before the recent war. Rice, sweet potatoes and peppers are the leading produce of
  the lowlands. Fishing villages dot the coast.

There are several historical sites in Quảng-Trị.
The La Vang Basilica is located near the capital.
It was founded around 1900 after a reported
appearance of the Virgin Mary. The Village of
Ái-Tử was the headquarters of Nguyễn-Hoàng when
he first came south to serve as Governor of Thuận-
Hóa (present-day Quảng-Trị and Thừa-Thiên pro-
vinces) in 1558. See BẾN-HẢI RIVER, DEMARCATION
LINE, DEMILITARIZED ZONE, KHÊ-SANH, LA VANG BASIL-
ICA, QUẢNG-TRỊ CITY.

QUANG-TRUNG (ruled 1788-1792). (Nguyễn-Huệ). The
second of the Tây-Sơn brothers who led the Tây-
Sơn Rebellion (1771-1788). He took the name
Quang-Trung when he proclaimed himself Emperor in
1788. He led the campaign against the Chinese
occupation forces resulting in the expulsion of
the Chinese from Vietnam in 1789. Quang-Trung
immediately paid tribute to the Chinese court and
gained recognition as King of An-Nam. He managed
to consolidate and strengthen his regime. He
selected the best and most willing of the former
mandarins, encouraged land development, revised
the tax system, and upgraded the army. He opened
new schools at all levels and emphasized the
development of the Vietnamese national language.
Many classics were translated into chữ nôm.
Poetry and scholarship flourished under his reign.
He died in 1792 at the age of forty. See NGUYỄN-
HUỆ, NGUYỄN-LỮ, NGUYỄN-NHẠC, TÂY-SƠN DYNASTY,
TÂY-SƠN REBELLION.

QUẢNG-YÊN PROVINCE. See QUẢNG-NINH PROVINCE.

QUI-NHƠN. The capital city of Bình-Định Province in
central Vietnam. Population 188,717. Qui-Nhơn
was the name of the entire province under the
Tây-Sơn regime (1788-1802). Several battles for
control of the Qui-Nhơn citadel ensued between
the Tây-Sơn and Nguyễn-Anh. Finally, in 1799
the citadel fell into the hands of Nguyễn Anh's
forces and the province was renamed Bình-Định,
although the name Qui-Nhơn was retained for the
capital city. The city is located 680 kilometers
(422 miles) north of Sài-Gòn just off highway
number one. It is also connected to An-Khê and
Kontum via highway number nineteen. Qui-Nhơn is
situated on the coast and has commercial port
facilities. There is a technical high school and
a normal school located in the city. On September 30, 1970 Qui-Nhơn became a separate municipality. See BÌNH-ĐỊNH PROVINCE, NGUYỄN-NHẠC, TÂY-SƠN
REBELLION, NGUYỄN-ANH.

QUỐC-NGŨ. (National language or script). A Romanized
writing system used to write the Vietnamese language. Quốc-Ngũ was developed in the early
seventeenth century by Catholic missionaries as
a means of translating the catechisms and prayer
books. One central figure, Father Alexander de
Rhodes, is credited with making major contributions toward the development of the script. This
Jesuit priest wrote a Vietnamese-Portuguese-Latin
dictionary which was published in Rome in 1651.
    Quốc-Ngũ was initially used only by the
Catholic church. The more prestigious Chữ Nho
(Chinese characters) was used for official state
business and by scholars as well as civil servants
and was thus essential for anyone who wanted to
advance himself. It was not until 1915-1918 when
the triennial examinations were abolished that the
Latin script began to increase in popularity. The
French encouraged the use of Quốc-Ngũ and it soon
became used in schools throughout Vietnam. Today
it is used exclusively in both the Democratic
Republic of Vietnam and the Republic of Vietnam.
Because of its simplicity, it has been responsible
for the rapid increase in the literacy rate and
because it is suited to the printing industry it
has made a great contribution to Vietnam's rich
literary tradition. See LANGUAGE, LITERATURE,
NHO, NÔM, RHODES, MONSIGNOR ALEXANDER DE, VIETNAM-
ESE LANGUAGE.

QUỐC-SỬ THỰC-LỤC. (Literally, True Records of the
National History). A history of Vietnam covering
the period from the reign of Emperor Lê Huyền-Tông
(1663-1671) through the reign of Lê Gia-Tông (1672-
1675). This work was written by Hồ Sĩ-Dương, Lê-
Hi and Nguyễn Quý-Đức at the command of the Trịnh
Lord Trịnh-Căn in 1676.

QUỐC-SỬ TỤC-BIÊN. (Literally, Supplementary part of
the National History). A history of Vietnam
covering the period from the reign of Emperor Le
Hi-Tong (1676-1705) through the reign of Lê Ý-Tông
(1735-1740). It was written by Nguyễn-Hoàn, Lê
Qúi-Đôn, Ngô Thời-Sĩ and Nguyễn-Du at the command
of the Trịnh Lord Trịnh-Sâm.

QUỐC TỬ GIÁM. National Royal College. The first in-
stitute of higher education to be established in
Vietnam. It was created in Ha-Noi in 1076 by
Emperor Lý Nhân-Tông (1072-1127). Only princes
and sons of high ranking dignitaries were admitted.
In 1253, it was enlarged and renamed Quốc-Học-Viện

and became accessible to commoners who could
achieve high scores on the regional examinations
(Thi Hương). In 1483 it was again enalrged and
renamed Thái-Học and located in the same complex
as the Văn-Miếu Pagoda (Temple of Literature)
which was built to honor the country's scholars.
Among the famous men who taught at the then
Quốc Tử Giám was Chu Văn-An (fourteenth century)
Nguyễn-Nghiễm, father of Nguyễn-Du (eighteenth
century), and Lê Quý-Đôn (eighteenth century).
Emperor Gia-Long (1802-1819) reestablished the
Quốc Tử Giám in Huế where it remained during the
Nguyễn Dynasty (1802-1945). The school's name
was changed to Quốc-Học under which it still
operates today as a public high school. Among
the more well-known figures in contemporary his-
tory who attended the school are Hồ Chí-Minh,
Ngô Đình-Diệm, and Phạm Văn-Đồng. See EDUCATION,
LITERATURE, LÝ NHÂN-TÔNG, VĂN MIẾU PAGODA.

QUY. (Also called Rùa). Tortoise. The tortoise is
an important character in Vietnamese mythology
and one of the four sacred animals (Tứ-Linh).
It represents longevity and perfection and is
usually found with a coral branch in its mouth,
and a crane on its back. The crane usually has
a lotus flower in its beak. It also symbolizes
longevity but is not usually used in Buddhist
temples. The tortoise is believed to live
10,000 years. Generally, the crane is found on
the tortoise's back in temples dedicated to Confucius, Emperors or local spirits. See TỨ-LINH.

QUỲNH-VĂN CIVILIZATION. (Also called Quỳnh-Văn Culture).
A prehistoric culture of the early neolithic
(late stone age) which existed on the coast of
central Vietnam. The archaeological finds of this
culture were discovered in 1963 north of Vinh in
Nghệ-An Province. The significance of this stone
age settlement lies in the fact that it is the
first example of prehistoric man living in the
open lowlands rather than in the sheltered caves
of the highlands. Consequently, their culture
was different from their contemporaries as represented by the cultures of Bắc-Sơn and Hòa-Bình.
The people of Quỳnh-Văn ate sea food as well as
vegetables and used seashells as cutting and shaping tools as well as stone implements. The most
distinguishing feature of this culture are the
shell mounds (also called kitchen middens) which
yielded not only the discarded shells of edible
molluscs, but also fragments of stone and pottery,

animal and fish bones, charcoal and ash. Some of
the pottery showed crude basketry impressions.
Beneath the shell mounds were found several human
burial sites. See PREHISTORY.

-R-

RẠCH-GIÁ. The capital city of Kiên-Giang Province in
south Vietnam. Population 104,161 (1971). The
city is located on the Gulf of Thailand and has
deep water port facilities. It is known as a
center for the fishing industry. There is a l
large Chinese population in the city. On
November 20, 1970 Rach-Gia was established as
a separate municipality. See KIÊN-GIANG PROVINCE.

RẠCH-GIÁ BAY. (Vịnh Rạch-Giá). A small bay on the
southwest coast of Vietnam. It is named for the
city of Rạch-Giá which is located on the bay.

RAGLAI. See ROGLAI.

RAILROADS. Construction of the railroad network in
Indochina was begun early in the French colonial
period. The main line connected Sài-Gòn to Hà-Nội
running along the coast through the major towns
in the central lowlands. It went north from Hà-
Nội to the Chinese border at Đồng-Đăng (near Lạng-
Sơn) and south from Sài-Gòn to Mỹ-Tho. Other
shorter lines emanated from Hà-Nội and Sài-Gòn.
Over 480 kilometers (300 miles) of the main line
were destroyed during the war years prior to 1954.
Extensive renovation has taken place since then
throughout Vietnam. All the railroads in Vietnam
are now government owned.
    Democratic Republic of Vietnam: The railroad
network in the Democratic Republic of Vietnam
radiates out from Hà-Nội. Three lines go northward to Lạng-Sơn, Lào-Cai and to the industrial
complex at Thái-Nguyên. One line runs south to
Vĩnh-Linh Special Zone in central Vietnam and
the third line runs southeast to the port city
of Hải-Phòng. There is a total of about 1,040
kilometers (650 miles) of rail lines in the Democratic Republic of Vietnam. However, the railroads, especially the railroad bridges, were
continual targets of United States air attacks
between 1965 and 1973 resulting in inestimable
damage.

Republic of Vietnam: There are about 12,500
kilometers (780 miles) of railroads in the Republic of Vietnam. The main line runs from Đông-
Hà in Quảng-Trị Province southward to Sài-Gòn.
There is a branch line from Phan-Rang to Đà-Lạt
and a short line from Sài-Gòn to Lộc-Ninh, in
Bình-Long Province. A branch line to Mỹ-Tho was
operative until 1962. The railroads have suffered
extensive damage during the war, especially in
the late 1960's and early 1970's.

RẰM. (Ngày Rằm). The fifteenth day (full moon) of the
lunar month. The day is observed by some as a
Buddhist holy day with special prayers and rituals.
Many of the more orthodox Buddhists abstain from
eating meat on that day. The fifteenth of the
seventh and eighth months are important holidays-
the Feast of the Wandering Souls (Lễ Vu-Lan) and
the Mid-autumn Festival (Tết Trung-Thu) respectively. See TẾT TRUNG-THU, VU-LAN.

RANG RIVER. (Sông Rang). A small river in north Vietnam which is actually a part of the larger Văn-Úc
River. See VĂN-ÚC RIVER.

RAO-NAY RIVER. (Sông Rao-Nay). See GIANH RIVER.

RAU MUỐNG. Bindweed. A vine-like vegetable that grows
on ponds or other marshy places. It is a favorite
food, especially of the north Vietnamese.

RED RIVER. (Sông Hồng-Hà, also known as Song Nhị-Hà,
Sông Côi or Sông Cái). The principal river of
north Vietnam. The Red River is about 1167 kilo-
meters (725 miles) in length. It originates in
Yunnan Province of China and has two main trib-
utaries - the Lô River and the Đà-Giang River.
Most of the Red River is located in China where it
is called the Yuan River. It enters Vietnam at
Lào-Cai and flows through the provinces of Lào-Cai,
Yên-Báy, Vĩnh-Phú and Hà-Tây where it passes
through the city of Hà-Nội. After leaving Hà-Tây
Province it serves to separate Thái-Bình Province
from Nam-Hà Province. It empties into the South
China Sea at five locations: Cửa Trà-Lý, Cửa Lớn,
Cửa Ba-Lạt, Cửa Đáy and Cửa Lục-Giang.
The Red River has an extremely large rate of
flow - as much as 2,270 cubic meters (800,000
cubic feet) per second, i.e., as much as the max-
imum flow of the Nile River. The river has deposited alluvium soil which actually formed the
entire delta region and has resulted in extremely
fertile and productive riceland. But the river

has also caused perennial death and destruction
through severe and sudden floods. At times the
river rises 7.6 meters (25 feet) above the surrounding countryside. The people of the delta
have developed an elaborate network of dikes and
canals over the centuries to contain the river
and utilize the water for irrigation. There is
a channel that accommodates larger craft between
Hà-Nội and the South China Sea. The river is
navigable beyond Hà-Nội past the cities of Sơn-Tây,
Việt-Trì, Phú-Thọ and Yên-Báy where it becomes
very deep but narrow. The Thái-Bình River
parallels the Red River and is situated about
fifty kilometers (thirty miles) to the northeast.
The two rivers are linked together by a system
of canals. See DIKES, RED RIVER DELTA, THÁI-BÌNH
RIVER.

RED RIVER DELTA. The flat lowlands area of north Vietnam centering around Hưng-Yên and Thái-Bình provinces. The delta region is triangular in shape
with Hải-Phòng, Phát-Diệm and Việt-Trì situated
at the three corners of the triangle. The delta
extends about 240 kilometers (150 miles) inland
and about 120 kilometers (75 miles) along the
coast. It covers approximately 14,990 square
kilometers (5,790 square miles).
     The Red River Delta is considered to be the
cradle of the Vietnamese civilization. It was
here that the first independent Vietnamese state
was established in 939 A.D. by Ngô-Quyền with the
capital at Cổ-Loa in Phúc-Yên Province. Although
the country came under long periods of Chinese
domination, the people of the Red River Delta
clung to their cultural identity. It was from
this area that the ethnic Vietnamese expanded
southward in their classic march to the south
(nam-tiến). The Red River Delta has the most
dense population in all of Vietnam. The delta
area also includes the delta of the smaller Thái-
Bình River with which it is linked by a system
of canals. The delta area is quite low, from
less than one meter (three feet) to 3.4 meters
(ten feet) above sea level. It is subject to
frequent and devastating floods. The high water
mark is 7.6 meters (25 feet) above the surrounding countryside in some places. An elaborate
system of dikes and canals have been developed
over the centuries to contain the floodwaters
and irrigate the rice paddies. The floods are
irregular and sometimes occur several times in
one season, rapidly and without notice. See BẮC-
PHẦN, DIKES, NORTHERN COASTAL PLAIN, RED RIVER.

RED THÁI. (Thái Đỏ). An ethnic minority group of
Thái speaking highland people found in Thanh-Hóa
Province. The Red Thái together with the Black
Thái, White Thái and the Tày (Thổ) are the prin-
cipal Thái speaking ethno-linguistic groups in
northern Vietnam. The Red Thái are the most
closely related to the Black Thái. Smaller in
number than either the White Thái or the Black
Thái, there are approximately 15,000 Red Thái.
See THÁI.

RELIGION. Vietnam is a composite of all the world's
major religions. The organized religions represented, in order of predominance, are: Buddhism
(both mahayana and theravada), Catholicism, Taoism, Cao-Daism, Hòa-Hảo (a form of Buddhism),
Protestantism, Hinduism, and Islam. Ancestral
worship, spiritualism and animism are also practiced. However, the most permeating and important
influence on Vietnamese life and thought is Confucianism and the accompanying institution of the
cult of the ancestors. The moral and ethical
precepts of Confucianism were introduced into
Vietnam by the Chinese and were incorporated into
the mandarinal civil service system, the imperial
dynastic form of rule and the very fabric of
village and family life. Especially important in
determining the Vietnamese individual and communal
system of values was the resultant attitude
toward authority. This was particularly exempli-
fied in the cult of the ancestors. It is also
compatible with the practice of the major religions.
    Buddhism was brought to Vietnam in the
second century A.D. simultaneously by Indian pilgrims and the Chinese monks. Consequently, both
forms of Buddhism (mahayana from the Chinese and
theravada from the Indians) became known in Vietnam. Today, the majority of Vietnam's Buddhist
population are of the mahayana (greater vehicle)
sect.
    Catholicism came to Vietnam in the sixteenth
century. Missionaries came from France, Spain and
Portugal. Prior to the 1900's Catholicism was
discouraged and at times was outlawed. Persecutions of Catholics were severe during the seventeenth and eighteenth centuries. However, under
the French rule the Catholic church enjoyed preferential status and grew rapidly. Today, approximately 8-10% of all Vietnamese are Catholic.
    Protestantism accounts for only a fraction
of a percent of Vietnam's population. The most
active denomination has been the Christian

Missionary Alliance, especially in the Republic of
Vietnam.
    Two religious groups which are native to
Vietnam are the Cao-Đài and the Hòa-Hảo sects.
Hòa-Hảo is an off-shoot of Buddhism and was founded in 1939. Its followers are centralized in
Châu-Đốc and An-Giang provinces. Cao-Daism can
be considered as a mixture of the major religions
and philosophies. The Holy See of the Cao-Đài
Church is located in Tây-Ninh Provnnce.
    The Cham population, which is centered in
two locations (Phan-Rang and Châu-Đốc provinces)
are the principal followers of Hinduism and Islam.
The highland tribal groups practice an assortment
and various combinations of animism, spiritualism,
and ancestral worship. See BUDDHISM, CAO-ĐÀI,
CHRISTIANITY, CONFUCIANISM, CULT OF THE ANCESTORS,
HÒA-HẢO, ÔNG ĐẠO DỪA.

RENGAO. An ethno-linguistic group of highland people
located in the central highlands in the region of
Kontum Province. The Rengao are closely related
to the Sedang and Bahnar and speak a Bahnaric
language of the Mon-Khmer language stock. They
number around 15,000 (1969).

REPUBLIC OF VIETNAM. See VIỆT-NAM CỘNG-HÒA.

RESTORED LÊ DYNASTY (1533-1788). (Nhà Lê Trung-Hửng).
The Restored Lê Dynasty was actually a continuation
of the royal dynasty founded by Lê-Lợi in 1428.
However, the succession of Le Emperors during this
period served only as figureheads whose role was
chiefly ceremonial.
    The dynasty was founded by Lê Trang-Tông
(1533-1548) who was proclaimed emperor by the son
of a former Lê General, Nguyễn-Kim during the
reign of the Mạc Dynasty (1527-1592). Nguyễn-Kim
and later, the Trịnh Lords, waged war against the
Mạc to restore the Lê Dynasty. The Mạc finally
relinquished control of all but one province (Cao-
Bằng) in 1592. From that time on to 1788 the
Restored Lê Emperors occupied the throne but the
power remained with the Trịnh Lords in the north
who passed it from generation to generation.
Meanwhile, the Nguyễn Lords (descendants of
Nguyễn-Kim) maintained control of the south. In
1627 the fifty years of internecine war began between the Trịnh and the Nguyễn. The Restored Lê
Emperors continued to occupy the throne until the
armies of the Tây-Sơn rebels drove the last Lê
monarch, Lê Mẫn-Đế (1787-1788) into China in 1788.

The Restored Lê Dynasty was only a puppet of the
Trịnh Lords. Ironically, both the Trịnh and the
Nguyễn factions claimed loyalty (albeit nominally)
to the Lê Emperors. See LÊ DYNASTY, NGUYỄN LORDS,
TÂY-SƠN REBELLION, TRỊNH LORDS, TRỊNH-NGUYỄN
INTERNECINE WAR.

RHADE. (Also known as Ete or Ede). An ethno-linguistic minority group of highland people located in
the Darlac Plateau in the central highlands. They
inhabit an area extending from Cambodia through
Darlac, Phú-Bồn and Tuyên-Đức provinces to western
Khánh-Hoa Province. The Rhade is one of the
largest highland groups in the Republic of Vietnam
and number over 100,000 as of 1972. The Rhade
language is a Chamic language of the Austronesian
language super-family and is related to the languages of the Jarai and Roglai. There is a phon-
etically designed writing system developed by a
French administrator in the early 1900's. A
colonial land rush in Darlac Province in 1925
brought the Rhade into early contact with both
French and Vietnamese. They have come to be
known as one of the more progressive and advanced
highland groups in the central highlands. Their
society is matrilineal and matrilocal. The extended family occupies a long-house and is the
most important corporate kin group. The long-
house is headed by a male, often the husband of
the senior woman, even though the property is
owned and controlled by the oldest woman in the
family. The Rhade religion is animistic, although
Catholic and Protestant missionaries have converted a significant number of people. The traditional Rhade economy is based on the slash-and-burn
method of dry rice cultivation. However, the
Rhade are increasingly growing wet rice in paddies.

RHEINHART, PIERRE-PAUL (1840-1902). The first French
Charge d'Affairs to An-Nam and Tongking. He
actually served three times in this post in Huế:
1875-1877; 1879-1880; and 1881-1883. He left
his post the first time because he suffered
constant insults by the population. He remained
aloof of the court in Huế. He took no active
part in relations with the Vietnamese until 1883
when he demanded that the Emperor disarm the Hà-
Nội citadel as France was moving to take Tongking.
He finally broke off relations with the court
and left Huế.

RHODES, MONSIGNOR ALEXANDER DE (1591-1660). A famous
    French Jesuit missionary who wrote the first
    catechism in Vietnamese and published a Vietnam-
    ese/Latin/Portuguese dictionary, both of which
    were the first to be printed in Quôc-Ngũ. He
    was born in the papal city of Avignon. He was
    sent to Hà-Nội in 1627 where he enjoyed an
    exceptionally successful two years as a diplomat,
    preacher, and organizer of the church. He was
    expelled from the north in 1630 as a result of
    a general policy against Christianity. He then
    established residence on the island of Macao and
    made several trips to Vietnam between 1640 and
    1645. Both the Trịnh in the north and the Nguyễn
    in the south forbade him to return to Vietnam.
    He continued his active interest in Vietnam by
    promoting the cause of the Vietnamese mission
    field. In 1649, Father de Rhodes went to Rome
    and later to Paris to solicit support for his
    scheme for developing an indigenous church. He
    was able to enlist a great number of priests for
    work in Vietnam and gain the support of the French
    Church. He also raised money and transportation
    from the French commercial sources. At this
    crucial moment, however, he was assigned to a
    mission in Persia. He died in Persia four years
    later.
        Alexander de Rhodes is most recognized for
    his work in perfecting the Vietnamese writing
    system, Quôc-Ngũ. An equally significant accom-
    plishment was his plan for Catholic missionary
    activity which was approved by the church in 1658.
    See CHRISTIANITY, LANGUAGE, QUÔC-NGŨ, VIETNAMESE
    LANGUAGE.

RICE CULTURE. The techniques of growing paddy rice
    (also called lowland or wet rice) was introduced
    into Vietnam from China during the period of the
    Chinese (Hán) domination (111 B.C. - 39 A.D.).
    The Governor of Giao-Châu, Tích-Quang, and the
    Governor of Cửu-Châu, Nhâm-Diên, initiated
    measures for irrigation and importation of
    agricultural tools from China. The new techniques
    spread quickly making rice the main agricultural
    crop. It can be said the very life cycle of a
    village revolves around the requirements and
    demands of the local rice culture. Today there
    are many kinds of rice grown in Vietnam. Upland
    rice is grown in the highlands without the aid
    of irrigation. Floating rice is cultivated in
    some areas of the Mekong Delta and adjusts to the
    fluctuating levels of the water. Glutinous or
    sticky rice is used for special dishes. And, most

important, white rice is the main staple of the
Vietnamese diet. It is grown extensively in the
rich alluvial soils of the Mekong and Red River
deltas. While rice is cultivated in the coastal
flatlands of central Vietnam, the poor soil and
unfavorable drainage conditions result in poor
yields.

RICHARD, ETIENNE-ANTOINE-GUILLAUME. Resident General
   for An-Nam and Tongking from November 1887 to
   April 1888 and Governor General of Indochina from
   April 1888 to May 1889.

ROBIN, EUGENE-LOUIS-JEAN-RENE. Governor General of
   Indochina from July 1934 to September 1936.

ROGLAI. (Also called Raglai). An ethno-linguistic
   minority group of highland people located in the
   central highlands. They are divided into the
   northern Roglai situated in western Khánh-Hòa and
   Ninh-Thuận provinces and the southern Roglai,
   located in parts of Bình-Thuận and Bình-Tuy provinces. Population estimates were given in 1972
   as 40,000, about equally divided between the two
   groups. The Roglai language is a Chamic language
   of the Austronesian stock. The Roglai cultural
   patterns have been heavily influenced by the Cham
   owing to their long standing interchange. The
   Roglai social organization is matrilineal, matriarchal, and matrilocal. The extended family is
   the basic social unit. Their economy is based
   around the slash-and-burn method of upland rice
   cultivation. Secondary crops include corn,
   manioc, cotton, squash, sugarcane, and fruits.

RON POINT. (Mũi Ron). A cape or point extending into
   the South China Sea in Hà-Tĩnh Province in central Vietnam.

ROUME, ERNEST-NESTOR. Governor General of Indochina
   from March, 1915 to April, 1916. He was responsible for the deposition of the young Emperor
   Duy-Tân who had attempted against the French.
   See DUY-TÂN.

ROUSEAU, PAUL-ARMAND. Governor General of Indochina
   from March, 1895 to December, 1896. It was under
   his authorization that the French undertook the
   pacification activities of Tongking and successfully dealt with the suppression of bands of
   rebels and pirates in Tongking.

RÙA. See QUY.

-S-

SA-ĐÉC CITY. The capital city of Sa-Đéc Province.
   Population 59,894 (1971). It is located on the
   left bank of the upper Mekong River (Sông Tiền
   Giang). The city is linked by road to Vĩnh-Long
   City and Long-Xuyên. See SA-ĐÉC PROVINCE.

SA-ĐÉC PROVINCE. An inland province in the Mekong
   Delta area of south Vietnam. It is situated
   south of Phong-Dinh Province, southeast of Kiên-
   Giang Province and north of An-Xuyên and Bạc-Liêu
   provinces. The population is 316,877 and the land
   mass is 818 square kilometers (315 square miles).
   The provincial capital, Sa-Đéc City, is located
   on the upper Mekong River (Sông Tiền-Giang). The
   area now occupied by Sa-Đéc Province was once
   part of Cambodia. It was given to the Nguyễn
   Lord Nguyễn Phúc-Khoát (1738-1765) by the Cambodian King Nac-Ton in return for the Nguyễn
   Lord's help in putting down a rebellion in Cambodia. Emperor Minh-Mạng (1820-1840) made it
   part of An-Giang Province. The French established
   the province under the name of Sa-Đéc, but it was
   dissolved in 1956. The area south of the upper
   Mekong River was incorporated into Vĩnh-Long Province while the territory north of the river was
   made a part of Kiên-Phong Province. In 1967, that
   part which had been absorbed by Vĩnh-Long Province
   was reestablished as Sa-Đéc Province. Thus, the
   present province of Sa-Đéc is quite smaller than
   the original province of the same name. The chief
   products of the province are rice, sweet potatoes,
   bananas and other fruits. The province is also
   well-known as a center for the production of
   shrimp chips (bánh phồng tôm). See SA-ĐÉC CITY.

SA-HUỲNH. The site of archaeological finds relating
   to the Bronze Age in Vietnam. Sa-Huỳnh is located on the coast of Quảng-Ngãi in central Vietnam. Several tombs were unearthed which also
   yielded in the funerary deposits a number of
   artifacts, including beads, split rings, axes,
   and bronze rattles, all of which were typical of
   the Đông-Sơn civilization further north. In fact,
   the Sa-Huỳnh site is believed to have been a
   colony of the Đông-Sơn civilization and is dated
   in the first century A.D. See ĐÔNG-SƠN CIVIL-
   IZATION, PREHISTORY.

SA-PHIN MOUNTAIN RANGE. (Dẫy Sa-Phin). A chain of
mountains in north Vietnam. It is actually a
part of the larger Hoàng-Liên-Sơn Mountain Range.
It extends from the Khao-Kim Pass to Chợ-Bờ in
Hoa-Bình Province. The highest peak in the chain
is Pou-Luong Mountain at 2,895 meters (9,498 feet).
See HOÀNG-LIÊN-SƠN MOUNTAIN RANGE.

SÀI-GÒN. (Also called Sài-Còn). The capital city and
major port of the Republic of Vietnam. It is located seventy-two kilometers (forty-five miles)
from the sea on the Sài-Gòn River (Bến-Nghé River)
and is a major Southeast Asian seaport. The
origins of the city and the name Sài-Gòn are
obscure. Most agree that the original settlement
was made by Cambodians. The name seems to be of
both Chinese and Cambodian influence. The site
of present-day Sài-Gòn was named Gia-Định Thành
after the citadel was built by Emperor Gia-Long
(1802-1819). The name Sài-Gòn was first used in
1861 when the French established themselves there
in preparation for the conquest of all of south
Vietnam. Adjacent to Sài-Gòn is the predominantly
Chinese community of Chợ-Lớn. Sài-Gòn became the
capital of the Republic of Vietnam in 1956. Today
the city of Sài-Gòn covers an area of seventy
square kilometers (twenty-seven square miles) and
has a population of 1,804,880 (1971). The Sài-
Gòn metropolitan area (including Chợ-Lớn and other
fringe areas) has a population of nearly three
million. Sài-Gòn has one of the largest population densities in the world. It is also the
major industrial, commercial and transportation
center in south Vietnam. See VIỆT-NAM CỘNG-HÒA.

SÀI-GÒN RIVER. (Sông Sài-Gòn, also called Sông Bến-
Nghé or the Bến-Nghé River). A principal river
in south Vietnam and a tributary of the Đồng-Nai
River. It originates in the Cambodian border
region north of Tây-Ninh City. It flows southeasterly through Tây-Ninh, Bình-Dương, and Gia-
Định provinces and through the city of Sài-Gòn
where it has become a major port facility. It
joins the Đồng-Nai River at Nhà-Bè and empties
into the South China Sea. See SÀI-GÒN.

SAM MOUNTAIN. (Núi Sam). One of seven mountains in
the Thật-Sơn Mountain Range. It is located in
Châu-Đốc Province in south Vietnam. Archaeologists
have unearthed several stone artifacts dating
back to the ancient kingdom of Funan. There are
several temples and grottoes in the side of the

mountain including the gravesite of Thoai Ngọc-
Hâu, a prominent mandarin, general and diplomat
under the early Nguyễn Dynasty (1802-1945).

SANCHI.   An ethno-linguistic minority group of highland
people located in Bắc-Thái, Quảng-Ninh and Hà-Bắc
provinces of north Vietnam.   They speak a Sino-
Thai language of the Sino-Tibetan language family.
The 1960 census recorded a Sanchi population of
14,382.

SANZIU.   An ethno-linguistic minority group of highland people located in the provinces of Bắc-Thái,
Hà-Bắc and Quảng-Ninh in north Vietnam.   They
numbered 33,913 in the 1960 census.

SARRAUT, ALBERT.   Governor General of Indochina from
November, 1911, to November, 1913, and from
January, 1917, to May, 1919.   He was the only man
to serve twice in this position.   He was an elo-
quent orator and, at the same time, was very
popular with the Vietnamese.

SEA SWALLOW'S NEST.   (Yễn-Sào).   A delicacy found off
the coast of Vietnam.   These edible nests are
made by four different species of the bird
Cypselideoe collocalia.   This small bird builds
its nests in the grottoes and caves of small
islands off the coast of Vietnam, from Quảng-Bình
Province in central Vietnam to Hà-Tiên in the Gulf
of Thailand.   The most important group of these
islands, from the standpoint of productivity and
quality, is located off the coast of Nha-Trang.
The nests are semi-oval, about two to three inches in diameter (average) and are made from
silk-like salivary secretions which dry rapidly
as they are exposed to the air.   Usually, two
crops are taken every year.   They are sorted and
packaged for sale.   The red nests are most valued,
after elaborate preparations they are used to
make soup or another expensive specialty - pigeon
with sea swallow's nest.   These nests are also
used in eastern medicine.   They are also said to
fortify the body and to have aphrodisiac qual-
ities.   Emperor Minh-Mạng (1820-1840), it is
said, owed his extraordinary virility to sea
swallow's nests.

SEDANG.   An ethno-linguistic minority group of highland people located in northwest Kontum Province
in the central highlands.   Estimates of the population in 1972 are placed at 30,000.   The Sedang
language belongs to the Bahnaric group of the

Mon-Khmer language family. The village is the
basic political unit and the extended family is
the basic social unit. Usually, each extended
family lives together in a longhouse. Although
the society is patriarchal, the kinship is
reckoned through both the male and female side of
the family. Their religion is animistic, involving the belief that spirits inhabit the lands,
vegetation, animals and objects around them. The
Sedang are composed of a number of subgroups, each
with a distinct dialact. The Sedang live on long-
houses on stilts. Each longhouse is inhabited by
one extended family. The eldest male is head of
the extended family and the father is the head of
the nuclear family. Polygamy is practiced but
is not common. In the recent past the young men
and women had their front teeth filed down and
lacquered black. This practice is now apparently
dying out. The major crop of the Sedang is upland
rice cultivated by the slash-and-burn method.
However, a limited amount of wet (paddy) rice is
grown. Secondary crops include corn, millet,
tobacco, and vegetables. The Sedang have always
been known as a war-like people, carrying out
frequent attacks on neighboring tribes, ethnic
Vietnamese and, later, the French. An interesting
and unusual development took place in 1888 when
the French soldier/adventurer David Mayrena established a loose confederation of tribes and declared himself King of the Sedang Nation. He
died in Singapore on a trip to solicit support
for his cause. The Sedang Nation fell apart only
a couple of years after it sfounding. More
recently, the Sedang have been among the groups
that have played a more belligerent role in the
armed conflict.

SEN. (Lotus). The lotus is one of the most popular
plants in Vietnam. The flower became a symbol
of early Asian religions. It was mentioned in
Hindu legends. Buddha used it as a symbol of
man's achievement potential. Since the beautiful
flower grows in the dirtiest of waters, the
analogy was made that man can achieve spiritual
serenity in spite of his environment. The lotus
flower thus became a popular offering in the act
of worship. The seed and root are not only
edible, but are used in a wide variety of dishes,
including as a fragrance for tea. The lotus
flower is also a common motif in Vietnamese art,
especially in Vietnamese sculpture and architecture.

SÊU. (Sêu Tết). The custom of a prospective bride-
groom presenting gifts to his future mother-in-
law and father-in-law. These offerings are made
on the major holidays anf family celebrations.

SĨ-NHIỆP (187 A.D. - 226 A.D.). A very popular and
venerated Governor of the Chinese district of
Giao-Chỉ. A native of Giao-Chỉ, he served as
administrator for the Chinese (Hán) during a
period of instability in China and neighboring
districts. Although banditry and disorder was
rampant in other areas, Sĩ-Nhiệp was able to
maintain peace and order in Giao-Chỉ. In fact,
cultural development (education, literature,
Buddhism, etc.) blossomed under his governorship.
     In the year 203 A.D. he successfully
petitioned the Chinese emperor to elevate the
colonial district of Giao-Chỉ to the status of
a normal Chinese province (Giao-Châu). Sĩ-Nhiệp
served as Governor for a total of forty years.
See GIAO-CHỈ.

SỞ-HỌC VẤN TÂN. First Inquiry into Learning. A compendium of Chinese history, Vietnamese history,
behavior rules, and study methods. This book
was written in Chinese and used as a textbook
for Vietnamese students in traditional Vietnam.

SƠN-LA CITY. The capital city of Sơn-La Province in
north Vietnam. It is located 310 kilometers
(192 miles) northwest of Hà-Nội and 77 kilometers
(48 miles) from the Lao border. See SƠN-LA
PROVINCE.

SƠN-LA PROVINCE. A highland province in north Vietnam.
It is located south of Lai-Châu Province and west
of Nghĩa-Lộ Province. Its western boundary is
also the Lào/Vietnamese border. The land mass of
the province is 11,000 square kilometers (4,247
square miles). The provincial capital, also
named Sơn-La, is only seventy-seven kilometers
(forty-seven miles) northwest of Hà-Nội. The Đà-
Giang River runs through the length of the province. Sơn-La is populated mainly by ethno-
linguistic minority groups of highland people,
chief among which are the Black Thái, Mèo, White
Thái and the Mường. Scattered throughout the
province are ethnic Vietnamese, Chinese and Man.
     Sơn-La Province is part of the Tây-Bắc Auto-
nomous Region (Khu Tây-Bắc Tự-Trị) which is
administered by the Thái. In fact, as far back
as the fourteenth century, the Black Thái controlled

the entire area around the Đà-Giang River. Việt-
namese influence in the area was nominal up until
the 1900's. There are many natural resources in
Sơn-La but most of them have not been exploited
fully. These include timber, gold, coal and
wildlife. The province is also noted for its
scenic beauty, especially along the Đà-Giang River.
Under the French administration, Sơn-La Province
also included what is now Nghĩa-Lộ Province. See
SƠN-LA CITY.

SƠN-MAI. See LACQUERWARE.

SƠN-TÂY PROVINCE. See HÀ-TÂY PROVINCE.

SƠN-TINH, THỦY-TINH. Two legendary spirits. The spirit
of the mountains (Sơn-Tinh) and the spirit of the
waters (Thủy-Tinh). Both spirits were vying for
the hand of Princess Mỵ-Nương, daughter of the
eighteenth King Hùng-Vương. The king, seeing that
both were equally matched suitors, promised his
daughter to the first to arrive with wedding
gifts. Sơn-Tinh was the first, bringing many
precious gifts. But, Thủy-Tinh was so angered
that he took revenge. He caused terrible floods
and tidal waves to occur, but Sơn-Tinh built a
tall mountain where he and his bride took refuge.
The higher the water rose, the taller he built
the mountain. Eventually, Thủy-Tinh realized the
futility of his battle and caused the floods to
recede. But the next year Thủy-Tinh again tried
to destroy Sơn-Tinh by flooding the land, and
again he failed. And, every year since then, in
the seventh and eighth lunar months, Thủy-Tinh
sends floods to plague the inhabitants of the
land. See TẢN-VIÊN MOUNTAIN.

SƠN-VI CIVILIZATION. One of the earliest prehistoric
civilizations that existed in what is now north
Vietnam. It is classified as Paleolithic (early
stone age). It is named for the village of Sơn-Vi
in Vĩnh-Phú Province in which the first vestiges
of this civilization were found. It is characterized by crudely shaped stone tools. In 1968,
archaeologists discovered many stone axes which
are considered to be representative of the culture in a transition period between the Paleolithic and Mesolithic eras. See PREHISTORY.

SÔNG. River. The word sông is used with the class-
ifier "con", as in con Sông Cửu-Long (Mekong
River). Individual rivers are listed under

separate entries. See BẮC-GIANG RIVER, BẠCH-ĐẰNG
RIVER, BẾN-HẢI RIVER, CAI RIVER, CẦU RIVER, CHU
RIVER, CON RIVER, ĐÀ-GIANG RIVER, ĐÀ-RẰNG RIVER,
ĐẠI-GIANG RIVER, ĐÁY-THƯỢNG RIVER, GẦM RIVER, HẬU-
GIANG RIVER, HIẾU GIANG RIVER, KHINH-TÂY RIVER,
KỲ-CÙNG RIVER, LẠCH-TRÀY RIVER, LẠI-GIANG RIVER,
LÔ RIVER, LUỘC RIVER, LŨY RIVER, MÃ RIVER, MEKONG
RIVER, PERFUME RIVER, RANG RIVER, SÀI-GÒN RIVER,
THÁI-BÌNH RIVER, TIỀN-GIANG RIVER, TRÀ-BỒNG RIVER,
TRÀ-KHÚC RIVER, RED RIVER, VĂN-ÚC RIVER, VỆ RIVER,
VÀM-CỎ RIVER.

SÔNG-ĐIỆP. A form of poetry in which each line contains
a pair of words, each of which is repeated once.

SÔNG GẦM MOUNTAIN RANGE. A chain of mountains extending from the Đồng-Quan highlands to Tam-Đảo in
Tuyên-Quang Province. The tallest peak is Pia-Ya
Mountain which stands 1,970 meters (6,463 feet).
The range follows the Gầm River for which it is
named. The area is noted for its scenery including the well-known Bà-Bể Lake. See BÀ-BỂ LAKE.

SÔNG HƯỜNG. See PERFUME RIVER.

SÔNG THẤT LỤC BÁT. (Also called Lục Bát Gian Thất).
A form of poetry in which there are two lines of
seven words followed by one line of six words and
one line of eight words. Each set of four lines
constitutes one verse. A rigid pattern of rhymes
is adhered to in the tradition of classical Chinese poetry. This form is one of the two most
popular forms used in the Truyện (narrative or
epic poem) written in nôm. The other being the
Lục-Bát or six-eight style. See LỤC BÁT, NÔM.

SOUTH CHINA SEA. (Biển Nam Hải). One of the seas in
the Pacific Ocean. It forms the entire eastern
border of Vietnam and provides resources for Vietnam's industry, including fishing, shipping and
salt production.

SOUTH VIETNAM. See NAM PHẦN.

SOUTHERN PLAIN. (Đồng-Bằng Nam-Phần). The lowland
area of south Vietnam which is dominated by the
Mekong Delta. It occupies the entire area south
of the southern limits of the central highlands
to Cà-Mau. It can be plotted on a map by drawing
a trapezoid between the following points: Vũng-
Tàu; Bù-Đốp (Phước-Long Province); Hà-Tiên; and
the Cà-Mau Peninsula. In addition to the Mekong

Delta, it also includes the delta areas of the
Đồng-Nai River, the Sài-Gòn River, and the Vàm-Cỏ
River and their tributaries. The inhabitants are
predominantly ethnic Vietnamese although there is
a significant minority of Cambodians (Khmer),
especially in the western and southern parts. The
total land mass of the southern plain is approximately 40,000 square kilometers (15,440 square
miles). It is characterized by rich, flat rice
land. However, it also includes two large jungle
areas (Rừng Sat and Rừng U-Minh) and scattered
small mountains such as the Bà-Đen Mountain in
Tây-Ninh and the Thất-Sơn Mountains in Châu-Đốc
Province. The southern part of the plain has a
vast and complex system of waterways (rivers and
canals) which are used for transportation, as
well as for water-level control. The major ports
of the southern plain are Sài-Gòn, Vũng-Tàu, Cần-
Thơ, Rạch-Giá and Hà-Tiên. See NAM-PHẦN, MEKONG
RIVER, MEKONG RIVER DELTA.

SPRATELY ISLANDS. (Quần Đảo Trường-Xa, or Trường-Xa
    Archipelago). A group of islands in the South
    China Sea about 545 kilometers (340 miles) east
    southeast of Vũng-Tàu. These islands have long
    been a source of tortoise shells and other marine
    products and, more recently, rich beds of phos-
    phates have been discovered and exploited there.
    The French claimed possession of the islands in
    1933. The Japanese occupied the islands during
    World War II. After the war, the islands were
    occupied by the Chinese naval forces. Based on
    that occupation, the Chinese governments (both
    communist and nationalist) contested the claim of
    the Republic of Vietnam over the islands. The
    matter has not yet been settled.

SRE. (Also called Cau Sre, which means the "People of
    the Rice"). An ethno-linguistic minority group
    of highland people located around Di-Linh in cen-
    tral Vietnam. They are actually a subgroup of the
    Koho. Official estimates in 1965 placed the Sre
    population at 21,000. Although the Sre share
    most of the cultural and social patterns of other
    Koho subgroups, there are some exceptions. For
    instance, the Sre do not use tattoos, neither
    do they file their teeth or stretch their ear-
    lobes. The Mongolian spot (a bluish mark at the
    base of the spine) is common in newborn babies of
    the Sre. The Sre are also considered to be one
    of the more advanced Koho subgroups. See KOHO.

STIENG.   An ethno-linguistic minority group of high-
    land people located along the Vietnamese/Cambod-
    ian border area, centering in the provinces of
    Phước-Long and Bình-Long in central Vietnam.
    They are of the Mon-Khmer language speaking
    group. Their population was estimated to be
    around 50,000 in 1972. The Stieng have a patri-
    archal society and live in villages which, indiv-
    idually, are the highest political unit. They
    have a subsistence level economy based primarily
    on swidden agriculture. Their chief crop is up-
    land rice which is supplemented by hunting and
    fishing. They have a reputation for belligerence
    and have traditionally resisted outside influences.
    The Stieng revolted twice (1869 and 1933) against
    the French.

SWIDDEN AGRICULTURE.   See LÀM RẪY.

                        -T-

TA DUNG MOUNTAIN.   (Núi Ta Dung).   A mountain in Quảng-
    Đức Province in the central highlands. It has
    an elevation of 1,971 meters (6,467 feet).

TAI. See THÁI.

TAM CƯỜNG.   The three basic elements of social ethics.
    These are based on the Confucianist teachings of
    the Chinese classics. These three elements con-
    cern the relationships between the ruler and his
    subjects (Quân-Thần), those between the father
    and son (Phu-Tử) and those between the husband
    and wife (Phu-Phụ).

TAM-ĐẢO.   A mountainous resort area in Vĩnh-Phú Province
    in north Vietnam. It is located about twenty-
    three kilometers (fourteen miles) from the city
    of Vĩnh-Yên and was made popular by the French.
    It is composed of three separate summits and has
    an elevation of about 1,000 meters (3,280 feet).
    Tam-Đảo is also the name of the mountain range
    in which the resort area is located.

TAM-ĐIỆP PASS.   (Đèo Tam-Điệp, also called Ba-Đội Pass).
    A strategic mountain pass in the Trường-Sơn Moun-
    tain Range. It is located on the Thanh-Hóa/Ninh-
    Bình border area. The main north/south highway,
    highway number one, runs through the pass connect-
    ing Hà-Nội with the provinces in central Vietnam.

Tam-Điệp Pass has three distinct sections: the
north section in Ninh-Bình Province; the central
section which serves as the actual border between
the two provinces; and the southern part in
Thanh-Hóa Province. The pass also separates
north Vietnam from central Vietnam.

TAM-GIANG LAGOON. (Phá Tam-Giang). A salt water
lagoon in Thừa-Thiên Province in central Vietnam.
It extends northward into Quảng-Trị Province and
southward to Cửa Thuận-An.

TAM GIÁO. The three traditional religions of Vietnam:
Buddhism, Taoism, and Confucianism (which is
actually a philosophy rather than a religion).
For political reasons, one of the three religions
dominated at various times in Vietnamese history,
and thus played an important role in the affairs
of state. However, the early part of the Lê Dynasty (1428-1788) is known as the Tam-Giáo Period
when all three religions prospered.

TAM-KỲ. The capital city of Quảng-Tín Province in
central Vietnam. Population 18,142 (1971). It
is located on highway number one.

TAM-KỲ RIVER. (Sông Tam-Kỳ). A river in central
Vietnam. It flows past the city of Tam-Kỳ, the
provincial capital of Quảng-Tín Province.

TAM THIÊN TỰ. Book of Three Thousand Characters. A
compilation of 3,000 Chinese characters and their
meaning in Vietnamese. This vocabular book
served as a primer to teach Chinese characters
to children in traditional Vietnam.

TAM TỰ KINH. The Three Character Classic. A textbook
in Chinese used by students in traditional Vietnam.
It was composed of 358 three character rhymed
sentences of Confucian philosophy and ethics and
of Chinese history. It concluded with incentives
to study in the form of noteworthy examples of
ancient times.

TÂN-AN. The capital city of Long-An Province in south
Vietnam. Population 55,441 (1971). It is located
fifty kilometers (thirty-one miles) south of Sai-
Gon on highway number four. Tân-An was also the
name of a province during the French period and
included what is now Kiến-Tường Province and part
of Long-An Province. See LONG-AN PROVINCE.

TẢN-ĐÀ (1888-1939). A poet, publisher, and Confucian
    scholar. He was born in Sơn-Tây Province and
    studied for the civil service examinations which
    he failed in 1912. He then went into publishing,
    and in 1921 he founded the influential An-Nam
    magazine. The An-Nam magazine closed down in
    1933. Tản-Đà retired to his native village and
    worked as an astrologer and teacher for an in-
    come. He died on June 7, 1939, in poverty at
    the age of fifty-one.

TẢN-VIÊN MOUNTAIN. (Núi Tản-Viên, also called Ba-Vì
    Mountain or Núi Ba-Vì). A small mountain in Hà-
    Tây Province in north Vietnam. It has an ele-
    vation of 1,280 meters (4,191 feet). On the
    mountain top is a temple (Đền Thờ Tản-Viên Sơn
    Thần) which is dedicated to the spirit of Tản-
    Viên Mountain. Legend has it that the Spirit of
    the Mountains (Sơn-Tinh) was a poor woodcutter
    when he met a fairy who gave him a magic wand.
    With this wand he saved the life of the Spirit
    of the Waters (Thủy-Tinh). Both spirits were
    close friends until they both fell in love with
    the Princess My-Nương. The Spirit of the Moun-
    tains finally married the Princess which angered
    the Spirit of the Waters so much that he caused
    terrible winds and rains to come in an effort to
    flood the mountains and drown Sơn-Tinh. But he
    was not successful. See SƠN-TINH, THỦY-TINH.

TÂN-VIỆT CÁCH-MẸNH ĐẢNG. (The New Vietnam Revolution-
    ary Party). A progressive political party formed
    in northern central Vietnam in 1926 from among
    the secret societies which were formerly allied
    with Phan Bội-Châu. It lasted only four years.
    In 1929 it was abosrbed into the Indochinese
    Communist Party. See PHAN BỘI-CHÂU.

TANG-CHẾ. Mourning. The custom of mourning the dead
    in Vietnam follows the Chinese tradition and tends
    to be very complicated in terms of who should
    mourn and to what degree. There are five classes
    of mourning or five different categories of mourn-
    ing requirements depending on the closeness of
    the relationship of the mourner to the deceased.
    In terms of time, these classes are as follows:

    1. Đại-Tang - 3 years
    2. Cơ-Phục - 1 year
    3. Cửu-Công - 9 months
    4. Tiểu-Công - 5 months
    5. Ty-Ma - 3 months

Each class also has different requirements for
the various kinds of mourning clothes. For instance, the parents would mourn a son one year,
a wife of the oldest son one year, other daughter-
in-laws nine months, daughters one year, married
daughters nine months and son-in-laws three
months. White is the color of mourning in Vietnam. In addition to the mourning clothes, a
person in mourning is expected to refrain from
participating in festive activities and certain
social events. Present-day Vietnamese do not
always adhere to the traditional mourning requirements as closely as in the past. See TANG-PHỤC.

TANG-CHỦ. A person who takes charge of the funeral
rites. It is usually the eldest child (Con-cả).
When the father of the deceased is still living,
he can be designated as the Tang-Chủ. See CẢI-
TANG, CON-CẢ, ĐƯA ĐÁM, HỘ-LỄ, MỘC-DỤC.

TANG-PHỤC. Mourning clothes. The traditional color
for mourning in Vietnam is white. The extent to
which one wears mourning clothes is determined
by the distince or closeness between the deceased
and the relative who is in mourning. Members of
the immediate family are required to wear ragged
white clothes during the funeral and to walk with
a walking stick. In traditional Vietnam, these
mourning clothes would be worn for as long as
three years. Distant relatives wear white clothes
for varying lengths of time. A khăn-tang (mourning cloth) is also a part of the mourning clothes
and is a white cloth or band worn on the head.
Red is infrequently used, but only very rarely.
The rationale for the use of red is that it is a
happy color and is considered appropriate whenn
the deceased is extremely old and to be called
to the world beyond is both timely and a relief.
In these cases, the smaller children usually
wear a red mourning cloth. It is also often
noticeable that, as a result of western influence,
a black armband or a black swatch of cloth is
worn to indicate mourning. See TANG-CHẾ.

TÁO-QUÂN. (Also called Vua-Bếp). The chief guardian
spirit of the household. Táo-Quân actually includes three distinct spirits: Thổ-Công (Ông-Công)
who guards the kitchen; Thổ-Địa, the guardian
spirit of the main house (the Vietnamese kitchen
is usually in a building separate from the living
quarters); and Thổ-Kỳ, the women's guardian spirit
in such things as marketing and child bearing.

The origins of Táo-Quân, according to legend, are
linked to a tragic love story. Trọng-Cao and Thị-
Nhi had been married for many years. Although
they were deeply in love, they were childless,
which was the cause of frequent quarrels. One
day, Trọng-Cao struck his wife who became so hurt
that she left him. She happened to meet a hand-
some young man who immediately fell in love with
her. His name was Phạm-Lang. Meanwhile, Trọng-
Cao was so overcome with remorse that he set out
to find her, but had no success. He continued
to search until one day he came to the house of
Phạm-Lang. His wife answered the door and the
two former lovers found themselves face to face.
She invited Trọng-Cao inside whereupon they became reconciled, and she prepared to return home
with her husband. Realizing that Phạm-Lang was
about to return she had Trọng-Cao hide in the
haystack. Phạm-Lang returned from the fields
and decided to burn the haystack to provide ashes
for fertilizer. Seeing the flames, the wife ran
to the aid of her husband but was too late.
Crazed with sorrow she threw herself into the
flames. Phạm-Lang, in trying to save her, also
burned to death. The Jade Emperor was so moved
by these three sacrifices that he made them
deities and assigned them the duties of the Táo-
Quân. Although incorporated into one, each
still retains a distinct identity: Phạm-Lang
became Thổ-Công, Trọng-Cao became Thổ-Địa, and
Thi-Nhi (the wife) became Thổ-Kỳ. See LÊ TÁO-
QUÂN, THỔ-CÔNG.

TAOISM. (Lão-Giáo or Đạo-Giáo). One of the three
    main religions (tam-giáo) which were introduced
    into Vietnam by the Chinese during their periods
    of domination. Taoism is derived from the doc-
    trine of Lao Tse, which is based essentially on
    the participation of man in the universal order.
    Although Taoism is not a major religion per se,
    in Vietnam today, it has strongly influenced
    Buddhism and Confucianism and accounts for much
    of the mysticism, magic, and sorcery that is
    popular in Vietnam. See RELIGION, TAM-GIÁO.

TẬP-CHÍ NAM-PHONG. See NAM-PHONG.

TAU-OI. An ethno-linguistic group of highland people
    located inland from Quảng-Trị City and extending
    eastward through the Lao province of Saravan.
    The Tau-Oi number approximately 11,000 and are
    of the Mon-Khmer language family.

TÀY. (Also called Thổ). An ethno-linguistic minority group of highland people located to the north and northeast of the Red River. This area is part of the Việt-Bắc Autonomous Region and includes the provinces of Cao-Bằng, Lạng-Sơn, Bắc-Thái, Tuyên-Quang, Hà-Giang and Yên-Bẩy. The Tày are the largest ethnic minority group in all of Vietnam. They numbered 503,988 in 1960. There are two distinct groupings of Tày: one in Cao-Bằng and Lạng-Sơn provinces and the other in the other provinces mentioned above. The Tày speak a Thái language and have a script which was based on the Vietnamese chữ-nôm. In the fifteenth and sixteenth centuries the Vietnamese emperors sent mandarins to administer over the Tày. Unlike other mandarins in the civil service, they married Tày women and passed their mandarinal authority on to their sons. A new class of socio-political elite was thereby established which still exists. As a result of the long established contact with the Vietnamese the Tày have become one of the most "Vietnamized" of the Thái groups. Their descent system is patrilineal and is similar to that of the Vietnamese. Polygyny is common among the well-to-do. Buddhism is practiced mainly among the elite and there are numerous Confucianist shrines in the Tày area. However, the main or most predominant religion is spirit worship. The economy is based on rice agriculture. Both glutinous and non-glutinous are cultivated in paddy fields and upland rice is grown by the swidden agriculture method. Cattle and buffalo are used for draft purposes and sometimes for sacrifices. The Tày are celebrated horse breeders and traders. They also raise a variety of small stock.

TÂY-BẮC AUTONOMOUS REGION. (Khu Tây-Bắc Tự-Trị, or literally, the Northwest Autonomous Region). A region of north Vietnam inhabited primarily by highland ethno-linguistic minority groups and encompassing the provinces of Lai-Châu, Sơn-La and Nghĩa-Lộ. It was established in April, 1955, and covers an area of 36,344 square kilometers (14,028 square miles), one fifth of the total area of north Vietnam. There are over 500,000 inhabitants in the region belonging to twenty-five different ethno-linguistic groups.

The region was originally called the Thai-Meo Autonomous Region, after the two largest ethno-linguistic groups. It was subsequently changed to Tây-Bắc in deference to the lesser sized ethno-linguistic groups. This administrative

zone is characterized by strong local (minority)
participation in the National Assembly and administration of the area. The people's councils and
administrative committees have broader than usual
discretionary powers to accommodate the many
cultural variations. The other similar zone in
the Democratic Republic of Vietnam is the Việt-Bắc
Autonomous Region.

TÂY-ĐÔ CITADEL. (Also called Hồ Thành). A fortified
citadel built in 1397 in Thanh-Hóa Province in
what is now Yên-Tôn Village. It is the largest
ancient stone structure in Vietnam. It is also
called the citadel of the Hồ Dynasty. The structure is rectangular, 900 X 700 meters (2,952 X
2,296 feet). The outer wall is made of large
square stones reinforced with battered earth.
It stands six meters (nineteen feet) high and has
four gates, one on each side. Inside the citadel
was located a knoll called Mount Thổ-Kỳ, the Phu-
Tường Lake and several palaces and temples. The
wall was surrounded by a ditch.
    Hồ Quý-Ly ordered the citadel built as a
capital for the Trần Dynasty (1225-1400). However, Hồ Quý-Ly usurped the throne in 1400 and
founded the Hồ Dynasty which lasted only seven
years (1400-1407). See HỒ QUÝ-LY, HO DYNASTY.

TÂY-NINH CITY. The capital city of Tây-Ninh Province.
Population 26,081. It is located about ninety-
seven kilometers (sixty miles) northwest of Sài-
Gòn. It has a large Khmer population. The city
of Tây-Ninh is most famous for being the center
of the Cao-Đài Church. The Holy See at the seat
of the religion and administrative headquarters
is located in Tây-Ninh City. The Cao-Đài Cathedral is one of the city's most important sites.
See TÂY-NINH PROVINCE.

TÂY-NINH PROVINCE. A province in south Vietnam which
borders on Cambodia to the west and Bình-Long,
Bình-Dương and Hậu-Nghĩa provinces to the east.
The population of the province is 386,738 and the
area is 3,925 square kilometers (1,515 square
miles). Tây-Ninh is the center of the Cao-Đài
Church and has large Khmer and Chàm populations.
Highway number one, which connects Phnom-Penh
with Sài-Gòn, passes through the province. The
provincial capital, Tây-Ninh City is located on
highway number twenty-two, 100 kilometers (62
miles) from Sài-Gòn. Tây-Ninh Province is a
large producer of rubber and rice, although a

large portion of the rubber plantations have been
destroyed by the recent conflict, particularly by
the large B 52's. The province also produces
vegetables and corn. Most of the province is less
than ten meters (thirty-three feet) above sea
level. The Vàm-Cô River flows from Cambodia
through the western part of the province. The
eastern border of Tây-Ninh Province is formed by
the Sài-Gòn River. Prior to the seventeenth century, Tây-Ninh was part of Cambodia. It was
annexed to Vietnam around the turn of the eighteenth century. In 1871 it was established as a
separate province. Because of the province's
strategic importance and the political importance
of the Cao-Đài sect, it has been a major battle-
ground during the French Indochina war and the
more recent Vietnam war. The best known landmark
in the province is the Núi Bà-Đen (Black Lady or
Bà-Đen Mountain). See BÀ-ĐEN MOUNTAIN, CAO-ĐÀI,
TÂY-NINH CITY.

TÂY-SƠN DYNASTY (1788-1802). The dynasty founded by
Nguyễn Huệ (Quang-Trung) during the Tây-Sơn Rebellion. The three Tây-Sơn brothers, Nguyễn-Huệ,
Nguyễn-Nhạc, and Nguyễn-Lữ set themselves up as
King of the North, King of the Center and King of
the South respectively, but still acknowledging
the Lê Emperors in Hà-Nội. But after the Lê Emperor Lê Mẫn-Đế (1787-1788) proved incapable and
solicited military assistance from China, Nguyễn-
Huệ marched into Hà-Nội, ousted the Chinese and
overthrew the Lê Emperor and proclaimed himself
Emperor Quang-Trung (1788-1792).
    Although unable to effect the long hoped for
social revolution, the Tây-Sơn rulers were able
to make remarkable advances. Quang-Trung retained
as many able officials as would stay. He made
attempts at land reform to encourage agricultural
development. The army was greatly improved and
expanded. Taxation was refined and great emphasis
was placed on education. Quang-Trung died in
1792. The throne passed to his son, Nguyễn Quang-
Toàn who ruled for only four years. He was overthrown by Nguyễn-Anh who then became Emperor Gia-
Long (1802-1819). See NGUYỄN-ANH, NGUYỄN-HUỆ,
NGUYỄN-LỮ, NGUYỄN-NHẠC, QUANG-TRUNG, TÂY-SƠN
REBELLION.

TÂY-SƠN REBELLION (1771-1788). A successful general
uprising in the late eighteenth century led by
three brothers from Bình-Định Province (Tây-Sơn

Village, An-Khê District). The ancestors of the
three brothers were from Nghệ-An Province but had
come south as settlers. The brothers adopted the
name Nguyễn, possibly to avoid suspicion. They
were Nguyễn-Nhạc, the eldest; Nguyễn-Huệ, the
second eldest; and Nguyễn-Lữ, the youngest. At
the time of the uprising, the Lê emperors were
occupying the throne in the north, but the Trịnh
Lords held all the power while the Nguyễn Lords
ruled the south.

Nguyễn-Nhạc began to attack the Nguyễn Lords
in 1771. First he captured Quảng-Nam and then
Bình-Định. The Nguyễn Lords were further weakened
when the Trịnh Lords attacked from the north and
took Thuận-Hóa and Phú-Xuân (Huế). The Tây-Sơn
brothers then turned toward Sài-Gòn which they
captured and lost again several times. Finally,
in 1783 Nguyễn-Lữ and Nguyễn-Huệ captured Sài-Gòn
and the rest of the south. Nguyễn-Anh (later to
become Emperor Gia-Long 1802-1819) was forced to
flee to Phú-Quốc Island then to Poulo Condore
Island and finally to Thailand. The Tây-Sơn then
attacked the Trịnh in the north. Quang-Trung
(Nguyễn-Huệ) captured the capital, then called
Thăng-Long, and proclaimed full support to the Lê
Dynasty. The Tây-Sơn brothers and their forces
returned to the south where Nguyễn-Nhạc proclaimed
himself King of the Center headquartered in Qui-
Nhơn. Nguyễn-Huệ became King of the North stationed in Thuận-Hóa and Nguyễn-Lữ was made King
of the South operating out of Gia-Định (present-
day Sài-Gòn).

After the fall of the Trịnh in the north, the
Lê emperor was too weak to maintain his power. However, rather than ask help from the Tây-Sơn, the Lê
Emperor Lê Mãn-Đế (1786-1788) called on the Chinese.
Seizing on the unstable situation in Việt-Nam, the
Chinese sent 200,000 troops into the country, ostensibly in support of the Lê. In response to the
development, and in reaction to public sentiment,
Nguyễn-Huệ proclaimed himself Emperor Quang-Trung
and proceeded to march against the Chinese occupational forces. At midnight on the fifth day of Tết
(lunar new year) in the year Kỷ-Dậu (1789) the Tây-
Sơn troops attacked the Chinese near Thăng-Long. It
was an overwhelming victory for the Tây-Sơn. One
Chinese General committed suicide in order to avoid
capture. The Chinese army fled to China. This military victory by Quang-Trung, known as the Đống-Đa
Battle, is presently celebrated as one of the greatest military achievements in Vietnamese history.

The Tây-Sơn Rebellion had widespread popular
support and offered the peasants hope for social
reform. Unfortunately the Tây-Sơn regime proved
both short-lived and unable to cope with the
social ills of the peasant class. See NGUYỄN-ANH,
NGUYỄN-HUỆ, NGUYỄN-LỮ, NGUYỄN-NHẠC, QUANG-TRUNG,
TÂY-SƠN DYNASTY.

TEMPLE. See ĐỀN, ĐÌNH, MIẾU, PAGODA.

TEMPLE OF LITERATURE. See VĂN MIẾU PAGODA.

TÊN HÈM. (Also called Tên Thụy or Tên Cúng Cơm). A
name given to a deceased person and used when
referring to the dead person in prayers during
the rituals and ceremonies such as the death
anniversary (ngày giỗ). If possible, the tên
hèm is chosen by the dying person. If not, it
is chosen by his son and spoken to the one who
is dying. See CULT OF THE ANCESTORS, NGÀY GIỖ.

TẾT. (Tết Nguyên-Đán). The lunar new year festival
and the most important Vietnamese holiday. Tet
is the celebration of the beginning of spring
as well as a new year. It is the time for family
reunions, special foods, new clothes and new
beginnings.
     Literally, Tết Nguyen-Đán means the first day
or first morning of the new period. Officially
it marks the beginning of a new year on the
lunar clanedar. In reality, it is a friendly,
festive, family holiday. Painstaking care is
given to starting the year out right, since it
is believed that the first day and first week of
the new year will determine the fortunes or mis-
fortunes for the rest of the year.
     Legend has it that the spirit of the hearth
or household (Táo-Quân) must travel to the Palace
of the Jade Emperor and report on the family
affairs. Therefore, the first pre-Tết ceremony
is the Lễ Táo-Quân which is designed to send Ông
Táo off on his journey in a favorable frame of
mind. In his absence, a special Cây Nêu (New
Year's Tree) is constructed of bamboo and red
paper to ward off evil spirits. Shortly before
the new year's eve ends a sacrifice is offered
to the deceased members of the family. At midnight on the eve of Tết, the family performs the
ritual of Giao-Thừa which ushers out the old year
and welcomes the new. The ritual is also observed
by the pagodas and temples. Firecrackers, drums,
and gongs welcome the new year and the arrival of

a new spirit of the hearth.

In order to start the new year right and set the best precedent, the houses are painted and whitewashed, new clothes are purchased for the first day of Tết and old debts are cleared. Great care is taken to avoid arguments. Families ex-change visits. The first visitor to the house on the first morning of Tet is of special importance. Particular care is taken to arrange in advance to have the visitor be rich, happy and prestigious.

The holiday is also observed by a family visit to the church or pagoda to pray for good fortune and happiness. A sprig of the yellow blossomed cây-mai (plum tree) is used to decorate the home. Tết officially lasts for seven days and ends with the Lễ Khai-Hạ ritual during which the cây nêu is taken down. See ÂM-LỊCH, GIAO-THỪA, LỄ TÁO-QUÂN, TÁO-QUÂN, CÂU ĐỐI, CÂY NÊU.

TẾT ĐOAN-NGỌ. (Also called Tết Đoan Dương). The Double Five Festival. The feast of the double five falls on the fifth day of the fifth lunar month. The holiday marks the changing of the seasons, the beginning of the hot, sunny season. This is a season of many common illnesses so Vietnamese often pray for a summer of health in the family. The holiday also commemorates a heroic scholar, Khuất-Nguyên. Legend has it that Khuất-Nguyên tried courageously but unsuccessfully to dissuade the King of So from making a journey to the Kingdom of Tần where he would be assassin-ated. Khuất-Nguyên composed a poem which he left for posterity then he drowned himself in the Mịch-La River. The dead king's successor was so moved that he ordered a celebration to take place on the banks of the river on the fifth day of the fifth month.

TẾT TRÙNG-CỬU. See LỄ TRÙNG-CỬU.

TẾT TRÙNG-DƯƠNG. See LỄ TRÙNG-CỬU.

TẾT TRUNG-THU. (Also called Tết Trong Trăng or Moon watching festival). Mid-autumn Festival. Accord-ing to legend, Tết Trung-Thu was started by Em-peror Minh-Hoàng of the T'ang Dynasty in China. While walking on the palace grounds one moonlit night he was suddenly transported to the moon by an old Taoist mystic. There he met spirits of enchanting beauty and danced to celestial music. He was intoxicated by the surroundings, but the interlude was short-lived. He was soon

back on earth. In order to commemorate the
experience, the fifteenth day of the eighth lunar
month is designated as Tết Trung-Thu.
      Today the holiday is celebrated by processions
of multi-colored lanterns, dancing, and special
cakes which are eaten only on that day. It is
considered to be a holiday especially for children. It is also a time for young boys and girls
to sing alternating songs to each other in order
to tease the opposite sex about being taken up
to the moon.

THẠCH-HÃN RIVER. (Sông Thạch-Hãn). A river in cen-
    tral Vietnam. It originates in the Trường-Sơn
    Mountains in the western part of Quảng-Trị Pro-
    vince. It flows past the provincial capital of
    Quảng-Trị city and empties into the South China
    Sea at Cửa-Việt. The two major tributaries of
    the Thạch-Hãn River are the Hiếu-Giang (Cam-Lộ)
    River and the Vĩnh-Phước River. It is sometimes
    called the Quảng-Trị River.

THÁI. (Also called Tai or Thay). An ethno-linguistic
    group of highland people in north Vietnam. The
    Thái are located in the Northwest Autonomous
    Region (Khu Tây-Bắc Tự-Trị) in the provinces of
    Lai-Châu, Nghiã-Lộ and Sơn-La, and in lesser num-
    bers, in the provinces of Nghệ-An, Thanh-Hóa and
    Hòa-Bình. They are the third largest ethno-
    linguistic minority group in Vietnam. The 1960
    census listed 385,000 Thái, representing 2.4%
    of the total population of the Democratic Re-
    public of Vietnam. By the end of 1965 official
    estimates placed the total Thái population at
    446,000 showing an annual increase of 3.2%. The
    Thai are closely related to the Tày who are lo-
    cated to the north and northeast of the Red River.
    Both groups are part of a larger ethnic family
    which includes various Thái speaking groups in
    Burma, Thailand, Laos and Southern China. Lin-
    guistically, these groups are included in the
    super family of languages called Tai-Kadai. The
    Thái speaking peoples originated in China. The
    early history of the southward expansion is un-
    clear. But by the fourth century the Thái were
    settling in small groups in north Vietnam.
    Towards the eleventh and twelfth centuries they
    arrived in north Vietnam in greater numbers form-
    ing two major migratory currents: the Thái came
    from the west following the Red River or across
    Laos while the Tày came via an eastern route,
    entering Vietnam through Cao-Bằng and Lạng-Sơn
    provinces. Unlike the Tày, the Thái had little

contact with the ethnic Vietnamese and consequently maintained their own distinct cultural identity with little or no Vietnamese influence.
The Thái are divided into three separate
groups named according to the color of the female
blouse which is common to that group. The Black
Thái are located in Nghiã-Lô and Sơn-La provinces
between the Black River (Sông Hắc-Giang) and the
Red River. The Black Thái are closely related to
the White Thái who are located on both banks of
the Red River from the Delta to the Chinese border as well as along the Black River and its tributaries. The Red Thái, a considerably smaller
group, are mainly found further south in the highlands of Thanh-Hoá Province. The Thái have long
had their own script based on Chinese ideographs.
Most Thái are literate and many also speak Vietnamese. The principal economic activity is paddy-
rice culture. The kinship system is bilateral
although descent is patrilineal. The worship of
spirits is the principal religion. Like the Mương,
the Thái also have a hereditary elite and a common
class in their tradition, although this is probably fading out now. See BLACK THÁI, RED THÁI,
TÀY, WHITE THÁI.

THÁI-BÌNH CITY. The capital city of Thái-Bình Province
in north Vietnam. It is situated on the Trà-Lý
River and is about 110 kilometers (68 miles) southeast of Hà-Nội. See THÁI-BÌNH PROVINCE.

THÁI-BÌNH PROVINCE. A heavily populated coastal province in north Vietnam. The province is located
south of Hải-Hưng Province and east of Nam-Hà
Province. The provincial capital, Thái-Bình City,
is located 110 kilometers (68 miles) from Hà-Nội.
Many parts of the province are actually below sea
level. There are three main rivers in the province: the Red River, the Luộc River and the Trà-
Lý River. Thái-Bình is a prosperous province due
mainly to the silt deposited by the rivers which
empty into the sea. It is among the top rice
producing provinces in north Vietnam. Thái-Bình
is inhabited by ethnic Vietnamese and has a population of around 1,230,000 (1969) and a land
mass of 1,229 square kilometers (474 square miles).
The population density is almost 1,000 persons per
square kilometer (2,595 persons per square mile).
The main crops of the province are rice, sweet
potatoes, taros, corn, sugarcane, and jute. The
principal industrial facilities include sugar
refineries, paper mills, distilleries, pickling

factories and silk mills. Pork and poultry are
also significant products of the province. See
THÁI-BÌNH CITY.

THÁI-BÌNH RIVER. (Sông Thái-Bình). A major river in
the eastern part of north Vietnam. The river
originates at Phả-Lại near Bắc-Ninh where the
three tributaries to the Thái-Bình meet. It then
flows past Hải-Dương and empties into the sea at
several locations in the vicinity of Hải-Phòng.
The river is 140 kilometers (86 miles) long. The
three main tributaries of the Thái-Bình are the
Cầu River, the Thương River, and the Lục-Nam
River. In addition, two rivers (the Đuống and
the Luộc Rivers) connect the Thái-Bình River with
the Red River. A system of canals also connect
the two rivers. See HẢI-PHÒNG.

THÁI-NGUYÊN. The capital city of Bắc-Thái Province in
north Vietnam. It is located on the Cầu River
(Sông Cầu). It is also situated on the road from
Hà-Nội to Cao-Bằng, seventy-six kilometers (forty-
seven miles) from Hà-Nội. It was the capital city
of the former province of Thái-Nguyên. The city
is an industrial center and is especially well-
known for its steel mills. Significant deposits
of iron have been located nearby and are being
mined. It is connected by rail to Hà-Nội. See
BẮC-THÁI PROVINCE.

THÁI-NGUYÊN PROVINCE. See BẮC-THÁI PROVINCE.

THÁI-NGUYÊN REVOLT (1917). An uprising against the
French in the mountain province of Thái-Nguyên
(now part of Bắc-Thái Province) in north Vietnam.
The revolt took place in a Vietnamese garrison
and prison and was led by a local sergeant, Đội-
Cấn and a political prisoner, Lương Ngọc-Quyến.
Lương Ngọc-Quyến had studied in Tokyo as part of
the Đông-Du Movement and was an activist in the
Việt-Nam Quang-Phục Hội (Association for the
Restoration of Vietnam). After several abortive
attempts to stage an uprising, the Vietnamese
troops in the garrison finally took action on the
night of August 30, 1917. They killed the French
Commander, the Deputy Commander, and the Warden
and his wife, and released all the prisoners. The
insurgents took the town of Thái-Nguyên and held
it for three days. The rebels were expecting help
from the Chinese nationalists but it never came.
The French sent reinforcements and dispersed the
insurgents. Lương Ngọc-Quyến was a cripple. He
committed suicide rather than slow down his

comrades' escape. The French relentlessly pursued the rebels until almost all were killed.
The uprising became a source of inspiration and
a symbol of sacrifice for the Vietnamese in the
anticolonial struggle against the French. See
ĐÔNG-DU MOVEMENT, LƯƠNG NGỌC-QUYỄN, VIỆT-NAM
QUANG-PHỤC HỘI.

THÁI-PHIÊN (1882-1916). A scholar and revolutionary
during the Nguyễn Dynasty (1802-1955). Born in
Quảng-Nam Province he became active in the resistance movement against the French. He was involved with Phan Bội-Châu in the Đông-Du Movement.
He was a close friend of Trần Cao-Văn and together
they joined the Việt-Nam Quang-Phục Hội (Association for the Restoration of Vietnam). In 1916
he played a key role in the abortive uprising of
1916 together with Emperor Duy-Tân and Trần Cao-
Văn. He was captured by the French and ex-cuted
by guillotine on May 17, 1916. See ĐÔNG-DU
MOVEMENT, DUY-TÂN, TRẦN CAO-VĂN.

THÁI-THƯỢNG-HOÀNG. A royal title used to designate an
Emperor who abdicates the throne in favor of his
son. A Thái-Thượng-Hoàng assumes the function of
advisor to his son the Emperor, but in fact, retains a great deal of power.

THẦN-TÀI. One of the important spirits of the household. Thần-Tài is believed to bring good fortune
to a household. According to the legend, there
was once a poor man named Âu-Minh. One day, when
passing by the Thanh-Thảo Lake, the Goddess of
Waters gave him a girl child named Như-Nguyện.
Âu-Minh brought Như-Nguyện home to raise her.
Âu-Minh prospered and his riches accumulated. Then
one New Year's Day he hit Như-Nguyện. Như-Nguyện
was frightened and hurt, so she faded away into
the kitchen refuse, never to return again. From
that moment on, Âu-Minh's riches also slipped
away until he was poverty stricken, as before.
It is said that Như-Nguyện became Thần-Tài. Many
Vietnamese continue to worship her spirit and
maintain an altar in the home dedicated to her.
This is also the origin of the custom by
which Vietnamese refrain from taking garbage from
the house during the first three days of the lunar
new year. The fear is that the spirit of Thần-
Tài might also be thrown away which would result
in bad fortune and poverty for the household.

THĂNG-LONG. See HÀ-NỘI.

THANH-GIANG RIVER. See LÔ RIVER.

THANH-HÓA CITY. The capital of Thạnh-Hóa Province in
central Vietnam. See THANH-HÓA PROVINCE.

THANH-HÓA PROVINCE. The northernmost province in central Vietnam. Thanh-Hóa is located north of
Nghệ-An Province and south of Ninh-Bình Province.
It borders on Laos to the west and the South China
Sea to the east. The population of the province
is estimated at 1,870,000 (1968). It covers an
area of approximately 9,992 square kilometers
(3,830 square miles). The principal products of
the province are cotton, fish, rice, timber, oxen,
chromium, and phosphate. Iron mining and brick
making are also done in Thanh-Hóa. Although the
majority of the population is ethnic Vietnamese,
small numbers of Mường and Red Thái are found in
the western part of the province. Thanh-Hóa is
the native province of Lê-Lợi and the site of the
Lam-Sơn Uprising. It is also the site of the important archaeological finds of the Stone Age at
Núi Độ (Độ Mountain) and of the Bronze Age at Đông-
Sơn. The Tây-Đô citadel which was used during
the Hồ Dynasty (1400-1407) is also located in
Thanh-Hóa Province. See ĐÔNG-SƠN CIVILIZATION,
LAM-SƠN UPRISING, NÚI ĐỘ CULTURE, TÂY-ĐÔ CITADEL,
THANH-HÓA CITY.

THÀNH-HOÀNG. The patron saint or guardian spirit of a
village. The Thành-Hoàng is one of the highest
ranking spirits in the hierarchy of the supernatural world. He is the patron saint of the
village and is the only one who is venerated by
the entire community and sanctified by the emperor,
the son of heaven. By this sanctification, he is
also the representative of the Supreme Being.
     Because of the unanimous respect and honor
accorded him by the entire village, the patron
saint serves as a symbol of unity and historical
continuity for the community. The cult of the
guardian spirit represents that awesome supernatural power which is a product of the combined
faith of all the members of the village. It is
also indicative of the individuality and unique
personality of any particular village.
     The patron saint is chosen by the village and
ratified by the emperor. There are three levels
of patron saints, according to their notoriety.
Many villages have selected famous personalities

in Vietnamese history, such as the founders of
dynasties, national heroes, or great literary
figures. The founding fathers of a village are
often deified as the guardian spirit. In some
instances, a person of exceptional achievement
is chosen while still living.

The place of worship of the patron saint is
the Đình, or communal hall. It is here that the
altar of the cult of the guardian spirit is located along with a statue and a recorded history
of the guardian spirit. The entire village cele-
brates the anniversary of the death of its patron
saint on the holiday known as the Ngày Giỗ Làng.
This is a major holiday in the life of a village.
See ĐÌNH, NGÀY GIỖ, NGÀY GIỖ LÀNG.

THANH-MINH. See LỄ THANH-MINH.

THANH-NGHỆ-TĨNH PLAINS. (Đồng-Bằng Thanh-Nghệ-Tĩnh).
The part of the central coastal plain extending
from the Tam-Điệp Pass in Thanh-Hóa Province to
the Hoành-Sơn Mountains in Hà-Tĩnh Province. It
includes the lowland areas of Thanh-Hóa, Nghệ-An
and Hà-Tĩnh provinces and measures about 6,750
square kilometers (2,595 square miles). Also
included in the plains are the deltas of the Mã,
Chu and Cả Rivers. See CENTRAL COASTAL PLAIN.

THANH-NIÊN TIỀN-PHONG. (Advanced Guard Youth, or Van-
guard Youth). A youth movement formed in 1942
by Phạm Ngọc-Thạch. This paramilitary unit played
a decisive role in the August Revolution in the
south where they fought tenaciously against the
reoccupying French. Its formation was heavily
influenced by the Indochinese Communist Party.
See AUGUST REVOLUTION.

THÁNH-SỬ. (Also called Tiên-Su or Nghệ-Su). See TIÊN-
SỬ.

THÀNH-THÁI (1889-1907). The tenth emperor in the Nguyễn
Dynasty (1802-1945). He was the son of Emperor
Dục-Đức. Thành-Thái was only ten years old and in
prison with his mother when the French retrieved
him and placed him on the throne. He was very intelligent and progressive and he quickly displayed
anti-French sentiments. During his reign the
French forced the Vietnamese court to cede to
France the ports of Tourane (Đà-Nẵng), and Hải-
Phòng and the city of Hà-Nội. When the French
discovered that he was conspiring against them,
they forced him to abdicate (September 3, 1907).

Eight years later, in 1915, they deported him to Reunion Island off the coast of Africa. He was returned to Vietnam in 1947 and died seven years later in Sài-Gòn. See NGUYỄN DYNASTY.

THAO RIVER. See LÔ RIVER.

THẮP HƯỞNG. The act of burning a joss stick (cây nhang) during the process of worship. It is thought that the fragrant smoke will please the spirit or God to whom worship is being made or to whom prayers are being offered. This practice is of Chinese origin. See NHANG.

THẤT NGÔN. A form of poetry in which each line of poetry contains seven words.

THẤT-SƠN MOUNTAINS. A group of seven small mountains in Châu-Đốc Province in south Vietnam. These are not very tall but are well-known for their grottoes and attract large numbers of visitors. The seven mountains include Núi Sam, Núi Két, Núi Dài, Núi Tà-Béc, Núi Cấm, Núi Voi, and Nui Cô-Tô. See NÚI SAM.

THẤT-TỊCH. See LỄ THẤT-TỊCH.

THÀY. See THÁI.

THÀY PAGODA. (Chùa Thày, also known as Thiên-Phúc-Tự Pagoda). A famous pagoda located at the foot of Sai-Sơn Mountain in Hà-Tây Province in north Vietnam. It was built during the reign of Lý Thân-Tông (1128-1138), and is patterned on the Chinese model. It is very ornate and is divided into three sections. The outer part is used for ceremonies. The middle part houses the Buddhist temple. The inner sanctuary contains the temple dedicated to Từ-Đạo-Hạnh, an eminent Buddhist monk who lived during the Lý Dynasty (1010-1225).

THÀY THUỐC. (Also called Thày Gia-Truyền or Ông Lang). A medicine man trained in traditional Sino-Viet-namese medicine (thuốc bắc or thuốc nam). Usually for every few villages there was one Thày Thuốc who would visit and treat the sick in traditional Vietnam. He had no formal education but was considered a highly skilled person. He used only natural medicines from trees and other plants. Often in the market place or privately in his home, he would sell his wares. Sometimes an assistant could sell the medicine but would not be able to diagnose or treat the illness. See

THUỐC BẮC, THUỐC NAM, Y-DƯỢC.

THEATER. Vietnamese theater can be traced to the
    spring festivals which have taken place since the
    beginning of recorded history. The classical
    theater, while distinctly Vietnamese, shows strong
    Chinese influence. In fact, a Chinese actor, Lý
    Nguyên-Cát, is credited with having introduced
    Chinese opera to Vietnam and training Vietnamese
    artists.
        There are four basic forms of Vietnamese
    theater:

    1. Hát Bộ (songs with gestures), later
        known as Hát Bội (songs with show
        dress). This is the classical Viet-
        namese theater.

    2. Hát Chèo, a popular, satirical theater
        form found mainly in north Vietnam.

    3. Cải Lương, a modern or reformed Viet-
        namese theater. Cải-Lương originated
        in south Vietnam in the early 1900's
        and contains strong western influence.

    4. Kịch or Kịch Nói refers to the play
        or drama. The regular play is not
        nearly as popular as the musical
        theater forms.

    See HÁT BỘI, HÁT CHÈO, LÝ NGUYÊN-CÁT.

THI ĐÌNH. (Court examinations). Triennial examinations,
    often referred to as civil service examinations
    which were held in traditional Vietnam to select
    candidates on a competitive basis for the mandarin
    civil service. These examinations were held in
    the imperial palace. Each examination consisted
    of only one essay composition on a topic chosen
    by the emperor. The candidates receiving the
    highest marks were awarded a Tiến-Sĩ degree (
    (approximaetly equivalent to a Ph.D.) and were
    given high positions in the provincial adminis-
    tration. An elaborate ceremony was held in
    honor of the successful candidates who knelt down
    to receive their caps and gowns from the mandarin
    in charge of examinations. They then went to the
    court where they prostrated themselves before the
    emperor while their names were solemnly called.
    An imperial banquet followed for both the examiners
    and participants. The Thi Đình was the highest

and most difficult of the triennial examinations.
See EDUCATION, VĂN-MIẾU PAGODA.

THI-HỘI. (General examinations, also sometimes called
metropolitan examinations). Triennial examinations held in traditional Vietnam to select candidates for the mandarin civil service. These
examinations were held in the imperial capital
(Hà-Nội and later Huế). The examinations were
similar in content to the regional examinations,
but were more detailed and difficult. The candidates receiving the highest marks were allowed
to participate in the court examinations (thi-
đình) and their names were recorded on the Chảng-
Bảng (register). See EDUCATION.

THI HƯỚNG. (Regional examinations). Triennial examinations held in traditional Vietnam to select
candidates on a competitive basis for the mandarin
civil service. These examinations were held in
various provincial capitals throughout Vietnam
every three years. The examination usually consisted of three or four sections in which the
candidates were asked to (a) write essays on
ancient or classical literature, philosophy, etc.
(b) interpret excerpts from the Chinese classics,
(c) compose poems or rhythmic dissertations on
certain topics and (d) compose administrative reports. The frequency, content, and methodology
of the examinations varied with eachddynasty.
The candidates had already passed the provincial
examinations (thi-khoa). Those who received the
highest marks were awarded the degree of Cử-Nhân
(rising man, approximately equivalent to the
Master of Arts degree). These might receive posts
as mandarin/teacher or positions in the provincial
administration. Many of them continued their
studies in preparation for the general examinations (thi hội). Those with low grades were
awarded the Tú-Tài degree (blossomed talents,
approximately equivalent to a bachelor of arts).
See EDUCATION, THI HỘI, THI KHOA.

THI KHOA. (Provincial examinations). Semiannual
examinations at the provincial level in traditional Vietnam. These examinations were part fo the
competitive civil service examinations system
which was used for selecting candidates for the
mandarinal corps. It was also designed to stim-
ulate the interest of the people in formal education. It was necessary to pass the thi khoa in
order to participate in the regional examinations.

See EDUCATION, THI HƯƠNG.

THIÊN-MỤ PAGODA. (Also known as the Thiên-Mẫu-Tự
    Pagoda). A famous seven-story pagoda located on
    the bank of the Perfume River (Sông Hương) in
    Huế. The pagoda was built by the Nguyễn Lord
    Nguyễn-Hoàng, who had a vision on that site in
    1601. One of his successors, Nguyễn Phúc-Tần had
    it restored in 1665. The great bell, the sound
    of which is renouned, was cast by another Nguyễn
    Lord, Nguyễn Phúc-Chu in 1710. The seven-story
    tower was constructed by Emperor Thiệu-Trị (1841-
    1847) in 1844. Inside the main pavilion are
    many Buddhas and a bronze gong cast by Jean de la
    Croix in 1674.

THIÊN TỰ VĂN. The Essay of One Thousand Characters.
    A textbook in Chinese used by students in tradi-
    tional Vietnam. This book was a compilation of
    1,000 Chinese characters arranged into four-word
    rhythmical sentences. It was written during
    the Sung Dynasty in China.

THIỆU-TRỊ (ruled 1841-1847). The third emperor of the
    Nguyễn Dynasty (1802-1945). He ruled only seven
    years. Thiệu-Trị continued the basic policies
    of his father, Minh-Mạng (1820-1840), except that
    his persecutions of the Christians were less
    severe until the last year of his reign when in
    1847, the French ship Victorieux fired on and
    sank several Vietnamese ships in the Đà-Nẵng Har-
    bor. He also continued to fight with Thailand
    over Cambodia.
        Thiệu-Trị was a poet and left behind several
    volumes of his writings. He died in 1847 at the
    age of thirty-seven. See NGUYỄN DYNASTY.

THỊT BÒ BẢY MÓN. Seven Dishes of Beef. One of the
    more popular specialty dinners in Vietnam. Each
    dish is prepared in a different manner. Some
    have vegetables added to them, others have the
    beef diced, sliced, minced or made into a pate.
    Each dish is eaten in a special way and all have
    their own distinct sauce. The seven dishes are
    served as one meal.

THỔ. See TÀY.

THỔ-CÔNG. (Also called Ông-Công). The guardian spirit
    of the kitchen. Most traditional Vietnamese
    households have an altar dedicated to the Thổ-Công.
    Many times this is placed next to the altar for

ancestral worship. There are actually three
guardians of a household: Thổ-Công guards the
kitchen; Thổ-Địa guards the main house (Vietnamese
kitchens are usually in a separate building from
the living quarters); and Thổ-Kỳ protects the
women in such things as marketing and child bearing. These three spirits are incorporated into
the one spirit called Táo-Quân. See TÁO-QUÂN,
LỄ TÁO-QUÂN.

THOMSON, CHARLES-ANTOINE-FRANCIS. Governor of Cochinchina from 1883-1885. The Patenotre Treaty (1885)
was negotiated during his tenure in office.

THÔN. Hamlet. See ẤP.

THU-BỒN RIVER. See CÁI RIVER.

THỦ DẦU MỘT PROVINCE. A former province in south Vietnam. See BÌNH-DƯỚNG PROVINCE.

THỦ-TỰ. A custodian of a temple. He is chosen by the
village to reside in the temple (Đình or Đền) and
oversee its upkeep and maintenance. It is his
duty to keep the grounds clean and the altar and
religious paraphernalia in good order. He is
paid a small sum by the villagers. He is also
exempt from the local taxes and receives special
bonuses on major holidays. See ĐỀN, ĐÌNH, MIỄU.

THỦ-VĨ-NGÂM. A form of poetry in which the first line
of the verse is the same as the last.

THỪA-THIÊN PROVINCE. A coastal province in central
Vietnam located south of Quảng-Trị Province and
north of Quảng-Nam Province. Thừa-Thiên has a
land mass of 4,971 square kilometers (1919 square
miles) and a population of 555,514 (1971). The
province is most well-known for the imperial city
of Huế and the related structures, institutions
and artifacts. The Perfume River (Sông Hương) is
also a famous land mark flowing through the city
of Huế and out to the sea at Thuận-An, thirteen
kilometers (seven miles) from Huế.
     Thừa-Thiên is mountainous to the west and
flat, almost at sea level to the east. National
highway number one and the railroad run through
the province from north to south. Thừa-Thiên
is separated from Quảng-Nam by the breathtaking
Hải-Vân Pass. Bạch-Mã is the most well-known
mountain. It reaches 1,410 meters (4,626 feet).
Most of the people are farmers, although the land
is not very productive. Ocean fishing is the

occupation of many but has been restricted recently because of the war. The province, especially Huế, is noted for the private backyard gardens. The biggest tourist attractions are the imperial buildings inside the citadel which still stands, and the imperial tombs near Huế which house the remains of the Nguyễn Emperors. The beaches at Thuận-An and Lăng-Cô are also popular in the summer. See HUẾ, NGUYỄN DYNASTY, PHÚ-XUÂN.

THUẬN-NGHỊCH-ĐỘC. A form of poetry in which each line can be read either frontwards or backwards. Often times it is read one way in Vietnamese and the opposite way in Chinese.

THỤC DYNASTY (257-207 B.C.). The second dynasty in Vietnamese history. The founder of the dynasty was An Dương-Vương, who established his capital at Cổ-Loa in present-day Vĩnh-Phú Province. The name of the kingdom during the Thục Dynasty was Âu-Lạc. See AN DƯƠNG-VƯƠNG, ÂU-LẠC.

THUẾ ĐIỀN. A land tax which was paid by the village to the state in traditional Vietnam. It was assessed according to the official land register (Điền-Bộ) in each village.

THUẾ THÂN. (Also called Thuế-Đinh). A head tax paid by the village to the state in traditional Vietnam. It was assessed according to the official register (Đinh-Bộ) of each village.

THUỐC BẮC. (Literally, northern medicine). A form of traditional Vietnamese medicine. Thuốc Bắc is of Chinese origin and is characterized by the use of dried or preserved natural medicines from herbs and medicinal plants. These are from all parts of the plant and can include seeds, leaves, bark, shoots, roots, fruits, tubers, whole plants, powder, ointment or other preserves. It is sold by a medicine man called Ông Lang or Thầy Thuốc. Thuốc bắc is one of two popular forms of traditional Sino-Vietnamese medicine - the other being thuốc nam which uses freshly gathered herbs and medicinal plants. Thuốc bắc is more popular because it is usually more convenient and is considered more exact even though it is more expensive. Some of the medicines used in thuốc bắc are Chinese, but most are native to Vietnam. See THUỐC NAM, Y-DƯỢC.

THUỐC LÀO. Tobacco smoked with a water pipe. The
use of thuốc lào is more popular in north Vietnam than it is in south or central Vietnam. And,
it is used mainly by men rather than women.
Thuốc lào, as distinguished from regular cig-
arette tobacco, is stronger and more habit forming. It is also unique to Vietnam and nearby
areas. Three kinds of water pipes are used:
điếu cầy, made from a hollowed out tree branch
or piece of bamboo; điếu sành or điếu sứ, made
from a wooden or porcelain bowl, and điếu đồng,
a preshaped or formed pipe made from wood or
ivory. A small bit of tobacco is rolled up with
the fingers and placed in the bowl of the pipe,
which is no larger than the head of a thumbtack.
The tobacco is lit and the smoke is inhaled deep
into the lungs in one deep breath. Thuốc lào
usually causes dizziness and lightheadedness,
especially to the novice smoker. Thuốc lào is
not to be confused with thuốc phiện (opium).
See THUỐC PHIỆN.

THUỐC NAM. (Literally, southern medicine). A form
of traditional Vietnamese medicine. Thuốc nam
is of Chinese origin and consists of freshly
gathered herbs and medicinal plants. It is one
of two popular forms of Sino-Vietnamese medicine,
the other form being thuốc bắc which utilized
dried or otherwise preserved natural medicines.
Because many of the medicines can often be
gathered in the locale it is usually cheaper
than thuốc bắc. However, thuốc bắc is usually
more popular because the fresh herbs are often
not available in the urban areas and it is more
convenient and practical for a sick person to
buy thuốc bắc medicine than to go gather the
thuốc nam medicine. It is a common misconception
that the medicines used in thuốc nam are found
in Vietnam while the medicines used in thuốc
bắc are from China. Actually, many of the thuốc
bắc medicines are native to Vietnam but not used
in thuốc nam such as lotus, cinnamon, cardamon,
and nutmeg. See THUỐC BẮC, Y-DƯỢC.

THUỐC PHIỆN. Opium. Opium dens were quite common
in Vietnam under the French. In fact, the sale
of opium and liquor was controlled and sold
through the government licensed stores. The sale
and use of opium is now illegal in all of Vietnam.

THƯỢNG-ĐẾ NGỌC-HOÀNG. The Jade Emperor or the King of
    Heaven. The Jade Emperor is the highest and
    supreme deity in Vietnamese mythology.

THƯỢNG-ĐIỀN CEREMONY. See LỄ THƯỢNG-ĐIỀN.

THƯỢNG-DU. 1. A mountainous area of north Vietnam
    which includes the provinces of Quảng-Ninh (nor-
    thern part or what used to be Hải-Ninh), Lạng-Sơn,
    Cao-Bằng, Tuyên-Quang, Hà-Giang, Sơn-La, Lai-Châu,
    Yên-Báy, Lào-Cai and Hòa-Bình. The area has
    historically served as a natural defense barrier
    between Vietnam and China and between Vietnam
    and Laos. It is inhabited mainly by highland
    ethno-linguistic minority groups. The Thượng-Du
    area is distinguished from the other two geo-
    graphical areas of north Vietnam - the Trung-Du
    and Trung-Châu areas. See BẮC-PHẦN.
    2. Thượng-Du is also a term used principally
    in the Republic of Vietnam to refer to the high-
    land peoples - người thượng-du or người thượng -
    similar to the French word "montagnard".

THƯỢNG-TÂN CELEBRATION. See LỄ THƯỢNG-TÂN.

THỦY-TINH. Spirit of the Waters. See SƠN-TINH THỦY-
    TINH, TẢN-VIÊN MOUNTAIN.

TỊCH-ĐIỀN CEREMONY. See LỄ TỊCH-ĐIỀN.

TÍCH-QUANG. A Chinese Governor who governed the
    district of Giao-Chỉ during the first period of
    post Hán domination (25-40 A.D.). He is re-
    membered and honored as a concerned administrator
    who taught the Vietnamese people about rituals
    and other facets of Chinese culture. See GIAO-
    CHỈ.

TIÊN-CHỈ. The first notable on the Council of Notables
    in the traditional Vietnamese village. He was
    chosen on the basis of age and/or academic achieve-
    ments. In this capacity he headed the Council of
    Notables and was the official spokesman of the
    council. During the Nguyễn Dynasty (1802-1945) the
    Tiên-Chỉ was charged with acting as the head of
    the village court. He was usually assisted on
    the council by the second notable (Thứ-Chỉ). See
    HỘI-ĐỒNG KỲ-MỤC, XÃ, XÃ TRƯỞNG.

TIÊN-CHỦ. The first head of household to occupy a
house. It is believed that, although the owner-
ship of any house may change hands frequently,
the house will always be remembered in a special
way by the original owner. Therefore, the
spirit of the original owner (Tiên-Chủ) will
frequently visit the house. Since nobody wants
to be in bad standing with the Tiên-Chủ, an altar
is maintained in honor of the first head of
household to have occupied the house. This altar
is usually constructed outside the house on a
single pillar. Rituals in honor of the Tiên-Chủ
are performed on the first and fifteenth of the
lunar month and at Tết, the lunar new year.
Prayers are also sometimes o-fered to the spirit
of the Tiên-Chủ when there is trouble in the
household.

TIÊN-GIANG RIVER. (Sông Tiền-Giang). The upper
branch of the Mekong River. It flows from Châu-
Đốc Province through Long-Xuyên, Sa-Đéc, and
Vĩnh-Long provinces. There it splits up into
several smaller branches and empties into the
sea. The six main outlets of the Tiền-Giang are
Cửa-Tiểu, Cửa-Đại, Cửa Bà-Lại, Cửa Hàm-Lưởng,
Cửa Cổ-Chiên, and Cửa Cung-Hầu. See MEKONG RIVER.

TIÊN-SƯ. (Also called Thánh-Sư, Tổ-Sư or Nghệ-Sư).
The patron saint of a particular profession or
trade. Members of the same profession or business-
men who deal in the same commodity often organize
into a fraternal professional organization called
a phường. A separate temple dedicated to the
patron saint of their trade is built by the organization. The celebration of the anniversary
of the death of that patron saint (ngày giỗ
phường) is held by the phường. If the members
of the phường are wealthy, the festivities are
likely to be quite elaborate.
    An altar in honor of the Tiên-Sư is main-
tained in the home of the individual tradesmen.
The altar is simple and is located alongside the
ancestral altar. Rituals in honor of the Tiên-
Sư are performed on all major holy days which are
observed by the family. The term Tiên-Sư referred
to the sage Confucius when referring to him
directly. See NGÀY GIỖ, PHƯỜNG.

TIEN TSIN TREATY. (1884). A treaty between France and
China in which China relinquished her claim of
suzerainty over Vietnam and agreed to withdraw
the Chinese forces which were at that time
stationed in Tongking. The treaty was brought
about by the French who were resisting the Chinese
attempts to establish sovereignty over Vietnam.
A French naval force landed in Formosa, bombarded
Fu-Chow and occupied the Pescadores. The treaty
was signed on May 11, 1884.

TIẾT-HẠ. A form of poetry in which each line is in-
complete, although the intended meaning is clear.

TIỂU-TƯỚNG. (Ngày Tiểu Tướng, or Ngày Giỗ Đầu). The
first anniversary of the death of someone. In
traditional Vietnam the ngày tiểu-tướng was celebrated by friends and relatives as well as the
immediate family. It is an act of mourning and
is also a family ritual honoring the deceased.
See CULT OF THE ANCESTORS, NGÀY GIỖ.

TIN-LÀNH. (Literally, Good News). Protestantism. See
CHRISTIANITY.

TỈNH. (Formerly called Lộ, Trấn, and Châu). Province.
The administrative unit in Vietnam which would
most closely compare to the state in the United
States. The number and size of the provinces has
varied throughout history. The province is traditionally headed by a Province Chief (Tỉnh Trưởng)
and is divided into districts (Quận in the Republic of Vietnam and Huyện in the Democratic Republic of Vietnam). There are at present twenty-
three provinces in the Democratic Republic of
Vietnam and forty-five provinces in the Republic
of Vietnam. See ADMINISTRATIVE DIVISIONS.

TÔ HIẾN-THÀNH (ruled 1138-1175). A military mandarin
under the reign of Lý Anh-Tông. He is credited
with putting down the Thân-Lợi uprising, destroy-
ing the Ngưu-Hồng rebels and pacifying the Lao
invaders. He was placed in charge of the army.
In this position he upgraded the quality of the
army and carefully selected the officer corps.
He was also educationally accomplished. In 1175
Lý Anh-Tông became ill and entrusted the powers
of state to Tô Hiến-Thành as well as the regence
of the crown prince, Long-Cần. After the death
of Lý Anh-Tông, Long-Cần took the throne at the
age of three under the regency of Tô Hiến-Thành.
However, the Queen wanted to place her first son
on the throne and tried to bribe Tô Hiến-Thành's

wife but was not successful. Tô Hiến-Thành served
as regent until his death in 1179. He is well-
known for his military skill, wise leadership and
above all, his loyalty. See LÝ ANH-TÔNG, LÝ
DYNASTY.

TÔ-HỮU (1920-   ). Poet, member of the Lao-Động
Party Central Committee and head of the propaganda and education board of the Democratic Republic of Vietnam. He is sometimes referred to
as the poet-laureate of the Democratic Republic
of Vietnam. He was born in Thừa-Thiên Province
in central Vietnam. His real name is Nguyễn Kim-
Thanh. He was educated in Huế and became active
in the commnnist party at an early age and rapidly
advanced in the ranks of leadership. Tô-Hữu has
served in many positions of responsibility in
the Democratic Republic of Vietnam, including
Minister of Culture, Director General of Information and Director of the Propaganda and Training School. In 1954-55 he was awarded the Vietnam Literary Prize for his revolutionary poetic
cycle, Việt-Bắc.

TÔ-NHƯ. Penname of Nguyễn-Du. See NGUYỄN-DU.

TÔN ĐỨC-THẮNG (1888-   ). President of the Democratic Republic of Vietnam. Also President of
the Vietnam Fatherland Front and member of the
Lao-Động Central Committee. He was born in
Long-Xuyên Province in south Vietnam. He was
educated in Sài-Gòn and worked as a mechanic while
at the same time becoming a political activist.
In 1912 he fled to France to avoid arrest. He
became a seaman but was discharged in 1919 for his
role in a mutiny to oppose French intervention
in the Russian Communist Revolution. He returned
to Vietnam in 1927 and joined Hồ Chí-Minh's
Revolutionary Youth League. In 1929 he was
arrested by the French and sentenced to twenty
years on the island of Poulo Condor where he
spent the next seventeen years. After the August 1945 revolution, he moved to north Vietnam
and joined the Việt-Minh. He was named Vice-
President of the National United Front of Vietnam (Liên-Việt). Tôn Đức-Thắng served in several
high ranking positions, including Minister of
Interior. In 1960 he was appointed Vice-President of the Democratic Republic of Vietnam and
succeeded Hồ Chí-Minh as President in 1969. He
was awarded the Stalin International Peace Prize

(now called the Lenin Peace Prize) in 1955 and
the Order of Lenin, the highest decoration in the
Soviet Union, in 1967. See VIỆT-NAM DÂN-CHỦ
CỘNG-HÒA.

TỔNG. Canton. An administrative subdivision of a
district. The Tổng has never been considered to
be a true administrative unit of the central
government. Rather, it is a local grouping of
villages headed by a member of the local population (Chánh Tổng) with narrowly prescribed
functions. The Tổng has always played a secondary role in governmental administration in Vietnam. In most provinces, the Tổng no longer
exists. See ADMINISTRATIVE DIVISIONS.

TONGKING. (Or Tonkin). The term referring to the
area of present-day north Vietnam centering
around the Red River Delta. This area was declared a French Protectorate by the treaty between France and the Vietnamese court at Huế in
1883. Tongking ceased being a protectorate in
1954 when the French rule in Indochina ended.
The word Tongking is derived from the Chinese
word "Đông-Kinh" which means the capital of the
East.

TORTOISE. See QUY.

TOURANE. See ĐÀ-NẴNG.

TRÀ-BỒNG RIVER. (Sông Trà-Bồng). A river in Quảng-
Ngãi Province in central Vietnam. It originates
in the mountains in the western part of the province and flows in an easterly direction through
Bình-Sơn District to Sơn-Tra where it empties
into the South China Sea.

TRÀ-KHÚC RIVER. (Sông Trà-Khúc). A river in central
Vietnam. It originates at Ly-Lang in Quảng-Ngãi
Province where its three tributaries (the Ong,
Drinh, and Selo Rivers) join together. It flows
past Quảng-Ngãi City where it empties into the
South China Sea.

TRÀ-KIỆU. A village in Quảng-Nam Province. It is an
important archaeological site and has yielded
many vestiges of the early kingdom of Champa.
It was apparently the capital of Champa until the
eighth century at which time the capital was transferred to Panduranga (Phan-Rang). Among the most

important finds were three rock inscriptions, one
of which is the oldest existent text in the Chàm
language (and indeed, in any Indonesian language).
This inscription dates back to the fourth century. See CHAMPA.

TRÀ-VINH PROVINCE. One of the five provinces of the
south during the French period. In 1956 it was
changed to Viñh-Binh Province. See VĨNH-BINH
PROVINCE.

TRÀM-HƯƠNG WOOD. (Aloes wood or incense wood). A
type of wood used for incense in Vietnam. It
belongs to the family Thymelaeaceae and is found
in many parts of the world.

TRẤN. Province. The word Trấn was used during
various periods of Vietnamese history to designate a province. It is no longer in use. See
ADMINISTRATIVE DIVISIONS, TĨNH.

TRẦN ANH-TÔNG (ruled 1293-1314). (Trần-Thuyên). The
fourth emperor in the Trần Dynasty (1225-1400).
He ruled a total of twenty-one years, most of
which were peaceful. He did have to send General
Phạm Ngũ-Lão to the Lao border to stop the border
raids.
     In 1301, Trần Anh-Tông went on a tour to
Champa. There he promised his daughter to the
Chàm king in return for the two northern Chàm
provinces (which extended from Quảng-Trị to
northern Quảng-Nam Province). In 1306, the
Princess Huyền-Tran left for Champa. The next
year the Chàm king died. It was the custom for
the king's wives to sacrifice themselves and be
buried with the king. However, Trần Anh-Tông
sent for his daughter and had her brought home.
This angered the Chams and caused them to attack
Vietnam. They were defeated and the Chàm king
was captured.
     Trần Anh-Tông stepped down from the throne
in 1314 in favor of the Crown Prince. He then
assumed the position of Thái-Thượng-Hoàng, a
semi-retirement type of status which provided a
strong role in the affairs of state. He died in
1320 at the age of fifty-four. See TRẦN DYNASTY.

TRẦN BINH-TRỌNG (?   -1285). A general during the
Trần Dynasty (1225-1400). He gained recognition
for his military skill in putting down local
insurrections under Trần Thái-Tông (1225-1258).
He fought against the Mongols under Trần Hưng-
Đạo. He was captured in Hưng-Yên Province. The

Mongol general tried to win him over by offering
to make him king of the north to which he is
said to have replied, "I would rather be a head-
less devil in the south than be a king of the
north". See TRẦN HƯNG-ĐẠO, TRẦN NHÂN-TÔNG, TRẦN
THÁI-TÔNG.

TRẦN CAO-VĂN (1866-1916). A patriot and scholar, he
was a central figure in the uprising of 1916.
Born in Quảng-Nam Province, he used several
names. He became a teacher and took his family
to Bình-Định Province. He used the classroom
to express his anti-French feelings. In 1898 he
was arrested for participating in an unsuccessful
revolt in Phú-Yên but was released. He returned
to Phú-Yên and went back to teaching. But, again
he was arrested and sentenced to three years of
hard labor for his political activities. He was
no sooner released than he was in jail again in
1908 for six years. In 1915 he became active in
the Việt-Nam Quang-Phục Hội (Association for the
Restoration of Vietnam) and there he met Thái-
Phiên, another well-known patriot.
          Trần Cao-Văn and Thái-Phiên arranged with
Emperor Duy-Tân (ruled 1907-1916) to stage a
national uprising against the French. Vietnamese
troops were to rise up in coordinated assaults
on the French. But, an informer in Quảng-Ngãi
alerted the authorities. The revolt was a failure and Duy-Tân was captured and exiled. Trần
Cao-Văn and Thái-Phiên were executed in Huế on
May 17, 1916. See DUY-TÂN, THÁI-PHIÊN, VIỆT-NAM
QUANG-PHỤC HỘI.

TRẦN DỤ-TÔNG (ruled 1341-1369). (Trần Hạo). The
seventh emperor in the Trần Dynasty (1225-1400).
Emperor Trần Hiến-Tông (1329-1341) died childless
so his father placed a younger relative, Trần Hạo
on the throne. For the first half of his reign,
the political power was in the hands of Trần Hiến-
Tông's father, former Emperor Trần Minh-Tông
(1314-1329). However, after the death of Trần
Minh-Tông and other important and skilled mandarins of the court like Trương Hán-Siêu, the
political and domestic affairs began to dis-
integrate. Natural catastrophes such as the
loss of crops, floods, etc., caused suffering
among the people. Trần Dụ-Tông drank excessively
and gambled with the rich citizens.

Fortunately, the Ming Dynasty in China had just come to power and were not in a position to attack Vietnam. They did ask Trần Dụ-Tông to pay tribute. He complied and sent an envoy to the Ming court. On the southern front, Champa realized the weakened condition of the Trần court and repeatedly and openly invaded Vietnam. As Vietnam lost her strength and prestige, Champa grew stronger in every respect.

Trần Dụ-Tông died childless in 1369. The court intended to put his brother, Cung Định-Vương Phu on the throne but the Queen objected and wanted instead to put Dương Nhật-Lễ, the adopted son of Cung Túc Vương on the throne (which would mean an end of the Trần Dynasty). Dương Nhật-Lễ actually was proclaimed emperor. He wanted to change the name of the ruling house to Dương, but the members of the Trần family had him killed. Trần Nghệ-Tông was then proclaimed emperor. See TRẦN DYNASTY.

TRẦN DUỆ-TÔNG (ruled 1374-1377). (Trần Kính). The ninth emperor in the Trần Dynasty (1225-1400). His reign was short and most of the power was held by the former Emperor Trần Nghệ Tông (1370-1372). In 1376 he led an army against Champa. He invaded Champa in what is now Quảng-Bình Province and advanced southward to what is now Khánh-Hòa Province. There he was killed as he led his troops into what he was told was an empty citadel. See TRẦN DYNASTY.

TRẦN DYNASTY (1225-1400). (Nhà Trần or Triều Trần). The second great dynasty in the history of Vietnam (the first being the Lý Dynasty (1010-1225). The Trần Dynasty lasted 175 years and included the reign of twelve emperors. Although constantly and heavily attacked by the Mongols and the Chàm as well as having to deal with sporadic minor local insurrections, the country developed and prospered under the Trần.

A program of extensive land reform was carried out accompanied by a new system of taxation. The field of public administration was improved with greater emphasis on the examination system for recruitment and more prestigious titles. Literature (in Chinese) flourished although much of the work has perished. Manuals of ritual, legal codes, military treaties, poetry and historical works comprised the bulk of the literary products of the dynasty. Among the most famous authors of this era are Nguyễn Trung-Ngạn, Chu Văn-An, Nguyễn Phi-Khanh and Lê Văn-Hưu.

The decline of the dynasty started with Emperor Trần Dụ-Tông (1341-1369) who was primarily a playboy at the expense of the country. He was followed by Trần Nghệ-Tông who also contributed to the demise of the dynasty by putting blind trust in the mandarin Lê Qúy-Ly, who in turn used his power for his own end. Lê Qúy-Ly eventually usurped the throne thus ending the Trần Dynasty and founding the Hồ Dynasty.

TRẦN GIẢN-ĐỊNH-ĐẾ (ruled 1407-1409). (Trần Qúi). The first Emperor in the Post Trần Dynasty (1407-1413). In 1407 he led a revolt against the occupying Ming forces and successfully defeated the Chinese at Bô-Cô. However, he accepted bad advice and had one of his high officers killed. The troops became demoralized and a faction deserted and invited a nephew of former Emperor Trần Nghệ-Tông (1370-1372) named Trần Qúi-Khoách to replace Trần Giản-Định-Đế as emperor. Trần Qúi-Khoách accepted and, in turn, asked Trần Giản-Định-Đế to serve as Thái-Thượng-Hoàng, an influential position which usually included much of the actual control of the monarchy. In 1409, while leading his armies against the Chinese (Ming) forces, Trần Giản-Định-Đế was captured. See POST TRẦN DYNASTY, TRẦN QÚI-KHOÁCH.

TRẦN HIẾN-ĐẾ. See TRẦN PHẾ-ĐẾ.

TRẦN HIẾN-TÔNG (ruled 1329-1341). The sixth emperor in the Trần Dynasty (1225-1400). Trần Hiến-Tông was only ten years old when he took the throne. Although he reigned for thirteen years, the power was always in the hands of the former Emperor Trần Minh-Tông (1314-1329) who had the title of Thái-Thượng-Hoàng. There were two minor uprisings that occurred during his reign. The first was by a Mường leader named Ngưu-Hồng and the second was another in the constant series of attacks from the Kingdom of Laos. Both incidents were successfully dealt with. Trần Hiến-Tông died in 1341 at the age of twenty-three. See TRẦN DYNASTY.

TRẦN HƯNG-ĐẠO. (Trần Quốc-Tuấn, also known as Hưng Đạo-Vương). (? - 1300). A famous and heroic general who is credited with having defeated the Mongol invaders under the Trần Dynasty (1225-1400). He was born in Nam-Định Province. In 1283 the Mongol army of 500,000 under Kublai Khan invaded Vietnam. The Vietnamese army, under Trần

Hưng-Đạo was pushed to the south to Thanh-Hóa.
After a period of regrouping and strengthening
his forces, his armies counterattacked. After
a series of victories during which the Mongols
land and sea forces were defeated, the invaders
withdrew to China.

Once again, in 1287, the Mongols returned
with 300,000 men. Trần Hưng-Đạo allowed the
Chinese to penetrate deep into Vietnam then
dealt them a stunning defeat on the Bạch-Đằng
River during which the entire Mongol fleet (400
craft) and thousands of Mongol troops were captured. The rest of the invading army retreated
toward China, but suffered another defeat from
Trần Hưng-Đạo's army at Nội-Bàng Pass.

Trần Hưng-Đạo is one of the most venerated
Vietnamese heroes. Besides his military feats,
he also wrote several outstanding works. His
Proclamation to his officers and soldiers, Binh-
Thư Yếu-Lược., written in classical Chinese to
inspire his men in 1284 has become a classic
in Vietnamese literature. He served as a mandarin until the reign of Emperor Trần Anh-Tông
1293-1314) at which time he retired to Vạn-Kiếp.
He was over seventy years of age when he died
in 1300. See BẠCH-ĐẰNG BATTLE, KIẾP-BẠC TEMPLE,
TRẦN DYNASTY, TRẦN QUANG-KHẢI, TRẦN QUỐC-TOẢN.

TRẦN MINH-TÔNG (ruled 1314-1329). The fifth emperor
in the Trần Dynasty (1225-1400). His reign was
peaceful except for border incursions by Champa
which caused Trần Minh-Tông to send an army
against Champa in 1318 which succeeded in occupying the Chàm capital. He had several highly
talented mandarins in his service including Mạc
Đỉnh-Chi, Chu Văn-An, Phạm Ngũ-Lão, Trương Hán-
Siêu and Nguyễn Trung-Ngạn. He also made several
domestic reforms including a law prohibiting
members of the same clan (họ) from suing each
other and a prohibition on soldiers against
tatooing. That also marked the end of tatooing
among the ethnic Vietnamese. Trần Minh-Tông
stepped down from the throne in 1329 and took
the title of Thái-Thượng-Hoàng which was a semi-
retirement type of status which afforded him a
strong voice in the affairs of state. The throne
was turned over to the crown prince, Trần Hiến-
Tông. See TRẦN DYNASTY.

TRẦN NGHỆ-TÔNG (ruled 1370-1372). The eighth emperor
in the Trần Dynasty (1225-1400). During his
short reign, the Chàm army invaded and succeeded
in pillaging the capital of Thăng-Long (Hà-Nội).
Trần Nghệ-Tông was a feeble ruler. He gave
practically all the power to Lê Qúi-Ly, a mandarin
of Chinese lineage. In 1372 he abdicated in favor
of his younger brother, Trần Duệ-Tông. He then
assumed the title of Thái-Thượng-Hoàng, a type of
semi-retirement status which allowed a strong
role in the affairs of state. He died in 1394 at
the age of seventy-four. He ruled directly for
only three years, but served as Thái-Thượng-Hoàng
for twenty-seven years. See TRẦN DYNASTY.

TRẦN NHÂN-TÔNG (ruled 1279-1293). The third emperor
in the Trần Dynasty (1225-1400). It was during
his reign that the Mongolian armies, under Kublai
Khan, twice ferociously attacked Vietnam, both
times unsuccessfully. The Mongols repeatedly
tried to place demands of servility on the Trần
Dynasty and the Trần Dynasty repeatedly refused.
Finally, in 1284 with 500,000 troops, the Mongols
invaded, ostensibly in order to pass through Vietnam to Champa where they wanted to attack the
Chams. They made their way to Thăng-Long (Hà-
Nội). The Vietnamese army (200,000 strong) under
the command of Trần Hưng-Đạo engaged the invaders.
For six months both sides fought fiercely until
the Mongols were driven out. The second invasion
came in 1287 as the Mongols invaded with 300,000
troops. Again the invaders were driven out by
Trần Hưng-Đạo with the famous decisive battle on
the Bạch-Đằng River. Both times the Vietnamese
armies enjoyed strong and active support from
the populace.
        After the fighting stopped in 1288, Trần
Nhân-Tông requested China to agree to a tributary
relationship, reasoning that Vietnam was so much
smaller and weaker than China that they could not
hold out forever. China agreed and the Mongols
accepted tribute from the Trần until they were
overthrown.
        On the other front, Trần Nhân-Tông had to
fight the Lao who were causing turmoil along the
borders. In spite of the wars with the Mongols
and the Lao, classical studies developed significantly during the reign of Trần Nhân-Tông. The
address of Trần Hưng-Đạo to his troops is considered
a masterpiece. Other literary works were produced
by such people as Phạm Ngũ-Lão and Hàn-Thuyên.
Trần Nhân-Tông stepped down in favor of the crown

prince in 1293. He then assumed the position of
Thái-Thượng-Hoàng, a semi-retirement type of
status which allowed him a strong role in the
affairs of state. He retained this title for
thirteen years. He died in 1308 at the age of
fifty-one. See BẠCH-ĐẰNG BATTLE, TRẦN HƯNG-ĐẠO,
TRẦN DYNASTY.

TRẦN PHẾ-ĐẾ (ruled 1377-1388). (Also known as Trần
Hiển-Đế). The tenth emperor in the Trần Dynasty
(1225-1400). Most of the power was still in the
hands of the former emperor Trần Nghệ-Tông (1370-
1372) when Trần Phế-Đế took the throne. His was
a trouble-filled reign. Champa invaded and
pillaged Thăng-Long (Hà-Nội) several times. The
court gave no attention to civil matters. The
population was taxed oppressively (the head tax
originated in the era), and the draft took people
into the army with no hope of returning to
civilian life. The Ming Dynasty had just come
to power in China and demanded very heavy tribute
from Vietnam.

Although most of the authority was still in
the hands of Trần Nghệ-Tông, the mandarin Lê Quý-
Ly was heavily entrusted with authority. Trần
Nghệ-Tông realized that Lê Quý-Ly was abusing
his position and, in fact, had designs on the
throne. So he planned to assassinate Lê Quý-Ly.
However, Lê Quý-Ly convinced Trần Nghệ-Tông to
demote the Emperor to the rank of King and place
Trần Nghệ-Tông's own son on the throne. Lê Quý-
Ly then moved his officers against the deposed
emperor who was killed along with other officers
who plotted against Lê Quý-Ly. Therefore, Trần-
Hiển is known as Trần Phế-Đế (deposed Trần) instead of having received a posthumous name. See
HỒ QUÝ-LY, TRẦN DYNASTY, TRẦN NGHỆ-TÔNG.

TRẦN QUANG-KHẢI (ruled 1241-1294). The son of Emperor
Trần Thái-Tông (1225-1258) and General under Emperor Trần Nhân-Tông (1279-1293). He was exceptionally intelligent and academically accomplished.
He mastered several languages including Mường, Mán,
Chàm, and Lao. He was expert in military affairs
as well as a scholar and poet. He was defending
Nghệ-An when the Mongols invaded and took Nghệ-
An. Trần Quang-Khải took to the mountains and
then led his men against the enemy in the battle
of Chương-Dương Warf. He continued the campaign
under Trần Hưng-Đạo which led to the recapture
of the capital (Thăng-Long or present-day Hà-Nội)
in 1385 and the subsequent expulsion of the Mongols in the summer of the same year. See TRẦN

HƯNG-ĐẠO, TRẦN NHÂN-TÔNG, TRẦN QUỐC-TOẢN.

TRẦN QÚI-KHOÁCH (ruled 1409-1413). (Also known as
  Trần Quý-Khoang). The second emperor in the
  Post Trần Dynasty (1407-1413), and a nephew of
  former Emperor Trần Nghệ-Tông (1370-1372). In
  1409 Trần Qúi-Khoách forced the abdication of
  Trần Giản-Định-Đế. He then continued the resistance against the occupying Chinese armies. He
  fought against the superior Ming armies and the
  Chinese General Trường-Phụ. In 1413 he was forced
  to retreat to the province of Hoa-Châu. Trường-
  Phụ pursued him and captured him and several of
  his generals. As they were being taken back to
  China, Trần Qúi-Khoách committed suicide by
  jumping into the river. See POST TRẦN DYNASTY,
  TRẦN GIẢN ĐỊNH-ĐẾ.

TRẦN QUỐC-TUẤN. See TRẦN HƯNG-ĐẠO.

TRẦN QUỐC-TOẢN. A brave and outstanding general during
  the Trần Dynasty (1225-1400). He fought against
  the Mongols (1284-1288) and assisted Trần Nhật-
  Duật in the battle of Hàm-Tử Warf in mid-1288 which
  sparked a series of decisive victories by the
  Vietnamese. Then, together with Phạm Ngũ-Lão and
  Trần Quang-Khải, he led the Vietnamese against
  the Chinese at the Chương-Dương Warf which
  routed the enemy. See PHẠM NGŨ-LÃO, TRẦN NHÂN-
  TÔNG, TRẦN QUANG-KHẢI.

TRẦN QUÝ-CÁP (? - 1908). A revolutionary scholar
  during the anti-colonial movement in the early
  twentieth century. Born in Quảng-Nam, he passed
  his doctoral examinations (tiến-sĩ) in 1904. In
  1905, together with his comrades Phan Chu-Trinh
  and Huỳnh Thúc-Kháng, he travelled to the south
  in order to generate support for their protests
  against the court. Upon his return to Quảng-Nam
  in 1907 he opened a school to teach French. The
  traditionalists objected and had him transferred
  to Khánh-Hòa. In 1908 the violent demonstrations
  erupted in Quảng-Nam resulting in the arrests of
  many of the local intelligentsia. Trần Quý-Cáp
  sent a letter of support to the Quảng-Nam activists. He was summarily arrested and executed
  by being chopped in half at the waise. See PHAN
  CHU-TRINH.

TRẦN TẾ-XƯƠNG (1870-1907). (Also known as Tú-Xương).
  A well-known poet in modern Vietnamese literature.
  Born in Nam-Định Province, he passed his bacca-
  laureate examinations (tú-tài) at the age of

twenty-three. Although he tried several times, he never passed his bachelor exams (cử-nhân). He died at the age of thirty-seven, a failure in his attempted career as a scholar. His writings often reflected his frustrations with life. He wrote in many poetic forms, including hát nói, thất ngôn and sông thất.

TRẦN THÁI-TÔNG (ruled 1225-1258). The first emperor and founder of the Trần Dynasty (1225-1400). When Trần Thái-Tông was eight years old he married the seven year old monarch of the Lý Dynasty (1010-1225), Lý Chiêu-Hoàng (1224-1225). However, the real power was in the hands of Trần Thủ-Độ, a cunning and ruthless mandarin who was dedicated to the maintenance of the Trần Dynasty. After twelve years of childless marriage, Trần Thái-Tông was forced to abandon his wife and marry instead, her older sister who was the wife of Trần Liễu and three months pregnant. This distressed both the emperor and Trần Liễu. Trần Thái-Tông attempted to abdicate but was prevented by Trần Thủ-Độ. The emperor finally gave Trần Liễu a section of land and proclaimed him a local king.

　　Under the reign of Trần Thái-Tông, the civil service system started by the Lý was reorganized, a comprehensive system of taxation was instigated, a system of dikes was built on the Red River, the first doctoral examinations were given, and the army is said to have stood at 200,000 strong. In 1252 the Vietnamese invaded Champa in response to continuous raids by Champa. The Chàm king and many troops were captured. In 1257, the Mongols, under the command of Kublai Khan, invaded the country from the north and occupied and sacked Thăng-Long (Hà-Nội). However, they suffered from disease and the heat as well as heavy Vietnamese attacks and were forced to retreat. Trần Thái-Tông stepped down from the throne in 1258 in favor of the Crown Prince. He assumed the position of Thái-Thượng-Hoàng, a type of semi-retirement status which left him with a strong voice in the affairs of state. He ruled for thirty-three years and was Thái-Thượng-Hoàng for nineteen years. He died at the age of sixty. See TRẦN DYNASTY.

TRẦN THÁNH-TÔNG (ruled 1258-1278). The second emperor in the Trần Dynasty (1225-1400). Trần Thánh-Tông was known for his informality, generosity, loyalty, and concern for the people. Under his reign, education progressed. His brother, Trần Ích-Tắc organized a school of letters. Lê Văn-Hưu completed the first national history, Đại-Việt Sử-Ký.

Although the reign of Trần Thanh-Tông was peaceful, he was constantly negotiating with the Mongols, who were then in control of China. The
Mongols persisted in placing demands of servility
on the Vietnamese. Trần Thanh-Tông, with equal
persistence, avoided giving in to the demands.
    In 1278, Trần Thanh-Tông stepped down from
the throne in favor of the Crown Prince, Trần-
Khâm (Emperor Trần Nhân-Tông (1279-1293). He
then assumed the title of Thái-Thượng-Hoàng, a
semi-retirement type of status which left him
with a strong role in the affairs of state. He
ruled for twenty-one years, served as Thái-Thượng-
Hoàng for thirteen years and died at the age of
fifty-one. See TRẦN DYNASTY.

TRẦN THIẾU-ĐỀ (ruled 1398-1400). The twelfth and last
monarch in the Trần Dynasty (1225-1400). He was
only three years old when his father, Trần Thuận-
Tông was forced off of the throne by Lê Quý-Ly.
Many of the court officials plotted against Lê
Quý-Ly but were discovered. In retaliation, Lê
Quý-Le had 370 people killed for their plans to
overthrow him. Trần Thiếu-Đề was monarch for
two years. In 1400, Lê Quý-Le usurped the throne
and founded the Hồ Dynasty (1400-1407) thus
bringing an end to the Trần Dynasty. See HỒ QUÝ-
LY, TRẦN DYNASTY.

TRẦN THỦ-ĐỘ. The cousin of Trần Thị, wife of Emperor
Lý Huệ-Tông (1211-1224). He was made chief mandarin of the court in 1229. From that time forward he assumed effective control of the country
throughout the remainder of the Lý Dynasty and
during the early years of Trần Thái-Tông's rule.
After Lý Huệ-Tông abdicated the throne to his
seven year old daughter, Trần Thủ-Độ had an
affair with the Queen Mother. He used his influence to arrange a marriage between his eight
year old nephew (Trần Thái-Tông) and the seven
year old monarch. The rule then passed from Lý
Chiêu-Hoàng to Trần Thái-Tông thus ending the
Lý Dynasty (1010-1225) and beginning the Trần
Dynasty (1225-1400). The Queen Mother relinquished
her title to marry Trần Thủ-Độ. The former
Emperor Lý Huệ-Tông had entered the monastery.
Trần Thủ-Độ's overriding concern was the stability and preservation of the Trần Dynasty. He
therefore goaded Lý Huệ-Tông into committing
suicide and then proceeded to have the royal
family killed.

Trần Thái-Tông and Lý Chiêu-Hoàng were
married twelve years and did not yet have a child.
Trần Thủ-Độ forced the emperor to abandon his
wife and take, instead, her older sister, the
wife of Trần Liễu, who was three months pregnant.
Trần Thủ-Độ then took the armies against the
rebellious warlords, but unable to defeat them
he parceled out sections of land and proclaimed
two of them as local kings. He also put down
an uprising of the Mường people, an ethno-linguistic minority group living in north Vietnam.
He participated in the campaign against the Mongols and died in 1264, over seventy years of age.
See LÝ CHIÊU-HOÀNG, LÝ HUỆ-TÔNG, TRẦN THÁI-TÔNG,
TRẦN DYNASTY.

TRẦN THUẬN-TÔNG (ruled 1388-1398). The eleventh
emperor in the Trần Dynasty (1225-1400). Trần
Thuận-Tông was the son of Trần Nghệ-Tông (1370-
1372) who placed him on the throne after deposing
his nephew, Trần Phế-Đế (1377-1388). However,
the mandarin, Lê Quý-Ly still retained much of
the power in the court. As soon as he was named
emperor he had to deal with numerous insurrections
in the countryside. Also, the armies of Champa
invaded and created a serious threat to the country until the Chàm King Chế-Bồng-Nga was killed
in battle. At the death of their leader, the
Chàm armies broke ranks and retreated.
When Trần Thuận-Tông's father, former Emperor
Trần Nghệ-Tông, died, Lê Quý-Ly assumed effective
control of the decision making process. He
initiated the issuance of paper money, instituted
land reform and reorganized the court and the
political administrative structure of the country.
In 1397, Lê Quý-Ly sent Taoist priests to urge
Trần Thuận-Tông to abdicate and enter the monastery. Thus was Trần Thuận-Tông forced to relinquish the throne to his son and retire from
public life. He entered a temple on the Đại-Lai
Mountain in Thanh-Hoa Province. See TRẦN DYNASTY.

TRẦN TRỌNG-KIM (1883-1953). A teacher and historian.
For over thirty years Trần Trọng-Kim served in
the field of education. He taught high school
in Hà-Nội, was made education inspector of the
northern region and finally became Principal of
the boy's elementary school. He retired in 1942.
After the Japanese coup in March, 1945, he
accepted an invitation to serve as Prime Minister
under Emperor Bảo-Đại (1925-1945). His government was weak and soon overthrown by the August

Revolution which took place immediately after the
surrender of the Japanese armies in the same year.
His best known works are Việt-Nam Sử-Lược and Nho-
Giáo. See BẢO-ĐẠI, AUGUST REVOLUTION.

TRẦN VĂN-GIÁP. (1898-1973). Scholar, author, historian
and bibliographer. He was born in Hà-Nội and
studied classical Chinese since his youth. He
received his advanced education in France. He
actively supported the government of the Democratic Republic of Vietnam since its founding in
1945 and served in the Ministry of Education in
the early years. He was associated with the
Historical Studies Institute in Hà-Nội and travelled
to the People's Republic of China in 1952 to work
on historical Chinese manuscripts. Trần Văn-Giáp
retired in 1970. His book length publications include: Lược-Truyện Các Tác Gia Việt-Nam; Tìm Hiểu
Kho Sách Hán Nôm; and Lưu Vĩnh-Phúc. He also
authored many scholarly articles which were published in numerous periodicals. He is equally
well known as a bibliographer as he is as an
historian.

TRẠNG-NGUYÊN. See LỄ TRẠNG-NGUYÊN.

TRẠNG-TRÌNH. See NGUYỄN BỈNH-KHIÊM.

TRANSPORTATION. Roadways and waterways compose the
chief forms of transportation in Vietnam. In the
delta areas of the Red River and the Mekong River,
water transport is used extensively and, in some
cases, almost exclusively. Barges, river taxis,
ferries, and small commercial craft travel the
complicated system of rivers and canals. The
basic network of roads and railways was constructed by the French. The railroad extended from the
Chinese/Vietnamese border south to Mỹ-Tho. The
chief ports are Hải-Phòng, Đà-Nẵng, and Sài-Gòn.
Both domestic and commercial air routes have
been established in the Democratic Republic of
Vietnam and the Republic of Vietnam. At the
local level, ox carts and small horse drawn carts
are used, varying from place to place. Bicycles
are a basic means of personal transportation for
the population and pedicabs and sometimes taxis
are used in the urban areas. The bamboo carrying pole (đòn gánh) is even more basic in the
rural areas and is used to carry a wide variety
of loads. See CYCLO, ĐÒN GÁNH, HIGHWAYS, RAIL-
ROADS, PORTS.

TRẦU. Betel nut. A masticatory made from the betel
    palm, lime and sometimes tobacco. The chew con-
    sists of a slice of betel (areca) nut, a chip of
    bark from the betel nut tree, and a betel leaf
    upon which a lime paste is smeared. The leaf is
    rolled and chewed with the other ingredients,
    which sometimes include a small amount of tobacco.
    The chew is bitter, spicy and has a slightly
    numbing effect which may be why many chewers
    dribble. The novice chewer may become light-
    headed after chewing for fifteen-twenty minutes.
    The ingredients, when masticated, produce a
    bright red juice which is spit out in a fashion
    similar to chewing tobacco juice. Habitual chew-
    ing will stain the teeth, but contrary to popular
    belief, the blackened teeth, common throughout
    Vietnam, particularly among the older women, are
    a result of the custom of teeth dyeing (nhuộm
    răng) and not from chewing betel.
        The act of chewing betel nut has great
    symbolic significance as a symbol of love. It is
    used during the wedding ceremony and other rituals
    in the engagement/marriage process. It is also
    an act of fellowship and a social institution.
    Usually at large gatherings, the older people
    will sit around talking and chewing betel. The
    practice can be said to be declining in popular-
    ity, especially in the urban areas. But it is
    still quite common among the older rural people.
    Betel chewing is widely practiced throughout
    Southeast Asia and Oceania. See NHUỘM RĂNG.

TRE. See BAMBOO.

TREATY OF PROTECTORATE (1883). (Also known as the
    Harmond agreement or the Hòa-Ước Quý-Mùi). The
    treaty between France and Vietnam which estab-
    lished central Vietnam and north Vietnam as
    French protectorates, thus ending the indepen-
    dence of Vietnam. The treaty was a result of a
    year long ruthless French campaign to gain control
    of all of Vietnam. There were twenty-seven points
    to the treaty. It was signed on August 25, 1883.

TREATY OF 1874. (Hòa-Ước Giáp-Tuất). A treaty be-
    tween France and Vietnam which officia-ly ceded
    all of Cochinchina to France. The Treaty of 1874
    actually replaced the Treaty of Sài-Gòn (1862).
    This treaty authorized the free exercise of the
    Christian religion, opened Tongking to foreign

trade, and opened the Red River to navigation
up to the Chinese frontier. It was later replaced by the Treaty of Protectorate (1884)
which established French control over all of
Vietnam. The treaty was signed on March 15,
1874.

TREATY OF SÀI-GÒN (1862). The treaty between the
court at Huế (Emperor Tụ-Đức 1848-1883) and the
French which ceded the three southern provinces
to France. In February, 1861, the French initiated military action against the Vietnamese, taking
Sài-Gòn by July. Within a year the French had
penetrated beyond Mỹ-Tho. The officials of the
court decided to try to appease the French by
suing for peace. The treaty called for:

> 1. French possession of the three pro-
> vinces of Biên-Hòa, Định-Tường and Gia-
> Định and the island of Phú-Quốc.
>
> 2. opening of three Vietnamese ports
> for trade with the West.
>
> 3. free passage of French warships up
> the Mekong to Cambodia.
>
> 4. unrestricted proselytizing by
> Christian missionaries.
>
> 5. a war of indemnity of four million
> piasters to France.
>
> 6. French veto over Vietnam's right to
> cede any other part of her territory to
> another country.

The treaty was negotiated by Phan Thanh-Giản and
Admiral Bonard. It was signed on June 6, 1862.

TREATY OF VERSAILLES (1787). The first treaty concluded between France and Vietnam. The treaty
was a result of Nguyễn-Anh's request for French
support in his attempt to regain the throne.
Under the terms of the treaty, Nguyễn-Anh, later
to become Emperor Gia-Long (1802-1819), promised,
as soon as he regained his power, to transfer to
France the territory and Bay of Đà-Nẵng, the
islands in the vicinity, and the island of Poulo
Condor (Côn-Sơn Island). He promised to cease
the persecution of missionaries and to allow
religious freedom. He also promised to grant
France trade advantages.

In return, France committed herself to fur-
nish Nguyễn-Anh with four frigates and 1,000
fully equipped troops. The treaty was signed on
November 28, 1787 at Versailles by Bishop Pierre
Pigneau de BeHaine in the name of Nguyễn-Anh and
by Count de Montorin, representing Louis XVI.
See PIGNEAU DE BEHAINE BISHOP, GIA-LONG, NGUYỄN-
ANH.

TRI-TÔN CANAL. (Kinh Tri-Tôn). A canal which extends
from the Ba-Thắc River past the village of Tri-
Tôn (An-Giang Province) to the Hà-Tiên/Rạch-Giá
Canal.

TRIỆU AI-VƯƠNG (113-112 B.C.). The fourth king in the
Triệu Dynasty (207-111 B.C.). See TRIỆU DYNASTY.

TRIỆU-ÂU. (Triêu Thi-Chinh). A Vietnamese girl who,
in the year 248 A.D. at the age of twenty-three,
led a revolt against the Chinese. She met the
enemy in golden armor riding high on an elephant.
She killed herself after her army of only one
thousand men had been destroyed. The revolt
failed, but she became a national heroine. A
shrine was built in her honor by Emperor Lý Nam-
Đế (544-548). It is located in Phu-Điền Village
of Thanh-Hoa Province.

TRIỆU-ĐÀ. The Chinese General who conquered the kingdom
of Âu-Lạc in 207 B.C. and established the first
kingdom independent of China. The kingdom was
named Nam-Việt. In 111 B.C. the Chinese army
recaptured this kingdom and divided it into
nine districts. Triệu-Đà ruled Nam-Việt under
the royal name of Triệu Vũ-Vương. See AN DƯƠNG-
VƯƠNG, NAM-VIỆT.

TRIỆU DƯỜNG-VƯƠNG (ruled 111 B.C.). The fifth and last
king in the Triệu Dynasty (207-111 B.C.). He was
killed by the Chinese when, in 111 B.C., the Hán
king sent his armies south to take the kingdom of
Nam-Việt. See TRIỆU DYNASTY.

TRIỆU DYNASTY (207-111 B.C.). (Nhà Triệu). The dynasty which ruled over the kingdom of Nam-Việt
from 207-111 B.C. The kingdom was founded by
Triệu-Đà who took the royal name of Triệu Vũ-
Vương. This dynasty is significant in that it
was the first rule independent of China. The
dynasty ended in 111 B.C. when the Chinese armies
of the Hán Dynasty invaded and conquered the
kingdom of Nam-Việt, thus beginning the first
period (one thousand years) of Chinese domination.

See TRIỆU-ĐÀ.

TRIỆU MINH-VƯƠNG (ruled 125-113 B.C.). The third king
in the Triệu Dynasty (207-111 B.C.). See TRIỆU
DYNASTY.

TRIỆU VĂN-VƯƠNG (ruled 137-125 B.C.). The second king
in the Triệu Dynasty (207-111 B.C.). See TRIỆU
DYNASTY.

TRIỆU VIỆT-VƯƠNG (ruled 549-571). The second emperor
in the Early Lý Dynasty (544-602). Triệu Việt-
Vương took over the leadership of the loyal
followers of Lý-Bôn (also known as Lý Nam-Đế,
544-548) after Lý-Bôn's death. Although most
of Giao-Châu was occupied by the Chinese, the
Early Lý Dynasty continued to struggle against
the Chinese. Triệu Việt-Vương is considered an
usurper because he was not of royal lineage.
He was challenged and defeated in 1571 by a
member of the royal Lý family, Lý Phật-Tử, who
took the name of Lý Nam-Đế, but is known as Hậu
Lý Nam-Đế (or the later Lý Nam-Đế) as distinguished
from the founder of the dynasty. See EARLY LÝ
DYNASTY.

TRIỆU VŨ-VƯƠNG. See TRIỆU-ĐÀ.

TRING. An ethno-linguistic minority group of highland
people centered in northwest Ninh-Thuận Province
in central Vietnam. The Tring are actually a
subgroup of the Koho linguistic group and, as
such, speak a dialect of Koho, a Mon-Khmer language. Official estimates in 1965 placed the
Tring population at over 4,000. See KOHO.

TRỊNH BỒNG (ruled 1787). (Also known as Án-Đô Vương).
The twelfth and last lord of the Trịnh faction
during the Restored Lê Dynasty (1533-1788). He
was placed in power after the armies of the Tây-
Sơn withdrew from the north in 1786. But the Lê
Emperor Lê Mẫn-Đế (1787-1788) asked the Tây-Sơn
General Nguyễn Hữu-Chỉnh to intervene. Accord-
ingly, he came immediately to the north and de-
feated Trịnh Bồng, ending once and for all the
Trịnh faction. See TRỊNH LORDS.

TRỊNH CĂN (ruled 1682-1709). (Also known as Định
Vương). The fifth lord of the Trịnh faction
during the Restored Lê Dynasty (1533-1788).

He was in power during a time of relative peace which allowed the court to develop the civilian administration. See TRỊNH LORDS.

TRỊNH CƯỜNG (ruled 1709-1792). (Also known as An-Đô Vương). The sixth lord of the Trịnh faction during the Restored Lê Dynasty (1533-1788). The period under his leadership was one of many reforms, especially in the areas of public administration and public taxation. See TRỊNH LORDS.

TRỊNH DOANH (ruled 1740-1767). (Also known as Minh-Đô Vương). The eighth lord of the Trịnh faction during the Restored Lê Dynasty (1533-1788). He was the younger brother of his predecessor, Trịnh Giang (1729-1740). He ruled for twenty-six years but was preoccupied most of the time with quelling local revolts and uprisings. He died in 1767. See TRỊNH LORDS.

TRỊNH GIANG (ruled 1729-1740). (Also known as Uy-Nam Vương). The seventh leader of the Trịnh faction during the Restored Lê Dynasty (1533-1788). He was known as a cruel and ruthless lord. Many revolts and uprisings took place during the period of his rule. This period marked the beginning of the decline of the Trịnh faction in terms of progress and domestic stability. In 1732 he forced the abdication of the Le Emperor Lê-Đê-Duy-Phường because the emperor had an affair with the wife of Trịnh Cường. Three months later he had the former emperor assassinated. See TRỊNH LORDS.

TRỊNH KHẢI (ruled 1783-1786). (Also known as Đoan-Nam Vương). The eleventh lord of the Trịnh faction during the Restored Lê Dynasty (1533-1788). He was in power for only three years when he was captured by the Tây-Sơn army after the fall of the capital (Thăng-Long or Hà-Nội). He committed suicide by cutting his neck with his sword. See TÂY-SƠN REBELLION, TRỊNH LORDS.

TRỊNH KIỂM (ruled 1539-1569). The founder of the Trịnh faction that in effect, controlled the north from 1539-1787 and fought the Nguyễn faction in the south for forty-five years from 1627-1672. A native of Thanh-Hoa Province, Trịnh-Kiểm joined Nguyễn Kim in exile in support of the deposed Lê Dynasty. When Lê Trang-Tông was proclaimed emperor in 1533, Trịnh Kiểm was given the rank of

General. He fought the Mạc Dynasty (1527-1592) in
an effort to restore the Le to the throne. In
1545 when Nguyễn Kim was poisoned by a surrendered
enemy general, all control of the armed forces
went to Trịnh Kiểm, who was also the son-in-law of
Nguyễn Kim. Trịnh Kiểm was very successful in his
campaign against the Mạc. In 1555 he defeated the
Mạc armies at Thanh-Hóa and in 1560 he delivered
the Mạc a serious blow at Lam-Sơn. He captured
the capital of Thăng-Long (Hà-Nội) in 1564. He
died in 1572 under the reign of Emperor Lê Anh-
Tông. His authority passed on to his son, Trịnh
Cối (1569-1570). See NGUYỄN-KIM, MẠC ĐĂNG-DUNG,
TRỊNH LORDS.

TRỊNH LORDS (1539-1787). (Chúa Trịnh). The family
that governed the northern part of the country
during the period of the Restored Lê Dynasty
(1533-1788). Because the Lê Emperors were retained, the Trịnh rulers took the title of Lord
(Chúa), as did their southern rivals, the Nguyễn
Lords. This title was inherited as a crown would
be passed on in a royal family. The Trịnh were
responsible for toppling the Mạc Dynasty (1527-
1592) and restoring the Lê family to the throne.
They also engaged in a forty-five year civil
war with the Nguyễn Lords in the south.
    After consolidating their power, the Trịnh
instigated a number of significant reforms in
such areas as public administration, military
organization, education and taxation. Scholarship
also flourished during most of this period.
Local uprisings and rebellions marked the decline
of the Trịnh government in the last half of the
eighteenth century. The Trịnh and the Restored Lê
were overthrown by the Tây-Sơn brothers in 1787.
See NGUYỄN LORDS, RESTORED LÊ DYNASTY, TÂY-SƠN
REBELLION, TRỊNH-NGUYỄN INTERNECINE WAR.

TRỊNH MÁN (ruled 1782). The tenth lord of the Trịnh
faction during the Restored Lê Dynasty (1533-1788).
He was only two years old when he succeeded Trịnh
Sâm as the head of the Lê government. However,
in a few months, officials loyal to Trịnh Khải,
the rightful heir to the position, forced the
abdication of the child and placed Trịnh Khải in
power. See TRỊNH LORDS.

TRỊNH-NGUYỄN INTERNECINE WAR (1627-1672). The war
between the Trịnh Lords in the north and the
Nguyễn Lords in the south. Both factions originally fought together against the Mạc in order

to restore the Lê Emperor to the throne. But, by
1600 the Trịnh generals became so powerful and
repressive that the founder of the Nguyễn faction,
Nguyễn Hoàng, arranged to go south as Governor of
Thuận-Hoá and Quảng-Nam.

The actual war broke out in 1627 when Nguyễn
Hoàng's son, Nguyễn Phúc-Nguyên, after occupying
some of the border areas in the south of the
Trịnh territory, was attacked by Trịnh Tráng. The
attack was unsuccessful as were the next three
expeditions against the Nguyễn. In 1665, the
Nguyễn Lord Nguyễn Phúc-Tần went on the offensive
but was equally unsuccessful. There were a total
of seven major encounters between the two factions
until an agreement was reached and a demarcation
line established in 1672. The agreement was
honored by both sides until the Tây-Sơn Rebellion
in 1771-1788. See NGUYỄN HOÀNG, NGUYỄN KIM,
NGUYỄN LORDS, TÂY-SƠN REBELLION, TRỊNH KIỂM, TRỊNH
LORDS.

TRỊNH SÂM. (ruled 1767-1782). (Also known as Tĩnh-Đô
Vương). The ninth lord of the Trịnh faction during
the Restored Lê Dynasty (1533-1788). He succeeded
in putting down the revolts in the north. He also
conquered the provinces of Thuận-Hoá and Quảng-Nam
from the Nguyễn. He had designs on the throne and
made an abortive attempt to gain recognition from
China as the new emperor. Trịnh Sâm was in love
with Đặng Thị-Huệ. He named her son as successor
to his position in preference to his first son.
Consequently, he was succeeded by the two year old
son of Đan Thị-Huệ rather than his own son, Trịnh
Khải. See TRỊNH LORDS.

TRỊNH TẠC (ruled 1657-1682). (Also known as Tây Vương).
The fourth lord of the Trịnh faction during the
Restored Lê Dynasty (1533-1788). He was the son
of Trịnh Tráng and led the Lê government from 1657-
1682. He continued the campaign against the Mạc
who were, by that time, limited to Cao-Bằng Province. In 1667, the Mạc were at odds with the
Chinese whereupon the Chinese captured the Mạc
ruler Mạc Kính-Hoan and turned him over to the
Trịnh.

On the southern front, Trịnh Tạc continued
the fight against the Nguyễn until 1672 when a
cease fire agreement was reached. There followed
a period of peace which allowed the Trịnh to develop their civilian administration. Trịnh Tạc
specifically ordered several histories to be
written. See TRỊNH-NGUYỄN INTERNECINE WAR, TRỊNH
LORDS.

TRỊNH TRÁNG (ruled 1623-1657). (Also known as Thanh-
    Đô Vương). The third lord of the Trịnh faction
    during the Restored Lê Dynasty. He was the son
    of Trịnh Tùng and the son-in-law of Nguyễn Hoàng.
    He assumed the leadership of the north upon the
    death of his father in 1623. The forty-five year
    war between the Trịnh and Nguyễn actually started
    in 1627 when Trịnh Tráng engaged Nguyễn Phúc-Nguyên
    in battle. Trịnh Tráng unsuccessfully attacked
    the Nguyễn four times (1627, 1633, 1635, and 1648).
    See TRỊNH LORDS, TRỊNH-NGUYỄN INTERNECINE WAR.

TRỊNH TÙNG (ruled 1570-1623). (Also known as Bình-An
    Vương). The third lord of the Trịnh faction
    during the Restored Lê Dynasty (1533-1788) and
    son of the famous General Trịnh Kiểm. Trịnh Tùng
    fought his brother Trịnh Cối for the leadership
    of the Trịnh faction. He proclaimed himself
    Lord (Chúa) in 1570. The Trịnh forces under
    Trịnh Tùng waged a constant campaign against the
    Mạc. The armies of the Trịnh progressed to the
    point where, in 1591, they occupied the Mạc cap-
    ital of Thăng-Long (Hà-Nội). Trịnh Tùng also
    managed to capture the Mạc Emperor Mạc Mâu-Hợp,
    who was tortured and executed. Within a short
    time Trịnh Tùng's forces captured Mac Mâu-Hợp's
    successor, Mạc Kính-Chí. The campaign waged
    by Trịnh Tùng was directly responsible for the
    effective downfall of the Mạc Dynasty (1527-1592).
    From 1592-1667, the authority of the Mạc Dynasty
    was limited to one province (Cao-Bằng). Trịnh
    Tùng died in 1623 after fifty-three years of
    leadership. His authority and title was passed
    on to his son, Trịnh Tráng. See MẠC DYNASTY,
    TRỊNH LORDS, TRỊNH TRÁNG.

TRÚC-GIANG. The capital city of Kiến-Hoà Province.
    Population 75,224. It was formerly known as Bến-
    Tre. See KIẾN-HOÀ PROVINCE.

TRUNG-BỘ. See TRUNG-PHẦN.

TRUNG-CHÂU. An area of north Vietnam characterized by
    lowlands, dense population and intensive rice
    cultivation. The area includes the provinces of
    Hà-Bắc, Hà-Tây, Nam-Hà, Hải-Hưng, Thái-Bình, the
    municipality of Hải-Phòng, and parts of Vĩnh-Phú
    Province. This area is distinguished from Thượng-
    Du and Trung-Du. It is inhabited almost entirely
    by ethnic Vietnamese. It is also the most in-
    tensively farmed area in north Vietnam, predomin-
    antly in rice cultivation. It has a significant

fishing industry and contains the two largest
cities in north Vietnam - Hà-Nội and Hải-Phòng.
See BẮC-PHẦN, RED RIVER DELTA.

TRUNG-CỬU. See LỄ TRÙNG-CỬU.

TRUNG-DU. An area of north Vietnam characterized by
flatlands and plains and located between the
mountainous area (Thượng-Du) and the populous
lowlands (Trung-Châu). The area includes the
province of Ninh-Bình and portions of Bắc-Thái,
Vĩnh-Phú, Quảng-Ninh, Hà-Bắc, Yên-Báy and Tuyên-
Quang provinces. The area is inhabited by both
ethnic Vietnamese and highland people of various
ethno-linguistic minority groups. It is a
scenic area in which numerous coffee and tea
plantations are located. See BẮC-PHẦN.

TRUNG-DUNG. The Doctrine of the Mean or Middle Way.
One of the four famous Chinese books (Tứ-Thư)
dealing with the philosophy and doctrine of
Confucius. Trung-Dung is an exposition of the
philosophical presuppositions of Confucian
thought dealing particularly with the relationships between human nature and the moral order
of the universe. This book was used by scholars
and students in traditional Vietnam. It was
particularly important because the civil service
examinations were, in part, based on it. See
TỨ-THƯ.

TRUNG-KỲ. See TRUNG-PHẦN.

TRUNG-NAM PLAIN. (Đồng-Bằng Trung-Nam). A lowland
coastal area extending from the Dinh (Padaran)
Peninsula in Ninh-Thuận Province to Long-Hải in
Phước-Tuy Province and including the lowland
parts of Bình-Thuận, Bình-Tuy, and Phước-Tuy
provinces. It is called the Trung-Nam Plain
(Central-Southern Plain) because it lies partly
in central Vietnam (Bình-Thuận), and partly in
south Vietnam (Bình-Tuy and Phước-Tuy). It covers
an area of about 7,000 square kilometers (2,072
square miles). It is the largest plains area in
the Central Coastal Plains. See CENTRAL COASTAL
PLAINS.

TRƯNG NHỊ. The younger of the two Trưng sisters (Hai
Bà Trưng) who are credited with leading the first
Vietnamese revolution against the Chinese in 40
A.D. See HAI BÀ TRƯNG.

TRUNG-PHẦN. (Also known as Trung-Kỳ, Trung-Bộ, and
    Miền Trung). Central Vietnam. That portion of
    Vietnam which extends from Thanh-Hóa Province
    south to the southern fringes of the Trường-Sơn
    Mountain Range. It includes the entire Trường-
    Sơn Mountain Chain, the Central Highlands and
    the Central Lowlands. It is located between Laos·
    and Cambodia to the west and the South China Sea
    to the east. The region is characterized by a
    narrow strip of relatively poor rice land sand-
    wiched in between the seacoast and the mountains.
    The coastal area is sandy and barren in most
    places except for groves of coconut and evergreen
    trees. It is broken in many spots where the
    mountain spurs jut into the sea. In many areas,
    like at Ninh-Hòa and Cam-Ranh, an elaborate
    system of lagoons are sites for the production
    of salt, which is important to the Vietnamese
    economy. The southern part of the coast is lined
    with natural bays, the most well-known of which
    is Cam-Ranh, one of the finest natural harbors in
    Asia. See CENTRAL HIGHLANDS, CENTRAL COASTAL
    PLAIN, TRƯỜNG-SƠN MOUNTAIN RANGE.

TRƯNG TRẮC. (Also known as Trưng-Vương). The older
    of the Trưng sisters who are credited with lead-
    ing the first Vietnamese revolution against the
    Chinese in 40 A.D. See HAI BÀ TRƯNG.

TRỨNG VỊT LỘN. See HỘT VỊT LỘN.

TRƯỜNG CHINH (1908-   ). (Also known as Đặng Xuân-
    Khu). A leading Communist ideologist, founding
    member of the Indochina Communist Party, Chairman
    of the Standing Committee of the National Assembly
    of the Democratic Republic of Vietnam and member
    of the Lao-Động Politburo. He was born in Nam-
    Định Province. As early as 1928 he was expelled
    from school for political agitation. He joined
    Hồ Chí-Minh's Revolutionary Youth League and there
    began a career which took him to jail under the
    French (1931-1936), to China in exile in 1939,
    and to the forefront of the political leadership
    of the Democratic Republic of Vietnam. He has
    served as Deputy Premier, on the Council of
    Ministers (1958-1960), as Chairman of the sci-
    entific Research Commission (1958-1961), and as
    a member of the Presidium (1961-   ). He was
    also elected Deputy to the Fourth National Assembly
    from the municipality of Hà-Nội.

TRƯỞNG CÔNG-ĐỊNH (1820-1864). A patriot and leader in
the anti-French resistance movement in Cochinchina.
He was born in Quảng-Ngãi Province. His father
became the military commander of Gia-Định Province.
Trưởng Công-Định accompanied his father where he
first took part in the battle against the French
in 1858 and later, under the command of Nguyễn
Trị-Phương, he participated in the battles of
Gia-Định and Ky-Hòa fortresses (1859 and 1861
respectively). He then moved to Tân-Hòa in Gò-
Công Province to continue his forays against the
French. In 1864 he was betrayed by a former
associate, captured by the French and executed
at Kiên-Phước on August 20, 1864. His son carried
on establishing a new base in Cambodia near Tây-
Ninh.

TRƯỞNG MINH-GIẢNG. A famous mandarin during the early
Nguyễn Dynasty (1802-1945). Born in Gia-Định, he
commanded the Vietnamese troops in the south
against the Thái invaders in 1883. He pursued
the Thai armies across Cambodia and established
a base near Phnom Penh to protect Cambodia. The
Emperor put him in charge of civilian affairs. In
1841 Emperor Thiệu-Trị (1841-1847) decided to
abandon Cambodia. Shamed and depressed, Trưởng
Minh-Giảng rrturned to Vietnam and died the same
year. See MINH-MẠNG, NGUYỄN DYNASTY, THIỆU-TRỊ.

TRƯỞNG MINH-KÝ. A journalist and scholar during the
late nineteenth century. A southern writer, he
was a main contributor to Gia-Định-Báo, Vietnam's
first newspaper. He was instrumental in promoting the use of the Romanized script (quốc-ngữ).
See GIA-ĐỊNH-BÁO.

TRƯỞNG-SƠN MOUNTAIN RANGE. (Also called the An-Nam
Cordillera, or the Chaine Annamitique). A chain
of mountains over 1200 kilometers (750 miles) in
length and extending from the Mã River in Thanh-
Hoá Province southeastwardly to the southern
extreme of the Central Highlands (Lâm-Đồng Province) about eighty kilometers (fifty miles)
north of Sài-Gòn. The northern portion of the
chain is rugged and narrow. The southern portion
contains the large plateau known as the Central
Highlands. The peaks of the Trưởng-Sơn Mountain
Range vary from 1,525 meters (5,000 feet) to
over 2,500 meters (8,500 feet). The tallest peak
is Ngọc-Linh Mountain in Kontum Province which
stands at 2,598 meters (8,521 feet). The limits

of the Trường-Sơn Range are also the north-south
borders of central Vietnam. See CENTRAL HIGHLANDS,
TRUNG-PHẦN.

TRƯỞNG TỘC. The head of the extended patrilineal family.
The patrilineage is reckoned through the male
line to a male ancestor in the fifth ascending
generation. The Trưởng Tộc or head of the patrilineage is selected by the adults in the extended family (họ) primarily on the basis of age.
     He is responsible for settling disputes
within the extended family, keeping and managing
the patrimonial land and maintaining the ancestral
graves. He uses the income from the patrimonial
land to defray the cost of the rituals and feast-
ing which is an integral part of the cult of the
ancestors. He is thus also responsible for organizing the religious ceremonies (ngày giỗ)
which venerate the common ancestor. As Trưởng
Tộc, he also maintains the family register or
genealogy book (gia-phả) if one is kept. See
ĐÍCH-TÔN, GIA-PHẢ, HƯỞNG-HỎA, KINSHIP SYSTEM,
NGÀY GIỖ.

TRƯỞNG VĨNH-KÝ (1837-1898). (Also known as Petrus Ky).
A scholar, journalist, translator, and linguist
of world renown. Born in Vĩnh-Long Province (in
a village that is now in Kiến-Hòa Province), he
studied classical Chinese at the age of five, and
then the Vietnamese Romanized script (quốc-ngữ).
When only eleven years old he went to Cambodia
and then to Penang with his mentor, Father Long.
He was a brilliant student and a devoted Catholic.
During his six years in Penang he learned French,
English, German, Italian, Spanish, Greek, Hindi,
and Japanese. He was cited as being particularly
outstanding in Latin literature and philosophy.
     In order to play a role of moderator, and
hopefully to help avoid war between France and
Vietnam, he became an interpreter for the French.
In this position he went to France with Phan
Thanh-Giảnh in 1863 to negotiate with Napoleon
III. While there he was elected a member of the
Paris Ethnology Society. He toured Europe and
was received in audience by the Pope. He returned
to Vietnam in 1865 and took a position in a
local school and published a local newspaper, the
first of many that he published.
     Emperor Đồng-Khánh (1885-1889) appointed him
special Counsellor at the court. He later retired
and devoted himself full time to his writing for
which he received the highest awards from the

French Academy. His literary genius was a hall-
mark in the development of modern Vietnamese
literature. Trường Vĩnh-Ký died in poverty on
September 1, 1898 at the age of sixty-one. See
PHAN THANH-GIẢN.

TRƯỜNG-XA ARCHIPELAGO. See SPRATLEY ISLANDS.

TRUYỆN. Narrative verse. Truyện is a literary art
form written in nôm. It is written in the lục-
bát style (alternating sentences of six and eight
words) or in the style of biến thể lục bát (a
modification of lục bát).

TỬ. Viscount, a rank of nobility. See NOBILITY.

TỨ DÂN. The four social classes in traditional
Vietnam. These classes include: scholars (sĩ);
farmers (nông); craftsmen (công); and merchants
(thương).

TỨ ĐỒ TƯỜNG. The four social evils in traditional
Vietnam. These include: wine (tửu); women (sắc);
opium (yên); and gambling (đổ).

TỰ-ĐỨC (ruled 1848-1883). The fourth emperor in the
Nguyễn Dynasty (1802-1945). He was known as
highly cultured and educated. He was a poet of
renown. Tự-Đức continued the policy of the
earlier Nguyễn emperors with respect to the
persecution of missionaries. In 1848 and 1851,
in particular, there were two edicts which, if
they would have been carried out, would have
resulted in mass executions. The French used
this issue as a reason for invading Vietnam. Đà-
Nẵng was shelled in 1856 and 1858. Three southern
provinces were ceded to the French in 1862.
Three more were lost to the French in 1874. In
1873, Hà-Nội was invaded and the whole of Tongking became a French protectorate along with
central Vietnam in 1883.
     Tự-Đức's policy had been to compromise in
the south to preserve the north. Since the
Nguyễn Dynasty was characterized by the development of an elite mandarinal corps at the expense
of the peasant, Tự-Đức had little popular support
in his fight against the French. In fact, his
reign was plagued with local revolts and uprisings.
He died in July, 1883 at the age of fifty-five
after a reign of thirty-six years. See NGUYỄN
DYNASTY, FRENCH INDOCHINA WAR.

TỨ ĐỨC. Four virtues. The four important virtues
for women as based on the Chinese classics and
repeated throughout Vietnamese literature. These
include: công (industriousness); dung (proper
countenance); ngôn (proper speech); and hạnh
(proper behavior).

TỨ LINH. The four sacred animals in Vietnamese mythology. These include the dragon, unicorn, tortoise, and phoenix (long, ly, quy, and phượng
respectively). See LONG, LY, PHƯỢNG, QUY.

TỰ-LỰC VĂN-ĐOÀN. (Literally, Self-Reliant Literary
Group). A literary school or movement founded
in the 1930's. The movement sought to promote
progressive social and literary reform. The
founders of the movement included Khái-Hưng,
Nhất-Linh, Thế-Lữ and Tú-Mỡ. The members published their ideas in the newspaper, Phong-Hóa
Tuần-Báo (1932-1935) and Ngày Nay (1935-1940).
The publishing house Đời Nay was also associated
with the movement. See KHÁI-HƯNG, NHẤT-LINH.

TỨ-THƯ. The Four Books. The famous four Chinese
classics: Luân-Ngũ (The Analects); Đại-Học (The
Great Learning); Trung-Dung (The Doctrine of the
Mean); and Mạnh-Tử (The Book of Mencius). These
books, all dealing with the philosophy and
doctrine of Confucius were used by scholars and
students in traditional Vietnam. They were
especially important for a person's preparation
for the civil service examinations which were
based, in part, upon these four classics. See
ĐẠI-HỌC, LUÂN-NGỮ, MẠNH-TỬ, TRUNG-DUNG.

TỨ-TUYỆT. A form of classical poetry (đường-luật)
in which each verse has four lines.

TÚ-XUONG. See TRẦN TẾ-XƯỜNG.

TÙNG-NGHĨA. The capital city of Tuyên-Đức Province.
Population 16,342. The town is located in the
Di-Linh Plateau on highway number twenty between
Đà-Lạt and Di-Linh. Tùng-Nghĩa is best known
for its settlements of north Vietnamese highland
minority groups, including the Nùng, White Thái,
and Black Thái. See TUYÊN-ĐỨC PROVINCE.

TƯỜNG RIVER. (Sông Tường). A river in north Vietnam.
It originates in the highlands of the Bắc-Sơn
Mountain Range (Lạng-Sơn Province) and follows

the Bắc-Sơn Mountains flowing past Bố-Hạ, Phủ-Lạng-Thượng, and Phả-Lại where it meets the Thái-Bình River.

TƯỞNG-TÂN. See LỄ TƯỞNG-TÂN.

TUY-HÒA. The capital city of Phú-Yên Province. Population 65,087. It is a coastal town located just off highway number one about 560 kilometers (347 miles) north of Sài-Gòn. See PHÚ-YÊN PROVINCE.

TUYÊN-ĐỨC PROVINCE. A mountainous province in the southern part of the central highlands. The province is located south of Darlac Province and Khánh-Hòa Province, north of Lâm-Đồng Province and it borders on Quảng-Đức to the west and Ninh-Thuận to the east. The population of Tuyên-Đức Province is 116,205 and the area is estimated at 4,916 square kilometers (1,898 square miles). The province is best known for the popular mountain resort city of Đà-Lạt which, until recently, was also the provincial capital. The provincial capital is now Tùng-Nghĩa. The area is a major producer of cool weather vegetables such as cabbage, lettuce, onions, and fruits, including strawberries. Timber is also among its chief products. While most of the inhabitants are members of the Koho ethno-linguistic minority group, there are small settlements of Nùng, White Thái and Black Thái around the town of Tùng-Nghĩa. The Vietnamese population is centered primarily in the city of Đà-Lạt. One of the country's best known scenic attractions is the series of waterfalls on the Đa-Nhim and Cam-Ly Rivers. These include the Cam-Ly, Prenn, Liên-Khương, and Pongour waterfalls. The Đồng-Dương hydroelectric plant, which was built under a war reparations agreement with the Japanese, is located on the Đa-Nhim River, southeast of Đà-Lạt. See ĐÀ-LẠT, ĐA-NHIM RIVER DAM, KOHO, TÙNG-NGHĨA.

TUYÊN-QUANG CITY. The capital city of Tuyên-Quang Province in north Vietnam. It is situated on the Lô River (Sông Lô) and connected by road to Hà-Giang and Hà-Nội. It is 161 kilometers (100 miles) from Hà-Nội, 52 kilometers (32 miles) from Phú-Thọ, and 185 kilometers (114 miles) from Hà-Giang. Long established coal mines are located nearby. See TUYÊN-QUANG PROVINCE.

TUYÊN-QUANG PROVINCE. An inland, mountainous province
in north Vietnam. It is located south of Hà-
Giang, west of Bắc-Thái, east of Yên-Báy and north
of Vĩnh-Phú Province. The land mass of the province is 5,524 square kilometers (2,132 square
miles). The population is estimated at 245,000
(1969). The province is inhabited by ethnic Vietnamese as well as by members of the Thổ, Man,
Mèo and Mường ethno-linguistic minority groups.
There are four main rivers in the province: Hồng-
Hà (Red River), Chảy, Lô and Gâm rivers. These
are separated by mountain ranges that measure
from 800-1200 meters (2,600 - 3,900 feet) tall.
    Tuyên-Quang was originally controlled by
the Thái. But, since the thirteenth century, it
has been governed by the ethnic Vietnamese. Much
of the province was occupied by the Black Flags
(Cờ Đen) when they fought against the French in
the early 1800's. The province is rich in
valuable timber. Under the French there were
many plantations ranging in size from 100-5,500
hectares (247-13,500 acres).

-U-

U-MINH FOREST. A large undeveloped jungle area along
the coast of the Gulf of Thailand in the southernmost part of Vietnam. This mangrove forest covers
an area of approximately 100,000 hectares (240,000
acres). The forest is divided into two distinct
parts: the upper U-Minh (U-Minh Thượng), which is
in Kiên-Giang Province, and the lower U-Minh (U-
Minh Hạ), in An-Xuyên Province.

UNG HOE. See NGUYỄN VĂN-TỐ.

UNICORN. See LY.

UNIVERSITY OF HÀ-NỘI. An institution of higher learning established in Hà-Nội under the name of the
Indochinese University by the French colonial
administration in 1907. The following year it
was closed except for the school of medicine,
due to the political agitation. The university
was fully restored by 1919 and included six schools
or faculties: Medicine and Pharmacy; Law and
Administration; Pedagogy; Agriculture and Forestry;
and Veterinary Science. A School of Fine Arts was
established in 1924 and then a School of Commerce.
Graduates of the university were originally awarded

diplomas and received no recognition from the
French universities. The standards were gradually
raised so that by the mid-1930's the medical and
law degrees were considered equivalent to those
granted by the French universities. The university was renamed the University of Hà-Nội which
is still used today. It now has eleven faculties
and an enrollment of 20,000 students (1963). See
EDUCATION.

-V-

VÀM-CỎ RIVER. (Sông Vàm-Cỏ). A principal river in
south Vietnam. It originates in Cambodia and has
two main branches: Vàm-Cỏ Tây (Western Vàm-Cỏ);
and Vàm-Cỏ Đông (Eastern Vàm-Cỏ). Both branches
meet at Cần-Đước in Long-An Province. From Cần-
Đước it flows northeasterly to join the Sài-Gòn
River and then empties into the South China Sea
at the Cửa Soai-Rạp.

VẤN-DANH. See LỄ VẤN-DANH.

VAN-KIỀU. An ethno-linguistic grouping of highland
people in central Vietnam. They are located
mostly in Quảng-Trị, Quảng-Bình and Thừa-Thiên
provinces along the Vietnamese/Laos border and
actually extend further into Laos than they do
into Vietnam. They are divided into distinct
subgroups which include the Brũ, Katu, Pacoh and
Phương. They belong to the Mon-Khmer language
family and take their name from the Van-Kiều
Mountain (west of Quảng-Trị). Sources in the
Democratic Republic of Vietnam estimated in 1960
that the Van-Kiều numbered around 30,000. See
BRŨ, KATU, PACOH.

VĂN-LANG. The name of the country ruled by the Hồng-
Bang Dynasty (the legendary eighteen Hùng-Vương
Kings 2879-258 B.C.). Văn-Lang is considered the
first Vietnamese nation and is said to have been
composed of fifteen provinces (bộ), extending from
parts of present-day Kwangsi and Kwang Tung in
China to Quảng-Trị Province in central Vietnam.
Văn-Lang was taken over by Thục-Vương-Phán, who
founded the Thục Dynasty (257-208 B.C.) and ruled
with the title of An-Dương-Vương. See HỒNG-BÀNG
DYNASTY, AN-DƯƠNG-VƯƠNG.

VĂN MIẾU PAGODA. (Chùa Văn Miếu, or Temple of Literature). A temple built in 1070 by Emperor Lý Thanh-Tông (1054-1072). It is located in Hà-Nội and was dedicated to Confucius in order to honor scholars and men of literary fame. In 1484, Emperor Lê Thanh-Tông (1460-1497) ordered that stone slates be erected in the temple, one for each triennial examination, to record the names, places of birth, and achievements of all men who received the doctoral degree (Thái-Học-Sinh). Since 1442, this practice continued until 1778. Although 116 examinations were held during this period, only eighty-two slates remain. In 1802, the Khuê-Văn Các (Khuê-Văn Pavillion) was built in the temple and has become known as a fine example of early Vietnamese architecture. The Văn Miếu Pagoda is situated in the heart of the city and covers an area 350 meters (1,148 feet) long by 70 meters (223 feet) wide and is surrounded by a brick wall nearly one kilometer (.62 miles) long. See LÊ THANH-TÔNG, LÝ THÁNH-TÔNG, QUỐC-TỬ-GIÁM.

VĂN-TẾ. A funeral oration. A literary art form written in one of several poetic forms.

VĂN-ÚC RIVER. (Sông Văn-Úc). A small river in north Vietnam. It is actually a branch of the Thái-Bình River from which it originates at Hải-Dương. It splits into two sections (Hương and Rang rivers) and empties into the South China Sea at Cửa Văn-Úc.

VẠN-XUÂN. (Literally, Ten Thousand Springs). The name of the kingdom established by Lý-Bôn in 544. Lý-Bôn led a popular revolt against the Chinese in what was then the Chinese province of Giao-Châu. He succeeded and proclaimed himself King of Vạn-Xuân, an early precursor state of Vietnam. See LÝ-BÔN.

VANGARD YOUTH. See THANH-NIÊN TIẾN-PHONG.

VARENNE, ALEXANDRE. Governor General of Indochina from November, 1925, to January, 1928. His term as governor is generally considered as successful. He was the first to create a core of Vietnamese military officers.

VC. See VIỆT-CỘNG.

VỆ RIVER. (Sông Vệ). A river in central Vietnam and

and a tributary of the Trà-Khúc River. The Ve
River originates in Kontum Province and joins
the Trà-Khúc River near Quảng-Ngãi City.

VĨ-TAM-THANH. A form of poetry in which the last word
in each line is repeated three times.

VI-THANH. The capital city of Chương-Thiện Province.
Population 24,477. See CHƯƠNG-THIỆN PROVINCE.

VIỆT-BẮC AUTONOMOUS REGION. (Khu Việt-Bắc Tự-Trị).
A region of the north Vietnamese highlands inhabited primarily by ethno-linguistic minority
groups of highland people and encompassing the
provinces of Lạng-Sơn, Cao-Bằng, Bắc-Thái, Tuyên-
Quang, and Hà-Giang. Its population includes
1,510,000 people representing fourteen different
ethno-linguistic groups. The two largest groups
are the Tày and Nùng. The region was established
in April, 1956. It is characterized by strong
local (ethnic minority) participation in the
local administration and national assembly. The
People's Councils and administrative committees
have broader than usual discretionary powers to
accommodate the many cultural variations. The
other similar zone in the Democratic Republic of
Vietnam is the Tây-Bắc Autonomous Region.

VIỆT-CỘNG. (Also called VC). An abbreviation for
Việt-Nam Cộng-Sản (meaning Vietnamese communist).
The word is a pejorative term used by the Republic
of Vietnam and other anti-communist belligerents
in the recent Vietnam war. The word has been in
use since 1956.

VIỆT-MINH. See VIỆT-NAM ĐỘC-LẬP ĐỒNG-MINH HỘI.

VIỆT-NAM CÁCH-MỆNH ĐỒNG-MINH HỘI. Vietnam Revolutiɒn-
ary League. An association established in October,
1942, by Vietnamese nationalist political exiles
in southern China. It had the sponsorship of the
Chinese military commander, Chang Fa-K'wei. The
association was composed of several factions in-
cluding the Việt-Nam Quốc-Dân Đảng, Việt-Nam Phục-
Quốc Đồng-Minh Hội, and the Việt-Nam Độc-Lập Đồng-
Minh Hội. The league was first headed by Nguyễn
Hải-Thanh who was succeeded by Hồ Chí-Minh in 1943.
The league remained in existence until the August
Revolution of 1945. See VIỆT-NAM ĐỘC-LẬP ĐỒNG-
MINH HỘI, VIỆT-NAM PHỤC-QUỐC ĐỒNG-MINH HỘI, VIỆT-
NAM QUỐC-DÂN ĐẢNG.

VIỆT-NAM CÁCH-MỆNH THANH-NIÊN ĐỒNG-CHÍ HỘI. Vietnam
    Revolutionary Youth League, popularly known as the
    Thanh-Niên. This party was formed in 1925 by Hồ
    Chí-Minh upon his arrival in Canton. Composed of
    Vietnamese exiles in southern China the league
    maintained close ties with indigenous cells in
    Vietnam, especially northern Vietnam. The Thanh-
    Niên continued to function until 1930 when the
    Indochinese Communist Party was created. See ĐÔNG-
    DƯƠNG CỘNG-SẢN ĐẢNG, HỒ CHÍ-MINH.

VIỆT-NAM CỘNG-HÒA. The Republic of Vietnam. The country,
    sometimes referred to as South Vietnam, extending
    from the Bến-Hải River (at approximately the
    seventeenth parallel) southward to the Gulf of
    Thailand. It is bordered on the west by Laos and
    Cambodia and to the easy by the South China Sea.
    The present boundaries were determined by the July,
    1954, Geneva Accords. Ngô Đình-Diệm became the
    Prime Minister under Emperor Bảo-Đại (1925-1945)
    in 1954 when the former emperor was serving as the
    Chief of State. In October, 1955, Ngô Đình-Diệm
    was chosen by referendum as the Chief of State.
    The following year a constituent assembly drew up
    the first constitution which was adopted on
    October 26, 1956, and which proclaimed the
    southern half of Vietnam to be a republic, with
    Ngô Đình-Diệm as President. Diệm was overthrown
    by the military in 1963. After a series of short
    governments, a new constitution was adopted and
    Nguyễn Văn-Thiệu was elected President in 1967.
        The country occupies an area of 173,809 square
    kilometers (67,108 square miles). The population
    in 1971 was estimated 18,800,000 with an average
    density of 108 persons per square kilometer (280
    per square mile) and an annual rate of increase of
    2.6 per cent. The literacy rate is estimated at
    fifty per cent. The official monetary unit is the
    piastre, the dollar value of which fluctuates wide-
    ly. The gross national product was estimated at
    $4,000,000 in 1971. The national capital is Sai-
    Gon. Administratively, the country is divided into
    forty-five provinces (tỉnh) and eleven autonomous
    municipalities (thị-xã). The provinces are sub-
    divided into districts (quận), villages (xã) and
    hamlets (ấp). The main ports of the country are
    Sài-Gòn, Vũng-Tàu, Cam-Ranh, and Đà-Nẵng. The
    chief products are rice, pork, rubber, coffee and
    tea. See EDUCATION, NGÔ ĐÌNH-DIỆM, NGUYỄN VĂN-
    THIỆU, POPULATION, PORTS, SÀI-GÒN, AGRICULTURE

VIỆT-NAM CỨU-QUỐC HỘI. Vietnamese National Salvation
    Association. Local front organizations set up
    by the Indochinese Communist Party. The purpose
    of the associations was to provide a network for
    popular participation in politics which would
    complement and supplement the Communist Party
    (Việt-Minh). Organized in 1941 to operate in
    concert with the local units of the Việt-Minh, the
    Cứu-Quoc organizations were merged into the Mặt-
    Trận Liên-Việt (Vietnamese United Front) in 1946.
    See ĐẢNG LAO-ĐỘNG VIỆT-NAM, VIỆT-NAM ĐỘC-LẬP ĐỒNG-
    MINH HỘI.

VIỆT-NAM DÂN-CHỦ CỘNG-HÒA. The Democratic Republic of
    Vietnam. The country sometimes referred to as
    North Vietnam, extending from the Chinese border
    southward to the Bến-Hải River (at approximately
    the seventeenth parallel). The Democratic Re-
    public of Vietnam was officially established on
    September 2, 1945, when Hồ Chí-Minh, President of
    the Provisional Government read the Proclamation
    of Independence in Hà-Nội. The present boundaries
    were determined by the 1954 Geneva Accords. The
    constitution, adopted in 1959, provides for a
    National Assembly, the Office of the President of
    the Republic and a Government Council consisting
    of the Prime Minister, Vice-Premiers, and other
    ministerial level officials. People's Councils
    are elected at the local levels. They are charged
    with the election and supervision of the Adminis-
    trative Committees and People's Courts. The
    Administrative Committees are the executive organs
    of the People's Councils which are the chief
    administrative bodies at the provincial, district
    and village level. The ruling party is the
    Marxist-Leninist party, Đảng Lao-Động Việt-Nam
    (Vietnamese Worker's Party). Hồ Chí-Minh served
    as President from 1945 until his death in 1969.
    He was succeeded by Tôn Đức-Thắng. Phạm Văn-Đồng
    has served as Premier since 1954.
        The country occupies an area of 158,750 square
    kilometers (61,294 square miles). The population
    was placed at 15,916,995 in the last official cen-
    sus in 1960. In 1970 it was estimated at 21,150,000
    with a density of 134 persons per square kilometer
    (345 per square mile), and an annual rate of in-
    crease of 3.5 per cent. The literacy rate was
    estimated at 65 per cent in 1960. The official
    monetary unit is the dong, (2.94 dong equal US$1.00
    1971). The gross national product was estimated
    at $1,600,000,000. The national capital is Hà-Nội.

The country is divided into twenty-three provinces, (tỉnh) and two autonomous municipalities (thành-phố trực-thuộc trung-ương). The provinces are sub-divided into districts (huyện), villages (xã) and hamlets (thôn). In addition there are two auto-nomous regions (Việt-Bắc and Tây-Bắc), encompass-ing several provinces each in the highland areas. See AGRICULTURE, EDUCATION, AUGUST REVOLUTION, HÀ-NỘI, HỒ CHÍ-MINH, POPULATION, PORTS.

VIỆT-NAM DÂN-CHỦ ĐẢNG. Vietnam Democratic Party. A political party founded in June, 1944. It con-sisted primarily of students and bureaucrats in Hà-Nội. It was founded by Dương Đức-Hiền, Presi-dent of the Association of Students. Members of the party participated in the August Revolution of 1945. The party continues to operate in the Democratic Republic of Vietnam where it represents the progressive capitalists and intelligentsia. As of 1971, it had about 300,000 members. The party organ is the newspaper Độc-Lập.

VIỆT-NAM ĐỘC-LẬP ĐỒNG-MINH HỘI. League for the Inde-pendence of Vietnam. (Also known as the Việt-Minh). Formed in May, 1941, by Hồ Chí-Minh, the Việt-Minh developed a broad nationalist, liber-ation program with an extensive political organiza-tion during World War II. Although it inherited a network of cells from the Indochinese Communist Party, it greatly extended its base during the war years. By 1945 it had recruited and organized an army of some ten thousand men under the leader-ship of Võ Nguyên-Giáp.

In March, 1945, it called on the Vietnamese to rise up against the Japanese. This culminated in the August Revolution and the abdication of Emperor Bảo-Đại (1925-1945). It was under the banner of the Việt-Minh that Hồ Chí-Minh estab-lished the Provisional Government of the Demo-cratic Republic of Vietnam. When the French tried to reassert themselves in Indochina, the Việt-Minh carried on the prolonged French Indochina War which ended in 1954 with the Geneva Accords. In 1951, the Việt-Minh was absorbed by the newly formed Lao-Động Party. See AUGUST REVOLUTION, ĐẢNG LAO-ĐỘNG VIỆT-NAM, VIỆT-NAM DÂN-CHỦ CỘNG-HÒA, VÕ NGUYÊN-GIÁP, HỒ CHÍ-MINH.

VIỆT-NAM DUY-TÂN HỘI. The Association for the Modernization of Vietnam. A political organization
founded by Phan Bội-Châu and Tăng Bạt-Hổ while
in exile in Japan in 1906. The organization had
three main goals: national liberation; restoration
of the monarchy; and the promulgation of a constitution on the Japanese model. The association was
dissolved in 1910 when the Japanese deported Phan
Bội-Châu and Prince Cường-Đế out of Japan. See
CƯỜNG-ĐẾ, PHAN BỘI-CHÂU.

VIỆT-NAM PHỤC-QUỐC ĐỒNG-MINH HỘI. The League for the
Restoration of Vietnam, known also as the Phục-
Quốc. An outgrowth of the Việt-Nam Quang-Phục
Hội (Association for the Restoration of Vietnam),
it came into being in February, 1939, and was
headed by Prince Cường-Đế. The Phục-Quốc was
responsible for the uprising in 1940 by Trần
Trung-Lập in the border area of Lạng-Sơn. The
league was later reorganized under the Japanese
and operated with Japanese protection. See CƯỜNG-
ĐẾ, PHAN BỘI-CHÂU, VIỆT-NAM QUANG-PHỤC HỘI.

VIỆT-NAM QUANG-PHỤC HỘI. The Association for the Restoration of Vietnam. This association was founded
in 1912 by Phan Bội-Châu as a means of uniting most
nationalist groups which were in exile in China at
that time. The organization was formed in Canton
with Prince Cường-Đế named as President of a
Provisional Government. In February, 1939, the
association was reorganized and renamed the Việt-
Nam Phục-Quốc Đồng-Minh Hội (League for the
National Restoration of Vietnam). See CƯỜNG-ĐẾ,
PHAN BỘI-CHÂU, VIỆT-NAM PHỤC-QUỐC ĐỒNG-MINH HỘI.

VIỆT-NAM QUỐC-DÂN ĐẢNG. (Popularly known as the VNQDD).
The nationalist party founded by Nguyễn Thái-Học
and other nationalist leaders in 1927. It was
modeled after the Chinese Koumintang and is still
active as a major political party in the Republic
of Vietnam. The VNQDD was composed largely of
middle class Vietnamese but was penetrated early
by the French authorities. They attempted the
abortive general uprising in February, 1930,
which materialized only at Yên-Bay. Many leaders
of the party were arrested including Nguyễn Thái-
Học who died on the guillotine in June, 1930. The
party received financial support from the Chinese
Koumintang during the 1930's. See NGUYỄN THÁI-
HỌC, YÊN-BÁY UPRISING.

VIỆT-NAM TỔNG LIÊN-ĐOÀN LAO-ĐỘNG. The Vietnamese
General Confederation of Labor, or TLD. The first
Vietnamese labor union, it was founded in Hà-Nội
in April, 1946. It later became the Vietnam
General Federation of Trade Unions in 1961. The
General Federation of Trade Unions is the official
federation of all the trade unions in the Demo-
cratic Republic of Vietnam and operates within
the Fatherland Front (Mặt-Trận Tổ-Quốc). See MẶT-
TRẬN TỔ-QUỐC.

VIỆT-NAM SỬ LƯỢC. An early history of Vietnam written
by an unknown author. The work includes three
volumes and covers the period from the Hồng-Bàng
Dynasty (2879-250 B.C.) to the reign of Trần Phế-
Đế (1377-1388). Although it was first published
in China, it seems to have been written from the
standpoint of a Vietnamese rather than by a
Chinese.

VIỆT-SỬ TOÀN-THƯ. A history of Vietnam covering the
period from the Hồng-Bàng Dynasty (2879-250 B.C.)
to the reign of Emperor Lê Thần-Tông (1649-1662).
The work was written by Phạm Công-Trứ at the
command of Lord Trịnh-Tạc. It was written in
twenty-three volumes but was never printed. The
work was incorporated into the larger history,
Đại-Việt Sử-Ký Toàn-Thư.

VIỆT-THƯỜNG. The name of a country which was apparently a precursor state of Việt-Nam. Some scholars
think that it was located south of Giao-Chỉ which
would mean that it later became Lâm-Ấp and
occupied an area in central Vietnam. Others lo-
cate Việt-Thường in southern China and think that
it became a part of the kingdom of Văn-Lang. In
any case, the area or country of Việt-Thường was
mentioned in ancient Chinese annals. It either
preceeded or existed concurrently with the kingdom
of Văn-Lang (2879-258 B.C.).

VIETNAM DEMOCRATIC PARTY. See VIỆT-NAM DÂN-CHỦ ĐẢNG.

VIETNAM REVOLUTIONARY LEAGUE. See VIỆT-NAM CÁCH-MỆNH
ĐỒNG-MINH HỘI.

VIETNAM REVOLUTIONARY YOUTH LEAGUE. See VIỆT-NAM
CÁCH-MỆNH THANH-NIÊN ĐỒNG-CHÍ HỘI.

VIETNAM WORKER'S PARTY. See ĐẢNG LAO-ĐỘNG VIỆT-NAM.

VIETNAMESE, GENERAL CONFEDERATION OF LABOR. See VIỆT-
     NAM TỔNG LIÊN-ĐOÀN LAO-ĐỘNG.

VIETNAMESE LANGUAGE. Vietnamese is a tonal, mono-
     syllabic language that is placed in the Viet-
     Muong group of the Mon-Khmer family of languages-
     which in turn is part of the Austroasiatic lan-
     guage superfamily. There are three principal
     spoken dialects: northern, central and southern
     Vietnamese. These dialects vary primarily in
     pronunciation, but there are slight differences
     in vocabulary.
          Vietnamese was first written in Chinese
     characters (chữ-nho, or scholar's language).
     Later, probably around the thirteenth century,
     the Vietnamese devised their own writing system
     called chữ-nôm (also referred to as a demotic
     or vulgar language), which borrowed from Chinese
     but was not intelligible by the Chinese. In
     the seventeenth century a Romanized script was
     developed by Catholic missionaries and was called
     quốc-ngữ, or the national script. This was set
     forth in a Vietnamese-Portuguese-Latin dictionary
     by the famous Father Alexandre de Rhodes. This
     script is now used exclusively throughout all of
     Vietnam, the other forms (nho and nôm) having
     fallen into disuse. See LANGUAGE, LITERATURE,
     NHO, NÔM, RHODES, ALEXANDRE DE, QUỐC-NGỮ.

VIETNAMESE, NATIONAL SALVATION ASSOCIATION. See VIỆT-
     NAM CỨU-QUỐC HỘI.

VIETNAMESE NATIONALIST PARTY. See VIỆT-NAM QUỐC-DÂN
     ĐẢNG.

VIJAYA. The capital city of the kingdom of Champa be-
     tween the years 1000 and 1471. Vijaya was lo-
     cated in the vicinity of Bình-Định Province. In
     1000 the Chams moved their capital from Indrapura
     because it was vulnerable to attacks. Vijaya
     remained the capital until 1446 when the city was
     taken by the Vietnamese. The Chams reconquered it
     only to abandon it permanently to the Vietnamese
     in 1471. In the final battle, the Vietnamese
     killed 60,000 people and took away 30,000 prisoners,
     including the king and fifty members of the royal
     family. See CHAMPA, INDRAPURA, VIJAYA.

VILLAGE. See XÃ.

VINH. The capital city of Nghệ-An Province in central
Vietnam. See NGHỆ-AN PROVINCE.

VINH. Gulf or bay. Individual bays or gulfs are
listed under separate entries. See CAM-RANH,
GULF OF THAILAND, GULF OF TONGKING, HẠ-LONG BAY.

VĨNH-BÌNH PROVINCE. A coastal province in the Mekong
Delta area of south Vietnam. It is situated
north of Ba-Xuyên Province and south of Kiến-Hòa
Province. The population is 411,190 (1971) and
the area is 2,263 square kilometers (873 square
miles). The provincial capital is Phú-Vinh. The
province was named Trà-Vinh under the French. In
1956 it was changed to Vĩnh-Bình. The chief
products are rice and fish. See PHÚ-VINH.

VĨNH-LINH SPECIAL ZONE. The southernmost administrative
zone in the Democratic Republic of Vietnam. It is
located in central Vietnam, south of Quảng-Bình
Province. It is bordered on the south by the
Bến-Hải River. The Special Zone was established
as a demilitarized zone in accordance with the
terms of the Geneva Accords in 1954. Prior to
the partition of the country, Vĩnh-Linh was part
of Quảng-Trị Province. It has approximately
77,000 inhabitants and covers an area of about
680 square kilometers (262 square miles). See
DEMILITARIZED ZONE, GENEVA ACCORD.

VĨNH-LONG CITY. The capital city of Vĩnh-Long Province.
Population 35,304 (1971). It is located on highway number four between Mỹ-Tho and Cần-Thơ. Vĩnh-
Long has traditionally served as the focal point
of the Catholic Church in the Mekong Delta. There
is a rather old Catholic school and a large Catholic cathedral located in the city. See VĨNH-LONG
PROVINCE.

VĨNH-LONG PROVINCE. An inland delta province in south
Vietnam. It is located north of Cần-Thơ, south
of Định-Tường Province, east of Sa-Đéc Province
and west of Kiến-Hòa Province. It is populated
almost entirely by ethnic Vietnamese numbering
around 563,282 and covering an area of 1,705
square kilometers (658 square miles). The capital
of Vĩnh-Long Province is Vĩnh-Long City which is
located on highway number four connecting Cần-Thơ
with Sài-Gòn. The upper Mekong River (Tiền-Giang)
flows through the province and out to sea. The
soil is fertile and manageable. The chief products
of the province are rice, pineapples, pork, soybeans, sweet potatoes, and coconuts. Vĩnh-Long

was one of the six pre-French provinces of the
south. The French divided these into twenty. In
1956, Sa-Đéc was added as a district of Vĩnh-Long
Province, but was reestablished as a separate
province in 1967. See VĨNH-LONG CITY.

VĨNH-PHÚ PROVINCE. (Formerly Phú-Thọ, Vĩnh-Yên and
Vĩnh-Phúc provinces). An inland province in the
Red River Delta area of north Vietnam. It is
bordered on the north by Yên-Báy, Tuyên-Quang,
and Bắc-Thái provinces, on the west by Nghĩa-Lộ
Province, on the south by Hà-Nội and Hà-Tây and
Hoà-Bình provinces, and by Hà-Bắc to the east.
The population of the province was given at
1,098,855 in 1960. The capital of the province
is Phú-Thọ. The principal crop is rice, although
agriculture is diversified and includes tea,
lacquer trees, sugar, timber, and various fruits
and vegetables. The two industrial centers in
the province are Việt-Trì and Phú-Thọ which produce plywood, chemicals, fertilizer, and insect-
icide. See PHÚ-THỌ.

VĨNH-PHÚC PROVINCE. See VĨNH-PHÚ PROVINCE.

VĨNH-TẾ CANAL. (Kinh Vĩnh-Tế). A major canal running
from Châu-Đốc to the Giang-Thành River which
empties into the Hà-Tiên Bay. The Vĩnh-Tế Canal
runs parallel to the Cambodian/Vietnamese border.

VĨNH-YÊN PROVINCE. A former province in north Vietnam.
The provincial capital was Vĩnh-Yên City. Vĩnh-
Yên was merged with Phuc-Yen Province to form
Vĩnh-Phúc Province. Vĩnh-Phúc was later merged
with Phú-Thọ Province to form Vĩnh-Phú Province.
See VĨNH-PHÚ PROVINCE.

VNQDD. See VIỆT-NAM QUỐC-DÂN ĐẢNG.

VỢ CẢ. First wife. In traditional Vietnam, when a
man would take more than one wife, the first wife
(vợ cả) would dominate over the others in terms
of authority, responsibility and prestige. The vợ
cả would, in effect, become the person in charge
of the housekeeping and domestic affairs.

VÕ-NGHỆ. (Also known as Võ-Thuật). The art of self-
defense or the art of hand-to-hand combat. Võ-
nghệ is a traditional art of Vietnam. It was
taught and practiced up until and even into the

French colonial period. A person became accomplished in the art of võ-nghệ by practice and
perfection of the following eight subdisciplines:
1. weight lifting (tập xách tạ); 2. gymnastics
(tập du); 3. body exercises (luyện chân tây);
4. jumping (tập nhảy); 5. shadow boxing (tập quyền
thuật); 6. weaponry (tập khi giới); 7. archery
(tập bắn cung); 8. wrestling (tập đánh vật).

VÕ NGUYÊN-GIÁP (1912-   ). Deputy Prime Minister,
Minister of Defense, Commander-in-Chief of the
Armed Forces, and member of the Lao-Động Party
Politburo of the Democratic Republic of Vietnam.
He was born in Quảng-Bình Province of a peasant
family. He became an activist as early as 1926
with the Revolutionary Party of New Vietnam (Tân-
Việt Cách-Mệnh Đảng) and then with the Indochina
Communist Party in 1933. He then became a teacher
while continuing his studies at the same time at
the University of Hà-Nội. He graduated in 1937
in law and political economy. In 1939 he was
forced into exile to southern China where he
participated in the founding of the Việt-Minh in
1941. From 1941-1945 he operated secretly in the
mountains of north Vietnam raising an army. In
August, 1945 he was active in the Việt-Minh seizure
of power and its proclamation of the Democratic
Republic of Vietnam. He was promoted to General
and Commander-in-Chief in 1946.

Võ Nguyên-Giáp is the single person most
responsible for engineering the military defeat of
the French in Indochina which culminated in the
battle of Điện Biên-Phủ in May, 1954. After the
establishment of the Democratic Republic of Vietnam
as an independent state in July, 1954, General Giáp
became Deputy Prime Minister, retaining the posts
of Defense Minister and Commander-in-Chief which he
has held ever since. He has written and spoken
frequently on guerrila and military strategy and
tactics. See AUGUST REVOLUTION, ĐIỆN-BIÊN-PHỦ,
HỒ CHÍ-MINH, VIỆT-NAM ĐỘC-LẬP ĐỒNG-MINH HỘI, VIỆT-
NAM DÂN-CHỦ CỘNG-HÒA.

VOLLENHOVEN, JOOST VAN. Governor General of Indochina
from January, 1914, to March, 1915.

VỌNG-CỔ. A type of tune or form of song used in the
modern theater (cải-lương). The vọng-cổ is the
most popular part of cải-lương and primarily
represents sadness and nostalgia. This could take

the form of a love song, lullaby or even an
expression of anger. See CẢI-LƯƠNG.

VỌNG-PHU MOUNTAIN. (Núi Vọng-Phu). A mountain in
Khánh-Hòa Province, east of M'Drak in the central
highlands. It has an elevation of 2,019 meters
(6,627 feet).

VOTIVE PAPER. See HOÁ-VÀNG.

VU-LAN. Feast of the Wandering Souls. One of the three
most important Buddhist holidays, the other two
being the full moons on the first and eleventh
months. This holiday falls on the fifteenth day
of the seventh lunar month. The origins of the
holiday go back to the time when Buddha lived.
An outstanding monk named Mục-Liên discovered that
his mother was in hell. Through his magic powers
he took rice for her, but each time she reached
out for it the rice turned into fire. He returned
and asked Buddha to intercede. Buddha instructed
him that of the fifteenth day of the seventh
month he should prepare fruits and flowers as an
offering. Through the collective holiness of the
monks in the pagoda, his mother could be saved
from the agony of hell. He followed the advice and
freed his mother from the bonds of hell. Thus it
is that on this day every year, the Vietnamese
Buddhists pray fervently for the redemption of
souls. See BUDDHISM.

VŨ QUỲNH. An historian during the Lê Dynasty (1428-
1788). Born in Hải-Dương Province he passed his
doctoral examinations in 1478. At the request of
Emperor Lê Tương-Dục (1510-1516) he wrote Đại-Việt
Thông-Giam Thông-Khảo, which he completed in 1511.
See ĐẠI-VIỆT THÔNG-GIAM THÔNG-KHẢO.

VUA. (Also called Vương). King. The Vietnamese
monarchs assumed the title of Emperor (Hoàng-Đế)
and established their various dynasties accordingly. However, in their relations with China they
always referred to themselves as King (Vương or
Vua) thus acknowledging their inferiority to the
Chinese Emperor and Vietnam's tributary relationship to China.

VUA BẾP. (Literally, King of the Kitchen). See TAÓ-
QUÂN.

VŨNG-TÀU. (Also known as Cap St. Jacques). A seaside
    resort city located 120 kilometers (75 miles)
    southeast of Sài-Gòn. It is located in Phúóc-
    Tuy Province on the Ganh-Rai Bay which is locate
    main channel entrance to Sài-Gòn. The city has
    always been popular among the westerners in Sài-
    Gòn as well as the Saigonese because it has
    pleasant beaches and is a short drive from Sài-
    Gòn. The city was made an autonomous municipality
    on October 4, 1965.

VƯỞNG. See VUA.

                             -W-

WATERWAYS. The waterways, especially in the delta
    areas of the Red River and the Mekong River, have
    always been used as major routes for both passen-
    ger and freight transportation. River taxis and
    ferries travel over prescribed routes and can be
    rented individually. Cargo craft, barges and
    rafts provide commercial transportation, and for
    those who live along the waterways, sampans and
    small boats are used for personal transportation.
    In many cases, the people live on the river and
    reside in a sampan. Small river craft have
    traditionally been oared by hand but recently, an
    increasing number of these small boats are motor-
    ized. Fishing boats also work the rivers and
    canals primarily using nets.
        Democratic Republic of Vietnam: There are
    more than 4,800 kilometers (3,000 miles) of
    navigable waterways in the Democratic Republic
    of Vietnam. However, only about a third are
    usable by larger craft year round. The rest are
    accessible to shallow-draft vessels only during
    highwater season, generally from May through
    October. In the highlands, only small locally
    made boats and rafts are used. The Red River and
    its tributaries constitute the most important
    network of waterways. Of secondary importance is
    the shorter Thái-Bình River system which parallels
    the Red River some forty-five kilometers (thirty
    miles) to the northeast. It joins the delta net-
    work of the Red River about fifty-five kilometers
    (thirty-five miles) northwest of Hải-Phòng.
    These two waterways are linked by canals and
    small streams. Other rivers in lower north Viet-
    nam and central Vietnam flow directly into the
    South China Sea.

Republic of Vietnam: There are about 4,400 kilometers (2,750 miles) of navigable waterways in the Republic of Vietnam. Approximately 2,100 kilometers (1,350 miles) are canals. Most of these waterways are located in the Mekong River Delta area. Sampans and other shallow-draft vessels are mostly used, although steamers do travel the Sài-Gòn River to the port of Sài-Gòn, some seventy kilometers (forty-five miles) inland. The rivers in central Vietnam are short, swift, and used very little for navigation by boats other than sampans and small fishing boats.

WHITE THÁI. (Thái Trắng). An ethno-linguistic group of highland people (Thái speakers) in north Vietnam concentrated along the banks of the Red River and Black River. The White Thái, together with the Black Thái, Red Thái and the Tày (Thổ) are the principal Thai speaking peoples of north Vietnam. The population estimates for the White Thái and the Black Thái together is given at 350,000. See THÁI.

WILD GAME. Big game hunting has been a traditional attraction for westerners. Among the many types of wild game native to Vietnam are the tiger, panther, leopard, elephant, gaur, capricorn, wild buffalo, deer, bear, and rhinoceroses. Small game includes rabbit, monkey and porcupine. A number of different varieties of birds are found in Vietnam including the peacock and are hunted for meat. Although an accurate estimate has not yet been made, the effects of the recent war, especially the carpet bombing, artillery and defoliation have been devastating for the wildlife of Vietnam.

-X-

XA. An ethno-linguistic minority group of highland people located in the Tây-Bắc Autonomous Region of north Vietnam and in the Trường-Dương District of Nghệ-An Province in central Vietnam. According to the 1960 census they numbered 22,500.

XÃ. (Also called làng). Village. The village is the basic administrative unit in Vietnam and is composed of several hamlets (thôn or ấp). Many villages comprise a district (quận or huyện).

Traditionally, the village is considered more or
less autonomous to the central government. A
popular saying states that the imperial orders
give way to village customs (Phép Vua Thua Lễ
Làng). The village in traditional Vietnam, was
governed by an executive body called the Council
of Notables (Hội-Đồng Kỳ-Mục). The Village
Chief (Xã Trưởng) was the executive agent of the
Council of Notables, as well as the intermediate
between the village and central government. The
village levied taxes, owned land, maintained
shrines, and temples, constructed roads and dikes
and dug canals. The village customs and traditions
as well as the spiritual and moral foundations,
were inscribed in the village charter (hương-ước).
See ADMINISTRATIVE DIVISIONS, HỘI-ĐỒNG KỲ-MỤC,
HƯƠNG-ƯỚC, KHAO-VỌNG, XÃ TRƯỞNG, XÃ QUAN.

XÃ QUAN. Village Mandarin. The administrator of the
village prior to 1467. He was a mandarin appointed by and responsible to the imperial court. He
was charged with directing all communal affairs
and representing the Emperor or central government at the village level. This position was
abolished in 1467 in favor of the more autonomous
Village Chief (Xã Trưởng). See XÃ, XÃ TRƯỞNG.

XÃ TRƯỞNG. (Also called Lý Trưởng). Village Chief,
the executive agent of the village (xã). The
Village Chief was not the highest authority at
the village level. The Council of Notables (Hội-
Đồng Kỳ-Mục) was the decision making body in the
village. The Xã Trưởng was responsible to the
Council of Notables. He represented the village
in relations with the central government and was
charged with carrying out the decisions of the
Council of Notables. His specific duties included
tax collection, military recruitment and provision
of labor for the Emperor. At times, he also
selected candidates for the provincial examinations
(khoa-cử). Prior to 1467, during the reign of
Emperor Lê Thánh-Tông (1460-1497), the village
was administered by a village mandarin (Xã Quan)
who was appointed by and responsible to the
royal court. In 1497, Lê Thánh-Tông abolished
this system and created the system using a Village
Chief (Xã Trưởng) who was chosen by the village
and ratified by the royal court. In 1828,
Emperor Minh-Mạng (1820-1840) changed the term
Xã Trưởng to Lý Trưởng. The Village Chief usually
had from one to three assistants called the Phó
Lý Trưởng or Phó Lý, and a police agent called

the Trưởng Tuần. See HỘI-ĐỒNG KỲ-MỤC, XÃ, XÃ
QUAN.

XÂM MINH. Body tatoo. Since the beginning of recorded
history, the Vietnamese have practiced the art of
tatooing. Fishermen had pictures of sea monsters
on their bodies to protect them from sea serpents.
The emperors had a dragon tatooed on their thigh
until the custom was broken by Emperor Trần Anh-
Tông (1293-1314) who refused to be tatooed. In
1323 Emperor Trần Minh-Tông (1314-1329) decreed
that his officers should no longer be tatooed.
In present times tatooing is practiced by only
a few--chiefly among the highland people.

XÍCH-LÔ. See CYCLO.

XÍCH-QUỶ. (Literally, Red Devil). The name of the
country over which Kinh Dương-Vương is said to
have reigned beginning in the year 2879 B.C.
The country, actually in southern China, was
bordered on the north by Hồ-Nam Province, on the
south by Chiêm-Thành, on the west by Ba-Thục and
on the east by the South China Sea. See HỒNG-
BÀNG DYNASTY, KINH DƯƠNG-VƯƠNG.

XÓM. A subdivision of a village (xã). A xóm is
usually formed by a group of houses built along
a common road or alleyway. A gateway marks the
entrance to the xóm. The members of the xóm are
loosely organized and are sometimes headed by
a xóm chief (Trưởng Xóm). Many xóm have their
own pagoda, but never do they have their own
communal house (đình). See ẤP, KHÓM, XÃ.

XUÂN-LỘC. The capital city of Long-Khánh Province.
Population 37,087. It is located on highway
number one between Bien-Hòa and Phan-Thiết. See
LONG-KHÁNH PROVINCE.

-Y-

Y-DƯỢC. The formal study of medicine and pharmacy.
Vietnamese medicine dates back to the time of
Emperor Đinh Tiên-Hoàng (9680979) when a mandarin
named Tuệ-Tĩnh from Hải-Hưng Province was sent to
China to study medicine. After ten years he
returned and practiced medicine. He also wrote
a book entitled Nam-Dược. His reputation and

success was so great that Emperor Lê Trung-Tồng
(1005) had a temple built in his honor. There
are two traditional types of medicine practiced
in Vietnam - thuốc-bắc and thuốc-nam - plus
various physical treatments such as châm-cứu
(acupuncture), đấm-bóp (massage) and giác (cupping). Western medical and pharmaceutical
facilities are now available throughout Vietnam.
However, traditional medicine is still quite
popular and is often practiced in combination
with western medicine. See CHÂM-CỨU, ĐẤM-BÓP,
GIÁC, THẦY-THUỐC, THUỐC-BẮC, THUỐC-NAM.

YANG SIN MOUNTAIN. (Núi Yang Sin). A mountain in
Darlac Province in central Vietnam. It has an
elevation of 2,404 meters (7,890 feet).

YAO. See DAO.

YÊN-BÁY CITY. The capital city of Yên-Báy Province
in north Vietnam. It is situated on the Red
River and is connected by road to Hà-Nội and Lào-
Cai. It is 147 kilometers (91 miles) from Hà-Nội.
Due to its location on the river and road it is
an important transportation center. There is a
large market in the city where the Mèo highland
people come to trade.

YÊN-BÁY PROVINCE. (Also written Yên-Bái). A moun-
tainous province situated north of Vĩnh-Phú
Province, east of Nghĩa-Lô, and south of Lào-Cai
Province in north Vietnam. Yên-Báy is most
famous for the political revolt against the
French that took place in the capital town on
February 1930. The Yên-Báy Uprising is always
associated with the Vietnamese Nationalist Party
(Việt-Nam Quốc-Dân Đảng). The most important
river in north Vietnam, the Red River, runs
through the province from northeast to southwest.
The provincial capital is located on the banks
of the Red River at only twenty-eight meters
(ninety-one feet) above sea level. The Red River
is an important transportation artery. Although
there are many small tributaries, most are too
shallow and rocky to be used for communication.
The province is inhabited principally by the
highland people of the Thái, Thổ, Mán, and Mèo
ethno-linguistic groups. Ethnic Vietnamese,
Chinese and Nùng are also represented.
     Yên-Báy was the Prefecture of Quy-Hóa during
the Trần Dynasty (1225-1400) and the District of
Trần-Yên during the Lê Dynasty (1428-1788). In

1832, Emperor Minh-Mạng (1820-1840) placed it
under the control of the court. Actually, since
the area was part of the Thái territory, the
extent to which the court exercised authority
varied. In the late 1800's the province was
occupied by the Black Flag armies of Lưu Vĩnh-
Phúc and later by bands of Chinese pirates. The
province was substantially reduced in size when
the district of Nghĩa-Lộ was made a separate
province after the partition of the country in
1954.
The province is strategically located in
relation to China and the mountain areas of Vietnam. Important military outposts have always
been maintained in the province. Yên-Bảy is also
rich in natural resources. Rice is the main crop
followed by corn, fruits, and sugarcane. Under
the French, there were many plantations, most of
which were owned by Frenchmen ranging in size from
eighteen hectares (forty-three acres) to 500 hectares (1,200 acres). See YÊN-BẢY CITY, YÊN-BẢY
UPRISING.

YÊN-BẢY UPRISING (February 10, 1930). The revolt
against the French led by the founders of the
Vietnam Nationalist Party (Việt-Nam Quốc-Dân Đảng,
or VNQDD). In late 1929, members of the VNQDD,
after failing to assassinate the French Governor
General of Tongking, murdered a Frenchman named
Bazin. This brought repressive measures by the
French against the VNQDD. In reaction to this,
the VNQDD planned a mass uprising. They infil-
trated the Vietnamese garrison at Yên-Bảy. On
the night of February 9-10, 1930, the soldiers
rose up against the French authorities and officers,
killing eleven and wounding ten. Because of poor
coordination, the uprisings in the cities (including Hà-Nội, Sơn-Tây, Phú-Thọ, etc.) were
complete failures.
The French reacted with severe repression.
The VNQDD party members and leaders were arrested.
The French used airplanes to bomb Vietnamese
villages for the first time. The violence continued through 1932 which caused that year to
become known as the year of white terror. The
leader of the VNQDD and of the uprising itself,
Nguyễn Thái-Học, was arrested on June 17, 1930.
He and twelve of his comrades died on the
guillotine at Yên-Bảy. The Yên-Bảy uprising is
significant because it ushered in the popular
based revolutionary or anti-colonialist movement
in Vietnam that resulted in the eventual defeat

of the French. The event is celebrated by the
VNQDD as a milestone in the life of the party.
See NGUYỄN THÁI-HỌC, VIỆT-NAM QUỐC-DÂN ĐẢNG.

YÊN-BINH MOUNTAIN RANGE. A chain of mountains in
north Vietnam. It is located between the Lô-
Giang River and the Chảy River and extends from
the western part of Hà-Giang Province down through
Yên-Báy and Tuyên-Quang provinces.

YÊN-LẠC MOUNTAIN RANGE. A chain of comparatively small
mountains extending from northern Bắc-Thai Province over to the Thất-Khê Highlands to Cao-Bằng
Province.

YÊN LÃO. A village feast or celebration in honor of
all the aged people in the village. The age
above which the people are included in the honored
group varies from village to village, although it
is usually around fifty years. All the men and
women above this age are honored guests of the
rest of the village. The celebration includes a
procession and a banquet.

YÊN SÀO. See SEA SWALLOW'S NEST.

YÊN-TỬ MOUNTAIN. (Núi Yên-Tử). An historic and scenic
mountain located in Quảng-Ninh Province in north
Vietnam. There are many pagodas located on the
mountain. Especially noteworthy is the Đồng Pagoda
(Chùa Đồng) where Emperor Trần Nhân-Tông (1279-
1293) retired from the throne and took up the
monastic life. Legend has it that 300 of his
harem followed him to the pagoda. He would not
let them stay, but they refused to return. So,
they settled nearby at a fresh spring which is
now called Suối Giải-Oan. See TRẦN NHÂN-TÔNG.

YERSIN, ALEXANDRE (1863-1943). A medical doctor who
was probably the Frenchman most well-known and
beloved by the Vietnamese. Born in Swedin of
French parents, he began the study of medicine
at the age of twenty at the Lausanne Medical
Institute. He also studied at Marbourg, Germany
and at Paris, France. In Paris he had occasion
to work under Pasteur. In 1887 he was awarded a
doctor of medicine degree and also took on
French citizenship.
        Dr. Yersin signed on as the medical officer
for the Messageries Maritimes Company and started
for Asia in 1889. Upon arriving in Nha-Trang he

was intrigued by and attracted to the mountainous
landscape of central Vietnam. For four years
(1890-1894) he travelled throughout central Vietnam recording his observations and impressions.
It was during this period that he came upon the
site of what is now Đà-Lạt. He recommended to
the authorities that a town be established there
for a leisure and health resort. His proposal
was later implemented.

In 1894 he went to Hong-Kong to study an
epidemic of the plague. He determined the relationship of the disease to the rat (which was the
carrier) and discovered the plague bacillus.

He founded the Pasteur Institute at Nha-Trang
in 1885. In 1902-04 he was instrumental in
founding the College of Medicine in Hà-Nội. From
1905-18, he served as the Director of the Pasteur
Institutes in Nha-Trang and Sài-Gòn. He was
made Inspector General of all Pasteur Institutes
in French Indochina.

Dr. Yersin was a specialist on animal diseases.
He also became an authority on horticulture and
experimented on the adaptability of various plants
such as coca and cacao to the climatic conditions
of Vietnam. He introduced the first rubber and
quinine producing trees to Vietnam. His lifestyle was simplistic. He was a humanitarian and
mingled with the common people, especially the
fishermen around his home. He was buried on the
Suối-Dầu plantation, 100 hectares (247 acres) of
which he gave to the Pasteur Institute. The Lycee
Yersin was founded in his honor in Đà-Lạt. See
ĐÀ-LẠT.

YẾT-HẬU. A form of poetry in which the last line of
each four-line verse has only one word.

-Z-

ZAO. See DAO.

APPENDICES

Appendix I: Outline of Vietnamese History.
This outline was prepared tenta-
tively by Professor Chingho A. Chen
of the Chinese University of Hong
Kong. Because there has been no
standard established for dividing
Vietnamese history into major
periods, the reader is advised that
there may be variants of this time-
table.

Appendix II: Dynastic Chronology

Appendix III: Maps. The series of maps #1 through
#7 is designed to show the his-
torical progress of the southward
expansion movement (nam-tiến).
These were taken from Sử Địa,
No. 19-20, 1970 and were originally
based on Đào Duy-Anh, Đất Nước Việt
Nam Qua Các Đời, Khoa Học, Hà-Nội.
Map #8 was adapted from Huard and
Durand (1954).

339

APPENDIX I

OUTLINE: HISTORY OF VIETNAM

I. Prehistoric age (? - 300 B.C.)

   Paleolithic (300,000 B.C.):   Bình-Gia (Lạng-Sơn)
                                 Núi Độ (Thanh-Hóa)
                                 Sơn-Vị (Vĩnh-Phú)

   Mesolithic (10,000 B.C.):   Hòa-Bình (Nghệ-An)

   Neolithic (3,000 B.C.):   Bắc-Sơn
                                 Quỳnh-Văn (Nghệ-An)

   Bronze age   Phung-Nguyên (2,000 B.C.)

                                 Đông-Sơn (Thanh-Hóa
                                 700 B.C. - 300 A.D.)

II. Ancient history (257 B.C. - 938 A.D.)

   Kingdom of Âu-Lạc (An-Dương-Vương): 257-208 B.C.
   Nam-Việt (Triệu Đà): 207 B.C. - 111 B.C.
   West Hán and Tần period: 111 B.C. - 39 A.D.
                                 Trưng Sisters: 40-43 A.D.
   East Hán, Three Kingdoms, West and East Tần Period,
       Northern and Southern Dynasties Period: 44 A.D.-
       621 A.D.
   T'ang Protectorate (An-Nam Đô-Hộ-Phủ): 622 - 938.

III. Medieval history (939 - 1427)

   Ngô (Ngô Quyền): 939-965 (twelve lords: 965-968)
   Đinh (Đinh Bộ-Lĩnh): 968-980
   Tiền Lê (Lê Hoàn): 980-1009
   Lý (Lý Cộng-Uẩn): 1010-1225
   Trần (Trần-Cảnh): 1225-1400
   Hồ (Hồ Quý-Ly): 1400-1407
   Hậu Trần (Post Trần): 1407-1413
   Minh rule: 1414-1427

IV. Early Modern History (1428-1788)

   Lê (First part): 1428-1527
   Lê (Second part): 1533-1788 (Confrontation between
       the Trịnh and the Nguyễn)
   Mạc (Mạc Đăng-Dung): 1527-1788

V. <u>Later Modern History</u> (1788-1945)

Tây-sơn (Nguyễn-Huệ): 1788-1802
Nguyễn (Nguyễn Phúc-Anh): 1802-1945
(French Protectorate: 1883-1954)

IV. <u>Contemporary</u> (1945-   )

The independence and the partition of two Vietnams.

APPENDIX II

DYNASTIC CHRONOLOGY

HỒNG-BẰNG DYNASTY (2879-258 B.C.)*

Kingdom: Văn-Lang
Capital: Phong-Châu, Province of Sơn-Tây

Reign of eighteen Hùng kings (Hùng-Vương I through Hùng-Vương XVIII)

THỤC DYNASTY (257-208 B.C.)

Kingdom: Âu-Lạc
Capital: Loa-Thành (Cổ-Loa), Province of Vĩnh-Phú

257-208 B.C.   An-Dương-Vương

TRIỆU DYNASTY (207-111 B.C.)

Kingdom: Nam-Việt
Capital: Phiên-Ngung, Canton, China

207-137 B.C.   Triệu Vũ-Vương
137-125 B.C.   Triệu Văn-Vương
125-113 B.C.   Triệu Minh-Vương
113-112 B.C.   Triệu Ai-Vương
111   Triệu Dương-Vương

WEST HÁN AND TẤN PERIOD (111 B.C.-23 A.D.)

Province of Giao-Chỉ under Chinese domination

TRƯNG SISTERS (40-43 A.D.)

Capital: Mê-Linh, Province of Sơn-Tây

40-43 A.D.   Trưng-Trắc (Trưng-Vương) and Trưng-Nhị

EAST HÁN PERIOD (25-220)

Province of Giao-Chỉ under Chinese domination (Name changed to Giao-Châu in 203)

*Legendary

THREE KINGDOMS PERIOD (220-265)

Province of Giao-Châu under Chinese domination

WEST AND EAST TẤN PERIOD (265-420)

Province of Giao-Châu under Chinese domination

SOUTHERN DYNASTIES PERIOD (420-589)

Province of Giao-Châu under Chinese domination

EARLY LÝ DYNASTY (544-602)

Kingdom: Vạn-Xuân
Capital: Vạn-Phúc, Province of Hà-Nôi (544-550)
          Long-Biên, Province of Ha-Nôi (550-571)
          Phong-Châu, Province of Viñh-Yên (571-602)

544-548   Lý Nam-Đế
549-571   Triệu Việt-Vương
571-602   Hậu Lý-Nam-Đế

T'ANG AND FIVE DYNASTIES PERIOD (622-938)

Province of Giao-Châu under Chinese domination (622-679)

Protectorate of An-Nam (An-Nam-Đô-Hộ Phủ) under Chinese domination (679-938)

NGÔ DYNASTY (939-965)

Capital: Cổ-Loa, Vinh-Phuc Province

939-944   Ngô Quyền
945-950   Dương Tam-Kha
950-965   Ngô Xương-Văn (950-965)
          Ngô Xương-Ngập (950-954)
965-967   Ngo Xương-Xí (period of the rule of the Twelve Lords)

ĐINH DYNASTY (968-980)

Kingdom: Đại-Cổ-Việt
Capital: Hoa-Lu, Province of Ninh-Bình

```
968-979    Đinh Tiên-Hoàng
979-980    Đinh Tuệ
```

EARLY LÊ DYNASTY (980-1009)

```
Kingdom:   Đại-Cồ-Việt
Capital:   Hoa-Lư, Province of Ninh-Bình
```

```
980-1005   Lê Đại-Hành
1005       Lê Trung-Tông
1005-1009  Lê Long-Đĩnh
```

LÝ DYNASTY (1010-1225)

```
Kingdom:   Đại-Việt
Capital:   Thăng-Long (Hà-Nội)
```

```
1010-1028  Lý Thái-Tổ
1028-1054  Lý Thái-Tông
1054-1072  Lý Thánh-Tông
1072-1127  Lý Nhân-Tông
1128-1138  Lý Thần-Tông
1138-1175  Lý Anh-Tông
1176-1210  Lý Cao-Tông
1211-1224  Lý Huệ-Tông
1224-1225  Lý Chiêu-Hoàng
```

TRẦN DYNASTY (1225-1400)

```
Kingdom:   An-Nam
Capital:   Thăng-Long (Hà-Nội)
```

```
1225-1258  Trần Thái-Tông
1258-1278  Trần Thánh-Tông
1279-1293  Trần Nhân-Tông
1293-1314  Trần Anh-Tông
1314-1329  Trần Minh-Tông
1329-1341  Trần Hiến-Tông
1341-1369  Trần Dụ-Tông
1369-1370  Dương Nhật-Lễ
1370-1372  Trần Nghệ-Tông
1372-1377  Trần Duệ-Tông
1377-1388  Trần Phế-Đế
1388-1398  Trần Thuận-Tông
1398-1400  Trần Thiếu-Đế
```

HỒ DYNASTY (1400-1407)

Kingdom: Đại-Ngu
Capital: Đông-Đô (Hà-Nội)

1400   Hồ Qúi-Ly
1401-1407 Hồ Hán-Thương

POST TRẦN DYNASTY (1407-1413)

1407-1409 Giản Định-Đế
1409-1413 Trần Qúy-Khoách

MING PERIOD (1414-1427)

Province of An-Nam under Chinese domination

LÊ DYNASTY (1428-1788)

Kingdom: Đại-Việt
Capital: Thăng-Long (Đông Kinh; Hà-Nội)

1428-1433 Lê Thái-Tổ
1434-1442 Lê Thái-Tông
1443-1459 Lê Nhân-Tông
1460-1497 Lê Thánh-Tông
1497-1504 Lê Hiển-Tông
1504   Lê Túc-Tông
1505-1509 Lê Uy-Mục
1510-1516 Lê Tương-Dực
1516-1524 Lê Chiêu-Tông
1524-1527 Lê Cung-Hoàng
           Dynastic succession interrupted by the Mạc
           usurpation of the throne
1533-1548 Lê Trang-Tông
1548-1556 Lê Trung-Tông
1556-1573 Lê Anh-Tông
1573-1599 Lê Thế-Tông
1600-1619 Lê Kinh-Tông
1619-1643 Lê Thần-Tông
1643-1649 Lê Chân-Tông
1649-1662 Lê Thần-Tông (Second reign)
1662-1671 Lê Huyền-Tông
1672-1675 Lê Gia-Tông
1676-1705 Lê Hi-Tông
1705-1729 Lê Dụ-Tông
1729-1732 Lê Đế Duy-Phường
1732-1735 Lê Thuận-Tông
1735-1740 Lê Ý-Tông
1740-1786 Lê Hiển-Tông
1787-1788 Lê Mẫn-Đế

MẠC DYNASTY (1527-1592)

Capital: Thăng-Long (1428-1592)
          Cao-Bằng (1592-1667)

1527-1530 Mạc Đăng-Dung
1530-1540 Mạc Đăng-Doanh
1540-1546 Mạc Phúc-Hải
1546-1561 Mạc Phúc-Nguyên
1561-1592 Mạc Mậu-Hợp
1593-1629 Mạc Kính-Cung
1623-1629 Mạc Kính-Khoan
1638-1677 Mạc Kính-Hoan

THE TRỊNH LORDS OF THE NORTH (1539-1787)

1539-1569 Trịnh Kiểm
1569-1570 Trịnh Cối
1570-1623 Trịnh Tùng (Bình-An Vương)
1623-1657 Trịnh Tráng (Thanh-Đô Vương)
1657-1682 Trịnh Tạc (Tây Vương)
1682-1709 Trịnh Căn (Định Vương)
1709-1729 Trịnh Cương (An-Đô Vương)
1729-1740 Trịnh Giang (Uy-Nam Vương)
1740-1767 Trịnh Doanh (Minh-Do Vương)
1767-1782 Trịnh Sâm (Tĩnh-Đô Vương)
1782   Trịnh Mán
1783-1786 Trịnh Khải (Đoan-Nam Vương)
1787   Trịnh Bồng (Án-Đô Vương)

THE NGUYỄN LORDS OF THE SOUTH (1558-1778)

Court held at Phú-Xuân (Huế)

1558-1613 Nguyễn Hoàng (Chúa Tiên)
1613-1635 Nguyễn Phúc-Nguyên (Chúa Sãi)
1635-1648 Nguyễn Phúc-Lan (Chúa Thượng)
1648-1687 Nguyễn Phúc-Tần (Chúa Hiền)
1687-1691 Nguyễn Phúc-Trăn (Chúa Nghĩa)
1691-1725 Nguyễn Phúc-Chu (Quốc Chúa)
1725-1738 Nguyễn Phúc-Trú
1738-1765 Nguyễn Phúc-Khoát (Võ-Vương)
1765-1777 Nguyễn Phúc-Thuần (Định-Vương)
1778   Nguyễn Phúc-Anh (later became Emperor Gia-
          Long)

THE NGUYỄN OF TÂY-SƠN DYNASTY (1788-1802)

1788-1792 Quang-Trung
1792-1802 Canh-Thịnh

THE NGUYEN OF HUE DYNASTY (1802-1945)

Kingdom: Việt-Nam (1802-1832)
         Đại-Nam (1832-1945)
Capital: Huế

1802-1819 Gia-Long
1820-1840 Minh-Mạng
1841-1847 Thiệu-Trị
1848-1883 Tự-Đức
1883   Dục-Đức
1883   Hiệp-Hòa
1883-1884 Kiến-Phúc
1884-1885 Hàm-Nghi
1885-1889 Đồng-Khánh
1889-1907 Thành-Thái
1907-1916 Duy-Tân
1916-1925 Khải-Định
1925-1945 Bảo-Đại

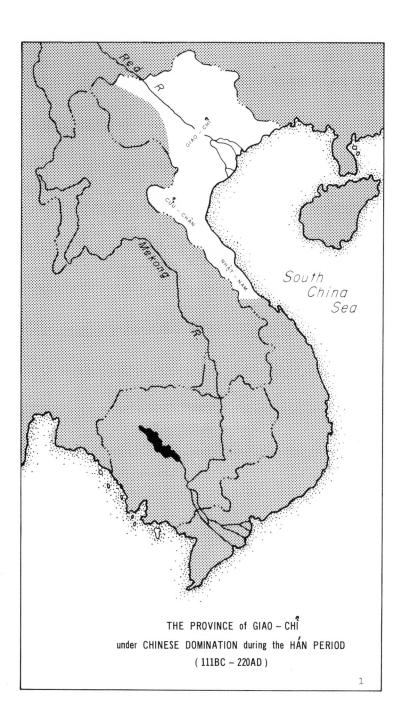

THE PROVINCE of GIAO – CHỈ
under CHINESE DOMINATION during the HÁN PERIOD
(111BC – 220AD)

1

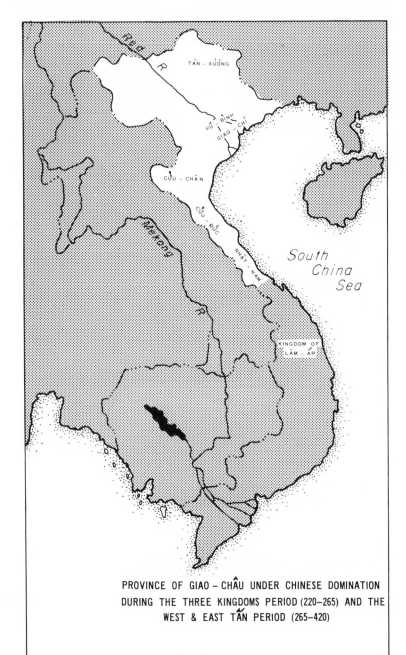

Red R

TẤN – XƯƠNG

VŨ – BÌNH

GIAO – CHỈ

CỬU – CHÂN

CỬU – ĐỨC

Mekong

NHẬT – NAM

South
China
Sea

KINGDOM OF
LÂM – ẤP

PROVINCE OF GIAO – CHÂU UNDER CHINESE DOMINATION
DURING THE THREE KINGDOMS PERIOD (220–265) AND THE
WEST & EAST TẤN PERIOD (265–420)

2

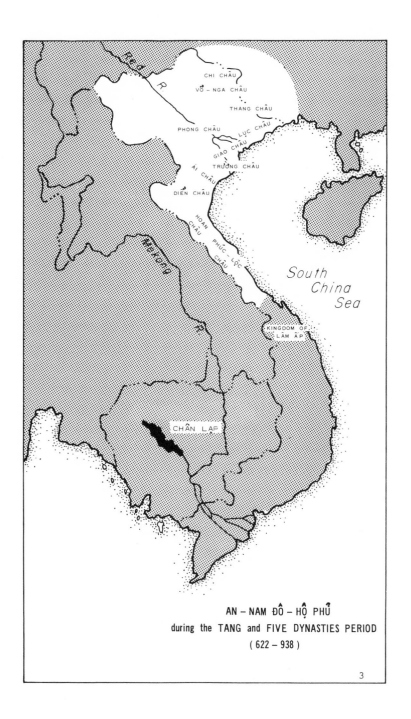

CHI CHÂU

VÕ – NGA CHÂU

THANG CHÂU

PHONG CHÂU

LỤC CHÂU

GIAO CHÂU

TRƯỜNG CHÂU

ÁI CHÂU

DIỄN CHÂU

HOAN CHÂU

PHÚC LỘC CHÂU

South
China
Sea

KINGDOM OF
LÂM ẤP

CHÂN LẠP

AN – NAM ĐÔ – HỘ PHỦ
during the TANG and FIVE DYNASTIES PERIOD
(622 – 938)

3

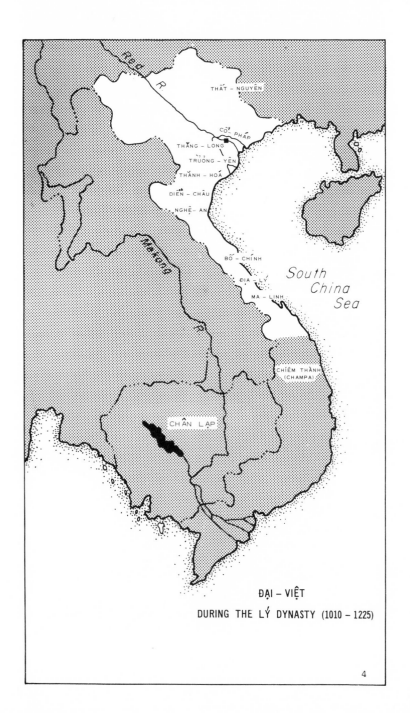

ĐẠI – VIỆT

DURING THE LÝ DYNASTY (1010 – 1225)

4

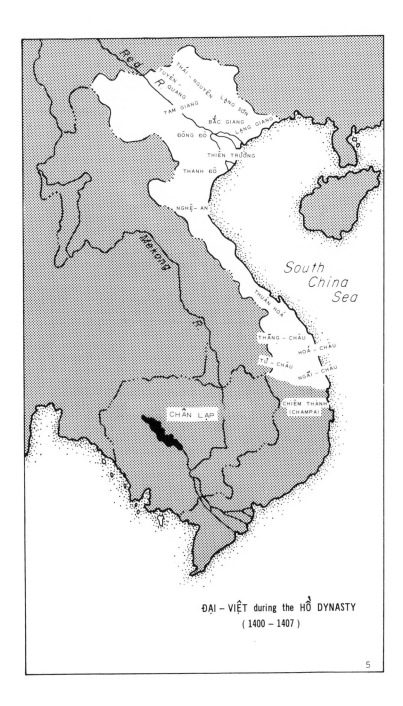

ĐẠI – VIỆT during the HỒ DYNASTY
(1400 – 1407)

5

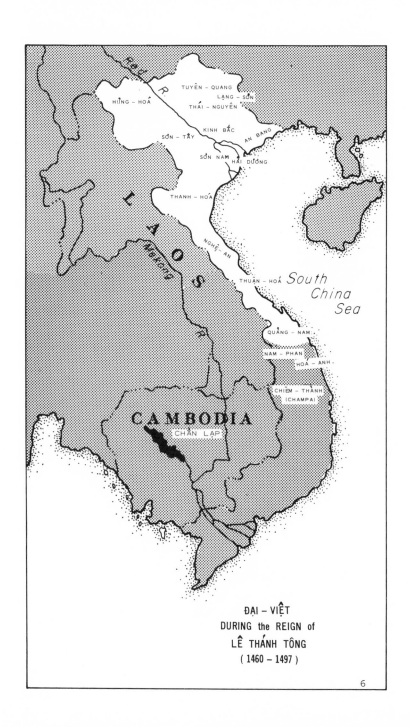

ĐẠI - VIỆT
DURING the REIGN of
LÊ THÁNH TÔNG
(1460 - 1497)

6

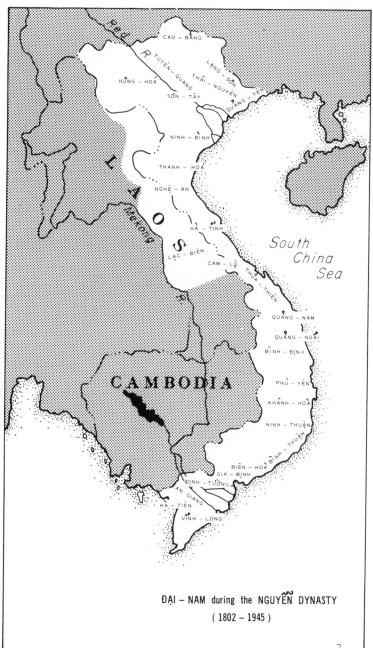

CAO – BẰNG

LẠNG – SƠN

TUYÊN – QUANG   THÁI – NGUYÊN

HƯNG – HOÁ

SƠN – TÂY   QUẢNG – YÊN

NINH – BÌNH

THANH – HOÁ

NGHỆ – AN

HÀ – TĨNH

LẠC – BIÊN

CAM – LỘ   THỪA – THIÊN

QUẢNG – NAM

QUẢNG – NGÃI

BÌNH – ĐỊNH

PHÚ – YÊN

KHÁNH – HOÀ

NINH – THUẬN

BÌNH – THUẬN

BIÊN – HOÀ

GIA – ĐỊNH

ĐỊNH – TƯỜNG

AN – GIANG

HÀ – TIÊN

VĨNH – LONG

CAMBODIA

L A O S

South China Sea

ĐẠI – NAM during the NGUYỄN DYNASTY

(1802 – 1945)

7

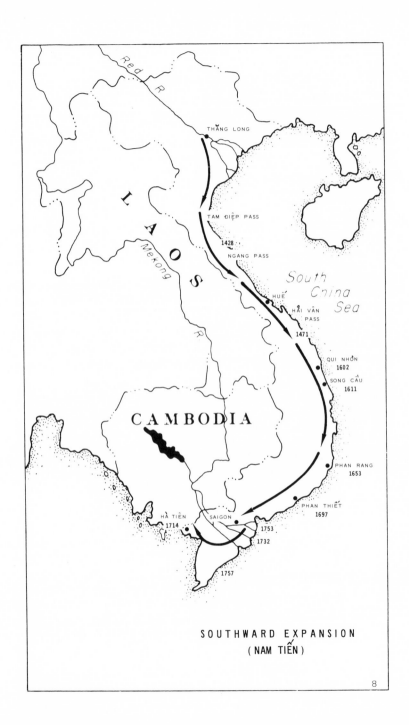

RED R

THẮNG LONG

TAM ĐIỆP PASS

LAOS

1428

NGANG PASS

Mekong R.

HUẾ
HẢI VÂN
PASS

South
China
Sea

1471

QUI NHƠN
1602
SONG CẦU
1611

CAMBODIA

PHAN RANG
1653

PHAN THIẾT
1697

HÀ TIÊN
1714

SAIGON

1753

1732

1757

SOUTHWARD EXPANSION
(NAM TIẾN)

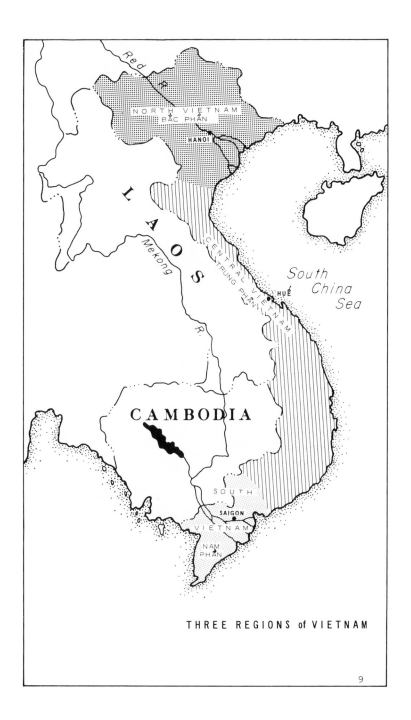

Red

NORTH VIETNAM
BẮC PHẦN

HANOI

L A O S

Mekong

R.

CENTRAL VIETNAM
TRUNG PHẦN

South
China
Sea

HUẾ

CAMBODIA

SOUTH

SAIGON

VIETNAM

NAM
PHẦN

THREE REGIONS of VIETNAM

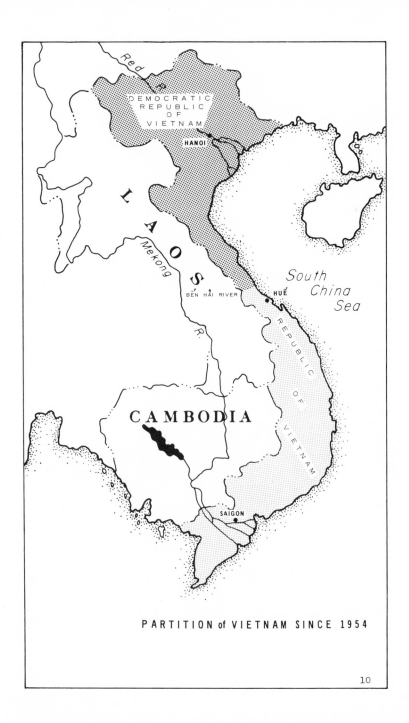

DEMOCRATIC
REPUBLIC
OF
VIETNAM

HANOI

L A O S

Red R.

Mekong R.

BẾN HẢI RIVER

HUẾ

South
China
Sea

CAMBODIA

REPUBLIC OF VIETNAM

SAIGON

PARTITION of VIETNAM SINCE 1954

10

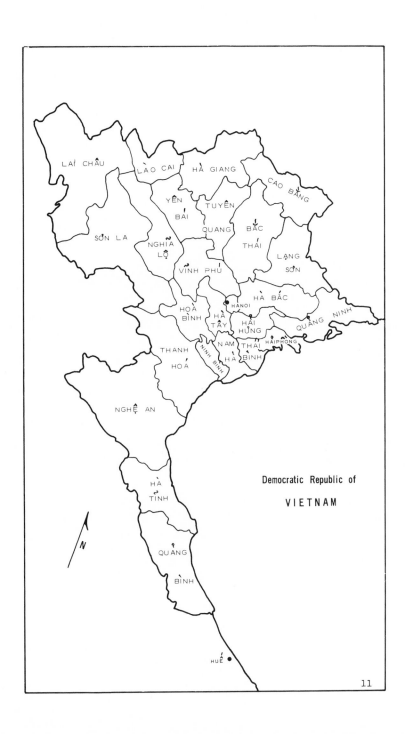

LAI CHÂU
LÀO CAI
HÀ GIANG
CAO BẰNG
YÊN BÁI
TUYÊN
QUANG
BẮC
THÁI
SƠN LA
NGHĨA LỘ
LẠNG SƠN
VĨNH PHÚ
HÀ BẮC
HOÀ BÌNH
HANOI
HÀ TÂY
HẢI HƯNG
QUẢNG NINH
THANH HOÁ
NINH BÌNH
NAM HÀ
THÁI BÌNH
HAIPHONG
NGHỆ AN

Democratic Republic of

VIETNAM

N

HÀ TĨNH

QUẢNG BÌNH

HUẾ

11

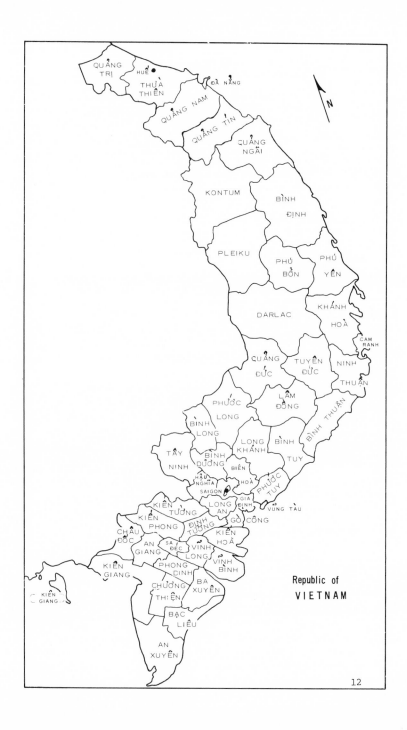

QUẢNG TRỊ

HUẾ

THỪA THIÊN

ĐÀ NẴNG

QUẢNG NAM

QUẢNG TÍN

QUẢNG NGÃI

KONTUM

BÌNH ĐỊNH

PLEIKU

PHÚ BỒN

PHÚ YÊN

DARLAC

KHÁNH HOÀ

CAM RANH

QUẢNG ĐỨC

TUYÊN ĐỨC

NINH THUẬN

LÂM ĐỒNG

PHƯỚC LONG

BÌNH LONG

LONG KHÁNH

BÌNH TUY

BÌNH THUẬN

TÂY NINH

BÌNH DƯƠNG

BIÊN HOÀ

PHƯỚC TUY

HẬU NGHĨA

SAIGON

GIA ĐỊNH

VŨNG TÀU

KIẾN TƯỜNG

LONG AN

KIẾN PHONG

ĐỊNH TƯỜNG

GÒ CÔNG

CHÂU ĐỐC

AN GIANG

SA ĐÉC

KIẾN HOÀ

VĨNH LONG

KIẾN GIANG

PHONG DINH

VĨNH BÌNH

CHƯƠNG THIỆN

BA XUYÊN

KIẾN GIANG

BẠC LIÊU

AN XUYÊN

Republic of
VIETNAM

12

BIBLIOGRAPHY

Addiss, Stephen. "Theater Music of Vietnam", South-
    east Asia: An International Quarterly. Vol. I,
    Nos. 1-2, Winter-Spring, 1971. Carbondale:
    Southern Illinois University, 1971.

_____. "Hat A Dao, The Sung Poetry of North
    Vietnam", Journal of the American Oriental
    Society. Vol. 93, No. 1, January-March, 1973.

Anonymous. "History of VN Buddhism." Vietnam Maga-
    zine. Vol. IV, No. II, 1971.

Barton, Thomas F. Southeast Asia in Maps. Chicago:
    Denoyer-Geppert, 1970.

Bastin, John Sturgis. The Emergence of Modern South-
    east Asia. Englewood Cliffs: Prentice Hall, 1967.

Bone, Robert C. Contemporary Southeast Asia. New
    York: Random House, 1962.

Boriskovskii, P. I. "Vietnam in Primeval Times."
    Soviet Anthropology and Archaeology. Vol. 7,
    No. 2, Fall, 1968; Vol. 7, No. 3, Winter, 1968-
    1969; Vol. 8, No. 1, Summer, 1969; Vol. 8, No. 3,
    Winter, 1969-1970; Vol. 8, No. 2, Summer, 1970;
    Vol. 9, No. 2, Fall, 1970; Vol. 9, No. 3, Winter,
    1970-1971. Moscow, 1968-1971.

Buttinger, Joseph. The Smaller Dragon. New York:
    Praeger, 1958.

_____. Vietnam: A Dragon Embattled. New York:
    Praeger, 1967.

_____. Vietnam: A Political History. New York:
    Praeger, 1968.

Bửu-Cầm. Quốc-Hiệu Nước Ta Từ An-Nam Đến Đai-Nam.
    Phụ Quốc-Vụ-Khánh Đặc-Trác Văn-Hoá. Saigon,
    1969.

Cadiers, Leopold Michel. "Vietnamese Ethnographic
    Papers." Human Relations Area Files, New Haven,
    Connecticut: 1953.

359

Cady, John Frank. Southeast Asia: Its Historical Development. New York: Ithaca, Cornell University Press, 1958.

Chen, King C. Viet-Nam and China 1938-1954. Princeton: Princeton University Press, 1969.

Chesneaux, Jean. The Vietnamese Nation: Contribution to a History--Translated by Malcolm Salmon, Current Book Distributors, Sydney, 1966.

Chaliand, Gerard.' The Peasant of North Vietnam. Middlesex, England: Penguin Books, 1969.

Coedes, George. The Making of Southeast Asia, Translated by H. M. Wright. Berkeley: University of California Press, 1966.

_____. The Indianized States of Southeast Asia, Translated by Susan B. Cowing. Honolulu, Hawaii East-West Center Press, 1968.

Cotter, Michael G. "Towards a Social History of the Vietnamese Southward Movement." Journal of Southeast Asian History. Vol. IX, No. 1, March, 1968.

Crawford, Ann (Caddel). Customs and Culture of Vietnam. Rutland, Vermont: Tuttle, 1966.

Cửu Long Giang and Toan Anh. Miền Bắc Khai-Nguyên, Tiến-Bộ. Sài-Gòn, 1969.

_____. Người Việt Đất Việt, Nam-Chi Tùng-Thư. Sài-Gòn, 1967.

Đào Duy-Anh. Việt Nam Văn-Hoá Sử-Cương Bốn-Phường, Huế, 1951.

Đào Trinh-Nhất. Việt-Sử Giai-Thoại, Tân-Việt. Sài-Gòn, 1950.

Devillers, Philippe. Histoire du Vietnam de 1940 a 1952. Editions du Sevil. Paris, 1952.

Đỗ Văn-Minh. Vietnam, Where East Meets West. Rome: Quatro Venti, 1962.

Đoàn-Bích. Famous Men of Vietnam. Vietnam Council on Foreign Relations. Saigon, 1970.

361

Dohamide, and Dorohiem. Dân-Tộc Chàm: Lược-Sử. Hiệp-
Hội Chàm Hội-Giáo Vietnam. Sài-Gòn, 1965.

Donnel, John C. Politics in South Vietnam: Doctrines
of Authority in Conflict. (Dissertation, ms.)
Berkeley: University of California, 1964.

Dournes, Jacques. God Loves The Pagans. New York:
Herder & Herder, 1966.

Dumoutier, Gustave. Annamese Religions. Translation
of Les Cultes Annamites, 1907. Human Relations
Area Files, Inc., New Haven Connecticut: 1955.

Duncason, Dennis J. Government and Revolution in
Vietnam. London: Oxford University Press, 1968.

Dương, Quảng-Hàm. Quốc Văn Trích Diễm. Bốn Phuong.
Sài-Gòn, 1952.

_____. Việt-Nam Thi-Văn Hợp-Tuyển. Trung-Tâm
Học-Liệu, Sài-Gòn, 1968.

_____. Việt-Nam Văn-Học Sử-Yếu. Trung-Tâm Học-
Liệu, Sài-Gòn, 1968.

Embassy of the Republic of Vietnam, Washington, D.C.
An Introduction to Vietnam. Washington, D.C.,
n.d.

_____. Industries of Vietnam, Viet-Nam Information
Series, No. 38. Washington, D.C., 1970.

_____. Vietnamese Agriculture. Viet-Nam Inform-
ation Series, No. 44, Washington, D.C., 1971.

_____. Vietnamese Handicrafts. Viet-Nam Inform-
ation Series, No. 43, Washington, D.C., n.d.

Embree, John F. Ethnic Groups of Northern Southeast
Asia. New Haven, Connecticut: Yale University,
1950.

Fall, Bernard B. Last Reflections on a War. Garden
City, New York: Doubleday and Company, Inc., 1967.

_____. The Two Vietnams. New York: Frederic A.
Praeger, 1967.

_____. Viet-Nam Witness 1953-1966. New York:
Frederic A. Praeger, 1966.

Foreign Languages Publishing House. Education in the DRV. Vietnamese Studies, No. 5, Hà-Nội, 1965.

_____. Glimpses of Vietnamese Classical Literature. Hà-Nội, 1972.

_____. Our President Hồ Chí Minh. Hà-Nội, 1970.

_____. Vietnam--A Sketch. Hà-Nội, 1971.

Gourou, Pierre. The Peasant of the Tonkin Delta: A Study of Human Geography. Human Relations Area Files, New Haven, Connecticut: n.d.

Gregerson, Marilyn J. "The Ethnic Minorities of Vietnam," Southeast Asia: An International Quarterly. Vol. II, No. 1, Winter, 1972.

Groslier, Bernard Philippe. The Art of Indochina, Translated by George Lawrence. New York: Crown Publishers, 1962.

Ha Van-Vuong (Mrs. A. L.). "The Pattern of Vietnamese Cooking." Viet-My, Vol. II, No. 2, 1957.

Hall, D. B. E. A History of Southeast Asia. New York: St. Martin's Press, 1968.

Hammer, Ellen Joy. The Struggle for Indochina 1940-1955. Stanford: Stanford University Press, 1955.

_____. Vietnam Yesterday and Today. New York: Holt, Rinehart and Winston, 1966.

Harrison, Brian. Southeast Asia, A Short History. New York: St. Martin's Press, 1954.

Hickey, Gerald Cannon. The Highland People of South Vietnam: Social and Economic Development. Santa Monica, California: Rand Corporation, 1967.

_____. Social Systems of Northern Vietnam. Chicago: University of Chicago, 1958.

_____. Village in Vietnam. New Haven, Connecticut: Yale University Press, 1964.

Hoskins, Marilyn W. and Eleanor Shepherd. Life in a Vietnamese Urban Quarter. Carbondale: Center for Vietnamese Studies, Southern Illinois University, 1971.

Huard, Pierre Alphonse and Haurice Durand. Connaissance du Vietnam. Ecole Francaise d'Extreme Orient. Hanoi, 1954.

Iredell, F. Raymond. Vietnam: The Country and the People. New York: The American Press, 1966.

Janse, Olov Robert Thure. Archaeological Research in Indo-China. Cambridge: Harvard University Press, 1947.

_____. "Vietnam Crossroads of Peoples and Civilization." Viet-My, Vol. 4, No. 2, June, 1954.

Kahin, George Mct. "Minorities in the Democratic Republic of Vietnam", Asian Survey, Vol. XII, No. 7, July, 1972.

Karamyshev, Viktor Pavlovich. Agriculture in the Democratic Republic of Vietnam. U.S. Joint Publications Research Service, 1961.

Karnow, Stanley. Life, Southeast Asia. New York: Time, Inc., 1962.

Lê Châu. Le Vietnam Socialiste: Une Economie de Transition Francois Maspero, Paris, 1966.

Lê Đinh-Tưởng. "Bành Trưởng Quốc Thổ Việt-Nam," Canh Tân Đất Việt No. 4, Winter-Spring, 1971-1972.

Lê Thành-Khôi. Le Viet-Nam, Histoire et civilization. Paris: (Edition de Minuit), 1955.

Lê Văn-Đức and Le Ngoc-Tru. Từ-Điển Việt-Nam, Quyển-Ha and Quyển Thưởng. Sài-Gòn: Khai-Trí, 1970.

Lê Văn-Siêu. Truyền-Thống Dân-Tộc. Sài-Gòn: Hoàng Đông Phưởng, 1968.

Lê Xuân-Thủy. Kim Vân Kiều by Nguyễn Du. Translation, footnotes and commentaries. Sai-Gon: Khai-Tri, 1968.

LeBar, Frank M., et al. Ethnic Groups of Mainland Southeast Asia. New Haven: Human Relations Area Files Press, 1964.

Lý Chanh-Trung. Introduction to Vietnamese Poetry. Vietnam Culture Series No. 3, Ministry of National Education, Sai-Gon.

Marr, David G. Vietnamese Anticolonialism. University of California Press, 1971.

Masson, Anore. Histoire du Vietnam. Paris: Presses Universitaires de France, 1960.

McAlister, John T., Jr. Vietnam: The Origins of Revolution. New York: Harper and Row, 1970.

Mole, Robert L. The Montagnards of South Vietnam: A Study of Nine Tribes. Tokyo: Charles E. Tuttle Company, 1970.

Nghiêm Đang. Vietnam: Politics and Public Administration. Hawaii: East-West Center Press, 1966.

Nguyễn Cửu-Giang. "Street Vendors in Vietnam." Viet-My, Vol. VI, No. 2, June, 1961.

Nguyễn Đang-Thục. Democracy in Traditional Vietnamese Society. Vietnam Culture Series, No. 4, Ministry of National Education, Sài-Gòn, n.d.

_____. "Nam-Tiến Việt-Nam." Sử Địa, No. 19-20, 1970.

_____. Viet-Nam Văn-Minh Sử. Tâp Thượng. Sài-Gòn: Bộ Giáo-Dục Trung-Tâm Học-Liệu, 1972.

Nguyễn Đình-Hòa. The Vietnamese Language. Vietnam Culture Series, No. 2, Ministry of National Education. Sài-Gòn, 1961.

_____. (ed.). Some Aspects of Vietnamese Culture. Carbondale: Center for Vietnamese Studies, Southern Illinois University, 1972.

Nguyễn Huyền-Anh. Việt-Nam Danh-Nhân Từ-Điển. Sài-Gòn: Khai-Trí, 1967.

Nguyễn Khác-Kham. Celebrations of Rice Culture in Viet-Nam. The Vietnam Council on Foreign Relations. Sài-Gòn, nd.

_____. Introduction to Vietnamese Culture. Vietnam Culture Series, No. 1, Ministry of National Education. Sài-Gòn, n.d.

Nguyễn Khắc-Ngữ and Phạm Đình-Tiếu. Địa-Lý Việt-Nam. Sài-Gòn: Cơ Sở Xuất Bản Sử-Địa, 1971.

Nguyễn Khắc-Viên. Mountain Regions and National Minorities in the D.R. of Vietnam. Vietnamese Studies No. 15. Hà-Nội, 1968.

_____. Traditional Vietnam: Some Historical Stages. Vietnamese Studies Vol. 21, Hà-Nội, n.d.

_____. (ed.). Ethnographical Data Vol. I. Vietnamese Studies No. 32. Ha-Noi, 1972.

Nguyễn Nang-Đạc and Nguyễn Quang-Đạc. Vietnamese Architecture. Vietnam Information Series 34. Embassy of the Republic of Vietnam. Washington, D.C., 1970.

Nguyễn Ngọc-Bich (comp.). An Annotated Atlas of the Republic of Vietnam. n.p., n.d.

Nguyễn Ngọc-Huy. Political Parties in Vietnam. The Vietnam Council on Foreign Relations. Sài-Gòn, 1971.

Nguyễn Nhân-Bằng. "Bác Sĩ Yersin, Người Đầu Tiên Tìm Ra Vùng Đất Đà-Lạt." Sử Địa, No. 23-24, 1971, pp. 33-41.

Nguyễn Như-Lân. 200 Nam Dưởng-Lich Và Âm-Lich Đối-Chiếu. Sài-Gòn: Khai-Trí, 1968.

Nguyễn Phúc-Tấn. A Modern History of Vietnam, 1802-1954. Sài-Gòn: Khai-Trí, 1964.

Nguyễn Tiên-Hùng. "The Red River, Its Dikes and North Viet-nam's Economy." Vietnam Bulletin Vol. VII, No. 17 and 18, September, 1972, pp. 23-28.

Nguyễn Trắc-Dĩ. Đồng-Bào Các Sắc-Tộc Thiểu Số Việt-Nam. Sài-Gòn: Bộ Phát Triển Sắc-Tộc, 1972.

Nguyễn Văn-Xuân. "Lịch-Sử Cuộc Nam-Tiến Của Dân-Tộc Việt-Nam." Sử Địa, No. 19-20, 1970, pp. 265-290.

Nhất Thạnh. Đất Lê Quê Thói. Sài-Gòn: Cơ-Sở Ấn-Loạt Đường-Sáng, 1970.

P.N.K. Việt-Nam Phong-Tục. Sài-Gòn: Đại-Hành, 1965.

Phạm-Quỳnh. "The Cult of the Ancestors." Viet-My Vol. 4, No. 1, March, 1959, pp. 48-51. (Translated from Franco-Vietnamese Essays, 1930).

Phạm Thê-Hùng. Village Government in Vietnam, 968-
1954. (Thesis), Carbondale: Southern Illinois
University, 1972.

Phạm Văn-Diệu. Văn-Học - Việt-Nam. Sài-Gòn: Tân-Việt,
1960.

_____. Việt-Nam Văn-Học Giảng-Bình. Sài-Gòn: Tân-
Việt, 1961.

Phạm Văn-Sơn. Việt-Nam Tranh-Đấu Sử. Sài-Gòn: Việt-
Cường, 1959.

_____. Việt-Sử Tân-Biên Vol. I through Vol. V.
Trần Hữu-Thoan; Văn Hữu Á-Châu, Phạm Văn-Sơn,
Sai-Gon, 1956-1962.

Phan Huy-Lê and Phan Đại-Doạn. Khởi-Nghĩa Lam-Sơn Và
Phong-Trào Đấu Tranh Giải Phóng Đất Nước Vào Đầu
Thê Kỷ XI. Hà-Nội: Nhà Xuất Bản Khoa Học Xã Hội,
1969.

Phan Kê-Bính. Việt-Nam Phong-Tuc. Taken from Đông-
Dương Tập-Chí 24-49 (1913-1914) Phong-Trào Văn-
Hóa. Sài-Gòn, 1972.

Phan Khoan. Việt-Nam Pháp-Thuộc-Sử 1885-1945. Sài-
Gòn, n.d.

Phan Phong-Linh. Thắng-Cảnh Việt-Nam Qua Thi-Ca.
Sài-Gòn: Văn Nghệ, 1956.

Pike, Douglas. Viet Cong. Cambridge: Massachusetts
Institute of Technology Press, 1966.

Rawson, Philip. The Art of Southeast Asia. New York:
Praeger, 1967.

Reischauer, Edwin O. and John K. Fairbank. East Asia
the Great Tradition. Boston: Houghton Mifflin
Company, 1962.

Republic of Vietnam. Ministry of National Planning
and Statistics National Institute of Statistics.
Vietnam Statistical Yearbook 1971. Saigon, 1972.

Schrock, Joan L., et al. Minority Groups in the Republic of Vietnam. Washington: U. S. Government
Printing Office, 1967.

Schroede, Albert. Chronologie Des Souverains De L-
    Annam. Paris: Impremere Nationale, MDCCCIV
    (1804).

Smith, Harvey H., et al. Area Handbook for North
    Vietnam. Washington, D.C.: U. S. Government
    Printing Office, 1967.

_____. Area Handbook for South Vietnam. Washington,
    D.C.: U. S. Government Printing Office, 1967.

Steinberg, David J. (ed.). In Search of Southeast
    Asia. New York: Praeger, 1971.

Summer Institute of Linguistics. Vietnam Minority
    Languages (Revised November, 1969). Saigon,
    1969.

Thái Văn-Kiêm. "A Historical Sketch of the Vietnamese
    Army." Viet-My Vol. 2, No. 3. Sài-Gòn, 1957.

_____. Viet Nam Past and Present. Commercial
    Transworld Editions. Sài-Gòn, 1956.

Thanh Lãng. Văn-Hoá Việt-Nam. Sài-Gòn: Phong-Trào
    Văn-Hóa, 1965.

"The Mekong Project: An International Undertaking."
    Impact. Manila: Vol. VIII, No. 6, 1963.

Thompson, Virginia. French Indochina. New York:
    Octagon Books, 1968.

Toan Anh. Nếp Cũ: Con Người Việt-Nam. Sài-Gòn:
    Khai-Trí, 1970.

_____. Nếp Cũ: Hội Hè Đinh Đám, Vol. I. Sài-Gòn:
    Nam Chi Tùng Thư, 1969.

_____. Nếp Cũ: Làng-Xóm Việt-Nam. Sài-Gòn, 1968.

_____. Nếp Cũ: Tin-Ngưỡng Việt-Nam, Vol. I, Sài-
    Gòn: Hoa-Đăng, 1969.

_____. Nếp Cũ: Tin-Ngưỡng Việt-Nam, Vol. II, Sài-
    Gòn: Kim Lai Ấn Quán, 1968.

_____. Phong-Tục Việt-Nam. Sài-Gòn: Khai-Trí,
    1968.

Tou Nan Azia Cho Sa Kai (Southeast Asia Research
    Association). Tou Nan Azia Yo Lan (A Random
    Glimpse of Southeast Asia). Tokyo, 1971.

Trần Đinh. Địa-Lý. Huế: Nhà In Đại-Học, 1959.

Trần Trọng-Kim. Việt-Nam Sử-Lược. Sài-Gòn: Tân-Việt, 1964.

Trần Văn-Giáp. Lược Truyện Các Tác Gia Việt-Nam, Vol. I & II. Hà-Nội: Nhà Xuất Bản Khoa Học Xã-Hội, 1971.

Trần Văn-Khê. La Musique Vietnamienne Traditionelle. Paris: Presses Universitaries de France, 1962.

Trần Văn-Tuyên. "Lịch-Sử Phát Triển Đà-Lạt" (1893-1954). Sử Địa No. 23-24, 1971, pp. 45-141.

Trịnh Văn-Thanh. Thanh-Ngũ Điển-Tích Danh-Nhân Tự-Điển, Vol. I and II. Sài-Gòn, 1969.

U. S. Army Special Warfare School. Montagnard Tribal Groups of the Republic of Vietnam. Fort Bragg, North Carolina, 1964.

U. S. Bureau of Naval Personnel. The Religions of South Vietnam in Faith and Fact. Washington, D.C.: U. S. Government Printing Office, 1968.

_____. Vietnamese Time Concepts and Behavior Patterns. Sai-Gon, 1968.

U. S. Department of Agriculture. Agricultural Economy of North Vietnam. Washington, D.C., 1965.

U. S. Department of State, Division of Foreign Languages. History of the Mountain People of Southern Indochina up to 1945. (translation) by Bernard Bourette. Agency for International Development, Washington, D.C., 1947.

U. S. Joint Publications Research Service. "Official Government Report on 1960 Census in North Vietnam." Translated from Nhan Dan, Ha-Noi, No. 2419, 2 November, 1960. Washington, D.C., 13 January, 1961.

U. S. State Department. Who's Who in North Vietnam, Washington, D.C., November, 1972.

Viện Quốc-Gia Thống-Kê Bộ Kế-Hoạch Và Phát-Triển Quốc-
Gia. Niên Giam Thống-Kê 1971. Sài-Gòn, 1971.

Vo Nhan Tri. Croissance Economique de la Republic
Democratic du Viet-Nam. Hà-Nội: Editions En
Langues Estrangeres, 1967.

Vu Huy-Chan. "Singing-From the Rice Field to the
Vietnamese Theater." Viet-My Vol. 3, No. 3,
June, 1958.

Vũ Tam Ích. A Historical Survey of Educational
Developments in Vietnam. Lexington, Kentucky,
1959.

Vương Hồng-Sển. Sài-Gòn Nam Xửa. Sài-Gòn: Khai-
Trí, 1969.

Vũ Ngọc-Phan. Nhà Văn Hiện Đại. Sài-Gòn: Thăng-Long,
1960.

Webster's Geographical Dictionary. Springfield,
Massachusetts: G & C Merriam Company, 1969.

Whiteside, Dale R. Traditions and Directions in the
Music of Vietnam. Museum of Anthropology
Miscellaneous Series No. 28. Greeley: University
of Northern Colorado, 1971.

Woodside, Alexander Barton. Vietnam and the Chinese
Model; A Comparative Study of the Nguyen and
Ch'ing Civil Government in the First Half of the
Nineteenth Century. Cambridge: Harvard
University Press, 1971.